HARDPRESS.NET
HOME OF HARD-TO-FIND BOOKS

Lectures on Ancient History
by Barthold Georg Niebuhr

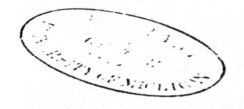

LECTURES

ON

ANCIENT HISTORY.

VOL. II.

LONDON :
PRINTED BY J. WERTHEIMER AND CO.,
FINSBURY CIRCUS.

LECTURES

ON

ANCIENT HISTORY,

FROM

THE EARLIEST TIMES TO THE TAKING OF
ALEXANDRIA BY OCTAVIANUS.

COMPRISING

THE HISTORY OF THE ASIATIC NATIONS, THE EGYPTIANS,
GREEKS, MACEDONIANS AND CARTHAGINIANS.

BY

B. G. NIEBUHR.

TRANSLATED FROM THE GERMAN EDITION OF DR. MARCUS NIEBUHR,

BY DR. LEONHARD SCHMITZ, F.R.S.E.
RECTOR OF THE HIGH SCHOOL OF EDINBURGH.

WITH ADDITIONS AND CORRECTIONS FROM HIS OWN MS. NOTES.

IN THREE VOLUMES.
VOL II.

LONDON:
TAYLOR, WALTON, AND MABERLY,
UPPER GOWER STREET, AND IVY LANE, PATERNOSTER ROW.
M.DCCC.LII.

CONTENTS OF VOL. II.

b

CONTENTS.

CONTENTS.

LECTURE LI.

LECTURE LII.

LECTURE LIII.

LECTURE LIV.

LECTURE LV.

LECTURE LVI.

LECTURE LX.

LECTURE LXI.

LECTURE LXII.

LECTURE LXIII.

LECTURE LXXV.

LECTURE LXXVI.

LECTURE LXXVII.

LECTURE LXXVIII.

LECTURE LXXIX.

CONTENTS.

LECTURE LXXX.

INSCRIPTIONS
ON
NIEBUHR'S TOMB AT BONN,
ERECTED BY FREDERICK WILLIAM IV., KING OF PRUSSIA.

(See Frontispiece.)

---

1. *On the frontispiece :* A ✠ Ω.

2. *On the arch :*

Ich bin der Erste und der Letzte und der Lebendige.

I am the First and the Last and the Living.

3. *Inside, round the head of Christ :*

Ich bin die Auferstehung und das Leben. Wer an mich glaubt, der wird leben, ob er gleich stirbt.

I am the Resurrection and the Life. He that believeth in me shall live, even though he die.

4. *On the large space on the left :*

Gott prüft die gerechten Seelen wie Gold im Ofen, und nimmt sie an wie ein völliges Opfer. Wisd. iii. 6.

God proves the righteous souls, as gold in a furnace, and receives them as a perfect offering. Wisdom, iii. 6.

Der Gerechten Pfad glänzet wie ein Licht, das da fortgehet und leuchtet bis auf den vollen Tag. Proverbs, iv. 18.

But the path of the just is as the shining light, that shineth more and more unto the perfect day. Prov. iv. 18.

Die Weisheit habe ich geliebt und gesucht von meiner Jugend auf, und gedachte sie mir zur Braut zu nehmen, denn ich habe ihre Söhne lieb gewonnen. Wisdom, viii. 2.

Wisdom have I loved, and sought from my youth up, and I thought to take her to me for a spouse, for I have won the love of her sons. Wisd. viii. 2.

5. *On the large space on the right :*

Die Weisheit kann errathen Weibes, was vergangen und zukünftig ist. Sie versteht sich auf verdeckte Worte und weiß die Räthsel aufzulösen. Wisdom, viii. 8.

Wisdom can divine both what is past and to come. She understands hidden words, and knows how to expound riddles. Wisdom, viii. 8.

O wie lerntest Du in Deiner Jugend und warest voll Verstand, wie ein Wasser das Land bedeckt, und hast Alles mit Sprüchen und Lehren erfüllt. Ecclus. xlvii. 14, 15.

O how wise wast thou in thy youth, and wast full of understanding, as a flood covers the land, and hast filled all things with wise sayings and doctrines. Ecclus. xlvii. 14, 15.

Quis desiderio sit pudor aut modus tam cari capitis. *Hor.*

6. *On the lower space :*

BARTHOLD GEORG NIEBUHR,
Born Aug. 27, 1776, Died Jan. 2, 1831.

MARGARET LUCY PHIL. NIEBUHR (HENSLER),
Born July 7, 1787, Died Jan. 1831.

CARL FRANZ PHIL. NIEBUHR,
Born March 24, 1814, Died Jan. 10, 1824.

ANCIENT HISTORY.

LECTURE XLI.

" THE state of peace between Athens and Sparta, after the beginning of the third Messenian war, was only artificial, and it was to be foreseen that war would break out as soon as an opportunity occurred." Under these circumstances, an event became a matter of importance, which by itself would have had no influence.

The Lacedaemonians still continued to regard the Dorians in their four towns with a certain reverence as their metropolis. The Dorians were hard pressed by the Phocians; and when the latter, during an expedition into their country, had taken one of the four towns, the Spartans considered it to be their duty to assist the Dorians. Accordingly, they crossed the Crissaean gulf with an army against the Phocians, and compelled them to give up what they had conquered.

Meantime an Athenian fleet had followed them into the gulf of Lepanto (gulf of Crissa), and a land army supported its operations. This army had taken possession of the Geraneian hills, which are nearly impassable, and which, in several ranges, join the principal chain from mount Helicon as far as Pindus.[1] The return of the Spartans thus seemed to be cut off, and the Athenians might, in that case, easily succeed in making their way across the Isthmus. The Athenians now entered Boeotia with a considerable army, under the command of Tolmides,

[1] This sentence occurs only in one MS. in this form—" had taken possession of hills from Helicon towards Pindus, joining the principal chain in several ranges." But this statement is not applicable to the Geraneian hills, which, according to other MSS. (in some they are called *Megarian*), Niebuhr, following Thucydides, mentioned.—ED.

who justly bears that name, for he was the boldest among the Athenian commanders of the time, and did not hesitate to offer battle to the Spartans and Peloponnesians, though they were superior in numbers; but he did so to his own ruin.   The Athenians, though they fought most bravely, were defeated at Tanagra (Olymp. 80, 4); the Peloponnesians, with the courage of despair, broke through the Athenian army, and forced their way home across the Isthmus, there being no army to pursue them immediately.   This defeat was severely felt by the Athenians, for many of their distinguished citizens had fallen; but otherwise the defeat was not very serious, nor was it followed by serious consequences.

The Athenians soon recovered themselves, and assumed the supremacy in Boeotia (Olymp. 80, 4).   The Boeotians and Thebans were at that time hostile to each other.   The Thebans stood to the Boeotians in about the same relation as that which at different times existed between Rome and Latium; Thebes being the one half of the state, and the Boeotians the other. There may have been a time, when the relation subsisting between Delphi and the Phocians was of a similar nature.   In the time of Servius Tullius, the relation between Rome and Latium was of such a kind, that the thirty Latin towns on the one hand corresponded with the thirty Roman tribes on the other; and this state of things was restored in the treaty of Spurius Cassius.   Such also was the relation between the Thebans and Boeotians.   It would seem, that at one time the Thebans and Boeotians conjointly appointed the Boeotarchs, so that, perhaps, Thebes, elected a greater number, and the supremacy belonged to both alternately; but at another, the Thebans possessed decidedly the same supremacy over Boeotia, as the Romans had over Latium in the time of Servius. This supremacy, however, was not firmly established, but had been shaken especially during the Persian war; and now the Thebans applied to Sparta to recover it through her assistance.   This eagerness, on the part of the Thebans, to gain the supremacy over Boeotia, led to the expedition of Myronides.   The details of this war are particularly obscure, and you will not find them described anywhere in the manner in which I shall here explain them; but I am perfectly convinced of the correctness of my views.

The account of these events in Thucydides is very brief;

and in such a brief sketch a writer may easily pass over some decisive circumstance. Thus Thucydides, in this instance, does not distinguish the different relations in which Athens stood to Boeotia and to Thebes, nor what were the relations between the Thebans and the body of the Boeotians. Thucydides' account was only an ἀνάμνησις; his object was not to write a history of that period, but only to give such explanations as were necessary to understand the Peloponnesian war, and to recall those well-known events as distinctly as possible to the minds of his readers. The work of Diodorus Siculus, though it is bad and utterly deficient in judgment, yet contains invaluable materials for a history of Greece (they are of course not his own) and abounds in matters which have never yet been made use of. All the moderns, who have written on the history of Greece, neglect him too much, when they have other authors for the same period. In regard to the times we are here treating of, we may take it for granted that, on the whole, he adopted the account of Ephorus; now as Ephorus did not, like Diodorus, proceed chronologically, Diodorus was obliged to find his own way, and hence the fearful and monstrous chronological blunders which he commits, in arbitrarily assigning dates to occurrences for which Ephorus mentioned no dates at all. Now Diodorus informs us, that after the battle of Oenophyta, the Athenians subdued the whole of Boeotia with the exception of Thebes; whereas Thucydides, without exempting Thebes, states that Boeotia was subdued by the Athenians. But Boeotia is to be understood in the same sense as in Diodorus, and his readers understood the distinction without being reminded of it. The distinction between Thebans and Boeotians must have been quite clear to his contemporaries, and the circumstance that it is no longer so to us, after the lapse of two thousand years, cannot be made a reproach to Thucydides.

I am therefore convinced, that a portion of the Boeotians, anxious to maintain their independence against Thebes, called in the aid of the Athenians; and after the battle of Oenophyta, all Boeotia submitted to them, with the exception of Thebes, Orchomenos and Chaeronea. We must understand the case thus—Thebes was at war with Boeotia, and Boeotia, with the exception of Orchomenos and Chaeronea, submitted to Athens.

" The Athenians, at that time, thoughtlessly extended their power on the continent of Greece, though they had no basis for it. They assumed the supremacy of Megara, Boeotia, Locris, and Phocis." Achaia, and a few places in the Acte of Argolis, also placed themselves under their protection. " It is true, this power was offered to them by circumstances, but the Athenians ought to have directed all their attention to the sea; and not to have attempted to establish a supremacy over nations of entirely different races on the continent; or else they ought to have maintained it by artificial combinations, which might, indeed, have been brought about. Had they introduced a municipal constitution among their allies, affording them the possibility of becoming Athenian citizens, a party favourable to Athens would have been formed, even in the oligarchical states which were hostile to them. But a democratic government acting according to feeling and impulse, is incapable of such prudent combinations. Rome indeed could form them, but not Athens; and hence those possessions contributed only to the ruin of Athens."

About the time of the battle of Tanagra, Cimon was sent into exile by ostracism; and that not, as was usually the case, merely for the purpose of removing him, but on account of a special personal suspicion, he being supposed to keep up a treacherous connection with Sparta. The self-sacrifice of his most intimate friends delivered him from that suspicion, for in that battle they greatly distinguished themselves: they fell fighting bravely, and Cimon was recalled, and recovered his former position in the state.[2]

Soon afterwards he was again sent out with a fleet of two hundred galleys, to complete the subjugation of Cyprus. This expedition is involved in great obscurity. According to some accounts it lasted for a considerable time, and ended in the conclusion of the celebrated peace of Cimon; but, according to others, Cimon died soon after the commencement of the war, during the siege of Citium (Olymp. 82, 4) and at the same time the Athenians were compelled, either by famine or by epidemic diseases,[3] to give up the war. .

[2] Niebuhr probably mentioned here, or at least intended to mention, the part which Cimon took in bringing about the five years' truce. He afterwards calls that truce simply " the peace of Cimon."—Ed.

[3] " $\Lambda\iota\mu\acute{o}s$ or $\lambda o\iota\mu\acute{o}s$, which are constantly confounded in the MSS. I think it more probable that in this case $\lambda o\iota\mu\acute{o}s$ was the cause."

The peace of Cimon is often mentioned, even by the orators of the age of Philip, especially by Isocrates, in his speech on the humiliation of the barbarians, where some details also are stated.[4] How often are we told of this glorious peace, in which the barbarians are said to have pledged themselves not to sail out of the Black Sea, nor beyond the town of Phaselis, nor to appear with any armed vessel in the west of the Chelidonian rocks; while on land they promised not to approach the coast with an army, within one, or according to others, within three days' march. The last point is not the same in all authorities. This is set forth as an event shedding brilliant lustre upon Greece. Some place it immediately after the battle on the Eurymedon; but this statement has been rejected, for it involves this difficulty: if the Greeks had at that time concluded such a peace with the Persians, they would afterwards have violated it in the basest manner; since after it the Athenians sent several expeditions to Cyprus and Egypt (for after the great expedition to Egypt, they sent another, though a trifling one, to assist Amyrtaeus). Hence this peace was disputed even by the ancients themselves. The best investigation of the subject is that by Dahlmann, the result of which is, that all the accounts of the peace (and they are very numerous, and even detailed, for it is said, *e.g.*, that the elder Callias was sent to Persia to conclude the peace) are without foundation, and that such a peace was never concluded. The war, it is true, was brought to a close, but only because it was forgotten. Such things cannot surprise us with Asiatics; they were tired of the war, and so long as the Greeks left them in peace, they were glad of the repose. One circumstance, however, makes me hesitate to adopt this view, and I should not wonder at all, if the same circumstance should be of weight even in our days; it is this, that Craterus, the Macedonian historian, who collected the psephismata at Athens from inscriptions and public records, had, in his work, a psephisma, containing a formal ratification of that peace. This circumstance is inexplicable if we deny the peace, for I am not prepared to declare that psephisma a forgery. Craterus did not commit such an act, and no one can think of charging him with it. If then there actually existed in the Acropolis a pillar on which the

4 Isocrat. *Panathen.*, p. 244, R.

peace of Cimon was engraved, this would have been a forgery made from mere vanity; we should, in this case, be obliged to suppose, that for some purpose or another, the Athenians afterwards forged the document of peace, and set it up engraved on a pillar; but this supposition is even less probable than the other, that Craterus fabricated it.

But why can we not view the matter in a different way? I see no difficulty if we consider what was actually possible under the circumstances, that is, if we suppose, that no peace was concluded, but only a truce, which was accepted by one of the satraps of Western Asia on his own responsibility; perhaps after the battle on the Eurymedon, and at the very time when the Athenians undertook the expedition to Egypt. We must conceive the Persian satraps to have been as independent of the great king, as such governors in the East still are. For while the sultan is at present carrying on war, the pasha of Egypt stands in a very different relation to the powers of Europe from that of his master. It does not seem to me at all improbable, that the satraps in Western Asia, in Lydia, etc., may have concluded such a separate peace with the Greeks, in order to enable themselves to direct their attention to other quarters, and pledged themselves to keep their cavalry within one or more days' march from the coast, and not to keep any ships of war within the Cyanean rocks, the Bosporus, nor to the west of the Chelidones. At a later time we find exactly similar cirumstances in the treaties concluded by Pharnabazus and Tissaphernes with the Spartan commanders Thimbron, Dercyllidas, and down to the time of Agesilaus. Tissaphernes was satrap of Lydia, and Pharnabazus of Phrygia; both were personal enemies, and each charged the other with having caused the invasion of the enemy; each concluded a truce with the enemy, and provided them with money in order to induce them to invade the territory of his rival and to spare his own. Such was the state of dissolution in the Persian empire.

If this supposition be true, the peace of Cimon was a separate peace; and I believe the accounts of it to be false only in so far as it is described as a formal peace between King Artaxerxes and the Athenians. But considered as a truce for that time, it at once and clearly shows, how the Athenians could direct all their forces against Egypt, without the satraps in Asia Minor availing themselves of the opportunity against Greece.

. For some time after the battle of Tanagra,[5] the Athenians were humbled; but this did not prevent them from perpetually increasing their fleet, and preparing and training themselves for war. And soon they became involved in other wars on the continent of Greece. The party among the Boeotians, which had called in the aid of the Athenians, was predominant indeed on the whole, but not so in all the particular towns. Moreover the blameless period of the Athenian supremacy was then already passed, the Athenians indulging in many acts of injustice and oppression. They then aimed at making all their allies tributary; and such things may have occurred also in Boeotia. In addition to this, the fact of the Boeotians being ἀλλόφυλοι was of great weight. This circumstance was of great importance among the Greeks, and formed a barrier, the strength of which becomes visible, if we consider the hereditary repugnance against the interference of foreigners even in modern Europe, where the nations have become so much assimilated. When we see how with them, manners and customs were in opposition to each other, which with us are matters of indifference, and which are the same, not only in the different branches of one nation, but even in different nations, it is clear that the interference of a strange race was disagreeable. Accordingly I here supplement the statement of Thucydides by the remark, that there arose great discontent among the Boeotians, because the Athenians extended their power in the Boeotian towns, and ruled too arbitrarily. Orchomenos and Chaeronea which had maintained their independence, now became places of refuge for those who were expelled from other Boeotian towns. The Athenians, therefore, turned against those two cities for the purpose of completing their dominion, and conquered Chaeronea only with great difficulty; but against Orchomenos they did not succeed, and on their retreat they met, near Coronea, the allied army of the revolted Boeotians, who were no doubt commanded by the Thebans. There a decisive battle was fought (Olymp. 83, 2) in which the Athenians were completely defeated; and this obliged

---

[5] The expression, " the battle of Tanagra," seems to be used here as a designation for the whole war.—ED.

them to conclude a peace, in consequence of which they had
to evacuate Boeotia.

Megara had even before revolted against the Athenians. [6]
After the Megarians had themselves invoked the assistance of
the Athenians, and after the latter had built harbours for them,
they suddenly and without any reason, treacherously revolted,
murdered the Athenian garrison, and invited the Spartans.
The Athenians were obliged to evacuate the country, and retained possession only of the two Megarian harbours, Pagae
on the Crisaean, and Nisaea on the Saronic Gulf. The Spartans
were already in arms, nay, had advanced as far as Eleusis,[7]
when the Athenians concluded a thirty years' truce with them
(Olymp. 83,3), in which they restored to the Peloponnesians
Achaia, which had placed itself under the protection of Athens,
and the ports of Megara.

Megara, considered geographically, does not indeed belong
to Peloponnesus, but politically it was justly regarded as a part
of it.   " This peace seems to have been very disadvantageous
for Athens; but no ancient author says so, and we may therefore suppose that it was so in appearance rather than in reality.
The possession of Megara would have been of great importance, if it had included the city of Megara itself; but as
the city had recovered its independence before, the two fortresses could not be of any use." Fourteen years of this thirty
years' truce had elapsed, when the Peloponnesian war broke
out; " and that period had been one of scarcely suppressed
anger and exasperation, and consisted of a series of mutual
provocations.   Neither party had any real desire for war.
Meantime the third Messenian war, which lasted ten years,
had been brought to a close (Olymp. 81, 4), and one of the
causes of hostility was the circumstance that the Athenians
received the fugitive Helots, and gave them a place to live in."

As in discoursing on general history, I cannot enter into a
detailed history of Greece, I have thought it superfluous to
give a minute account of several occurrences of this period
which were glorious for Athens; for example, of the expedition
of Pericles, of the circumnavigation of Peloponnesus by
Tolmides, during which the arsenal at Gythium was reduced

---

[6] According to Diodorus, xii. 5; but comp. Thucyd. i. 114.—ED.

[7] This name is here given from conjecture instead of Megara. The sentence
occurs only in one MS.—ED.

to ashes; in like manner, I have not related how Zacynthos and Cephallene did homage to Athens. For the same reason, I shall only mention briefly the wars with revolted allies, in which the Athenians were involved in the mean time. The most important among these feuds were those against Euboea and Samos (Olymp. 83, 2). All the Euboeans together formed one state of different races, consisting of about four or five independent cities, among which Chalcis and Eretria had lost their ancient greatness. When they revolted, the island was subdued by Pericles, and on the north-eastern promontory the Athenians founded the colony of Oreos in a district which had once been occupied by the Histiaeans, a Pelasgian people, whose name corresponds with that of Histiaeotis in Thessaly. That settlement was, in a military point of view, a post of great importance to the Athenians, especially during the last unfortunate years of the Peloponnesian war, since through it they were enabled to keep up a communication with Thessaly, Lemnos, and Scyros.

The war against Samos belongs to the time immediately preceding the Peloponnesian war (Olymp. 85, 1). The Samians had not indeed been one of the great states, and were less powerful than the Lesbians and Chians, but they had a great fleet. They had not only freed themselves from the domination of Athens, but had even formed connections with the Persian satraps, and received auxiliaries from Pissuthnes. " They were not ashamed of obeying barbarians rather than Greeks of their own race." Their defence was obstinate, and the Athenians were obliged to make immense efforts to conquer the island. At length, after a siege of nine months they succeeded. This war is remarkable, because it is the first in which the Greeks used an improved kind of besieging engines, which had been made by Artemon. But they were not then invented for the first time, for on the Egyptian monuments representing the victories of the great Ramses, we find the most perfect besieging engines of the Greek period, such as the battering-ram, and other engines which were employed by the Greeks of later times. But the besieging engines appear to have been as imperfect among the Greeks as they were afterwards among the Romans; and it is surprising that they were not used by the latter till so late a period.

After the subjugation of Samos, all the Greek towns which

had formerly stood to Athens in the relation of allies, had
become tributary and subjects. They had gradually lost their
own power, and given up their own constitutions. The
arrogance of the Athenians had increased in the same proportion,
and they soon went so far in their desire to strengthen their
own hands, as to forbid their subjects to build and keep any
ships of war.[6]

The conquest of Samos is one of the most brilliant feats of
Pericles, the son of Xanthippus. He belonged to one of the
greatest families in Attica, and his mother, Agariste, was a
grand-daughter of Cleisthenes, the Alcmaeonid, who after the
expulsion of the Pisistratids, reformed and changed the constitution of Athens. This statement about Agariste appears to
me to be true, and from it we may infer, that at the time when
he made his reforms, Cleisthenes was already a man of mature
age. Pericles was thus descended on the one hand from the
princes of Sicyon and the Alcmaeonids, the opponents of the
Pisistratids, while on his father's side, his family was connected
with the Pisistratids, and Pericles himself bore a family resemblance to Pisistratus, of which the effects were different:
with some it was a recommendation, in others it excited
jealousy and mistrust.

Some of the particulars which we know about him are
founded on rather weak evidence: Stesimbrotus is probably
the chief source of our accounts, and he is not a very good
authority; but all that is related of Pericles is so consistent,
and some points are so strongly confirmed by writers who
lived nearer his own time, that on the whole, and without
maintaining the correctness of every particular point, we can
form a fair conception of the great changes which took place
in the life and character of the Athenians at that time. Even
when Pericles was a youth, a literature had sprung up which
had not existed before. If we imagine the instruction which
Pisistratus may have received, it can have consisted only in
his learning songs and poems by heart, and in reading and
writing, unless we suppose what is impossible, that he first
brought the Homeric poems to Athens. But in the time of
Pericles, literature and science were already developed; he

---

[6] In the preceding part of this Lecture, the order adopted by Niebuhr in 1829
and 1830, has been considerably altered, for the purpose of rendering the subject
clearer and more intelligible.—ED.

accordingly received the best instruction, and is said to have listened to the discourses of Zeno of Elea, the acute and profound metaphysician, and afterwards to those of Anaxagoras. That he heard the latter, is quite certain, whereas in regard to Zeno, the statement may seem doubtful; but I believe it. Much that had before been the common property of all, and had been popularly cultivated, now separated itself, and became a distinct art or branch of art, and had already been so far developed, as to be taught as an art: thus Pericles learned music of Damon. Hence the instruction which he received was already essentially the same as that which we find among the Greeks of later times, with the exception of rhetoric, which as yet formed no part of it; for in the time of Pericles this art was not yet practised, and people entertained no other idea of oratory, but that it was a talent cultivated by practice; it was as yet unknown that there could exist such an art as rhetoric, which subsequently did so much injury to the character of the Greeks. In the education of the later times, war and the forum were quite distinct, as for example in the case of Demosthenes, who did indeed engage in a campaign, but that was only accidental and of no importance; his life was quite different. The man of the sword, on the other hand, did not appear in the forum: Iphicrates spoke badly, and Chabrias not at all. But in the period of Pericles both were inseparably connected; the statesmen then were obliged to be at the same time warriors; and there existed then altogether a much closer union among the different pursuits of life, in which division was not yet carried so far as was afterwards the case.

Pericles had inherited a large property from his ancestors; his father Xanthippus was one of the most distinguished citizens, and had acquired great reputation on the day of the battle of Mycale. On the whole, therefore, he was early received by the people with great favour, although there existed a certain distrust on account of his connection with Pisistratus. He put himself in opposition to Cimon, though he did not equal him in wealth; he was indeed rich, but did not possess as much wealth as Cimon had acquired in war. He, therefore, could not compete with him for popular favour; yet he himself, either from inclination, or from conviction, or perhaps from calculation, entered upon the career of a demagogue, that is, a man endeavouring to win the favour of the people. " The power which his birth could no longer secure to him, he endeavoured to obtain from the people. This demagogy of aristocrats by birth is not uncommon; we find it, for example, in the history of the French revolution." For this purpose he allied himself with a friend, Ephialtes.

" The source of his power lay in the magic of his eloquence and" in the fact that he applied the treasures and the wealth of the republic to the personal comfort of the people. " He adorned the city with buildings and works of art of every kind; and there can be no doubt, that his πολιτεία had great influence upon the embellishment of the drama. But with all this, he was a faithful administrator of the public property, and very skilfully increased the sources of the revenue; he contributed much to the wealth and comfort of the people.

Pericles has often been compared with Lorenzo de Medici, and that very justly; but Lorenzo is inferior to Pericles, who was not indeed a great man, but a distinguished man, and great as a statesman, full of great and brilliant ideas.

LECTURE XLII.

To call the most brilliant period of Athenian history " the age of Pericles," is indeed a modern idea, and the expression does not occur in antiquity, but it is perfectly appropriate. The name of the man who is in the possession of the greatest power, fully and accurately indicates the character of his age. If we look a little back to the time of Themistocles and Cimon, we perceive the greatest difference between it and that of Pericles. In the latter period, the age of art and perfection manifests itself in every respect; men advance and are conscious of it, continuing that of which the foundations lie in the past, and working out their own cultivation in every way.

His age, moreover, witnessed the great change, by which Athens became so entirely the centre of Greek intellect; something of a similar nature is found in Germany, nay, even in France. Before the time of Pericles, Greek intelligence, culture, and genius, were the common property of the whole nation, excepting the Spartans, who always were and remained barbarians, and a few of the other nations of Peloponnesus: neither the Eleans nor the Arcadians, nor even the Achaeans, had men whom they could boast of, if we except a few of later times. At Sparta, the common mechanical crafts, as those of smiths, carpenters, and the like, which might be carried on by slaves, were flourishing; but whatever required free intelligence lay prostrate. But otherwise the spirit of the Greeks was generally diffused. Poetry, *e. g.*, flourished indeed chiefly in Ionia and the Asiatic Aeolia, but it was not confined to Asiatic Greece; it was thriving most luxuriantly also at Thebes in the sublimest lyrics of later times, in southern Italy, and Sicily. In like manner, the arts, in their earlier periods, had different places where they were cultivated, as Corinth and Aegina. But, from the time of Pericles, a great change took place in this respect, and at a still later period Athens was everything; Athens alone had artists and orators and poets, both tragic and comic, in the real sense of the term. For the more ancient Sicilian comedies were of quite a different nature, and had sprung from quite different roots. The Sicilian comedy had no lyric element at all, whereas in regard to the poetical form, the lyric element was essential in Attic comedy. As far as its materials are concerned, Attic comedy moves in the political world, in the world of reality; whereas the Sicilian moved in a widely extended range of subjects. In its whole nature and tendency, it was essentially meditative and generally philosophical; ranging from heaven, through the earth, and down to the infernal regions. It is true, its philosophy, according to the nature of things in that age, was simple, practical wisdom, of the kind which we find in the writings of Saadi and the gnomic poets; but Epicharmus, in his comedies, also entered into philosophical speculations on nature.

Art in its state of perfection, no longer consisting of mere symbols and unfinished representations, but that art which strove to comprehend life even in its innermost recesses, and to represent truly living forms, true images of the inner man, and not mere mummies, very soon withdrew from all parts, with the exception of Corinth, to Athens. The mechanical parts of art continued to flourish at Corinth, and even at a later time Corinth was distinguished for the perfection of mechanical skill; but the spirit of art dwelt at Athens alone.

" The arts had, indeed, originated in other places, and risen to
a certain degree of mediocrity, but the sudden advance to
what was better and best, proceeded from Athens.   Athens
was the heart of the body," the real home of the arts; and in
the same manner it became the exclusive seat of literature.
The rest of Greece no longer produced anything worth naming.
If a great man sprang up in any other part of Greece, he
betook himself to Athens, cultivated his talents, and struck
root there only, just as at present every person of eminence
in France goes to Paris; though I must add, that this comparison is not accurate;[1] nor is the parallel which we find in
Germany, in the transition from the ancient popular poetry to
the attempt of raising poetry to the rank of an art, entirely to
the point.   This transition, the imitation of the foreign trou-
badours, extended all over Germany, though, it is true, it was
far greater in Upper Germany, than here on the Rhine and in
northern Germany.   In our part of Germany there was more
of imitation at second hand; as the dialect of Upper Germany
had become more firmly established, the North, with its
dialect could no longer make opposition, and hence the latter
countries preserved much more that was genuine ancient
German.   It was not till the sixteenth century that this state
of things became altered, when a great part of southern Germany, where intellectual culture and literature were widely
extended, had become effete, so that during that century we
can mention but few Austrian and Bavarian authors, and
northern Germany rose superior.   At present it has again
become generally diffused.   Such has also been the case in
France: the refinements of the civilisation of Europe in the
middle ages proceeded from southern France, Catalonia and
Valencia, and passed over to the north; but those southern
countries, if we compare them with the north of France, in
which, as in other Romanic countries, afterwards everything
was concentrated, are at present sunk into barbarism.   Thus
the spirit of intelligence often migrates and settles in a different quarter.   I do not mean to say, that the south of France
has not produced mighty minds, but then they no longer
belonged to the south of France, the whole activity of their
minds being of the character of northern France, and directed

[1] " In the modern world Florence has the greatest resemblance to Athens, in
regard to the moral and mechanical arts."—1826.

towards Paris. Had they lived in Marseilles as their centre, they would have been dead, as at Colophon or similar places. In Catalonia, things have become truly barbarous. One of the causes of such a change is the fact, that circumstances become quite different, when the culture and the results of a long period, must be made use of by art and reflection. The case is quite different, when every one must begin afresh, as a youth, and with nearly equal difficulties, from what it is, when an art has already sprung up, which must be regularly learned, and from which men must start.

The general culture in Greece now also displayed itself in the plastic arts, which afterwards contributed so much to the glory of the Greek name.[2] In the earlier times the Greeks did not excel in them; the mechanical skill necessary for working in brass and the like, may have been considerably developed even at an early time, but all that depends on the art of drawing was yet entirely in its infancy.

If we are here reminded of the fact, that in Egypt as early as the eighteenth dynasty, art, notwithstanding its barbarous stiffness, yet shows exquisite beauty, especially in the formation of statues, which were made of a most intractable material, and in the paintings on the ruins of Thebes even gracefulness and a considerable degree of truth and life, we must not lose sight of the other fact, that from the time when the arts had obtained that perfection in a foreign country, until the age of Pericles, at least nine hundred years had elapsed, and that from that time the arts had been stagnating in Egypt like everything else in the East. At present, and for a long time past, we see only imitations of what has been produced at a period of greater prosperity, and such also was the condition of the arts at that time among the Egyptians and other nations.

In order to comprehend and appreciate the merit and the genius of the fathers of Grecian art, we must transport ourselves into Italy in the period of the thirteenth and fourteenth centuries. Although there still existed at Constantinople a species of art which mainly imitated the works of the ancient school, yet its life had died out more than 1000 years before; and the great Italian masters recalled the dead art to life again

[2] As to what follows, comp. vol. i. p. 306 foll. The repetitions which here occur could not be removed without destroying the whole context.—ED.

and restored it to a state of consciousness. The relation of the fathers of Grecian art to the art which had existed before was of the same kind; though we cannot compare the arts in the age of Pericles with what they were in the thirteenth and fourteenth centuries.[3]

The formation of figures in clay was one of the principal branches of the plastic art in ancient Greece; hence the vessels which were at first called Etruscan, then Greek, and now again Etruscan.   Such vases of clay, of very beautiful forms, were made at a very early period; the drawing was monochromatic, with red or yellow colour on dark ground. On the most ancient vases, these paintings are quite grotesque, and their bad drawing renders them disagreeable to an unprejudiced eye.   It would seem that Greek drawing was first cultivated on such vases, and that thence painting was developed in two directions, namely, painting on tables and on walls; the latter was then certainly not fresco, but encaustic painting.   The art of painting occurs in Greece at a very early time.   The objects of the first great paintings were, as at Rome, very remarkable actions, battles and the like.   The first of which we have any definite information was a picture of the battle of Marathon by Panaenus, in the Poecile, in which the Athenian heroes and the Persian commanders were portraits of great excellence.   These pictures, however, were not perfect; but persons might delight in them nevertheless as much as we may delight in those of the great Giotto, than which they probably were not more perfect.   But Polygnotus is the father of the real Greek art of painting ; he at once raised it in all its branches, in the mechanical execution as well as in invention. When the Greeks were already accustomed to representations from mythical story, he painted in the portico at Delphi the magnificent scenes from Homer.   The descriptions which Pausanias gives of them, are so faithful that any one endowed with imagination can represent the pictures to his mind, even without his being able to paint; and it was a happy idea of Göthe to suggest a restoration of such a picture from the description of Pausanias;[4] but the attempt at restoration was

---

[3] This paragraph has been transferred to this place from the beginning of this Lecture.—ED.

[4] This alludes to the drawings by F. and J. Riepenhausen, 1805 and 1806. See Göthe, *Nachgelassene Werke*, vol. iv. p. 92, foll.

was made with very little success. The work of Polygnotus was distinguished above all the earlier productions, and we see that he came forward as a mighty genius. In an artistic point of view, the chest of Cypselus was nothing at all; there may have been much technical skill, but it was not a work of art.

Sculpture, which had been far more cultivated than painting, especially in the Aeginetan school, appears simultaneously with Polygnotus in a beautiful and even higher stage of development. The sculptures of Aegina (the Aegina marbles at Munich) are excellent; the heads are indeed detestable, but the figures are admirable. This cannot be well explained otherwise than by supposing that the heads were made according to ancient types, from which the artist did not venture to deviate, as is the case at present in the Greek church in Russia, where an artist is not allowed to make any alteration in the barbarously faulty attitudes of the figures without being decried as an infidel by the orthodox people. Thus Pericles found sculpture already at its height, that is to say, it had as yet nothing charming or lovely, it was severe and harsh, and there still was in it much that was strange ; but it was nevertheless highly developed. The art of working in marble, however, did not become really general till his time ; works in marble had indeed been executed before, but only rarely and imperfectly. In former times the carving in wood had existed along with brass-founding, and had been as customary as it was with our ancestors down to the fourteenth and fifteenth centuries, when the art of carving was excellent; some works were made in brass also, but no human figures. The working in marble rose to its highest perfection after the time of the Peloponnesian war. In the age of Pericles it was still customary to paint all marble statues, a custom which was not abandoned till afterwards ; but, throughout that age, they were painted from head to foot, the drapery was coloured, and the eyes consisted of coloured stones put in. The most beautiful specimen of this kind which we possess, is a Diana at Naples, on which much of the painting is preserved. I can quite understand, that it is possible to accustom one's eyes to it so much that it ceases to be offensive; but the omission of the colours was nevertheless a step in advance. At that time the graceful and beautiful became everywhere more

prominent, the purely severe forming the characteristic feature
of the preceding period.

Before the time of Pericles, no other style of architecture
was employed but the Doric, with its mighty columns, which,
being very thick at the base, become thinner towards the top,
almost like a cone, as we see in western Sicily, at Selinus and
Agrigentum.   I know this style of architecture only from
drawings, and do not think that I should be able to accustom
my eye to it.   It must, however, be observed, that gradually
the disproportion between the diameters of the upper and
lower ends (for a basis, properly so called, does not occur in
those columns) was diminished.   In the age of Pericles, the
Ionian style was first introduced in Greece, having unquestionably been in use in Ionia before that time.   To a man,
who, like myself, lives upon the ruins of antiquity, this
uncommonly beautiful style of architecture is the most perfect
of all beautiful forms, the emblem of the consummation of the
age of beauty, when gracefulness had reached the highest point,
without being over-refined.   The Corinthian style, on the
other hand, is decidedly indicative of the sinking condition of
Greece.   The influence of Pericles upon architecture was
extremely great ; for he made use of the treasures of the
republic for erecting the most magnificent buildings.   " The
Poecile, or the portico with the picture of the battle of
Marathon, had been built as early as the time of Cimon,
who also raised the temple of Theseus out of the booty
taken from the Persians."   Pericles built the ῾Εκατόμπεδον or
Parthenon, which had exactly 100 feet in front, a circumstance
which has afforded us an opportunity of becoming accurately
acquainted with the Greek and Roman foot: from it we know
exactly what a Greek foot was, and can be certain also of
estimating the Roman foot rightly.   The results of Cagnazzi's
investigations about the extent of the Greek and Roman foot,
are quite confirmed by that circumstance.   The Parthenon is
the real glory of Athens.   Pericles also built the Propylaea or
portico leading up to the Acropolis, from which it is evident
that all thoughts of making use of the Acropolis as a fortress,
had been given up.   The interior of the sanctuary contained
the statue of Athena by Phidias, which being composed,
according to our description, of ivory and gold, appears to us
strange; and yet it is only men of prejudiced minds that, as

we are so often told, can doubt the extraordinary beauty of the statue: that beauty consisted in its whole expression, its form, magnitude, and general magnificence. The use of ivory may have been somewhat strange, but it must not be forgotten, that it is extremely easy to work in it, and does not oblige the artist to waste so much labour as working in marble. The pieces were so put together that they could not be distinguished.

Another great change which belonged to the age of Pericles is the cultivation of oratory, which now became an art. Men had, no doubt, addressed the people long before that time, but it had been done in a natural manner and without artifice; and there can be no question that previously there had been men of great power of persuasion, who could give a lucid exposition, and stir up the passions of their audience, for even uncultivated nations often display powerful eloquence. Oratory, perhaps, shows itself least in times like those immediately preceding the age of Pericles; the passions of a rude age, on the other hand, create a wild eloquence of their own, as we see among the North American Indians, and among nomadic nations. But Pericles was the first who worked up his speeches with the intention to persuade his hearers. The evidence on this point is unquestioned. He was, however, not exactly the inventor, for it lay in the spirit of the age; and Gorgias was even then in a condition to raise eloquence to the rank of an art, which he did in so perverse a manner, that rhetoric from its very beginning was corrupted. No art, in fact, had from its very commencement been so corrupt as this: had Demosthenes learnt his rhetoric from a school, he would have been a still more mighty genius, if he had become the orator he really was; but his genius might have been crippled by the injurious influence of the rhetorical schools. The fact that he remained so free from the influence of the time arose, no doubt, from his not having gone through any school, but trained himself. Homer and Thucydides were his models; and the latter of these is a better rhetorician than Gorgias. He was a true orator, and had no such σχήματα as Gorgias; but of this I shall say more hereafter.[5]

The period from the Persian to the Peloponnesian war is

[5] This paragraph has been transferred to this place from an earlier part of the present Lecture.—Ed.

the one in which history began to unfold itself, and dramatic
poetry to rise to its height. History originated in another
part of Greece, but tragedy was developed at Athens.   I have
already spoken of the origin of dramatic poetry and the tragedy
of Thespis.   Phrynichus wrote in the time of the Persian war,
and Aeschylus had, no doubt, commenced even before it, so that
we may refer the development of the drama to the time of Cleisthenes. But it did not remain stationary at that point. The whole
character of Sophocles belongs to the age of perfect beauty,
which was the result of the great impulse given by the Persian
war.   Never in any nation has such an elevation and such an
all-animating enthusiasm manifested itself, as at Athens at
that time: " the youth of the great men fell in the time of the
Persian wars, and after them they developed themselves and
reached their culminating point, through the prosperity which
Greece enjoyed during the subsequent period.   All lyric poetry
became absorbed by tragedy: the poet no longer sings his own
feelings like the lyric bard, but he makes others sing as he
himself would have sung if he had been in their position.   The
dialogue is by far the smallest and most unimportant part; the
strength lies in the choruses."   The same impulse also affected
the excellent ancient comedy, " the child of the greatest
energy and enjoyment of life," which, as far as its form is
concerned, is somewhat younger than tragedy, for Attic
comedy does not commence till after the Persian wars.   " As
it is quite worthy of the ancient tragedy, so everything else
at that time was in harmony with tragedy, e. g., the earliest
Attic oratory, the orations of Antiphon, and the historical
narrative of Thucydides, who was somewhat younger."   What
an abundance of men of great genius and talent Athens at
that time possessed, may be easily seen by distributing them
into their respective classes.   Some are only mentioned here
and there, but ex ungue leonem, and from the little we know of
them, we can judge what extraordinary men they were.
" Even now we are amazed at the freshness of life in reading
the works of that period."   We may with truth assert, that
there never was a period when a nation was happier than the
Athenians then were; for how can a people, like any individual
man, be more happy than at a time when it lives more and
more intensely.   It was an important circumstance, that the
great simplicity in the mode of living was not altered by this

uncommon splendour—luxury did not enter the life of individual citizens, nay, the nobles were not allowed to display any luxuries. The wealthy at Athens were obliged to consider themselves the equals of the poor, and their general character was that of frugality and simplicity; just as was the case in the equality at Venice, where no nobleman was allowed to keep a more ornamented gondola than the others, in order that the poorer nobles might not be thrown into the shade. This is characteristic of the Greeks, and seems to be a peculiarity of their race. The Greeks live very frugally, and meat is eaten rarely. The strictness of fasting in the East is the consequence of this mode of life. " Olives, salad of wild herbs, fruit, salt fish, bread, ricotta, all kinds of dishes made of milk, and fresh cheese, have been the ordinary food of the Greeks at all times, and they are perfectly happy with it. Their wines, too, are, on the whole, not particularly good; there are, indeed, some of excellent quality, but the ordinary wines are not agreeable to the palate. Thus every one lived simply, and could not live otherwise, if he wished to enjoy influence and esteem among the people."

One advantage of riches was, that a wealthy man could do much for the people and the common good, and that he was enabled to institute festivals for the people, and this he was obliged to do. The wealthy were chosen according to certain lists to furnish the choruses, and to see that they were instructed; and the splendour and excellence of the choruses conferred honour and distinction upon those who furnished them. How many στῆλαι have come down to us containing the honourable record that this or that man provided the chorus for the tribe Acamantis, and that by it he gained the victory for his tribe ! Another burden which, however, was likewise a distinction, consisted in the trierarchy; the state furnished the naked galleys, but wealthy individuals were appointed to equip them; and in the earlier times a man who did this had also the command of the galley; but this was afterwards changed, and others were entrusted with the command. Whoever distinguished himself in the discharge of this duty, received a crown; and he who had equipped his galley most beautifully and most perfectly, who had the best rowers and gave them an addition to the pay which they received from the public

funds, and the like, had the honour of being publicly named
before the people, and of receiving a crown as his reward; and
the fact of his having obtained the crown was engraved on a
table with a representation of the crown.   Such were the
demands made upon the wealthy, and such their rewards.   A
very ingenious man, from whom we may always learn much,
though he has erred in particular points, has looked upon this
as a great hardship, and has lamented the heavy duties which
fell upon the wealthy Athenians.   In reference to a later period,
this remark is true; there certainly were times when the
demands were exorbitant, and the distinction was nothing but
a burden; but those were times of need and distress.   It
cannot, indeed, be denied that in those later times the demands
were carried to a point at which they became unfair; for when
times became less prosperous, the demands also ought to have
been diminished.   But I am here speaking of the period
of the highest prosperity of Athens, in regard to which
the arrangement was excellent.   What harm did it do to a
Nicias, a Callias, and other wealthy persons, if they had to
give up even the greatest part of their income for purposes,
which did them honour, and if thereby they promoted such
glorious objects?   For what could be more glorious than to
bring out in a splendid style a comedy of Cratinus, or a tragedy
of Aeschylus?   And does not the generosity of those men still
live in our recollection?   That assuredly is not a thing to be
lamented, of which the objects were great and sublime.   Have
those men whose names are remembered even after the lapse
of more than two thousand years, not gained more than if they
had lent out their money at a high rate of interest, or had
squandered it in pomp and luxury?

"The prosperity of Athens during this period was immense.
Three hundred galleys were equipped by private persons; the
great festivals were celebrated to some extent at their expense;
and they regarded this enormous burden as an honour worth
contending for.   But as nothing on earth is perfect, the habit
of flattering the people became developed amid this luxuriance
of strength; and when everything had risen to such a height,
that no one could think of the possibility of falling, the state
was undermined by laws which were proposed by demagogues,
because they afforded momentary gratification to the people.

Under Pericles the constitution became more and more formless and relaxed."[6]

———•———

LECTURE XLIII.

I SHALL now proceed to give you some account of the constitution of Athens during this period, and a brief sketch of its very obscure internal history.

It is perfectly true that we know far less about the history of the Attic constitution than about that of Rome, although in the case of Athens we have the immense advantage of contemporary writers, and although the orators furnish us with contemporary documents. We are more particularly ignorant of the transitions. In respect to the constitution, therefore, and especially in regard to its development, we are left to conjecture. The difficulty lies in this: the outlines, the essential characteristics of which are the same among all the ancient nations—and this is a remarkable fact—were preserved at Rome to a greater extent, and for a longer time, and the periods of transition were more marked, and were noticed much more by the Romans themselves, who paid special attention to their constitution. Although modern writers entertain confused and erroneous notions of the Roman constitution, yet fortunately all its main points are clear and distinctly stated in our authorities. The Attic constitution, on the other hand, had become changed at so early a period that its real principles were greatly modified even as early as the time of Solon; and there can be no doubt, that even before the Persian war, changes were made in accordance with the momentary exigencies and with expediency, and not, as at Rome, according to the analogy of what had been established before; for at Rome the new constitution was always adapted to the circumstances of the preceding one. Even at the time when contemporary history begins to be written, the standard of numerical relations, which in the history of Rome enables us to recognise so many things, had ceased to be applied at Athens. In

---

[6] Many passages have been transposed in the foregoing Lecture, in order to make the statements more coherent and intelligible.—ED.

regard to many important changes, all that a cautious critic can say is, that about the time of the Peloponnesian war, the Athenian constitution was in some points more and in others less advanced than is commonly believed. The dignity of the ἄρχων ἐπώνυμος, for example, which was afterwards a mere shadow, and still more so than that of the Doge of Venice ever was, had, until shortly before the Peloponnesian war, been a substantial magistracy and a real power in the state; and the first men of Athens did not disdain to be invested with it: Solon, Aristides, and Themistocles, had been ἄρχοντες ἐπώνυμοι. It is certainly not true that those high offices were obtained by lot as early as that time, they were not yet κληρωταί, a mistake under which even Plutarch laboured; for how should men like Aristides and Themistocles have obtained the office? But it is equally certain that in the time of Pericles the ἐπώνυμος ἀρχὴ was given by lot, and when we are told that Pericles was opposed to the Areopagus, because the office of ἄρχων ἐπώνυμος had not fallen to his lot, this is in all probability not true, but it proves the mode of election at that time, and shews that then the dignity was obtained by lot.

We are not only unable to trace step by step the changes in the Attic constitution, which were made during the period of about forty-eight years, from the Persian down to the Peloponnesian war, but we are in great uncertainty even in regard to the importance and the extent of several of them. At the beginning of that period the power of the council of the Five Hundred was, according to all appearance, still very considerable; it probably still enjoyed the privilege that no popular decree could be passed without its probuleuma. But this was gradually very much altered, and in later times everything was done in the form of a simple psephisma, which before had required a preliminary decree of the council (προβούλευμα). The importance of that principle lay in the fact that a decree of the people could not be proposed on a sudden, nor be passed in a hasty manner.

The following is a much disputed point, but no certain result has been arrived at: it is commonly said, that Ephialtes, the friend of Pericles, weakened the power of the ἄνω βουλὴ, or the βουλὴ ἐν Ἀρείῳ πάγῳ. But what the power of that council consisted in, is a very obscure question. To my mind, it is quite certain that its power consisted in something undefined, that in times of urgent necessity it obtained from the senate full power to govern the state, and to adopt extraordinary measures, just as the consuls did at Rome, when ordered *videant nequid res publica detrimenti capiat;* and that under particularly pressing circumstances it sometimes usurped that power. Certain it is, that at the time of the Persian war, that council exercised a kind of dictatorial power to manage public affairs during that dangerous period. But what were its authority and rights in ordinary times of peace, what share it took in the government, what judicial power it had, and what powers were taken from it by Ephialtes, these are questions which are quite obscure. In modern times it has been much discussed, with unequal arguments and without any results, as to whether through Ephialtes the Areopagus was deprived of the δίκαι φονικαί for a time, and afterwards recovered them. I have no opinion upon the question; but I do not think it impossible, that we may yet come nearer the truth, though I do not believe that we can get beyond mere probabilities. This much, in short, is certain, that the Areopagus, though not in a distinct form, could generally exercise an extraordinary power, and it was perhaps this extraordinary power itself, of which Ephialtes deprived it, "since by it the council was enabled directly to interfere in, and check the power of the people." Pericles and Ephialtes both aimed at extending the power of the commonalty; and we may say of both of them, that they did not know what they were doing, for there can be no doubt that through their measures they injured the republic. Where the circulation of the blood is so rapid as in the Athenian people, care ought to have been taken not to accelerate the pulse, but rather to introduce a retarding element in the proceedings, for there was no fear of torpor. Ephialtes certainly was a perfectly honest man, he cannot be charged with egotism and ambition, a charge which may with more justice be brought against Pericles, whom I would not in any way acquit of egotism. Pericles was conscious that he was ruling the people, which was identified with him; his convictions, expressed with spirit and enthusiasm, penetrated into the soul of the people, and whatever he proposed, was adopted. But to the Areopagus he stood in quite a different relation. He would not have possessed the same power, if he had spoken before a limited assembly like that of the Areopagus; nor could he have spoken there, if he had wished to make opposition, for he was not a member of it, nor had he any prospect of becoming a member, because the archonship was given by lot and no longer by election. Had the innovators not made the archonship attainable by lot, he would have become ἐπώνυμος, and a member of the Areopagus, which, perhaps, he might have swayed according to his own discretion. But as it was, he was obliged to adopt a different course.

The Areopagus is a remarkable instance of what is called *esprit de corps* in its noblest meaning, just as previously to the French revolution the parliament of Paris shewed a gravity and independence, which was communicated to all its members and remained with them through life and in all its relations. A frivolous member of parliament would have been despised even by those who would have liked to see all the world frivolous. The hereditary spirit in a family in free countries is an *esprit de corps* of this kind; it is the real bond which insures the continuance of a free constitution, and which exercises a great restraint from within, when outward restraint has ceased. Wherever in a free state such family sentiments exist, the family remains faithful to them, and supports them so that they become a principle which is maintained for centuries. Thus it is impossible for a Russell in England to become an advocate of absolutism; it would be regarded as monstrous. The same has been the case in other free states, and this is a true and beneficial aristocracy. In like manner the Areopagus had its peculiar sentiments; a frivolous and miserable man, says Isocrates,[1] at a time of dissolution, when becoming a member of the Areopagus, must assume a different spirit. Hence the Areopagus was an excellent institution. It consisted of men who had been members of the college of the nine archons, who at the expiration of their office became members of the Areopagus, and remained in it for life. But as the Areopagus was to represent the consistency and intelligence of the republic, a scrutiny was instituted, especially when the archons were appointed by lot, for otherwise it would have been a folly. Whoever had been appointed by lot had to undergo a δοκιμασία, before he entered on his office, and when the period of office terminated he had to submit to another

---

[1] *Areopag.*, p. 147, R.

δοκιμασία, before he was admitted into the Areopagus. A similar scrutiny is instituted in the Italian cities in regard to the Podesta.

The power of the Areopagus, then, was reduced by Pericles and Ephialtes; Aristotle, the profoundest connoisseur of the political constitution, in speaking of this fact, says, that Pericles and Ephialtes ἐκόλουσαν τὴν ἐν Ἀρείῳ πάγῳ βουλήν.[a]

There are yet other injudicious things which Pericles did from motives which we can perfectly excuse. If we consider that the greater part of the sovereign people were so fearfully poor, and the Athenian state, on the other hand, so extremely rich, I think it quite right that Pericles directed his attention towards relieving this condition, and to distribute among the individual citizens a portion of the riches of the state.[3] In like manner the *leges frumentariae* at Rome are unfairly judged of. But it was not wise that the law granted the money on condition of the people taking part in the assemblies and courts of justice. The payments were made in such a manner, that every one on entering the assembly or a court of justice received a ticket, for which he obtained a τριώβολον (about 4½d.) just as in certain Royal Academies, where the lectures are often so tedious, that those who do their duty and attend the meetings, receive a *jeton*, which is changed into money: a Periclean scientific institution ! This was a very great expense, and the evil consequence was, that all the poor people who had formerly remained at home looking after their own business, now deserted their trades, and crowded to the assemblies to get their triobolon.   " The popular assemblies were now attended by immense crowds, while formerly they had consisted of those who took a real interest in the business; and the people now gave their votes either according to the dictates of their passions or at random. This change, therefore, was very injurious. But it was almost worse that the popular courts now became so exceedingly numerous, and that not only for political offences but for civil cases. The popular courts often consisted of 5,000 citizens; 500 or 600 were the

---

[a] *Polit.*, ii. 9, 3.

[3] " We see these poor people, but contented with their poverty, vividly portrayed in the comedies of Aristophanes. However much of caricature there may be in them, the details of the life of the people are true.   It is true the bad features—we cannot call them wicked—are set forth rather prominently, but we must bear in mind that his works after all are but comedies."—1826.

ordinary numbers. These courts themselves were an innovation of that time, though popular courts had existed before, for they arise from the nature of republican and democratic states; but they had been of a different-kind.

These democratic courts are generally but unjustly compared with our trials by jury, in which the question is only as to whether an offence has been committed or not. The individual judges at Rome, who were appointed by the praetor, were of this nature: the *judex juratus* decided as to whether the accused was guilty or not. But beside these judices, Rome also had its popular courts, which tried offences against the state, or such as affected the state in any way; their object was quite different, for the question there was not only whether M. Manlius had committed an illegal act, or had disregarded the *majestas* of the magistrates? (this was only the first question); but the other question, Is he to be pardoned or not? was likewise decided. These trials came before the sovereign people, because it alone had the power of pardoning. The sovereign people had to judge also of the circumstances of the accused, and to determine as to whether he was responsible for his actions. This is everywhere the object of consideration in cases which are tried by popular assemblies, which in their capacity as courts, though not by a special act, exercise the right of pardoning. This is the meaning of all the popular courts, both in Greece and at Rome, in the earlier times. At the beginning of the seventh century of Rome, however, this power belonged to other courts, which we may term juries, and not to popular courts, which were no longer found suitable, because the manners of the people had become changed; and in this way the popular courts at Athens, also, in the course of time, produced bad effects. In this respect, the regulations of Pericles and Ephialtes were injurious, inasmuch as they multiplied the popular courts to such an extent, that not only offences against the state, but even civil cases, were tried by the people; and it was a mere abuse, that such a many-headed court was allowed to decide in cases where the only object was to ascertain whether a person was guilty or not. It was quite right, on the other hand, that the case of Socrates was tried by the popular court or *heliaea*, since it was certainly connected with the interest of the state. At Rome, all cases in which the question was simply whether the accused was guilty or not, were tried before a single judge, and the opinion now generally entertained, that several men must unanimously determine upon a man's guilt or innocence, would have appeared absurd to the Romans. Now considering the difficulty of establishing a person's guilt or innocence by the agreement of seven or twelve men, among whom a divergence is quite unavoidable, what must have been the result, when five hundred men, chosen by lot from among the most ignorant and reckless of the nation, were called upon to decide? There might occur such votes as are represented by Aristophanes, in his immortal comedy of the Wasps!

The opponent of Pericles was Thucydides of Alopece, an excellent man, who was probably not at all related to the great historian, and at any rate belonged to a different demos. He was at the head of what was then called the aristocracy, but which was an aristocracy in no other sense than that which in the United States is opposed to the democracy, and had no thought of any exclusive privileges. No importance could be attributed to it, and it could exert its influence only on particular emergencies. " Thucydides, at the head of this party, exerted himself to prevent the state of dissolution, at least, from spreading farther." He was an excellent man, and possessed of brilliant oratorical talent; but in the struggle against Pericles he could not, of course, maintain himself; he was unable to overcome his popular power of persuasion, and Pericles always could furnish that which was welcome to the sovereign people. Thucydides, moreover, was not without faults, one of which was, that in the popular assembly he and his friends occupied a separate place, and that they kept together, forming a sort of *côté droite*, which roused the suspicion of the people, and also allowed them to see how few they were, whence their designation of the ὀλίγοι. And as the people saw the smallness of their number, Thucydides lost his importance in their eyes.

Greece, in its unhappy career, had even then arrived at that point, where there exists no other criterion for estimating the worth of men, but wealth. At first the noble houses had alone constituted the state of Athens; afterwards the commonalty, which had risen by their side, and both together formed the whole body of the people; just as at Florence, the houses stood on one side and the commune on the other, until afterwards united

in seventy-two houses, they formed *il popolo*.   Powers had
thus been opposed to each other which could influence and
check one another.   But now one branch of the citizens, the
houses, had entirely disappeared, and this evil could not be remedied, because no one had ever thought of renewing the old
aristocracy in such a manner, as to enable it to continue to live;
but the aristocracy had to blame itself for this, for aristocrats
always wish that their body should consist of as few as possible.

As no attempt at renewal was made in Greece any more than
at Rome, all distinctions had gradually disappeared; and when
a distinction was to be made, there appeared no other criterion
than that of property; and into this the ancient notion of
aristocracy was fused.   The ancient idea of aristocracy was so
thoroughly lost, that even Aristotle, to whom otherwise nothing
is obscure, cannot quite comprehend its original meaning; he
knows, indeed, how to distinguish an aristocrat and an oligarch,
but he does not know that the ancient aristocracy was not at
all based upon a distinction arising from the possession of
money.   There is not a more wretched distinction than that
according to money.   How many things there are which have
a far higher value than property !   This mistake could never
be remedied, and hence it was afterwards impossible to form a
compact body able to maintain itself.   The Athenians often
thought of selecting a portion from the body of the citizens,
which was to be sovereign; and several momentary attempts
were made to remedy the evil.   Phrynichus and Antiphon of
Rhamnus, aimed at this, and Theramenes, in appointing the
Thirty, assuredly acted with this object in view.   After the
Peloponnesian war, there appeared symptoms of a plan of
selecting a portion of the citizens; and we find mention of it
in the fragments of Lysias; but it did not produce any results.
Afterwards an attempt was made by Demetrius Phalereus,
which for a time succeeded, because Cassander was ready to
support him with a powerful army, because all parties were
quiet, and the tyrannis was in the hands of a benevolent man,
who did not make use of it for selfish purposes.   But nothing
permanent could be created.

The great misfortune in all the Greek states was this:
" the internal relations were dissolved, and scarcely any other
distinction was known anywhere, except the vulgarest of all
distinctions, that arising from the amount of wealth, or else the

whole mass of the people ruled as sovereign. With an intellectual nation like the Athenians, the democratic form was indeed only a delusion, for the government was in the hands of individual great men, and the assembly only followed them; but wherever this is not the case, nothing is more wretched than this kind of democracy, which we see, for example, in Switzerland. The states no longer had the power to regenerate themselves, and" all the Greek constitutions in the time of the Peloponnesian war were ripe for revolutions, which however did not lead to lasting forms or permanent constitutions, but rather to usurpations.

There were yet several other causes which hastened the outbreak of the war. One of them was that the population had immensely increased, for Greece at that time was enormously populous. Imagine, for example, that Corcyra kept one hundred and twenty galleys: even if we suppose that the rowers were for the most part slaves, we may be sure that the marines in those galleys when completely equipped, amounted to 24,000 men: * and they were furnished by the single island of Corfu, all the inhabitants of which at present amount to no more than 60,000. The Zacynthians sent 1,000 hoplites to assist the Corcyraeans; Zante might, perhaps, even now raise 1,000 men, but what must have been its power to send them by ships out of the island! I have already expressed my opinion on the statements respecting the population of Aegina and Corinth, which are indeed ridiculous; but Athens at the beginning of the Peloponnesian war had 29,000 free armed hoplites, consisting of citizens and metoeci; if we estimate every family at five persons, we obtain a population of about 150,000 freemen. Now I do indeed believe that the number of slaves was less than that of freemen, but still the little country of Attica was incredibly populous, and we can scarcely

---

* Only one manuscript contains a qualification for these 24,000 men, for it has the additional word *other*, which, in opposition to the slaves, can only mean free men. The whole sentence, however, is very strange; for it suggests that Niebuhr here supposed every trireme to have contained at least 400 marines and, as there is evidently no fault in the manuscripts, it is obvious that Niebuhr made a slip. He probably intended to mention 12,000 freemen as the one-half of the complement, but forgot the division, and mentioned the number which ought to have been divided. It is possible that he meant to say: " the 120 galleys when completely manned contained 24,000 men, and even if the rowers were for the most part slaves, how enormous was this power for the single island of Corfu."—ED.

comprehend how the people were able to purchase even their
bread, which was imported from abroad. This over-population,
a portion of which consisted of poor people, was the principal
cause of the ferment then going on, and of the decline of the
Greek nation. In former times, the establishment of colonies
had been a suitable remedy, but it was now.no longer easy to
apply it; nor was it seasonable, for most countries were already
occupied. But some districts might still be taken possession
of. Athens did at that time send colonies to Amphipolis,
which ought to have been established in the north of the
Adriatic. This plan would indeed have been practicable, but
difficulties, of which we have no clear notion, prevented it at
that very time when the want of it was most strongly felt, and
the over-population produced poverty, uneasiness, and revolution.

The ancient manners, moreover, had everywhere undergone
a very rapid change: an extraordinary vivacity, a desire for
strong mental excitements, and a love of innovation, prevailed
throughout the people. The old views of things had disappeared, or had at least been shaken, and many new speculations sprang up in their place.

While things were in this condition, the conflict between
Athens and Peloponnesus could not be avoided. " The happy
period of Greece was gone, and the war broke out because
peace could not continue." The Peloponnesian war was one
of those events which might be delayed but could not be
averted, and in consequence of the mutual exasperation must
come to pass sooner or later; the necessity of it was felt,
the state of peace had something unnatural, and in the end
became unbearable.[5] The long-cherished exasperation between
the Athenians and a portion of the Peloponnesians, and the
envy of the Corinthians at the greatness of Athens, placed it
beyond the power of man to prevent the outbreak of the war.
It had become impossible to avert it by a peace, as had been
done before by the peace of Cimon: a decision was necessary,
and that decision could be brought about by war alone. The
subsequent peace of Nicias was only a truce.

This war was the vital crisis which put an end to the fresh
vigour of Greece: *propius periculum fuerunt qui vicerunt*, says

---

[5] The first part of this paragraph has been transferred to this place from the
beginning of the present Lecture.—ED.

Livy. It showed from the very beginning the character of a contest which had no definite object, and accordingly could terminate only with the destruction of one of the two parties. This feeling pervading even the thoughtless multitude, gave to the Peloponnesian war from the first the character of an internecine war.

LECTURE XLIV.

THE prosperous condition of Greece before the outbreak of the war, stands to the subsequent period in about the same relation as Germany before the thirty years' war to Germany after it, and as Italy before the wars beginning with the invasion of Charles VIII. to Italy after them. I say this not only in reference to the moral and intellectual condition of the country, but also in reference to its devastated state, although this was not quite so bad in Greece as in Germany and Italy. The youthful age of Greece had ceased even with the age of the epic and of the early lyric poets; but the vigorous age of manhood perished in the Peloponnesian war. If we compare even Demosthenes, one of the greatest geniuses that ever lived, and who stands almost alone in his time, with the men who flourished before the Peloponnesian war, we shall find that the poetical element has vanished. After the war, poetry still continued for a time to manifest a little life; but afterwards it disappears entirely, and what remains is only the reflex of the sun which has set, and illumines only the tops of the mountains. In the Augustan age, the men who had been young at the period of the civil wars, and before the battle of Actium, continued in comparative ease to produce immortal works, which as far as their origin is concerned, belonged to a by-gone age; and such also was the case in the Peloponnesian war. This observation is true in regard to all the arts of human speech, no less than to the whole mode of life. During the commotions which followed after the Peloponnesian war, all was in a state of weariness and exhaustion, just as ten years after the outbreak of the French revolution there existed no energy for new formations, representations and enterprises. All Greece had become fatigued and languid, all illusions and all hopes were exhausted and worn out. Such was the unfortunate result of the Peloponnesian war.

It was commenced with great vigour and energy: many things had then already reached their highest point, and others were just then attaining it. Tragedy had reached its highest perfection even before the war; the most distinguished plays were indeed brought out during the Peloponnesian war, but they were only the fruits of previous blossoms. Comedy still was cultivated by very many masters of the art, of whom we scarcely know more than their names; but Aristophanes was the greatest. The case of tragedy is different, for none can be compared with Sophocles. The plastic art was in a somewhat different condition: it steadily advanced during the war, and even after it, and reached a perfection, refinement, and gracefulness, of which no one had before had any idea. The art of prose composition reached its height during the war, while before it, it had scarcely existed at all: it was now produced and developed.

The power and wealth of Greece were destroyed by the war: before it had been a very flourishing country; but the riches were now drained, and even the districts which did not suffer directly from devastation, received a severe shock through the great levies of the Spartans. In addition to this, I must mention the general moral corruption and dissolution which was matured by the war: all the feelings of hatred and exasperation developed themselves; confidence and benevolence became extinct, and, what was worse than all, the youthful look towards the future was lost for ever. People lived on, as if it were a duty to do so; they lived without joyfulness, and without a prospect of bright and cheerful days, or any realisation of dreams and thoughts.

The Peloponnesian war, which in some respects resembles that against Hannibal, is the most immortal of all wars, because it is described by the greatest of all historians that ever lived. " Thucydides has reached the highest attainable point in historiography, both in regard to the positive historical certainty, and to the animated style of his work. In the latter point, Tacitus might perhaps be compared with him, if we possessed the lost books of his Historiae; for in those which have come down to us, he did not yet take an active part in public matters, as Thucydides did in the time which he describes. Tacitus, however, is not so unrestrained nor so graphic. Thucydides is, as it were, present everywhere, and sees what he relates. In this respect he is unique; it is possible that Livy, in his last books, was similarly graphic, though in quite a different way. Sallust has it in his speeches, and may have had it also elsewhere in his lost books. The charge which was formerly brought against Thucydides, is of the most absurd kind; in him and in Demosthenes every word has its full weight.

The opinion of some among the ancients, that the eighth book was not written by Thucydides, but was the work of Theopompus, is indescribably perverse. He was, indeed, unable to complete the whole history, but so far as the eighth book is finished, it is his work as certainly as the first seven books, and it is, moreover, such as he wished it to be. With the destruction of the Athenian expedition to Sicily, the ancient colossal greatness of Athens and the happy time of Greece came to their close, and the remaining period of the war was wretched and heart-rending: any one could foresee the issue. This is the reason why he wrote the eighth book differently from the others. Until the end of the seventh the solemnity of his narrative is constantly rising with the greatness of the events; but then the greatness was gone, there was nothing more to be related in a solemn and sublime style; there was no more free-will, the people were surrounded by misfortunes, and could no longer act otherwise than the iron necessity of fate decreed. The demegoriae also had become superfluous; they would have been quite out of place.

Xenophon in the first two books of his Hellenica is the continuator of Thucydides. They belong to a different time, and are quite a different work from the other books. As a continuation of Thucydides, they were composed in Xenophon's youth, and were published separately at a time when the heroes of the Peloponnesian war were still living. The interval between the second and third books is filled up by the Anabasis, and the third book of the Hellenica is so little connected with the two preceding ones, that the chronology which he otherwise faithfully notices, ceases all at once. The third book is a continuation of the Anabasis, so that two entire Olympiads are wanting in Greek history; the expedition of Agis against Elis alone is inserted, while other important occurrences are not touched upon at all. I may here observe that the Anabasis is evidently the work of Xenophon, and there can be no doubt that the person mentioned under the name Themistogenes,[1] is Xenophon himself. The Anabasis was certainly written before the last five books of the Hellenica; it is evidently the work of a man in the vigour of life, while the last five books of the Hellenica, which betray a man at a very advanced age, were probably composed in the middle of the Phocian war. Xenophon did not die before Olymp. 108. His history is worth nothing: it is untrue, written without care, and with perfect nonchalance. He has for a long time been considered as a model of Attic elegance; but how weak and dull are his narratives when compared with Thucydides! It is as if we were to compare Gleim with Göthe. The partiality towards Sparta is quite revolting: he glosses over their evil deeds, and acts the part of a calumniator and detractor towards his own country. His infatuation is inconceivable, for he imagined the supremacy of the Spartans to be salutary and beneficial to Greece: how could an Athenian say so?

As authorities for the period of the Thirty Tyrants, we have the speeches of Andocides and Lysias, who throw a much clearer light upon that time than Xenophon.

Besides Xenophon, Theopompus also continued Thucydides in his Hellenica; he carried the history from the point where his predecessor breaks off, down to the battle of Cnidus. This work may have been his best, for it was of a limited extent and without pretension, and his personal feelings did not come into play.

The outbreak of the Peloponnesian war, as I have already said, could no longer be avoided. Between Athens and the Peloponnesians, but especially between Athens and the Corinthians, there existed an invincible exasperation, which could not but lead to extremities. But the Corinthians could only endeavour to satisfy their spirit of revenge by stirring up the Spartans. This was not a very easy matter, as the Spartans were by no means inclined to commence war, not indeed from any scruples on account of the thirty years' truce, but from their own awkwardness, because a state living in such entirely

[1] *Hellen.* iii. 1.

obsolete forms, and existing in reality only as a remembrance of past ages, must have a natural aversion against all movements and convulsions, which might either produce unavoidable changes, or other mischief, if no change is allowed. " They also probably felt, that they could not bring the war to a speedy termination, and that it would be extremely troublesome to them because they had no revenues. This accounts for the great aversion of the Spartans to commence the war, although they cherished the bitterest hatred of Athens." But it was the leading men of the state who saw this difficulty rather than the great body of the Spartan citizens who had to decide upon the war. In cases, like this the real Spartans alone had a vote, but not the Lacedaemonians and Neodamodes; they formed an assembly like that of the curiae in ancient Rome, inferior to the democracy only in numbers, and the latter were pressing on for war. " The allies of the Spartans were divided in their opinions; a portion of them was quite barbarous and eager for booty."

In relating the history of a war which took place more than 2,000 years ago, it may appear superfluous to ask which of the belligerents was in the right, and which was in the wrong; but the question cannot be avoided. The Athenians certainly were not altogether wrong; it was here, as in many other cases, the weaker that occasioned the war, and not the more powerful. A dispute concerning Epidamnus had broken out between Corinth and Corcyra. Epidamnus was a Corcyraean colony, and according to the custom of the time an οἰκιστής had been taken from Corinth to conduct its establishment, because Corcyra itself was a colony of Corinth. When a colony was to be founded, the Roman people appointed triumvirs to make all the necessary arrangements, and sometimes even to draw up laws for the colony; and such also was the case in Greece, with this difference, that in the latter country a single person was appointed dictator to regulate the affairs of the new settlement. When a town which was itself a colony, sent out another, the custom was to apply to the mother city to furnish that dictator. Thus the colony of a colony stood to the metropolis in a relation similar to that existing at Rome, when a grandfather adopted the son of his own emancipated son. If he adopted him with the intention of afterwards emancipating him, the grandson had no other

obligation but that of *pietas*, and in like manner the colony
had no other duties.   Epidamnus can have been founded only
at a time, when the Illyrians were yet a very weak people, or
perhaps did not yet possess those districts at all.   The Illyrians
probably immigrated into those parts at a late period; they
advanced much later than is commonly believed, and hence it
is possible that at the time when Epidamnus was founded, the
Illyrians had either not yet settled in the country, or were
very weak.   From Aristotle's Politics² we know, that the
constitution of Epidamnus in ancient times was very oligarchical, whence we must infer that the Doric population was
very small, and that there were many strangers among the
inhabitants.   This explains the circumstances mentioned by
Thucydides, that the δῆμος and the ὀλίγοι were at war with
each other, and that the latter were overpowered and expelled
by the former.   The exiles fled to the neighbouring Illyrian
Taulantians, and thence applied to Corcyra.   This island
seems then to have had a mixed constitution, having previously
likewise been an oligarchy; for Corcyra too had a mixed
population, since even before the Corinthians settled in it, it
had been colonised by Eretrians who ruled over a Liburnian
population.   The Corinthian Corcyraeans, therefore, had two
classes of subjects, Eretrian colonists and hellenised Liburnians.
But as the Corcyraeans, like the ancient inhabitants whom
they found in the island, were a maritime people, the constitution could not remain long a strict and narrow oligarchy,
and there gradually arose a mixed constitution.   It is strange
and quite unnatural that the two great Italian republics of
Venice and Genoa, though commercial and maritime states,
yet were oligarchies. In Greece, an oligarchy never maintained
itself in a state given to navigation and commerce, which always
led to democratic institutions.   Even some among the ancient
politicians have noticed this phenomenon as a general axiom,
whence some who are always ready to establish maxims, are of
opinion that navigation must be regarded as an evil, because
it leads to democracy.   But the phenomenon is historically
correct.   At that time, however, Corcyra was not yet an
ἄκρατος δημοκρατία, that is, not so completely democratic that
the demos of Epidamnus necessarily allied themselves with it,
and to prevent the ὀλίγοι applying to it for aid; the fact that

² V. i. 6.

they were of the same race, was a point of more weight than the democratic constitution. The oligarchs were kinsmen of the Corcyraeans, while the demos was a mixture of several tribes, and foreign to them; hence the oligarchs applied to the Corcyraeans because they were related to them by blood. The Corcyraeans wished to bring about a reconciliation between the contending parties; but the Epidamnians of the city, that is, the demos, applied to the Corinthians (Olymp. 86, 1), after having in vain tried to form an alliance with Corcyra. From a legal point of view, much might indeed have been said on both sides, to justify the interference; and if the matter had been tried in a court of justice with all the trickery of lawyers, very different decisions might have been come to, as in a very learned law-suit of Lucifer against Christ for doing injury to paganism, which was composed in the seventeenth century. Corinth might have said, " the town is under our immediate protection because we have furnished the οἰκιστής," and this in fact they did say. But according to a very natural mode of reasoning, the town belonged more to the Corcyraeans than to the Corinthians. The men who then acted in this matter, did not come to a decision from a feeling of right or wrong; but to us it cannot be a matter of indifference.

In short the Corcyraeans and Corinthians became violently exasperated, for which causes had existed even before, as there had long been a misunderstanding between them, the Corinthians being jealous of the great power of the Corcyraeans. It is, however, surprising to find that they seem to have made so little use of their power. What was the object of their navy of more than 120 excellent galleys? They must have made some use of them; but we have no information as to how they employed them. They may have required many to pursue the pirates and to escort their merchant vessels, but this does not account for all. It is, moreover, not impossible that the hostility may have arisen in a great measure from the circumstance, that Corcyra impeded and drew towards herself the commerce of the Corinthians in those parts. That Corinth traded in those countries, is evident from her colonies there. The Corcyraeans, in conjunction with the exiles, laid siege to Epidamnus, into which the Corinthians had already introduced a garrison. This garrison and the demos were now blockaded, and suffered from famine. The Corinthians sent to their relief a fleet consisting partly of ships of their own, and partly of such as were furnished by their allies, the Leucadians, Ambracians, and others; but they were signally defeated, and Epidamnus now surrendered to the Corcyraeans.— (Olymp. 86, 2).

The Corinthians meditated only revenge, and made preparations which were almost beyond their strength, so that the Corcyraeans clearly saw, that they alone could not resist such a power. And thus they abandoned the wise principle which they had hitherto followed, of keeping aloof from treaties with larger states, and sought an alliance with Athens (Olymp. 86, 2). The Athenians accepted the offer, but made only a defensive alliance, a step for which they cannot possibly be censured. The means of judging as to whether a thing is reasonable or unreasonable, just or unjust, are always furnished by the speeches in Thucydides. It is one of his artistic excellencies that, by means of his speeches, he renders it unnecessary for us to make any further inquiries. He places before us the state of mind of all the persons concerned in a transaction; we see how they form their resolutions, we see them in the condition in which they really are before coming to a determination, and we see what ideas they had formed of it. He makes them speak not as they ought to have spoken, or as many others would have done, but in the manner in which they probably did speak. This shows the greatest mastery in the art of writing history. In Thucydides, the Athenian, the Corcyracan, and the Corinthian, do not speak as one would do after the things have already happened, and experience has been gained, but as persons speak at the time when a determination must be come to, when they are yet liable to be mistaken, and the future is yet buried in obscurity. I have read it, and heard men of judgment say, " This is wrong, for the event shows that the person ought to have spoken very differently ; how then could Thucydides make him speak thus?" Some persons thus blame him most unjustly, and others endeavour to improve the speeches by emendations. Thucydides knew all this ten times, nay, a hundred or a thousand times better than we; but he also knew, that persons would speak differently before matters were decided from what they did afterwards, and that before the decision persons might be mistaken. An historian of the revolution would not indeed put into the mouth of men speeches that were not actually delivered in the cabinet, but by means of memoirs and other documents, he would place before us the thoughts, and represent the facility with which they imagined that victory might be gained, with the same confidence with which people then looked forward to it.

If then we wish to inquire whether the Athenians ought to have accepted the alliance with Corcyra, we find all that can be said for and against it in Thucydides. We can never enough ponder his words: he does not on this occasion make the Athenians speak very wisely, but only the Corinthians and Corcyraeans, and yet we fancy we hear the Athenians. Had I been at Athens at that time, I would unhesitatingly have advised what Pericles no doubt did advise, namely, to accept the alliance with Corcyra. Athens must have been jealous of the increasing power of her bitterest enemies, and the thought must have struck her, that it was advisable to prevent the Peloponnesians obtaining possession of that wealthy and powerful island; a war with the Peloponnesians could not be avoided, and in that case Corcyra was of great importance to Athens. Nor was there any sufficient reason for the Peloponnesians to regard this as a violation of the peace. The thirty years' truce did not absolutely forbid to form new alliances, but only to admit those who were already allied with the opponents; and a short time before it had only been owing to an accident that the Peloponnesians did not receive the revolted Samians into their alliance, although they were allies of the Athenians, an act which would have been ten times more unjust, for Corcyra was allied with neither. The resolution was now formed with perfect justice; but the step was so serious in its consequences, that what was now done was very far from being sufficient. In carrying out their plan, the Athenians adopted the most inefficient measures, and sent a force which was far too weak. Had the Athenians equipped a large fleet, and attempted to mediate between Corinth and Corcyra, the war, or at least the battle which brought on the war, might perhaps for the moment have been averted. But many, no doubt, imagined, that the resolution would lead to a reconciliation between Corinth and Corcyra, and that if they appeared as mediators with a great force between the two, war would more probably be the result; and hence the Athenians sent only ten ships.

This squadron acted the part of spectators during a sea fight between the Corcyraean and a far superior Corinthian fleet,[3] in which the Corinthians gained a decisive victory (Olymp. 86, 4), and on the following day they would no doubt have driven the Corcyraeans into their harbour and destroyed the greater part of their fleet, had not, most fortunately for the Corcyraeans, on the very day of the battle, another Athenian squadron been signalled; this had been sent on second thoughts, for the Athenians saw that they had after all sent too small a force to Corcyra; and by this means the victory was snatched from the Corinthians.

This unexpected issue of the battle produced great exasperation among the Corinthians, who took revenge by inciting the colony of Potidaea, on the coast of Macedonia and Thrace (subsequently Cassander called the town Cassandrea and enlarged it), to revolt against Athens (Olymp. 87, 1). That town, and the small Chalcidian and the Bottiaean towns in the neighbourhood, now rose against Athens. The Bottiaeans, a Pelasgian people, south of Thessalonica, between this city and the peninsula of Pallene, were, moreover, encouraged by king Perdiccas of Macedonia, of whom I shall have to speak hereafter in treating of the history of Philip. There existed at that time a very large number of extremely small towns on that coast. Mount Athos, and the peninsula of Sithonia, between Pallene and mount Athos, as well as the eastern part of that projecting country, were occupied by a Thracian population; but the whole of the western coast was inhabited by Greeks and Pelasgians. The Corinthians carried out their plan with the greatest skill, for the revolt of the Potidaeatans threw the Athenians into great difficulty. They were obliged to send troops to the north; but instead of crushing the insurrection at once, they sent only a small force which was quite insufficient, and this circumstance protracted the war in a manner highly injurious to Athens.

While Corinth and Athens were thus at war with each

[3] " Thucydides (i. 29), in speaking of old ships, uses the expression ζευγνύναι, of which no definite explanation is given. There is no doubt, that it means to repair ships: the leaky parts were filled up with wadding and tar, and the places were then covered over with boards, so that the ships became thick. In regard to these ζευχθεῖσαι, it is often stated that they did not present to the waves a smooth and regular surface, but that they were uneven on account of the boards nailed over the leaks."

other, " Sparta and Athens were still at peace and were averse to war, as each felt that it would not gain any decided advantage over the other. It was a very singular state of excitement, which is described by Thucydides in a masterly manner." The Corinthians now demanded a general Peloponnesian congress, which assembled at Sparta. After many deliberations, it was decreed, amid great hesitation of the Spartans, and contrary to the advice of Archidamus, to make of Athens such demands as would necessarily lead to war, viz., to restore autonomy to the Aeginetans who had revolted, and to repeal the interdict against all intercourse between Athens and Megara, which the Athenians had pronounced against the latter city.

The accounts of the cause of this psephisma against Megara clearly show on what uncertain ground we are treading whenever we want to go beyond Thucydides, and how then we are moving among mere traditions and anecdotes. The fact that all intercourse between Athens and Megara had been done away with is quite certain; but why was this done? If Plutarch's account, which was probably derived from Ephorus,[*] is true, the Athenians in this case, also, deserve no blame. Athens had many reasons to complain of Megara: in order to demand reparation, a herald was sent, on the advice of Pericles, to Megara and Sparta; the envoy was murdered in the former city, though the Megarians denied it. The Athenians, therefore, were justified in regarding them as loathsome people (ἐναγεῖς). The other account is not true, and is founded on a joke which occurs in the Acharnians of Aristophanes. The poet belonged entirely to the opposition, and therefore took the liberty of representing the actual government as being wrong in all things, and of devising opportunities for censuring it on all occasions. His intention only was to make his audience laugh at the story, but he did not wish them to believe it; and the less he wished this, the greater was the boldness and the unconcern with which he related his story. It is inconceivable how historians, who had Ephorus and Plutarch before them, could so confidently believe the story of the poet.

[*] Plut. Pericl. 30.

LECTURE XLV.

THUCYDIDES says that in the time of Pericles the constitution of Athens was nominally democratic, but that, in truth, the state was governed by one man. The condition of Athens may be compared with that of Florence under the first two Medici—Cosmo, who is not quite justly called the father of his country, and Lorenzo il Magnifico. As under these two, though in general the people submitted, there nevertheless arose an opposition, so also in the case of Pericles; a resistance against him cannot be mistaken, though his power and influence were very great. His authority had even before been twice shaken, though only for a short time, and it had in each case been quickly restored; but at the beginning of the Peloponnesian war he was more seriously threatened, and it seems that at his advanced age the opposition against him had become stronger. However foolish and absurd the stories about the personal character of Pericles may be for a great man and a great people, yet it cannot be denied, that the feeling that his power was somewhat decreasing exercised an influence upon his policy; and that for this reason he was pleased with the outbreak of the war. But the senseless anecdotes which are related to account for this are mere fabrications. Thucydides, in every respect our most trustworthy and most unsuspected witness, has raised a monument to Pericles in his account of his character, according to which he occupies so lofty a position, that those who judge of him from the biography in Plutarch cannot admit that he deserved it. Thucydides represents him to us as an extraordinary genius and a truly great statesman, who, by his personal qualities, had become the manager of the greatest state. When we are told by him that his influence was so great, because he was entirely disinterested and far from desiring any base gain, we must despise those anecdotes which men like Hermippus derived from obscure sources and put on record; such as, that Pericles began the war, because he had been called upon to render an account of the money which had been spent upon building the propylaea. This is assuredly a wretched invention.

But it is nevertheless certain that a number of attacks was made upon Pericles; and this was the natural result of circumstances. According to his descent, he belonged to the aristocracy, but from inclination and conviction he strove to establish general liberty. As he completely broke the ancient bonds which had for the most part been already torn and loosened, the natural consequence was, that the state of things produced by him was not an organic one. His whole administration was not creative, or organically developing, but altogether personal: the prosperity and the influence of Athens depended upon his personal character; it was a happy anarchy under the influence of one great man, during which, however, nothing was firmly established for the future. Had he been able to work for the future, he would deserve serious censure. But who can assert that? And who is there that will cast the blame upon the great man? No one can assert that the course of events was not necessary. Those are often the happiest times, which are necessarily followed by a period of decay; and what constitutes the happiness of the individual, often produces the decay of the whole as a necessary consequence. Under the administration of Pericles, the individuality of both the nation and each particular citizen, showed itself in all its vigour; the condition of dependence perished and disappeared during that time, and thus it came to pass, that while in his youth Themistocles and Aristides, afterwards Themistocles and Cimon, next Cimon alone, then Pericles together with Cimon, and lastly Pericles and his opponent Thucydides of Alopece, constituted the sum total of the powerful Attic statesmen (πολιτευόμενοι and ἀντιπολιτευόμενοι), so during the last days of Pericles a great number of distinguished men came forward who aimed at placing themselves at the helm of the state. They were qualified for it by political skill, and a degree of intellectual culture, especially of free eloquence, which had not existed at all in Pericles' youth, except in the case of some extraordinary men, and which Pericles himself did not, perhaps, possess in any very high degree. But not one of the many who now came forward, had any basis for his system. There were only a few among them (Alcibiades was yet a youth), who wanted to conjure up again the spirit of the ancient aristocracy; the greater part were demagogues, people who wanted to be the first, who regarded Pericles as a man that was growing old and stood in their way, and whose high position every one desired to have for himself. Thus the hostility against him arose according to a sad but quite a natural course of human life, which often manifests itself also in literature and science. When great men have opened new paths, those who owe their existence to them, treat them as persons that are in their way; and this is the case especially in times of great excitement; when the pulse is beating less violently, the case may be different.

Pericles experienced this in a high degree; as he himself was unassailable, attempts were made to hurt him in the persons of those who were dear to him, and hence accusations were made against them. In this manner arose the shameful accusation against Phidias who was charged with having appropriated to himself a portion of the gold which he had received for the statue of Athena. But the artist had employed the gold in such a manner, that it might all be taken off and weighed.—Phidias was then charged with ἀσέβεια for having introduced his own portrait among the reliefs on the shield of Athena. The accusations of heresy, to which subsequently Socrates fell a victim, began as early as that time. Hence some hypocrite also came forward with charges of impiety against Anaxagoras, and Aspasia, the friend of Pericles, alleging that they neglected the duties of the established religion. It was only with great difficulty that Pericles saved both; Anaxagoras was even thrown into prison, but being liberated through the mediation of Pericles, he quitted Athens. The hatred against Aspasia was still greater. In this manner the arrows were always aimed at Pericles.

Considering these circumstances it is certainly very possible, that the sad conviction, that the people must necessarily be occupied in something, may have rendered Pericles inclined to embark in the war. But, in point of fact, he could not have prevented it. The war was no longer a matter depending upon any man's will; he might have deferred it, but he could not avert it; its breaking out could not be avoided, whether it broke out in the fourteenth or the twentieth year of the thirty years' peace. And although on the one hand it seems to be pretty certain that it would have been to the advantage of Athens to delay the war for a time, because a prolongation of the peace could not but strengthen the power of Athens, seeing that

Sparta was standing still while Athens was ever increasing in power and wealth, yet it was to be feared on the other hand, lest in a longer continuance of the peace, Lesbos and Chios should begin to think of revolting, and the rebellion of either of those places might bring on the war at a very inconvenient time for Athens. Negotiations between the two states could lead to no results.

Pericles advised the Athenians not to fear anything; but, according to the speech put into his mouth by Thucydides, he cautioned them not to engage in fantastic undertakings, and told them to carry on the war with calmness, and quietly to await what could not be avoided. It may be that this is only the opinion of Thucydides; but if, as is very probable, he here followed actual traditions of Pericles, the latter here appears as one of the most clear-sighted statesmen that ever ruled a state, as is proved by the event. For this much is certain, if the Athenians had continued the war in the same manner as during the first years, after the first devastation of Attica had taken place, and if they had attacked their enemies at a thousand points, they would have worn out the Peloponnesians, and might have obtained a favourable peace, like that of Nicias, but which would have secured to them more lasting advantages.

The description of the power of Athens which we read of in Thucydides, is as authentic as it can be. It is in the highest degree astonishing, and it is inconceivable how, after the devastations of the Persian war, and within a period of forty-eight years, such a power could grow up! Thus it might seem that nothing would have been more desirable for Athens, than the continuance of that state of things; but even then the restless and ambitious minds would not have been satisfied. We see that the citizens and metoeci together furnished 29,000 hoplites, and 1,200 horse; they had 300 galleys, and at different periods of the war even more; a treasure of 6,000 talents, and 600 talents in tribute from the allies, independently of the great revenue from Attica itself, of the import duties, and the produce of the land and the silver mines " which yielded at least £142,850. In addition to this, there existed an immense number of precious vessels and the like, and the galleys were equipped by private individuals." Considering this wealth, the Peloponnesians were comparatively poor people, with the exception of Corinth, which was an important commercial state, the trade of which, however, could not but be entirely ruined by the war with Athens. Attica was altogether a great power, and through its fleet and maritime ascendancy, it was a commercial state, which stood to the other Greek states in the same relation in which Great Britain stands to the states of the continent, which notwithstanding their wealth in natural products, are poor in capital. The Peloponnesians had no common fund; in the course of the war the Spartans indeed likewise levied tribute on their allies, but at first they had nothing but large armies; every state was obliged to provide for the contingents it furnished, and such provisions generally did not last longer than six weeks, or at the utmost two months; then, having no more provisions, the men could not be kept together, and all dispersed. Their fleet consisted of small contingents, some of which were manned with excellent sailors; those of Corinth were no doubt as good as the Athenians. But although they had good sailors for their merchant vessels, it does not follow at all, that in war they were a match for the Athenians. The several contingents consisting of two galleys from one state and ten from another, were as ill suited to one another, as the contingents of the army of the German empire. Such a power could not hold out against Athens; the only thing in which the Peloponnesians were formidable to the Athenians, was the fact that the latter were unable to defend their frontiers, and that they could not prevent the enemy traversing and laying waste Attica from one end to the other. The Spartans in Attica carried on the war in as barbarous a manner as Ibrahim Pasha in the Morea: they destroyed villages, cut down the olive and other fruit trees, etc. But they could not lay siege to Athens, and if they had done so, the Athenians had it in their power to ravage the countries of Peloponnesus.

The war broke out in the first year of the eighty-seventh Olympiad, that is, forty-nine or fifty years before the capture of Rome by the Gauls, if its date is correctly stated, not as is usually done, but according to the chronology of Fabius. " When Thucydides states, that Plataeae was taken in the beginning of spring, we have to understand the beginning of March; for spring in Greece commences somewhat later than in Italy, for the mountains are mostly covered with deep snow. At Rome spring begins about the 7th or 8th of February, just as it was marked by Caesar in his calendar. The Athenian archons at that time cannot have entered upon their office in Hecatombaeon at the beginning of the civil year, but must have done so in May; for Thucydides says, that Pythodorus continued in office for two months afterwards, whereas according to the civil year he would have remained only one month longer. When Thucydides says, "at the time when wheat was ripe," we have to understand the middle of June.

The war broke out at a time, when the Corinthians and Athenians had already fought against each other at Potidaea; and the first act was the attempt of the Boeotians to take Plataeae by surprise. "The Thebans cherished an implacable hatred of the Plataeans, who had revolted from them and joined the Athenians. At the same time, the laurels which Plataeae had won in the Persian war, were so many reproaches to the treacherous Thebans. The party which had then betrayed Greece continued to rule at Thebes during the Peloponnesian war, and it was headed by the son of the arch-traitor of Greece." The attempt partly succeeded, the town having been betrayed and one gate thrown open by the oligarchs. It was night; the Plataeans were roused from their sleep, and were terrified at finding the enemy in their town; but only a small number had been sent, that they might get into the town unobserved. When, therefore, in the morning the people recovered from their first fright, they perceived that the number of the enemy was so small, that they would soon repent of their undertaking. The people now pretended to be willing to negotiate with them, deceived the enemy—fraud in general was a common resource among the Greeks—and seemed to be ready to join Thebes. Meantime, however, they armed themselves in secret, barricaded the streets with waggons, closed the gates through which the Boeotians had entered, and then a general attack was made from all corners, and from all the windows and roofs. The Plataeans commenced on all sides to destroy the intruders with missiles. "The Thebans fled into a tower, mistaking it for a gate, and were shut up in it." Those who were to have come to their support, did not make their appearance, having been detained by heavy rains during the night, so that in the end the three hundred Boeotians were obliged to capitulate. This was the first act of the war, and even it shows the rage with which it afterwards continued to

be carried on; it was of that fearful kind we usually meet with
only in deplorable civil or religious wars. " The Thebans
sent a second expedition intended to lay waste the territory of
Plataeae; but the Plataeans send word to them, that if they
did not desist, all their prisoners would be put to death."
The Thebans then retreated, but all the three hundred prisoners were, nevertheless, murdered by the Plataeans. The
vengeance for this deed begot new vengeance, and thus things
went on from one to another until all Greece was frightfully
destroyed in this war. The Athenians were innocent of that
deed of blood, which the Plataeans committed of their own
accord, before the Athenians had time to advise them. It
cannot, however, be denied that the attempt of the Thebans
was disgraceful: it was made in the depth of peace and friendship, and so unexpectedly, that the Plataeans had not even
closed their gates or secured them by sentinels. The exasperation of the Plataeans, therefore, was quite natural, and their
rage is not without its excuse; but the bloody deed at the
same time shows, the great demoralisation and exasperation at
the very commencement of the war.

After the unsuccessful attempt against Plataeae, all intercourse between the two parties was suspended, nor were
κήρυκες, or sacred messengers, any longer employed between
them. Soon afterwards the Spartans assembled their whole
army on the Isthmus, and thence proceeded through Megara
towards Eleusis and the Thriasian plain, while their allies were
preparing to join them. They were met on the Isthmus by
all their Peloponnesian allies, except the Argives and Achaeans
of whom the Pellenians alone were present, but afterwards all
the Achaeans joined them. The Argives bore a grudge
against Sparta from early times, and refused to recognise her
as the first city, still insisting upon their ancient claim to the
supremacy for themselves. At the same time the Spartans
were joined by the army of their continental allies, the
Boeotians and Phocians, the latter of whom had formerly been
allied with Athens, but had then, for reasons unknown to us,
joined the enemies of Athens. But the fact that Phocians were
among the enemies of Athens saved her from destruction, for
it was the Phocian generals that at the termination of the war
prevented the destruction of Athens, which all the others
desired. The Argives were neutral, and on the continent the

Acarnanians were the only allies of the Athenians, all the others being islanders or inhabitants of the coast of Asia Minor. All the islands, with the exception of Melos and Thera, were on the side of Athens, as well as many of the cities in Asia Minor; they were all tributary to Athens, Chios and Lesbos alone enjoying autonomy, and by their tribute the Athenians were enabled to maintain their fleet.

The Spartan army, amounting to 70,000[1] men, invaded Attica, "and spread over the whole country; the Athenians were totally unable to resist such an overwhelming force." The Peloponnesians advanced to the very walls of Athens; the whole of the country population took refuge in the city, where many were kindly received, but most of them had to take up their abode between the long walls; many also were conveyed to Salamis and the neighbouring islands. Although few fell into the hands of the enemy (most men were enabled to save their lives, their freedom and their moveable property, for the Spartans as usual were slow), yet all immoveable property, houses and the like were left behind and ravaged by the enemy in the most cruel manner, and all the fields, olive plantations and vineyards were destroyed. It was fortunate for the Athenians that the people lived so extremely simply, nay, poorly. The houses were made of clay; and from the account of the attack on Plataeae we learn that the Greek towns at that time had no paved streets; for, in consequence of heavy showers, the mud in the streets was as deep as on the high roads, and the water remained standing in the streets. Even Athens was not paved till a later period; the streets of Rome were paved at an earlier time. Athens was now full of workshops of every description, and all agricultural implements had been carried into it. As the houses consisted only of clay, it was easy to break through the partition walls in order to get from one house into another or into the street without being observed. The destruction of houses, therefore, was but a slight injury, but that of the fruit trees (δενδροτομεῖν) was a fearful loss. The Athenians had not imagined that the miseries of war would be so great; they had indeed been aware that they would not escape unscathed, but as the last plans

---

[1] This statement is probably based upon Plutarch, *Pericl.* 33, where the number of heavy-armed men alone is said to have been 60,000. If we add the light-armed and the cavalry, we have at least 70,000 for the whole army.—ED.

against Attica had not been carried into effect, and as a
Spartan army had but once invaded Attica and advanced
only as far as Eleusis, they had always cherished a hope that
this time also the enemy would not be able to carry out their
design.   But as matters turned out differently, as the enemy
advanced irresistibly, as fire and destruction shewed themselves
all around, and as the distress became greater every day, the
general feeling soon changed, the people became desponding, and
all began to long for peace.   Against this feeling Pericles now
came forward, reminding them that he had foretold them, that
they must expect that all the country would be laid waste,
but that this was a necessary consequence of their not being
islanders, and that these were misfortunes against which
an island only could be protected.   Not even Themistocles
had been able to induce them to settle in Piraeeus and to
dwell there in safety ; but even if it had been possible to persuade them to establish a new home in an island, where could
they have found one to supply the place of Attica?   Attica is
indeed λεπτόγεως. a country with a thin and barren soil, but
it also has some beautiful districts, great natural treasures,
marble and silver mines, the latter of which, however, are now
exhausted.   Pericles had foretold them everything, and he now
added, that, as circumstances could not be altered, as it was impossible to stop the enemy's progress, and as nothing could be
done to check the enemy without certain defeat, there remained
nothing but to persevere until the storm was over, and to think
of retaliation, which would amply indemnify them. "The Peloponnesians were indeed soon obliged to return because they
received no pay, and provisions began to fail ; and the Athenians
retaliated upon them by an expedition against Peloponnesus; but
this was nothing in comparison with the loss they had sustained."
    In the mean time, however, the general distress was in-
creased by the fearful plague (Olymp. 87, 2), which visited
Athens in the second year of the war, at the moment when
the Peloponnesians had invaded Attica a second time.   It is
surprising that this plague made much more havoc among the
Athenians than among their enemies; some parts of Peloponnesus were indeed visited by it, but its effects were not to
be compared with the calamity of Athens.   Much has been
said about this plague: the description in Thucydides is
excellent.   Whatever may be said, no one will be able to form

a perfectly clear notion of the nature of the disease, or to say whether it was the real Oriental plague, which now prevails at Odessa and elsewhere, or whether it was only a typhus of the same species. That it was a typhus cannot be doubted. It resembled the yellow fever, inasmuch as it was most violent in the coast districts. It first appeared in Piraeeus; but it spread farther from the sea into the interior, and not along the course of rivers, as is the case with the yellow fever, which from the sea ascends the rivers, and does not seem to be conveyed by the air over soil which is quite dry. This is the great difference between the Attic plague and the yellow fever. My belief is, that it was neither the Oriental plague nor the yellow fever, but something between the two. Vomiting in which bile is thrown up rarely occurs in the Oriental plague, but is regularly connected with the yellow fever; whereas ulcers are extremely rare in the yellow fever, but general in the Oriental plague. This plague is a remarkable phenomenon, and an event in the history of the world: it broke the power and the spirit of the Athenians. It was a fearful blow to Athens, and it is only surprising that the Athenians could overcome its effects as they did; "for in the very same year they rallied and made a fresh expedition against Peloponnesus."

I shall devote particular care to the history of epidemics. I can prove that time to have been a period of epidemics, which extended over from thirty to forty years; it began in Italy about thirty years before, and there raged fearfully, assuming different forms, and manifesting a truly pestilential character.[2] Afterwards there appeared diseases, which were as destructive as the plague, though they were not typhus, but fevers connected with diseases of the eye. The history of diseases is a branch of universal history, which has not yet been investigated, though it is of great importance. Whole periods in history are explained by the appearance and disappearance of deadly epidemics. " They exercise the greatest possible influence upon the morality of nations; almost all great epochs of moral degradation are connected with great epidemics. Thus at Rome, the ancient intellectual culture, a certain high mindedness, and a noble spirit in art, remained down to the time of M. Antoninus; but then the great plague spreads from the army of Verus over Italy, and suddenly the whole character

[2] See *Hist. of Rome*, vol. ii. p. 272, foll., and p. 505, foll.

is entirely changed: the death-blow is given to literature and art, especially to the latter, and everything noble perishes. In the time of M. Aurelius, we find beautiful historical works of art, though no ideal or characteristic ones, and there was much technical skill; but immediately after everything becomes wretched. The artists who adorned the arch of Septimius Severus, had lost all knowledge of proportion in drawing. Africa was not visited by that plague, whence that country continued to be highly flourishing, and a peculiar literature maintained itself there, of which Tertullian and others are the representatives. Then came the plague under Gallienus, which carried off more than half the population, and after it antiquity is entirely gone: a perfectly barbarous period began, in which even the Latin language could no longer preserve its purity, but became corrupt. During the great plague under Justinian everything completely perished; even the few artificial remnants of antiquity disappeared, and what remained was only the dregs. Greek pronunciation and the whole system of writing became altered; the long and short syllables were no longer distinguished. In like manner, the plague of the fourteenth century in Italy and in the East marks distinct periods. At Athens, too, the plague marks a new era. Those who had reached a mature age, remained what they were, if they survived it, but the rising generation was quite different."

LECTURE XLVI.

THE plague and the repeated devastations of Attica, had thrown the Athenians into very great distress, which exercised an unhappy influence upon their disposition. They had commenced the war with spirit, but as until then nothing had turned out to their advantage, and as they had experienced nothing but misfortunes, their confidence was changed into great dejection, and the dejection of spirits at the same time increased the power of the plague. It became the general opinion—and that not quite without reason—that the plague was a necessary consequence of the war. The general despondency and discontent now turned against Pericles, as the man who had commenced the war, and was therefore regarded as the cause of all misfortunes. The people saw no safety any-where, except in negotiation with the Spartans, although it was evident no acceptable peace could be expected from them. The negotiations led to no results, nor could they lead to any, as the first demand of the Spartans was, that the Athenians should renounce the supremacy over all their allies, a demand to which the Athenians could not submit. Athens was then in the same situation in which England was in the years 1796 and 1797. A portion of the nation had strongly urged the necessity of the revolutionary war, but when in consequence of ill-management they began to be tired of it, they demanded of the ministers to make peace on any terms, as fair terms could not be obtained. Then negotiations were likewise com-menced, merely to convince the nation that there was no obstinacy in the minds of the ministers, but that peace ac-tually could not be obtained. Such wars must be judged of differently from ordinary wars, for in the former peace is attainable only when one of the belligerent parties is decidedly conquered. In these circumstances, Pericles endeavoured to quiet the minds of the Athenians.

But he himself was exposed to unreasonable accusations by persons who wanted to make him responsible for all the mise-ries of the war, and treated him as the cause of the plague. And yet none of them was visited by severer afflictions than he himself; for the two eldest of his three sons died of the epidemic. But notwithstanding all this, the charges brought against him were childishly and thoughtlessly listened to, and the exaspera-tion against him became so strong, that his enemies were enabled to carry a decree by which he was sentenced to pay a heavy fine. This state of feeling, however, did not last long; and as soon as he had assembled the people, and convinced them of his innocence, they repented of their act of injustice. Cordiality and good nature were peculiar characteristics of the Athenian people, and hence they now endeavoured to comfort him, not only by appointing him strategus, but by conferring the full franchise on his third son, whose mother was not an Athenian citizen, and thereby enabling him to be the heir of his father. Pericles was thus again strategus, an office to which he was elected year after year, just as Lorenzo il Magnifico, at Florence, was every year appointed Gonfaloniere.   But Pericles survived this event only for a short time, for he died two years and six months after the commencement of the war (Olymp. 87, 4). There can be no doubt that his life was shortened by his disappointment at the course of events, by his grief at the misfortunes of the state, and at there being no prospect of a speedy decision, because the people were unwilling to persevere; the grief at the death of his sons, though they were personally unworthy of him, also contributed to break his spirit.   His third son was likewise an insignificant person; there is nothing remarkable in his history, except that he was unfortunate, and shared the fate of the generals, who at a time of fearful moral confusion, were put to death on account of the battle of the Arginusae.

When the plague had ceased, and when the Athenians had become a little more hardened by misfortunes, they again undertook several expeditions, which although they were not followed by decisive results, yet had the effect of reviving the warlike spirit of the people, and of making them more satisfied.   Potidaea at length also surrendered, after a long siege (Olymp. 87, 3), which had cost enormous sums, "for at that time citizens only served in the army, and were paid so liberally that they could live comfortably in the field."   The Corinthians settled at Potidaea were sent away, and Potidaea became an Athenian city.   The war with the revolted Chalcidians, however, still continued.   I cannot here relate all the separate expeditions, which are described in so masterly a manner by Thucydides, such as the expeditions of Phormio, and those against Laconica and Argolis; to enter into them would lead me too far; and in the history of the Peloponnesian war I shall give you only broad outlines, and relate the great and important expeditions.

One of the most remarkable events, is the revolt of Mitylene (Olymp. 88, 1).   The island of Lesbos contained five Aeolian towns, which were indeed connected in a certain way, but were yet perfectly independent of one another; Mitylene, however, by the advantages of its position and by its excellent harbour, had risen far above the other four towns.   The three smaller ones among them, Pyrrha, Eresos, and Antissa, had absolutely joined Mitylene, and were guided by it; but Methymna had not done so, and the relation in which the

Lesbians stood to Athens was still very favourable: their contingent consisted in ships commanded by Lesbians, and they paid no tribute. But the fate of Samos had warned the few places standing in the same relation, Chios and Lesbos, and had rendered them suspicious of the intentions of the Athenians; and they feared lest the Athenians should treat them as they had treated the smaller islands, and should reduce them to the same state of dependence as Samos, by ordering them to deliver up their ships and pay tribute. But the more such places became aware of their importance, and the more they felt that by going over to the other side, they would cast a great weight into the scale, the more they naturally became inclined to revolt. Thus the Mitylenaeans were prepared for the step they took, and the revolt spread thence over the whole of Lesbos, with the exception of Methymna, which, as is always the case in confederations of states, from jealousy of Mitylene, sided with the Athenians, and directed their attention to the fact, that treasonable plots were formed in Lesbos, and that a revolt was near at hand. At first the Athenians, with incredible carelessness, paid little attention to the information, a neglect which was the consequence of the strange anarchical condition of Athens, where the government had in reality no power. There was no magistracy to take the initiative, or to form a preliminary resolution or probuleuma in such cases. The people might indeed meet, and did meet every day, and any demagogue might propose a measure; but when this was not done, there was no authority on which it was incumbent to introduce such measures, and nothing was done. At Mitylene, on the other hand, although under the supremacy of Athens democracy everywhere gained the upper hand, there seems to have been a powerful aristocratic element, and the government must have been very strong. Everything was carefully and cautiously prepared, and was kept profoundly secret. The revolt was determined upon, and public opinion was in favour of it. But as they wished to proceed safely, and provide themselves sufficiently with arms and provisions, the undertaking was delayed, and the Athenians, who at first had neglected everything, at last fitted out an expedition which was to take Mitylene by surprise. But on this occasion it became evident how injurious it was to Athens down to the end of the war, that at such times of urgent necessity the government still continued to be as before, and that there had not been instituted a separate magistrate for war to take such measures in time. As all proceedings were public, and neither the preparations nor their object could not be kept secret: all the plans were known to everybody, as they were discussed in the popular assembly. It was indeed resolved there to surprise Mitylene; but this decree was ludicrous, and its consequences might be foreseen. A Mitylenean, who was staying at Athens, or some one else, anxious to do them a service, on hearing of it, went to Euboea, took a boat, and informed the Mityleneans of the danger that was threatening them. Had this not been done, the revolt would have been prevented, and that for the good of the Mityleneans themselves. The intention of the Athenians was to surprise the city during the celebration of a festival, which the Mityleneans solemnised at a considerable distance from their city, in conjunction with the other Lesbians. Knowing the design of the Athenians, they did not go out to the festival, and determined to raise the standard of revolt at once. They quickly applied to the Peloponnesians, with whom they had, no doubt, been already negotiating, and requested the Spartans to send them succour of some kind or another. The Spartans sent them a commander without a force, which was anything but what they would have liked. He undertook the command in the city, and exhorted them to be courageous and persevering. They were expected to undergo the hardships of famine for the sake of the Spartans, but the general did not bring them any additional strength to repel the Athenians. They had nothing but their own forces.

The Athenian fleet now arrived and blockaded the city; after several little engagements, the Mityleneans were reduced to extremities. Their envoys had at length prevailed upon the Peloponnesians to send them a motley fleet to relieve Mitylene. But it set sail with the usual slowness of the Spartans, and did not arrive until Mitylene, compelled by famine, had surrendered (Olymp. 88, ⅓). Such was the care shown to save Mitylene! The long endurance of famine, shows how strongly the Mityleneans were bent upon escaping from the dominion of their enemies. How fearful it must have been, may be inferred from the fact, that in the end they preferred surrendering at discretion to an enraged enemy. The courage of the Mityleneans was like that of the Campanians in the Hannibalian war: they allowed themselves to be shut up like sheep in a fold, to be starved, and thus there remained nothing for them in the end, but to surrender. Many of those who had been most conspicuous, were taken prisoners by Paches, the Athenian general. The capitulation contained nothing else but a promise that the Athenian commander would not, on his own authority, order any one to be put to death, and that he would leave the decision to the people of Athens.

The war had already assumed the most fearful character: Alcidas, the Spartan admiral of the Peloponnesian fleet, which went to the relief of the Mityleneans, had, on his voyage, indulged in the most cruel piracy; he had captured all the ships he met with, without any regard as to what place they belonged to, and had thrown into the sea the crews of the allies and subjects of the Athenians, for whose deliverance the Spartans pretended to be anxious, as well as those of Athenian vessels. This barbarous mode of warfare was practised by the Spartans from the very beginning of the war. They not only captured the Athenian ships which sailed round Peloponnesus, but mutilated the crews, chopping off the hands of the sailors, and then drowned them. Such was their practice at sea, a practice altogether contrary to the law of nations, and similar to that adopted by the French during the revolutionary war against the English, when they imprisoned defenceless persons, and confiscated English goods wherever they found them, in violation of the law of nations. The cause of such conduct lay in the feeling that they were unable to cope with the English at sea; that is, the consciousness of their own weakness; and such also was the case with the Spartans. This inhuman cruelty of the Spartans excited in the minds of the Athenians a desire to make reprisals; and thus it unfortunately became quite a natural feeling among the Athenians to devise inhuman vengeance upon the Mityleneans. They felt that Athens had given the Mityleneans no cause for revolt, that the alliance with them had been left unaltered as it had been before, and that if the Mityleneans had succeeded in joining the Spartans, they would have brought Athens into great danger, partly by their power, and partly by their example. It was, moreover, thought necessary to terrify Chios by a striking example, in order that the oligarchical party there might not attempt a similar undertaking. Those who did not see the necessity for such a measure, at least imagined that they saw it, for reasons of this kind are never anything else than an evil pretext. With all enticements of this description, the people were induced to despatch orders to the general Paches to avenge on the Mitylenaeans what the Spartans had done to the Athenians. He was to put to death all the men capable of bearing arms, and to sell women and children into slavery. But the minds of the Athenians were too humane for such a design to be entertained by them for any length of time; and although it had been possible to carry out such a decree, through the existing confusion of ideas about morality, yet the better voice had not yet died away in their bosoms. The historian need not tell us that thousands could not close their eyes during the night in consequence of the terrible decree; and that through fear lest it should be carried into effect, they assembled early in the morning, even before sunrise. The morning after the day on which the decree had been passed, all the people met earlier than usual, and demanded of the prytanes once more to put the question to the vote, to see whether the decree should be carried into effect or not. This was done, and although the ferocious Cleon struggled with all fury to obtain the sanction of the first decree, yet humanity prevailed at this second voting. It was resolved, that only the leaders of the rebellion should be taken to account and conveyed to Athens, but that no harm should be done to the other Mityleneans. The Mityleneans were, of course, obliged to deliver up all their ships and arms; and their territory, with that of the other towns, except Methymna, became a cleruchia, that is, it was divided into equal lots, and given to Athenian citizens as fiefs. But this was, in point of fact, nothing else than the imposition of a permanent land-tax upon the former owners; for the Athenians let out their lots to the ancient proprietors for a small rent. The number of rebels who were carried to Athens and executed there, was, indeed, very great, sadly great; but they were real rebels, and their blood did not come upon the heads of the Athenians.

In the declamations of the sophists, we hear much of the evils of the Athenian democracy, of the misfortunes of the most distinguished men: and that of Paches is regarded as one of the more conspicuous cases. The people, it is said, were ungrateful towards Paches, the conqueror of Mitylene, who had, even before that conquest, distinguished himself as a general; and they now took him to account for the manner in which he had conducted the war; and he, in order to escape condemnation, made away with himself. This story is, I think, related by the father of all sophists and declaimers, Isocrates, and is mentioned also by the sophists of later times, and by a Roman writer on military affairs.[1] But the true account may be learnt from a poem of the Greek Anthology,[2] where Paches is said to have abused his power in subduing the island: he dishonoured two noble ladies of Mitylene, who went to Athens to appeal to the sense of justice of the Athenian people. On that occasion the Athenians showed their true humanity, for they forgot how dangerous enemies the Mityleneans had been to them, and notwithstanding the victory of Paches, they were inexorable towards him, and had he not put an end to his life, he would certainly have been condemned and handed over to the Eleven. Of this deed the friends of Athens need not be ashamed.

The conduct of the commander of the Spartan fleet, which appeared on the coast of Ionia, shows the Spartans in the same light in which they always appear, as immensely awkward and slow in all they undertook. It was in vain that the Corinthians and other enterprising people advised them to attack Mitylene, because the Athenians were in a newly-conquered city, and the appearance of a superior force of Peloponnesians would be sufficient to create a revolt in the city, and to crush the small force of the Athenians. But Alcidas, in torpid Spartan laziness, was immoveable, and returned to Peloponnesus without undertaking or having effected anything, except that he received on board the suppliants who threw themselves into the sea, and carried on the most cruel piracy. The Spartans followed the principle of not punishing their generals, which was the very opposite to that of the Athenians, who often made their commanders responsible when fortune had been against them; and when they had neglected an opportunity, or been guilty of any crime, they never escaped unpunished. Every genuine Spartan, on the other hand, was almost certain of impunity, as the Spartans cherished the idea of inviolability, which, according

---

[1] The Editor has not been able to find the passage in which Isocrates is said to have mentioned the story. The Roman writer alluded to is Frontin. *Strateg.* iv. 7, 17.

[2] Anthol. Graec. vol. iv. p. 34; comp. Agath. *Epigr.* 57, ed. Bonn.

to our views, a monarch may establish in regard to some prince, but not otherwise.

About the same time the Spartans formed a determination, which was the very opposite to that of the Athenians, regarding Mitylene, for the Spartans acted without any provocation; theirs was a decree of mere cruelty, and an instance of the grossest inhumanity. After their second invasion of Attica (Olymp 87, 3) they blockaded and besieged the little town of Plataeae. The Plataeans had sent to Athens the defenceless, their women and children, except a small number of women, who were necessary to prepare the food and the like for the men, who themselves refused to abandon their homes, and were determined manfully to hold out against the besiegers, and to defend their town. The art of besieging was then still in its infancy; they still used the ancient instruments of war, which had long been known in the East and in ancient Egypt. It is only the catapulta and balistae that do not occur on the Egyptian monuments; battering-rams are often seen in Egyptian paintings of the time of Sesostris. The Spartans employed no arts of besieging, but confined themselves to raising a mound against the wall. They endeavoured to carry it near to the walls, by constantly pushing it onward between wooden scaffoldings. They intended ultimately to establish themselves upon it, and to take the town. This method was as rude as that of the Romans, who, in the first Punic war, provided their ships with grappling-irons.[3] They also had battering-rams, which, however, seem to have been very weak. The description of the siege of Plataeae, in Thucydides, is remarkable, because it gives us an insight into the wretched condition of the art of besieging at that time. As the Spartans failed in all their efforts, they at length confined themselves to blockading the town, and enclosed it with a double wall as a double circumvallation, that no one might escape. A portion of their soldiers were left behind in winter quarters. During the winter, the Plataeans resolved, like the defenders of Missolonghi, to force their way through the fortifications of the enemy, for their provisions were exhausted. But only a portion ventured upon the bold enterprise, and escaped to Athens. It would have been better if all had united in the attempt. Some

---

[3] " The whole machinery described by Polybius consisted of nothing else but grappling irons."

wanted to remain behind, intending to apply to Athens for succour; which would perhaps have been possible, as the Spartans were always so slow in taking the field, and it would perhaps, not have been impossible to break through the besieging army. But as the remaining Plataeans received no aid, they were at last compelled by distress to capitulate with the Spartans (Olymp. 88, ¼). The Spartans now, as on many other occasions, had recourse to a cunning choice of words in their treaty. As it was to be expected, that in any future peace with Athens, it would be stipulated that conquests should be restored, but not those towns which had surrendered, they declared to the Plataeans that they must, of their own accord, surrender at discretion; for thus they might, in a peace with Athens, say that the Plataeans had spontaneously surrendered, and that, accordingly, Sparta was not bound to restore them. When Plataeae had in this manner fallen into their hands, they put the inhabitants in chains, and sat in judgment upon them. With the exception of a few, who had supported the interest of the Thebans, they and some Athenians, who were found in the place, were strangled; the town was destroyed, and its territory given to Thebes. All this was done, although the Plataeans had not wronged the Spartans in the least, and reminded them of the fact, that through the victory of Pausanias, the noblest trophies of the Spartans had been won in their neighbourhood, and that, at that time, they had quitted their town to fight with Sparta against the Persians. All this was of no avail: the Thebans insisted upon their being put to death, and the Spartans were too anxious to win over Thebes, and attach her to Sparta, by an atrocious deed. King Archidamus thus yielded to the Thebans. " All this did not hasten the issue of the war. After the events in Lesbos, the Peloponnesians lost their hopes, for they found themselves disappointed in the expectation of a revolt of the allies of Athens. The power of the Athenians was far more firmly established than at first, and the continuation of the war was, on the whole, not at all disagreeable to them. The first years had decidedly been the worst."

LECTURE XLVII.

DURING the discontent with the progress of the war, which had at first been so vehement at Athens, and which afterwards, though it had decreased, was yet revived by every new disaster, and continued to be the feeling of many, the comic poets acted the same part which in modern times is acted by the periodical press of the opposition, "in France and England, and produced even greater effects, because they courted the approval of the great mass of the people." In the extant plays of Aristophanes we thus see a reckless opposition gradually developing, and we perceive the same thing equally distinct in the fragments of Eupolis, most of whose plays likewise belong to the first period of the war. Cratinus, who lived somewhat earlier than Eupolis and Aristophanes, had probably given the first example of political comedy. When we delight in the plays of Aristophanes, that extraordinary genius, which is so masterly both in point of language and of spirit, we are somewhat in danger of being led away from the true aspect of the events; we are ready to give ourselves up to the poet, and to forget that he is a leading character of a decided opposition party, which by no means undertakes to answer for all its assertions: the poet's private thoughts were, no doubt, different from what he said and wrote in the spirit of the opposition. Such is the case with all oppositions: they are not very scrupulous in their assertions; and when you talk to them privately, they speak in quite a different tone. Often, when remonstrating with persons for such a mode of acting, I have been told, "Why should we not do so? we are of the opposition; our words need not be taken in their literal meaning." This is one of the great disadvantages of the absolute freedom of public discussion. If any one were to write the history of the French revolution from the opposition journals, he would be guilty of the most monstrous misrepresentations and errors; and, in like manner, we should be very far from the truth, if we were to consider the contempt with which Aristophanes treats many, and especially Lamachus, as fair and just, or if we were to agree with his way of describing the war from the very first as senseless and unfortunate. " He was above all responsibility, and inquired only into the faults which he saw distinctly, without taking any notice either of their causes or their possible justification. Thus he everywhere attacks the system of the war, although it was altogether beyond the power of the government to refrain from carrying on war. Aristophanes was certainly a good citizen; but such a system of constant attacks on the government could not but utterly destroy its patriotism and power."

The opinion that the war ought not to have been commenced at all, however, was gradually abandoned by the great mass of the people, as the first calamities began to be forgotten. A second outbreak of the plague (Olymp. 88, 2) did not produce the same effect upon the minds of the people as the first, although it was equally destructive. That period was remarkable in every respect; it was one of those in which, as the poet says in Hamlet, " The time is out of joint." A disturbance of the usual order of things was manifested throughout all parts of nature; and there appeared gigantic signs of an internal convulsion of nature, and of her decay through epidemics and earthquakes, such as were unknown in the traditions of former times. During a period of many years there were fearful earthquakes, not only in Greece, but also in other parts: the elements seemed to have left their spheres, and the seasons were changed. In the year before the second outbreak of the plague, there were no Etesiae, that is, no north-west winds in the Mediterranean, which until the dog-days blow for a period of fifty days, and contribute much to the health of the country. During the winter there were sudden changes, from fearful showers of rain to terrible droughts. Diodorus of Sicily, and the genuine books of Hippocrates on epidemics, which are of great importance to an historian, contain remarkable descriptions of changes in the elements. But to these things, also, the people became accustomed.

" The circumstances of the Athenians had considerably improved." The treasury had indeed become exhausted, but as the tribute of the allies was increased, and the few wealthy among the Athenians were heavily taxed, the bulk of the Athenian people was not oppressed by the war. And as the Spartans had not for several years crossed the borders of Attica, being perhaps convinced, that their exertions were greater than the results, the Athenians were again enabled to live in the country in ease and tranquillity, as if the Spartans had not been masters of the main land. " Having few wants, the people were soon comforted and forgot their losses. The Athenians, moreover, had obtained cleruchiae in Lesbos and Aegina, the Aeginetans having been driven on to retaliate— subsequently they also obtained cleruchiae in Cythera—and losses in their own country were thus more easily got over." In this manner confidence and tranquillity were restored among the people, " who gave themselves up to fresh hopes. They again became more and more enterprising, and" again turned their ambitious thoughts towards distant parts. They now extended their plans farther and farther.

" Their confidence and boldness were now so great, that they began to think of extending their power to Sicily, as they had extended it over the islands of the Aegean. The wealth of Sicily had even before attracted their attention,[1] and now its attraction was the more powerful, as they were masters of Corcyra. They hoped that at some time or other Sicily, and even Italy, might be made to acknowledge their supremacy like Corcyra. They forgot the fact, that they had no basis for such an undertaking; but circumstances were so favourable to them, and the prospects so brilliant, that, if the war had been conducted with circumspection, and if only glaring mistakes had been avoided, even the most reckless and thoughtless undertaking would have been successful. The cities of Sicily were divided among themselves; some of them which were opposed to Syracuse, petitioned the Athenians to come to their assistance, and the latter (Olymp. 88, 2) sent them a small fleet which, however, was so insignificant, that there could be no thought of its making conquests. For the present it was sufficient for them to gain allies there, who were after- wards obliged to support their interests; some towns, as a necessary consequence, had no choice but to join the Athenians with body and soul. This was the first step; but this first expedition led to very different and much more important things than had been aimed at or foreseen in the commence- ment of the undertaking.

First of all, it accidentally happened that the alliance between Athens and Corcyra was saved by it; for there was the

---

[1] Justin, iv. 3.

greatest danger lest the oligarchical party at Corcyra should gain the upper-hand. There existed in that island, as I have already remarked, two parties which opposed each other with the greatest bitterness. The demos, not the common people, but the inhabitants of the country, the Eretrian population and the ancient hellenised Liburnians, were opposed to the houses of Corinthian origin; and this demos had in the meantime recovered its ancient freedom and formed the majority; but the government was still wavering between the influence of the ὀλίγοι and the power of the demos. The latter as everywhere else naturally sided with the Athenians, and under these circumstances the ὀλίγοι had assumed a different character, by which they could gain over to their side many, who otherwise belonged to their opponents—they had assumed the character of a political party, whose watch-word was the independence of the republic of Athenian influence. In addition to this, it must be observed that several Corcyraeans who, during the last naval engagement with the Corinthians had been taken prisoners, had been treated at Corinth with particular kindness, and had thus been cunningly gained over by the Corinthians to assist them in subduing Corcyra; they were ransomed only for the sake of appearances, and returned home in freedom. At first the Corcyraeans were probably glad to see them restored to their country, but these liberated prisoners soon became the centre of a political party, which began to discuss the alliance with Athens, and exerted itself to get it done away with. The friends of Athens, the democratic party, on the other hand, insisted the more zealously on its being preserved and confirmed, because it was to their own interest. The most conspicuous among them was Pithias, the author of the alliance, who now aimed at making that, which had hitherto been only a protective alliance, an offensive and defensive one. The Athenian party prevailed; the ὀλίγοι at first made a violent opposition, and as they were out-voted, they created a violent revolution, murdered Pithias and some other partisans of Athens, and threw off the alliance with the Athenians.

This senseless step led to a general insurrection, and an exasperated civil war (Olymp. 88, 2). The different streets and quarters of the town were inhabited by the different parties, probably according to the different settlements, and it would be wrong to infer that the quarter of the demos was that of the poor people. The quarter of the sailors was indeed inhabited entirely by the demos; but the fact that the aristocrats lived near the agora, arises from the circumstance of their being ancient burgesses, and of the Corinthian settlers, their ancestors, having settled there. Afterwards, many of them may have moved to the quarter of the demos, and a few demotae perhaps lived about the agora. The history of Switzerland, by Meyer von Knonau, a book which is extremely instructive to every one who is interested in regard to the relations of ancient and modern states, contains a mistake about Geneva, for in the second volume the author says, that at Geneva the nobles accidentally lived in the upper town, and that this gave rise to the conflict between the inhabitants of the *cité* and those of the *bourg*. The *cité* alone was the real free town, the *bourg* St. Gervais was out of the pale of citizenship; such also was the case at Florence, and at Corcyra it must have been similar. Between those parts of the town a struggle now broke out, which raged for several days within the walls; the ὀλίγοι invited Epirots to come to their aid, while the demos strengthened itself by the country population. During the contest fire broke out in the town, for when the oligarchs saw that they would be defeated, they themselves set fire to the houses on the side from which the assault was made, in order to repel the attack of the demos; a great part of the place was thus laid in ashes. But the demos gained the victory nevertheless, and an Athenian squadron which was just arriving, completed it. The conquered oligarchs were now obliged to capitulate for their lives: the manner in which they were treated is dreadful; you may read the account of it in Thucydides, which shows to what a degree rage now prevailed, and how far the thirst of blood and revenge carried the people. The unhappy oligarchs had first commenced the bloodshed, and the wild passion to take revenge allowed the people no rest, until the murderers had atoned for their crime with their blood. The massacre was fearful, and the Athenians could save only a few of the wretched aristocrats.

Those who saved their lives, escaped to the main land, whence, full of despair, they returned to the island and fortified themselves in castles, from which they made ravaging excursions into the country. In this manner, they maintained themselves for a year, until the Corcyraean demos, with the aid of the Athenians, again compelled them to surrender (Olymp. 88, 4). The Athenians had effected a capitulation for them, in which it was stipulated that their lives should be spared; but the Corcyraeans, in their exasperation, did not observe it, and indulged in a second massacre. These scenes are real prototypes of the September massacres at Paris: all the prisoners, just as at Paris, were led from the prison between two rows of armed men and cut to pieces. In those struggles, Corcyra ruined itself for ever, and during the remaining period of the Peloponnesian war its name is rarely mentioned. After the war, when that part of the sea again became the scene of maritime combats, that splendid island, so distinguished for its rich olive plantations, was so powerless, that it surrendered to the one who first approached; afterwards it was taken without difficulty by Cassander, Agathocles, Pyrrhus, and the Illyrians. Its inhabitants themselves had given it the death-blow. But even during the period following the war, attempts at reaction must have been made, to which Thucydides alludes only in one word[2]—a circumstance which, as well as several others, proves that he wrote after the termination of the Peloponnesian war; but when and how these attempts were made, are questions to which history gives no answer.

This civil war in Corcyra and the expedition to Sicily also occasioned the enterprise of Demosthenes against Pylos. He was a son of Alcisthenes, and belonged to the Athenian nobility, as in general at that time, if we except Cleon and Hyperbolus, the leaders of the republic always belonged to the noble houses. This was not in consequence of any privilege which they possessed; but they bore illustrious names, and were supported by hereditary wealth, which was wanting to the *novi homines;* and to these means alone the nobles owed their promotion and power. Demosthenes was a very enterprising commander, but not always successful. During an expedition against the Aetolians, he had suffered a fearful defeat; while, on the other hand, in conjunction with the Acarnánians, he gained a great victory over the Ambracians. He enjoyed a great reputation at Athens, and created a great

[2] iv. 48.... ἡ στάσις.... ἐτελεύτησεν ἐς τοῦτο, ὅσα γε κατὰ τὸν πόλεμον τόνδε....
—Ed.

sensation; there and in the rest of Greece, the eyes of all were directed towards him.

The Athenians were now preparing to send reinforcements to the ships which had sailed to Sicily (Olymp. 88, 3). Demosthenes asked permission to accompany the expedition, and his request was granted. His object, however, he kept secret. His plan was by some bold enterprise, for which he might either be condemned or gain immortal praise, to give a different turn to the deplorable course of the war. In antiquity it was customary to sail with the galleys along the coast, and to land as often as possible to take in fresh water, which, considering the great number of marines, with 200 rowers, and the narrow space of a galley, had to be frequently renewed. Now as that fleet had to cross the whole of the Ionian sea, it was necessary to take in water before cutting across. The sad manner in which the Spartans managed their dominions, and which in many parts of Laconia, and especially in the conquered Messenia, allowed the country to lie waste, "and the towns to become heaps of ruins, had produced the effect that many harbours and places for anchoring on the coast, were neglected and deserted, so that the Athenians were accustomed to take in water in the hostile country as undisturbed as in a country of friends. The excellent port of Pylos, the modern Navarino, which is now celebrated throughout Europe, was then quite deserted. The population was extirpated far and wide, and the country was changed into a large forest. The soil was excellent and especially adapted for the cultivation of olives; but the Spartans, in their laziness, were indifferent as to whether a number of square miles were lying waste or not. The Athenian fleet thus landed at Pylos for the purpose of taking in water, and Demosthenes now declared to the two Athenian generals, Sophocles (not the dramatic poet, who had been the strategus in the war against Samos) and Eurymedon, that he had accompanied them for the purpose of taking possession of the harbour for the Athenian fleet, and of fortifying himself upon the ruins of the ancient Pylos, whence he hoped to harass the Spartans in their own country; because from this point serious injury might be done to them. There they were in the neighbourhood of the Helots, and Pylos might be a stronghold to them whither they might retreat and concentrate their strength. Demosthenes justly calculated, that, if the undertaking were conducted consistently and energetically, not only the Helots, but many of the towns of the Perioeci, would rise against Sparta, as they had done under King Archidamus scarcely forty years before, and that thus they might succeed in crushing Sparta, which was very weak in the number of its own citizens, and whose strength consisted only in its subjects over whom it tyrannised. This idea was great and correct, but was not well received by men of ordinary minds. The two strategi were vexed at it as an unauthorised interference in their own management of affairs, and rebuked Demosthenes, saying that he had no command, and that, as a mere volunteer, he must obey their orders. But fortunately the wind was unfavourable to the continuation of the voyage, and they were compelled to prolong their stay for some days. Here again we see the noble character of the Athenians, which is displayed on so many occasions: even a common Athenian was charmed by a great idea; he did not place difficulties in the way of its being carried out, but eagerly caught it up as a gift of fortune. As the wind continued unfavourable, and Demosthenes proposed to the soldiers to build a fort by way of experiment, the soldiers were immediately ready, and the commanders could not prevent it. With the greatest difficulty, and without any tools, they erected a fort within six days, and Demosthenes remained behind (for, having joined the fleet as a volunteer, he was at liberty to stay wherever he liked) with some galleys and a few hundred men. A pirate ship of the former Messenians, which was cruising from Naupactus against the Spartans, joined them and joyfully remained with them, and thus they abandoned themselves to the hope of recovering Messenia. Demosthenes thus had at his command a small band and six ships, and with this force he continued to fortify himself more and more.

The Spartans here again gave a striking proof of their utter incapacity and drowsiness: they allowed the Athenian general to establish himself in the best part of their country, and to make himself master of the best harbour in Greece, without even attempting to prevent it, " although Pylos was scarcely thirty miles distant from Sparta." They regarded it as a foolish undertaking, which, as soon as matters should become serious, would be given up. In this manner they delayed doing anything, until the Athenians had strongly fortified themselves; and now they equipped all their ships at Gythium, and sent their militia against the place. But they found the fortifications already too far advanced, to attempt to take them by storm. "Their attack was repulsed," after which they relapsed again into their inactivity, thinking that it would be easy to reduce the enemy by hunger, and that the small band was sure to fall into their hands, whether a few days earlier or later. In order to blockade them, they intended to block up the double entrance to the bay with ships at anchor, and thus to cut off their communication with the Athenian fleet, and to prevent them sailing out into the sea. In order completely to prevent the introduction of supplies from the sea, they landed a detachment of Lacedaemonians and Spartans in the island of Sphacteria, at the entrance of the bay. The Athenians sent a superior fleet to the relief of the besieged, who boldly prepared for an attack. Had the Spartans already taken their posts at the entrance, they might, perhaps, have been able to resist the Athenians; but they had not yet carried out their plan, and the Athenians surprised the enemy's ships, while they were yet within the harbour, and defeated them. The Spartans did not, indeed, lose many ships, because a portion of the fleet threw itself on the coast, and there defended itself; but the Athenians forced their way into the bay, put themselves in communication with the garrison of Pylos, and entirely surrounded the island of Sphacteria, on which was encamped a detachment of 420 men, partly Spartans and partly Lacedaemonians.

This disaster spread the greatest consternation among the Spartans: their ships lay on the coasts, their troops were cut off in the island, which, desert and without any provisions, was surrounded by the Athenians; and it was wholly out of their power to save them. "The fate of the Plataeans floated before their eyes, and it was feared, with good reason, that the Athenians would take bloody vengeance." The smaller the number of the Spartan citizens was, of the more importance was it to them to save those that were shut up in Sphacteria. There can be no doubt that half of the 420 prisoners in the island were Spartan citizens, and there was probably not a family at Sparta of which some member was not among them. The Spartans at all times were very sparing in sending their own men to war; generally they employed only a few as commanders, and large masses were sent out but rarely; the numbers of Spartan citizens who fell at Leuctra were but small, yet the grief at their loss was immense. The terror, therefore, with which the Spartans were now seized was indescribable, and they began to negotiate with Athens. The Athenians were then in great doubt as to the terms on which peace should be concluded; for it was evident that if a peace was brought about, it could not be of long duration. Accordingly, they could not now make peace without obtaining considerable advantages, nor were the terms which they demanded too hard. In the thirty years' truce the Athenians had ceded several points which they had previously possessed in Peloponnesus, and these they now claimed back, if peace was to be concluded, and the prisoners in Sphacteria to be set free. Those points were Troezen and Achaia, and also the two fortresses which commanded Megara, namely, Pagae and the port of Nisaea. These were the demands of the Athenians, and it is impossible to see what else they could have demanded. But the Spartans would not agree to them, imagining that matters would after all turn out differently, if they could but be protracted until the beginning of the stormy season of the year, for that then the Athenian fleet would be obliged to quit Pylos.

During the negotiations, however, a truce was observed, which enabled the Spartans to supply the prisoners in Sphacteria with provisions; but the Spartans had been obliged to deliver up their ships of war in the bay and at Gythium, that they might not attempt to rescue their prisoners; the ships were to be restored to them at the expiration of the truce. It cannot be denied, that here the Athenians were guilty of a breach of faith; for, under the pretext that the Spartans had not observed the truce, they refused to give back the pledged ships. It may be true, that the Spartans committed acts of hostility in violation of the terms of the truce, but it was, nevertheless, unfair on the part of the Athenians to keep back the ships.

LECTURE XLVIII.

FROM this time the Spartans consoled themselves with the
prospect of the stormy season of the year, which would compel
the Athenians to give up the blockade ; and, in the meantime,
they endeavoured in every possible way to supply the prisoners
with provisions.   They insured the vessels carrying provisions
to Sphacteria, and, by promising rewards and liberty, they
induced more especially the Helots to sail out on such expeditions.   When the wind was favourable, they succeeded
in this, with their small sailing boats, in defiance of the
Athenian galleys ; and it sometimes happened that individuals, swimming across, carried substantial provisions in
sacks covered with pitch.   By these means the small band in
Sphacteria was amply provided with supplies.   The Athenians, therefore, again began to feel very uneasy at not having
accepted the peace which had been offered to them.

The government of the republic of Athens, at that time,
was not in the hands of one great man, but several men of
talent, and of different characters, were at the head of affairs.
The most distinguished of the party of the nobles was Nicias,
who was now strategus, and conducted the war ; he was a
man of a good ancient family, and especially renowned for his
wealth, which, according to the standard of the Athenians,
was immense, but of which, according to the laws of Athens,
a great portion belonged to the commonwealth.   He was a
good and blameless general ; in his military undertakings, he
was, on the whole, successful, and, as far as we can judge of
him, he was a thoroughly honest and conscientious man, to
whom his country owed nothing but gratitude.   But he was
of a temperament not common at Athens—calm and phlegma-
tic ; and, as he had been successful in war, he was anxious not
to lose the reputation he had gained ; he wished to enjoy his
present good fortune until the end of his life, and not to com-
promise it by further undertakings.   He also dreaded the
calumnies of the sycophants, who were most tempted to
attack a man of his rank.   Hence he wished for peace, and
had wished for it in the very first negotiations.   Some of the

other generals sided with him. These few words may serve you as an introduction to Aristophanes, " from whose comedies we may form a clear picture of the condition of Athens at that time." One of the generals siding with Nicias was Lamachus, who does not at all deserve the scorn of Aristophanes, though the poet, as I have already observed, did not mean any great harm, and the two men might, perhaps, have lived together without any bitterness. But Laches was a man of a different kind.

The celebrated, or rather notorious, Cleon,[1] a man of a peculiar mind, a strange being, was the real opponent of Nicias. He, indeed, deserves the bad reputation which he has, and I know nothing that might be said in excuse of his conduct. Whenever Aristophanes speaks of him, it is always in a very different manner from that in which he mentions Nicias or Demosthenes, or even Lamachus : against Cleon he has a real aversion ; nay, he despises him. Cleon was a man of very low origin. What fifty years before would have been impossible, now came to pass — a tradesman succeeded in putting himself at the head of the state. Those trades, however, were carried on upon a large scale ; and the circumstances with which we become acquainted in the history of the father of Demosthenes, give us some idea of what they were. We seldom have people whose trade is as extensive as those whom we meet with at Athens ; they resembled our owners of manufactories. Cleon himself assuredly did not work ; he had only set up his tannery, and the work was done by slaves. The social position of Cleon, however, was not a thing that deserved blame — nobody but a fool could have opposed his being in the government on that account : in London, brewers sometimes are men of great distinction and members of Parliament ; but it is his personal character that deserves censure, and merits all that Aristophanes says about it ; the term βυρσοδέψης ought, perhaps, not to have been so often employed by the poet. In the excellent narrative of Thucydides, as well as in many anecdotes derived from other sources, his

[1] " This name, in the later Attic comedy, is the type of an ordinary citizen, just as that of Jérome is in the comedies of Molière, but in life the name no longer occurred, whereas, during the Peloponnesian war, it was still common in noble families. At a still later period, it reappears in illustrious families, and ceased to be ridiculous. The study of the names of the ancients is a very interesting subject."

whole conduct clearly appears like that of an entirely sense-less and unprincipled person, who has no idea of the sacred-ness of the relations, and of the duties, of a man who is placed at the head of a state. There are, indeed, others who have no notion of such things; but the recklessness with which he treated the republic in the manner in which people deal with an intimate acquaintance before whom they require no reserve, the audacity and the insolence with which he made proposals to the popular assembly, and accused and attacked persons who were a hundred times better than he—these things reveal to us a character like that of Cobbet in England, who is the true Cleon of our time; " but Cleon was not as bad as his modern counterpart."

" The people distrusted Nicias, it being known that he wished for peace; and he was suspected of having been un-willing to strike a serious blow at the Spartans. As the hostility between the nobles and the people was generally becoming worse and worse, it was an easy matter for Cleon to make the people listen to him." Thus he now came forward as the accuser of the Athenian generals, asserting that the war in Sphacteria was protracted through their fault alone, and that it was only their cowardice that had prevented their defeating the Spartans. The real truth was, that it was a very pre-carious matter to venture upon such a thing without an express order from the people; considering the fearful responsibility of Athenian generals, they could not venture upon the storming of an island which had no harbour, and where they had to make their way in boats through the strongest breakers. This difficulty was very great; but if the Athenians had sent troops, and the people ordered the island to be taken, Demosthenes would unquestionably have been the man to carry out the undertaking; and he did carry it out. The insolence of Cleon on that occasion had its good results; he urged the necessity of attacking the island, and if this had not been done before the arrival of winter, it would, perhaps, have been necessary to give up the whole of this gallant enterprise. He declared it to be owing to cowardice alone that the island was not already in their hands (though every one knew that he was the most cowardly person in the world), and offered to lead an army to Sphacteria, to take the Spartans prisoners and convey them to Athens. This amused the Athenians to such a degree, that, being fond of a good laugh, they immediately appointed the arch-coward commander, and ordered him to go, hoping that afterwards they would have an opportunity of laughing at him.   Then all at once the extraordinary man became modest, and begged to be excused; but all his evasions were of no avail, and the people told him that he must go.   He then thanked them, and set out with a considerable force (Olymp. 88, 4).

Cleon, who was not wanting in intelligence, now behaved very differently towards Demosthenes from what he had done behind his back; for he became uncommonly modest, showed great respect for him, and entrusted to him the whole management of the blockade.   Demosthenes was satisfied with this. "The conflagration of a forest in the island favoured his enterprise;" he succeeded in effecting a landing, and thus the matter was decided.   The Spartans occupied three posts, one behind another, and although they fought bravely, they were beaten out of two of them, and driven to the last and highest. It was now impossible to convey provisions to them, and the Athenians might now have stopped their proceedings and reduced the Spartans by hunger; but the matter was brought to a speedier termination.   The Athenians walked through the water, which was not deep at the foot of the rocky coast, and thus came round the height; and the Messenians, who knew the locality and all the footpaths well, ascended the summit of the height, which rose above the place where the Spartans had their fortification, and to which they had retreated.   Now, as the Spartans saw certain death before their eyes, they laid down their arms; but, from fear of responsibility, they asked permission to have an interview with the Spartan commanders on the main land.   But the latter refusing to take the responsibility upon themselves, declared to them with their usual hypocrisy, that they would not decide upon the course to be pursued, that the prisoners themselves should deliberate and decide upon their mode of action, but that they must not do anything against the honour of Sparta.   This was only a farce, for how could it be questioned whether their surrender would affect the honour of Sparta?   Thus the two hundred and ninety men, who alone survived of the four hundred and twenty, surrendered and were carried to Athens.   The result showed that they might have held out much longer, for they still had abundance of provisions.

Their appearance at Athens created the most enthusiastic delight. The Athenians now believed that everything was gained ; and had it not been for other intervening occurrences, the Spartans would have sacrificed everything to ransom their kinsfolks and relations.

That the affairs of Sparta were not brought to extremities was owing to Brasidas, the only great man that Sparta then had. The only other man who can, perhaps, be called great is Lysander, but between him and Brasidas there is a great difference. Lysander, in his way, was indeed a great man; but he was ambitious and very dangerous, because the unnatural relations of the Spartan constitution went so far that they interfered with him; and his just claims could not be reconciled with their obsolete forms. Brasidas, on the other hand, had the advantage of being a genuine Spartan, with all the rights of a Spartan, and of being in that condition that the state could grant him anything to which his ambition might be directed, and it would have been madness on his part to allow his ambition a wider range. He was, moreover, of all the Spartans, for a long period, the noblest and best; he was evidently a truly just, fair, and benevolent man, who did not, like his countrymen, with but few exceptions, see in every other Greek a kind of Helot, but knew how to estimate a man according to his personal worth, treated every Greek in the discharge of his duties with respect, and honoured the claims which others, great or small, made for their countries, while he endeavoured to place Sparta as only the first among other equal cities at the head of the Greek nation. This much we can gather from the actions which he was enabled to perform during his short career; and there is no ground for believing that, if he had lived longer, he would have acted differently, or that he would not have made an exception from the other Spartans; for he was not an ordinary man. Ever since the expedition of Alcidas to Ionia, Brasidas had distinguished himself everywhere, and in some campaigns he had risen above all others by his prudence and resolution; he was everywhere the boldest, and advised that which was most useful. It was probably at his own suggestion that the

Spartans now sent him to the coast of Thrace to make a diversion against the Athenians, which might afford the means by which they might purchase peace. He himself had, no doubt, formed this plan, and it was the most useful that could have been devised. The intention was to oblige the Athenians to direct their forces to quite a different quarter. I have already remarked how important the Thracian coast was to Athens. It was, in reality, the first true military move; for hitherto the war had been carried on in an almost childish manner. The idea of Demosthenes had been admirable, but its execution was unskilful in many respects.

Brasidas (Olymp. 89, 1) set out from Corinth with an army amounting not quite to 2,000 men; he marched through Boeotia, Phocis, Locris, and Thessaly, to the coast of Thrace, in order to support the Chalcidian and Bottiaean towns on the Thracian coast, which were already in arms against Athens, to deprive the Athenians of their other allied towns, but especially to take possession of Amphipolis on the Strymon, and thus to cut off the communication with those parts, and to prevent the exportation of timber from Thrace. This undertaking, with so small a force, was very bold.

But it is remarkable that this expedition, at the same time, afforded the means for averting another great danger which threatened the Spartan republic. Great as is the obscurity that envelops the relations of Sparta, it is clear that the Helots were extremely numerous. We are mistaken if we suppose that they were not only cruelly oppressed, but that they were also a degraded, insensible, and useless, mass of slaves. This was formerly my notion; we commonly imagine them to have been like the Lettes in Livonia and Kurland, who are treated as cruelly as the ancient Helots, and thus the common supposition has some semblance of truth. But it is erroneous; the Helots were rather in a condition of savageness, of constant rage and secret exasperation against their cruel tyrants, like the negroes in the sugar islands, who can never be reconciled to their fate; while other tribes of negroes are so weak that they become quite accustomed to their chains. The Helots were in a state of savageness, whence they were undoubtedly very useful, when the Spartans led them out to war. If there is any trustworthy authority in all history, that man is Thucydides, whose words may be unconditionally

relied upon, who says nothing but that of which he is perfectly convinced, and who is incapable of uttering an untruth
about a friend or about a foe. He relates, that shortly before
this time the Spartans had employed a body of Helots in the
war, and had promised them their freedom after the campaign.
When they returned, the Spartans actually declared them to
be free, but then ordered them all to be murdered one after
another. This occurrence, which furnishes us a satisfactory
standard by which we may estimate the value of Spartan
virtue, had created the most furious exasperation among the
Helots, as we may easily imagine. But yet, even after this
experience—such is often the power of circumstances which
exercise an inexplicable and magic influence—they were ready
to go to war as soon as the Spartans offered to enlist them,
and promised them their freedom, the prospect of which was
more powerful than anything else. Thus Brasidas enlisted a
corps of Helots for his undertaking. This was very advantageous to the Spartans, whether they were victorious, or
whether they sustained a defeat: for if they perished, the
oligarchs had reason to rejoice at having got rid of them; if
they were victorious, it was for the good of Sparta, and all the
Spartans had then to do, was to consider as to whether it was
advisable to poison them with bread, as they were said to have
done shortly before in Cythera, or to give them settlements
whereby again the interests of the ruling class were promoted.
An extraordinary man like Brasidas, understood those unhappy
outcasts, and it is evident that his troops were very much
attached to him personally, and admired him.

When the Athenians heard of the expedition, they saw the
danger at once; but what were they to do? An attempt of
their friends in Thessaly to prevent the Spartans from marching
through their country failed; Brasidas reached his goal, and
appeared on the Thracian coast between the Thermaic gulf
and the sea of Thasos. The expeditions of Brasidas in those
parts are details which do not belong to a general history of
antiquity, and we therefore pass them over; you may read
them in Thucydides. He took possession of one place after
another, and above all, he succeeded in making himself master
of the large city of Amphipolis on the Strymon. He accomplished this, because unfortunately the Athenian spirit in that
great settlement had been crushed. Had not the 10,000

colonists whom Athens had at first sent to the place, been destroyed soon after the Persian war, Brasidas would never have succeeded in taking that city. A second Athenian colony, which was sent thither under Hagnon at a considerably later time, was far too weak to be able to defend such a large place in the neighbourhood of the warlike Thracian tribes. Hence they were obliged to admit men from other Greek settlements, especially from the Chalcidian towns, which were then not hostile to the Athenians, and which could be trusted. These as epoeci soon formed a demos, which was opposed and hostile to the Athenian colonists. They stood to the Athenians at Amphipolis, in the relation of persons who were not perfectly ἔντιμοι; hence they formed a demos in opposition to the democratic Athenians, as if the latter had been the strictest oligarchs. This lay in the nature of circumstances, notwithstanding the democratic character of the Athenians, who cherished democracy for themselves only. In like manner, we see in our own days the settlers in the small cantons, who have come from the other Swiss cantons, treated very unfairly. Nay, in Freiburg there existed a patriciate consisting of persons that were not noble, and who obliged the nobles to give up their titles when they wished to be admitted: such is the changeable nature of an oligarchy! Now the epoeci in Amphipolis, the Chalcidians, and other Greeks, delivered the city up to Brasidas, and the immortal Thucydides, who had been sent from Athens with a fleet for the purpose of collecting a force in those parts, was unable to arrive in time to defend Amphipolis against the enemy: he could only maintain the port of Eion, which however was an important point, from which further maritime attacks on Thasos could be prevented.

At this time (Olymp. 89, 1) a truce for one year had been concluded between Athens and Sparta, according to which all the conquests which each party had made after a certain day were to be given up. On that occasion, the Spartans again showed their ever-recurring faithlessness in not fulfilling the terms of the truce. Thucydides, who is so just that he does not allow himself to be unfair towards his fellow citizens, although they had unjustly exiled him for having had the misfortune of being unable to save Amphipolis, and who is, therefore, certainly impartial, remarks, that the point might indeed have been disputed, but that justice was on the side of the Athenians,

and that the Spartans were untrue.   How could peace have
been maintained with the Spartans, who considered it lawful
to lie *ad majorem rei publicae gloriam,* and who had made it a
regular principle, that there was no obligation for a Spartan to
keep his faith towards a non-Spartan, if to break it was
advantageous to the republic ! Thus it was with some difficulty
that the year passed away without acts of hostility; but when
the year was over, arms were taken up again.   In the meantime, however, the Athenians had continued the war against
their other enemies, especially against the cities which had
revolted.

Matters had now come to that point, that Cleon looked
upon himself as a hero; and it would seem that, in consequence
of his good luck, the Athenian people also had changed their
opinion of him.   They exiled Thucydides, and entrusted to
Cleon the command against Brasidas in Thrace (Olymp. 89, 2),
that he might carry out what Thucydides had failed in.   The
beginning of the undertaking succeeded pretty well, for he
took from Brasidas some places which had revolted to him; but
when he directed his force against Amphipolis, in the hope of
recovering it, he miserably failed.   In the neighbourhood of
that city, an engagement ensued between only a few thousand
men; but in its consequences it was as eventful as the greatest
battle.   Brasidas there displayed his insight, and his arrangements show that he was a truly great general. It is remarkable
to see the interest which Thucydides takes in him: although
his heart was assuredly bleeding at the defeat of his countrymen; yet with his artistic talent he is evidently delighted with
the excellent arrangements of Brasidas, and we may still rejoice
with him, if we have but sufficient imagination; for he draws
the positions of the armies quite accurately, and we see the
battle distinctly before our eyes: the contrast between the
victorious energy of Brasidas, and the miserable awkwardness
of Cleon.   When Brasidas moved onwards, and his spears
were glittering in the sun, Cleon lost courage, and saw no
means of escaping, except by leading his troops back in a
column; but he made his retreat as stupidly as possible, and
the column was formed so badly, that its right wing was left
without protection, and exposed to the Spartans.   Cleon fell;
it is not probable that he should have sought death in order to
escape from the disgrace; life was too dear to him, and it

would not have been difficult for him to get over the disgrace. He certainly fell very reluctantly. Brasidas, too, fell bravely fighting, together with a very few of his men, while the Athenians lost a great many. The issue of this battle is painful to all who look to Athens for the salvation of Greece; but for the moment it led to a peace. "After Cleon's death, the party of peace could come forward more openly," the sanguine hopes of the Athenians had vanished; they had lost courage, and felt the want of peace.

LECTURE XLIX.

AFTER the capture of Sphacteria, the Athenians had experienced several things which tended to damp their sanguine expectations. Besides the painful occurrences at Amphipolis, they sustained a serious defeat near Delium in Boeotia. They had made an expedition into Boeotia, and there fortified the temple at Delium, in order to have a better point for crossing over to Chalcis and Euboea. The place was one of great importance. This undertaking being very dangerous to the Boeotians, roused them to a great operation, which was highly unfortunate for the Athenians (Olymp. 89, 1). The latter had marched into Boeotia with an army raised by a general levy, and which seems to have had extremely little discipline and training: the Greek phalanx required, indeed, little of these things, but yet more than the Athenian militia possessed. "The Thebans were far better troops of the line." The Athenians suffered a decided defeat with great loss ; their commander fell, and Delium was obliged to capitulate.

The great difficulty, or rather impossibility, of expelling the Spartans from the Thracian coast, together with this unfortunate catastrophe, induced the Athenians seriously to think of proposals of peace, of securing the advantages which they yet possessed, and of lowering their demands. By their connections in Thessaly, they had, indeed, gained so much, that the succour sent to the Spartan army in Thrace did not reach its destination; Perdiccas, king of Macedonia, also had abandoned the cause of Sparta and again joined the Athenians, and

G 2

although Macedonia was at that time an extremely weak state,
yet its alliance was of great importance on its frontier; but
still it was not of sufficient weight to enable the Athenians to
keep possession of those districts by force; and when the towns
of Macedonia, most of which were Greek places, in spite of
the king's alliance, more and more renounced their connection with Athens, and kept together among themselves,
the Athenians really began to wish for peace.   These circumstances led to the peace of Nicias (Olymp. 89, 3), whose name
it bears with justice, for the merit of having brought it about
belongs to him, and he did all the work.   He seems, like
Cimon in former times, to have possessed the confidence of
the Spartans; it is possible that he, like Cimon, was the only
Athenian in whom the Spartans had confidence, and who
wished them well.   This peace was concluded in spring, after
the war had lasted somewhat more than ten years.   It is the
subject of Aristophanes' comedy, entitled Εἰρήνη.[1]

This peace, "formally a truce of fifty years," met with no
difficulties on the part of the Athenians and Spartans, for both
were ready to conclude it, and everything was soon settled.
But it was rendered difficult by the relations subsisting between
the Spartans and their allies.   Athens had assumed such a
position, in regard to her allies, that they no longer had any
voice in the matter at all; but this was not the case with the
Spartans, whose allies were still entitled to take part in the
common assembly, and very few among them were inclined to
make peace.   It was, however, more particularly the Corinthians and Boeotians that would hear nothing of peace, and
they were joined by the Megarians.   This was most senseless
on their part; but they were, no doubt, urged on to this by
their neighbours.   "Sparta and Athens, however, believed
that it was sufficient if they agreed with each other, and
Sparta concluded the peace without consulting her allies.   The
latter accordingly began to feel great mistrust, and the peace
became from the first very insecure."

Sparta was particularly peaceably disposed.   One of the
chief reasons which made her so, was the circumstance
that another enemy had risen against her; for there was a
revival of the ancient enmity between Argos and Sparta,

[1] This paragraph has been transferred to this place from the end of the 48th
Lecture.—ED.

which had originated at the time of the first Doric settlements, and had continued ever since. The war had been renewed even before, and had been interrupted only by an indefinite truce; and at the present moment, too, there existed a fifty years' truce,[2] which had probably been concluded shortly after the great defeat, which the Argives had sustained through King Cleomenes in the Hebdome. On that occasion, nearly all the ancient Doric population of Argòs was cut off, being destroyed by fire and sword by the Spartans in a grove. This was at the same time the cause of the anomalous phenomenon that Argos was now almost a complete democracy. It is said that at that time, after the extirpation of the ancient citizens, many serfs, that is, clarotae, obtained the franchise; we must not, however, imagine that this statement refers to domestic slaves, but to the real serfs of the Argives, that is, the remnants of the ancient Achaeans. This truce had now very nearly terminated, and the Spartans had reason to fear lest the Argives, whose population had been restored, should now join the Athenians, and that the war should thus be transferred to Peloponnesus. They would then have been placed between two fires—the Athenians at Pylos, and the Argives on the other side; and this might have become very dangerous, as the Helots might be excited to revolt on two sides. It was, therefore, their fear of losing their unjust position that made them wish for peace. And as regards the peace itself, they might console themselves with the thought, that after all they would not observe it further than was agreeable to them: they were very ready with their promises, but afterwards they kept no more than they liked, or than they could help.

The terms of the peace were very simple: in the first place, both parties were to give back their conquests, and Sparta, in particular, was to restore the conquests on the coast of Thrace. There can be no doubt that both parties understood that Amphipolis and the Chalcidian towns, which Brasidas had conquered, should be restored and renew their former connection with Athens. It is true, the relation of the Chalcidian towns was not very distinctly set forth in the document; but the return to the former state of affairs sufficiently indicated what was meant. The Athenians promised to the revolted towns

- [2] According to Thucydides, v. 14, it was only a thirty years' truce.—ED.

an amnesty and autonomy, and that they would not raise the tribute above the amount fixed by Aristides. No possessions were ceded. All the prisoners, also, were to be restored to freedom, a point of particular importance to the Spartans, because they thus received back their prisoners of Pylos: in this respect the Spartans had by far the greater advantage. Lastly, both parties reserved for themselves the right of adding new terms to the treaty, or to modify those agreed upon. This was perhaps not badly meant, but it made a bad impression. The clause " to add and to modify the terms," is, in fact, one which was always added to ancient treaties; but as in this matter the Spartans took no notice of their allies, they excited distrust among them.

All the Spartan allies in Peloponnesus and the Boeotians refused to join in this treaty. The latter concluded with the Athenians only a truce of ten days (δεχημέρους σπονδάς), probably on condition, that, if no notice was given to the contrary, it was to be constantly renewed after the lapse of ten days. With Corinth there existed no truce at all.

" Some of the terms of the peace were not complied with, though this was the case much less on the part of Athens than on that of Sparta. At first the Athenians carried the stipulations into effect with perfect good faith; and it would have been better for Greece, if they had acted with more distrust towards the Spartans; but trusting the word of Sparta, they good-naturedly restored all the prisoners. The Spartans, on the other hand, acted quite differently: they indeed withdrew their garrisons from Amphipolis and the other towns, but instigated the inhabitants to refuse again to submit to Athens, and then declared to the Athenians that they had done their part, and that they had no means of compelling the towns. While thus they declined to do what was fair, and even opposed the Athenians when they wanted to use force, they themselves did not blush most peremptorily to demand the unconditional surrender of Pylos, where Athenian troops were still in garrison. Among other things, the Athenians expected that the fort Panacton, on the Boeotian frontier, which had been taken by the Boeotians with the assistance of the Spartans, and was still in their hands, would now be restored. But as it was in the hands of the Boeotians, the Spartans said that they had nothing to do with it.   The Spartans, from the first, were guilty of infamous deception, and this immediately gave rise to bitter feelings.

But before matters had come to this, and when the Athenians were were still in the full belief, that the Spartans were honest, all Greece was startled by a treaty of alliance between Athens and Sparta against their common enemies. This treaty was concluded very soon after the peace, just as has sometimes been done in modern times; Peter III, for example, concluded an alliance with Frederick II, and immediately ordered his troops to join him. In like manner, France, soon after the Spanish war of succession, allied itself with England against Spain, against the same Philip whom she had raised to the throne.   In 1790 war was on the point of breaking out between Prussia and Austria, and the very year after, an offensive and defensive alliance was concluded between these two states. In Greece this alliance made a very singular impression, not that suspicion was directed against Athens, for from it, the Peloponnesians had nothing to fear, but all suspected Sparta. All the Peloponnesians, the Arcadians, Eleans, etc., imagined that Sparta had concluded an alliance with Athens to induce the latter to allow her to reduce the states of Peloponnesus to complete submission; it was believed that such an arrangement had actually been entered into—although at Athens everything was done with the greatest publicity—and that Sparta had pledged herself to allow Athens to do the same.   The consequence was, that Sparta suddenly found herself deserted by all her allies; the Corinthians and Boeotians renounced her, because they found themselves given over to the Athenians, and the Boeotians perhaps thought, that the Spartans, if they could but reduce the Eleans to the condition of Helots, would readily allow Boeotia to be subdued by the Athenians. Thus Argos found the means of again following a policy which ever since the time of Cleomenes it had not ventured to think of, and again endeavoured to establish its ancient claims to the supremacy. " Argos had indeed been regarded from early times as a very illustrious city, especially on account of its renown in the Homeric poems; but it had not sufficient strength to inspire the other states with fear, and" it thus became the centre of an alliance with Mantinea, " which had always been opposed to the

Lacedaemonians," and some other Arcadian towns, Achaia, Elis, and some places of the Acte. The Arcadians had dissolved their union, the three people of the country had separated themselves, though sometimes they united again; and thus it happened that only some of their towns were allied with Argos. Corinth at first would listen to neither party, and chose to remain neutral; "for although for the moment it was highly exasperated against Sparta, yet it had at all times entertained a mortal hatred of Argos, and its own interests drew it towards Sparta."

But when, owing to Sparta's dishonesty, the affairs on the coasts of Thrace became more and more complicated, when the towns refused to submit to Athens, and when it became evident, that this was the consequence of the instigations of Sparta, then the relation subsisting between the two states became worse also in Greece, and various negotiations and cavillings ensued. As to the manner in which the negotiations became more artificially complicated, while the indignation of the Athenians was increasing, I must refer you to Thucydides. It was owing partly to intrigues and partly to accident, that the result was different from what had been anticipated. After much delay, the Athenians and Spartans were already on the point of taking up arms against each other; but then they came to the singular agreement (Olymp. 89, 4), that the Athenians should retain possession of Pylos, but keep in it only Athenian troops, and not allow the Helots and Messenians to remain there. After this the loosened bonds between the Spartans, Corinthians, and Boeotians, were drawn more closely. The Boeotians were at length prevailed upon to surrender Panacton to the Spartans, who now restored it to the Athenians. This was in accordance with the undoubted meaning of the peace; but the Boeotians had first destroyed the place, and the Spartans delivered it to the Athenians only a heap of ruins. The Athenians justly complained, that this was not an honest restoration, and that the place ought to have been given back to them with its fortifications uninjured. The Spartans do not appear to have had honest intentions in any way, for otherwise things might speedily have been altered and settled. Had they restored the fortress and caused the Boeotians to pay the expenses, they would have done only what was just; but this they did not do, because they did not wish it. While thus the alliance between Athens and Sparta, in the eyes of the world, still existed, it had in reality ceased and become an impossibility.

Another alliance, however, was formed between Athens and Argos (Olymp. 89, 4) through the influence of Alcibiades, who stood in the relation of an hereditary proxenus to Argos. A more natural alliance than this could not be conceived, and by it the Athenians gained the Mantineans, Eleans, and other Peloponnesians over to their side.

Alcibiades now exercised a decisive influence upon the fate of his country, and this is the place to speak of him. He is one of those men of antiquity whose name is familiar to every one; but that which is most characteristic in him is by no means sufficiently recognised. What is commonly related about him is, for the most part, incorrect; and, in speaking of his beauty and gracefulness, people forget the principal things which render him a really remarkable man. The advantages of his personal appearance were so great, that they have actually injured him, and thrown his brilliant qualities into the shade. We generally conceive Alcibiades as a man whose beauty was his ornament, and to whom the follies of life were the main thing, and we forget that part of his character which history reveals to us. There are only very few who know what he really was; and hence it often happens with modern writers, that he is not only judged of unfavourably, but even with a certain degree of contempt. Works which have been very much read, contain expressions altogether unpardonable, and opinions unjustifiably contemptuous about him. According to the judgment of the ancients, Alcibiades was not an ordinary man, but one of those demon-like beings whom we often meet with in history, who decide the fate of whole nations and countries, and whose personal influence is more powerful than the fortune and policy of states. Thucydides, who cannot be suspected of having been particularly partial to Alcibiades, most expressly recognises the fact, that the fate of Athens depended upon him, and that, if he had not separated his own fate from that of his native city, at first from necessity, but afterwards of his own accord, the course of the Peloponnesian war, through his personal influence alone, would have taken quite a different direction, and that he alone would have decided it in favour of Athens. This is,

in fact, the general opinion of all antiquity, and there is no
ancient writer of importance who does not view and estimate
him in this light.   It is only the moderns that entertain a
derogatory opinion of him, and speak of him as an eccentric
fool, who ought not to be named among the great statesmen
of antiquity.   Aristophanes, a man not inferior to Thucydides
in judgment and intellect, though in other respects he is
widely different from him, and whose opinion of Alcibiades is
expressed in the Frogs, with an air of joke, indeed, but at a
time when the object was to raise him again, describes his
worth and his position most strikingly in the words—

> Οὐ χρὴ λέοντος σκύμνον ἐν πόλει τρέφειν,
> (Or Μάλιστα μὲν λέοντα μὴ 'ν πόλει τρέφειν,
> Ἢν δ' ἐκτρέφῃ τις, τοῖς τρόποις ὑπηρετεῖν).

This opinion contains all that can be said about him ; Aristophanes tells the Athenians, that the appearance of such an
abnormal demon-like being, in a free state, may, indeed, be
regarded as a misfortune and a danger, but that, wherever
such a being exists, the people must accommodate themselves
to him and not oppose him.

Alcibiades is quite a peculiar character ; and I know no one
in the whole range of ancient history who might be compared
with him, though I have sometimes thought of Caesar ; for he
too, from early life, indulged in political licenses, by which he
violated the strict law established by custom.   But he is, after
all, quite a different man ; for he is infinitely superior to Alcibiades in thoughtfulness.   Alcibiades, as is agreed by all, was
not a φύσις πολιτική, he was, on the contrary, a φύσις τυραν-
νική ; for, to accommodate himself to the law and the regulations of the state, quietly to find for himself the position
which the constitution assigned to him, and to regulate his
life by the laws of the state, these were things which he
could not do.   Caesar could do it: he also, it is true, generally disregarded the laws, and strove upwards ; but, up to a
certain point in his life, this striving to rid himself from
restraints was, after all, only a secondary object, and, generally
speaking, he remained, up to his consulship, a citizen of the
republic.   Caesar, moreover, was a practical man of creative
powers in the forms and business of the state.   Alcibiades, on
the other hand, had no taste for activity in the state ; he

was a fearful ègotist ; he looked only to himself and his power, and the republic was obliged to give way. The republic had to endure things at his hands which no free state ought to submit to from a citizen, if it can be helped ; but these were the only terms on which the services of Alcibiades could be obtained. It must, however, be acknowledged that, as he grew older, he became better ; and during the last years of his life, when he had fallen out with his country a second time, he showed patriotic sentiments which prove that, when he had come to maturity, he had become an incomparably better citizen than he had been before.

There can be no doubt that, from his earliest youth, he claimed, in the most insolent manner, to exercise in the state that power, and to gain that ascendancy, which his guardian Pericles had reached. But all are agreed in acknowledging, that he was really great as a general and statesman, and in all those things which do not require labour, care, conscientious strictness, and perseverance. For such things he had neither taste nor conscience ; but wherever he could influence the minds, in or out of Athens—whenever he had to win over, terrify, and persuade the Athenians, to guide foreign states, and command armies, he was a great master. At the head of an army he was incomparable, and decidedly a great general. " His personal influence was truly magical, ruling everything around him ; and this had made him conscious that he might use his power in any manner he pleased. Characters of this kind seldom use their powers for good purposes. Nothing can resist them, everybody views them as something far above the rest, while they themselves recognise no law, human or divine, above them ; they may conform to law when it suits them—they may be noble, generous, affectionate—but, at the same time, they break through all restraints whenever they please, and when their own interests demand it ; men are then to them no more than insects which they can trample upon, and which they regard as nothing." Such a man was Alcibiades.[3]

[3] " In modern times this power was possessed in an eminent degree by Mira- beau, and in a less degree by Fox. They charmed every one approaching them, and chained them irresistibly to themselves: but neither in the same degree as Alcibiades. Napoleon was too practical a man. Demosthenes was a character of the same kind, but remained quite pure: this is the noblest phe- nomenon in history, and envy immediately begins to malign such a character.

Alcibiades was opposed to the peace of Nicias from entirely personal, perhaps even mean, motives. The statement, that, during the negotiations which the Spartans were carrying on with the Athenians, in order to prevent them from forming an alliance with Argos, he cheated the Spartans in a shameful way, seems to be perfectly credible, and it was on his advice that Athens concluded the alliance with Argos and Elis.

Athens now had two alliances which were equally binding, and yet altogether opposed to each other: the one with Sparta, and an equally stringent one with Argos, the enemy of Sparta. This treaty with Argos, the Peloponnesians, etc., was extremely formidable to the Spartans; and they accordingly, for once, determined to act quickly, before it should be too late. The alliance with Argos, however, did not confer much real strength upon Athens, for the Argives were lazy, and Elis did not respect them, whence the Spartans had time again to unite themselves more closely with Corinth, Boeotia, and Megara. When, therefore, the war between the Spartans and Argives broke out, and the former resolutely took the field, Alcibiades persuaded the Athenians to send succour to the Argives, and thus the peace with Sparta was violated in an unprincipled manner. But still no blow was struck between Argos and Sparta; there was, indeed, abundant cause for war, but both parties felt timid, and were unwilling to allow matters to come to extremities. King Agis had set out with a Spartan army, but concluded a truce with the Argives (Olymp. 90, 2); this, however, was taken very ill at Sparta, and the Argive commanders who had concluded it were censured by the people and magistrates of Argos. Soon afterwards the war broke out again, and, when the Athenian auxiliaries appeared, decided acts of hostility commenced. The occasion was an attempt of the Mantineans to subdue Tegea: the sad condition of Greece became more particularly manifest in Arcadia, by the divisions which tore one and the same nation to pieces. The country was distracted by several parties; had Arcadia been united, it would have been invulnerable. A battle was fought (Olymp. 90, 3) in the neighbourhood of Mantinea, between the Argives, their Athenian allies, the Mantineans,

But such natures rarely remain pure, and most of them have come under the influence of the evil spirit. Catiline, too, was a man of a similar nature, and by no means a vulgar miscreant."—1826.

and part of the Arcadians (" the Eleans, annoyed at the conduct of the Argives, had abandoned their cause"), on the one
hand, and the Spartans and a few allies on the other. The
Spartans gained a most decisive victory; and, although they
did not follow it up, yet the consequence was, that Argos
concluded peace, the Argive alliance broke up, and at Argos
a revolution took place, in which an oligarchical government
was instituted, and by which Argos was drawn into the
interest of Sparta (Olymp. 90, 4). This constitution, however did not last, and very soon gave way to a democratic
form of government.

Argos, even at this time, and still more at a later period,
is a sad example of the most degenerate and deplorable democracy, or, more properly speaking, anarchy. Down to the
Macedonian period, when it entered the Achaean state, it
was the scene of the most fearful horrors, and most bloody
revolutions; and, throughout that period, there did not appear
a single man who, by his personal character, exercised any
influence or commanded respect, and far less gained renown
for himself and his country.

This battle thwarted the hopes of Alcibiades. Soon after
these events, there followed the great expedition to Sicily, " one
of the most decisive events in the history of the world. Without this undertaking, on which Athens staked everything,
Sparta could never have gained the victory. It was not only
the material consequences that decided the contest, but the
opinions of men also were determined by the issue of that
undertaking."

— ◆ —

LECTURE L.

AT the time of the Peloponnesian war, Sicily was undoubtedly
at the height of its prosperity; more than three hundred years
had then elapsed since the first Greek settlement in the island,
and about one hundred and fifty since the last.

" The western Greeks, the Siceliots and Italiots, have their
history quite distinct from that of the eastern Greeks, as in
general they had their own literature, and more especially

their own range of poetry, consisting of the idyl and comedy, for they had neither tragedy nor epic poetry.

The earliest Siceliot historian is Antiochus of Syracuse, a contemporary of Herodotus, who perhaps knew him, and divided with him the history of the world; for it is an unfounded supposition, that Herodotus is silent about the West, because he knew nothing about it. It is surprising to find, that the work of Antiochus was still written in the Ionic dialect, as if the Doric had been considered unfit for prose composition. He wrote an account of the Greek settlements in Sicily and Italy down to Olymp. 89, and gave solid information. Much of what we read in Diodorus is taken from his work, though it may be at second or even at third hand.

He was succeeded by Philistus, whose loss is greatly to be lamented, for Cicero and Dionysius speak of him as an historian with great admiration. He was a bad man, and exercised great influence upon the tyrant Dionysius, but he must have possessed great talent. He is said to have imitated Thucydides; but whether this consisted simply in his imitating the style of Thucydides, or whether, as a practical man, he entered into his spirit and mode of thinking, cannot be decided. We may, however, suppose that he, too, did not write Doric, but perhaps Attic.

Shortly after Agathocles, Timaeus, of whom I have already spoken,[1] composed his work. It was written in the annalistic form, and was for a long period regarded as a great authority by the ancients. Timaeus was credulous, and fond of the marvellous; he was a diligent inquirer, but very uncritical, and his history contained much that was impossible and ridiculous. We see this from the book entitled "Mirabiles Auscultationes," and printed among the works of Aristotle, which is almost entirely taken from the history of Timaeus. But his great fault was his inclination to calumniate; he was a mean, wretched man, who hated all great characters, and took a delight in reviling them. But, notwithstanding all this, his history was of great value. He was probably still alive at the time when the Romans crossed over into Sicily, or at least died shortly before that event, for he related the war of Pyrrhus."

The earliest inhabitants of the island are called Sicani, and

---

[1] See vol. i. p. 176.

Thucydides distinctly recognises them as Iberians; it is, however, indifferent whether we adopt the tradition, that they immigrated from Catalonia because they were thence expelled by the Ligurians, which is highly improbable, or whether we regard them as autochthons (for such they believed themselves to be), that is, as people who had inhabited Sicily from time immemorial, and about whose immigration nothing can be said. The latter view is supported by the circumstance, that the most ancient population of Sardinia and Corsica was an Iberian race; and as it is highly probable, that at one time the whole of the north coast of Africa was inhabited by an Iberian population, while the whole of Spain was occupied by Celts, it may be that those Iberians had established themselves also in Sicily. This is at least very probable, and Thucydides expresses it with the greatest certainty. I must, however, notice that the name Sicani is very like Siculi, and that this change of the termination *anus* into *ulus* is of common occurrence among the Italian nations, as in Romanus and Romulus, and in like manner we have Aequus, Aequanus, Aequiculus, and Aequulus. Hence as the Aequians are called both Aequani and Aequuli, we might also say, that the Sicani and Siculi were one and the same people under different names. The circumstance, that Virgil calls the Siculi in Latium, Sicani, clearly shows that the learned among the Romans viewed the matter in this light. He uses the name Siculi for the inhabitants of the island, and Sicani is the name of the ancient Pelasgian and Tyrrhenian inhabitants of Latium.

But, however this may be, there existed in Sicily two different nations or two different tribes of the same people, viz., the Sicani and the Siculi. There can be no question that the latter were Pelasgians, just like the Siculi in Latium and the inhabitants of the southernmost parts of Italy; for, in fact, the inhabitants of southern Calabria are likewise called Siculi by the Greeks. This name came into use again in southern Italy at the time of the Byzantine emperors; and during the middle ages, the court of Byzantium, after having lost Sicily proper, still possessed a province called Sicily, in the south of Calabria, the ἐπαρχία of Calabria being called the ἐπαρχία of Sicily. Hence the name of the " kingdom of the two Sicilies." The expression *utraque Sicilia* occurs as early as the time of the first Norman princes, so that there was a Sicily on each side of the straits.

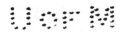

The great Gibbon saw in this only a piece of vanity of the
Byzantines; this may be true, but there can be no doubt that
it was at the same time a continuation of the ancient mode of
speaking, for in ordinary life the southernmost part of Italy
had been called Sicily, because in the earliest times it had
been inhabited by Siculi.   In like manner, Tuscany, under the
last Roman emperors, began to be called Tuscia, from the
ancient Tusci, although that name had not previously been
used.   In ordinary life, the people, no doubt, always called
themselves Tusci, although in the classical age of Cicero and
Caesar, we only hear of Etrusci.   In the time of Cato, the
name Etrusci does not occur, the people being called Tusci
and the country Etruria.   But each of these two names has a
different meaning, Etrusci being the ancient Rasena, and
Tusci the ancient Tyrrhenians.   " The Siculi had no doubt
immigrated into Sicily, being expelled from Italy by the
Opicans, and they again pushed the Sicani from the eastern
to the southern, and especially to the western parts of the
island.   Both nations appear in history as altogether different.
The Sicani formed small communities, while the Siculi had
larger ones and obeyed at least one king."[2]

Besides these two nations, whom the Greeks found on their
arrival in Sicily, there existed from the earliest times small
Phoenician settlements, both on the coasts and in the adjacent
islands, which had been established as commercial stations long
before the Greek colonies.   They resembled the German
colonies of the Hansa, e.g., in Russia and Scandinavia, being
places governing themselves, submitting sometimes to the
supremacy of the mother country, and being sometimes
altogether independent.   " But Sicily must have been very
thinly peopled, for the Greeks appear to have established their
settlements without any difficulty.   Their colonisation of
Sicily began immediately after the commencement of the
Olympiads, and these Sicilian colonies are the most ancient of
which we have any historical records; they were contemporary
with Croton, and more ancient than Tarentum.   They were
established very gradually: bands of warriors went out, and
having gained a firm footing, were followed by many others
from their native country."   They came from the most
different places, being partly Dorians and partly Chalcidians.

[2] With what has been said here, comp. *Hist. of Rome*, vol. i. p. 6-173.

Corinthian colonies existed there at an early period, a fact which cannot surprise us, since Corinth had from early times been a great commercial city; but it is surprising to find that there also existed an ancient Rhodian settlement. This Creto-Rhodian colony is a proof, that in the ante-historical period, Rhodes was much greater and more powerful than it afterwards is in history. It generally appears, as if Rhodes first became a place of importance during the Macedonian period; this is indeed true, but only in reference to the period immediately preceding, for during the Peloponnesian war, the island was of no importance. This is an instance of one of the fallacies which occur most frequently; for in historical inquiries we generally conceive things as in a progressive development, and do not take into consideration that the course of events often resembles a cycloid. When we see a state in the condition of progress, we imagine that, during the preceding period also, it was always in a similar state of advancement, and we overlook the fact, that a country often makes a great movement in advance, then goes backwards, then rises again, and again becomes retrograde, as we so often see in the history of Rome. Such also was the case with Rhodes. The mention of the Rhodian cities in the Catalogue of the Iliad, justifies the inference, that it must have been an important state even at an early period; but afterwards it fell back, nobody knows how. Now the establishment of a Rhodian colony in Sicily belongs to that period of the ancient prosperity of Rhodes.

This consideration is cheering; and it is something very depressing to cling to the prejudice, that a nation, when it has once gone backward, cannot recover itself. To what a degree, for example, has our state recovered since the calamity of 1806, when it had fallen into a condition of perfect exhaustion! It is indeed difficult for a state to recover as quickly as Prussia then did; but how much did Germany itself rise after the thirty years' war, when it had become so powerless, that Sweden, for a long time afterwards, even after the death of Gustavus Adolphus, could terrify it and tyrannise over it; and yet it grew strong, and that even without great men, until Frederic II. created a real national feeling. Many examples of this kind occur in the history of antiquity.

More unaccountable than these are the Sicilian colonies of Megara, which in Greece proper was always a very small state,

The Chalcidian colonies, on the other hand, may easily be accounted for by the evident greatness of the navigation and maritime power of Euboea, though the detail is unknown to us. Chalcis founded the so-called Chalcidian towns, in which the Chalcidian νόμιμα prevailed.

The Dorians and Chalcidians were everywhere opposed to each other, from the deplorable tendency of men to cherish an antipathy against those who are nearest to them. It was not only the jealousy so common among people of the same trade, which is described in Hesiod, καὶ κεραμεὺς κεραμεῖ κοτέει, etc., but it was also a wretched national jealousy. Towards our own relations we are the severest judges ; and we feel most deeply hurt by the superiority of those who belong to a nation of the same race with our own, but have a different political existence. Such was the case in Italy among the different cities, such in the German empire, such in ancient Greece, and such everywhere, through a *vitium ingenitum humanae naturae,* which is unconquerable, and cannot be avoided where a number of states of the same nation have independent centres. Many things, it is true, may be developed in such a state of things, but this does not counterbalance the advantages of union. If Bordeaux and Toulouse were jealous of each other, it would be a greater disadvantage than the fact that those places have no independent centres. The regret that so many free cities of the empire have ceased to exist in Germany, can only be of an aesthetical nature; for all had outlived themselves; three or four hundred years ago they had their advantages and their peculiarities, but at present they would be of no advantage whatever. They had become proud and conceited little communities, without anything peculiar to themselves. In countries consisting of several minor states, the first endeavour should be to abolish and overcome that unfortunate separation, and to unite all efforts to make one great empire. In the Greek states, this division and separation was in the highest degree unfortunate; and in Sicily, too, the cities were from early times hostile to one another, and they became still more so, when they had established themselves more firmly, and when the inhabitants of the interior had sunk into obscurity. " The Doric places were most numerous and most powerful : Syracuse, Gela, Agrigentum, Camarina, Megara, etc.; Catana, on the other hand, Zancle (originally

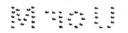

Chalcidian, afterwards Doric), Himera, and Naxos, were Chalcidian. Besides these, there were some other small towns, which had been founded by those already mentioned, such as Mylae, afterwards Tauromenium, and others." The two Doric places, Syracuse and Agrigentum, were distinguished from early times. " The latter was a colony of Rhodes (indirectly through Gela), and the former of Corinth." Agrigentum possessed a very fertile territory, but not so Syracuse; both arose from very small beginnings. Syracuse was originally confined to the island of Syracusa, the only part that is at present inhabited, in order to be safe against the attacks of the natives of Sicily. Subsequently there arose the suburb Achradina, on the main land opposite which, in the Peloponnesian war, was the real city, while the island had become the acropolis. There gradually also arose Tycha and Neapolis, whence Syracusa was changed into Syracusae.

The increase of these places was no doubt partly owing to the fact, that their Greek population formed indeed the original body of citizens, but that the ancient inhabitants among whom they settled, stood in a different relation to the Greeks, than, for example, the Libyans did to the Cyreneans. The Siculi, although quite different, were nearly akin to the Greeks in language and manners; their institutions were the same, many of their laws were the same, and their language being akin to that of the Greeks, they easily learned the latter. These Siculi were admitted by the Greeks as a demos or a commonalty, and thus was formed a numerous population; as many more settlers also arrived from the mother country and joined the commonalty, the latter became perfectly hellenised. The constitution of all those places was originally aristocratic, that is, the body of citizens had assumed a definite form, and maintained its ancient statutes: the Doric towns had three tribes, while those of Chalcidian origin had no doubt four. But this affected only the $\pi \acute{o} \lambda \iota \varsigma$; the demos, which had its own corporations ($\delta \hat{\eta} \mu o \iota$), did not belong to it.

The Greek towns in Sicily carried on agriculture and commerce, and the number of inhabitants and the amount of wealth which was accumulated there in early times are almost incredible. The very circumstance, that Greece proper was so densely peopled, constituted their prosperity; for they, in particular, provided the mother country with corn, especially in early times, before Greek navigators visited the Euxine and imported grain from the Ukraine; but even afterwards Sicily made great exports to Greece. It must, moreover, be observed, that at the time the olive was not yet cultivated at Carthage, and that the olive plantations of Sicily entirely supplied Carthage with oil.

" But the amount of population which those towns are said to have had, is quite incredible. Those enormous numbers have arisen from the circumstance of writers forgetting, that the registers of a town also contained the names of all those who stood to it in the relation of isopolites. No distinction then is made between those connected with the town, and the actual number of its citizens; and the sum total of the population is thus computed according to an incorrect calculation, each individual being supposed to represent a family of about three members. Such also was the case among the Romans: when the *capita civium Romanorum* are mentioned in a census, they include, 1st., the Romans themselves; 2nd, the *municipes* proper; and 3rd, the citizens of those places which stood to Rome in the relation of isopolity, because these latter, if they chose, might, without difficulty, be admitted among the number of citizens. The inhabitants of such isopolite towns, might, therefore, be enrolled twice or three times in the registers of different towns. Hence those statements must not be regarded as fabulous, nor must we suppose them to give any other numbers than those of grown-up men. This same custom existed among the Greeks of Italy and of Sicily, who were in many respects far more Italian than Greek.

Misled by the mistake I have here pointed out, some writers have inferred from a passage of Diodorus, without critical examination, that Agrigentum had 200,000 citizens, and as, according to the views of the ancients, this would give a population of 800,000 souls, they have assumed this enormous population; and this opinion is now repeated in all books of travel, because one traveller had copied it from Diodorus. Nay, one of the forgers of Pythagorean books has changed these 800,000 into 800,000 citizens, which would make a population of millions. The extent of the town of Agrigentum may be very accurately determined by the ruins, and if we bear in mind, that in Greek towns the houses were not crowded together, that houses were small and had for the

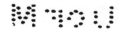

most part only one or at the utmost two stories (a house of three stories was regarded as something gigantic), it is clearly impossible that Agrigentum should have had 800,000 inhabitants. We may say, without hesitation, that the walls of Agrigentum never contained more than 100,000 inhabitants, nay not even so many as this. The statement, that Syracuse had 1,200,000 inhabitants, has no foundation at all, and seems to be merely an hypothesis: as Syracuse was a larger city than Agrigentum, it was assumed at random that its population was fifty per cent. larger than that of Agrigentum, and thus the ridiculous number of 1,200,000 inhabitants was made out. We know the precise circumference of Syracuse, and from it we can say with certainty, that its population amounted, at the utmost, to 200,000.[3] However, the ruins of those cities still attest their importance."

Their early history is altogether unknown,[4] and it is not till shortly before the Persian wars, when Greek history everywhere merges from legends and from obscurity, that some light is thrown upon it. We then find the ancient citizens of those places, in a hostile relation to the demos, and not with the demos alone, but the latter is united with the serfs. For the ancient inhabitants in the country had been reduced by the colonists to a state of helotism or servitude, "and the Greeks were the owners of the soil (γαμόροι)." The demos and the δοῦλοι καλεόμενοι Κυλλύριοι had revolted together against the nobles. The expression of Herodotus, which must here be carefully considered, clearly distinguishes between the real free demos and the serfs. The latter were persons in the same condition as originally the clients at Rome; but in Sicily the clients united with the demos against the gentes, and this revolution produced the same effects there as in other parts of Greece. While, on the one hand, the gentes were bent upon maintaining their antiquated claims, which were no longer compatible with the actual state of things, some of their number connected themselves with the demos, and, as the guardians of the state, made themselves dictators for life under the name of tyrants, while the constitution accommodated itself to the altered circumstances, and acquired consistency.

At Syracuse we hear nothing of tyrants previously to the

[3] Comp. *Hist. of Rome*, vol. ii., note 147.
[4] " We here want Diodorus from the 6th to the 10th Book."—1826.

insurrection of the demos, but in other places they do occur: Syracuse, until then, had been kept back, and prevented from becoming great and powerful by nothing else but by the government of the gentes. Gela was much more important; it had acquired its power chiefly through a usurper, Hippocrates, who extended his sway far and wide, and ruled not only over Gela, but over many other towns, such as Catana, Zancle, and, no doubt, also over the Siculians who inhabited the country between those towns. Phalaris of Agrigentum, whose history is quite fabulous, belongs to a somewhat earlier period; the only thing certain about him is, that, by placing himself at the head of the demos, he usurped the government in the city, and ruled over western Sicily, " and that he was a contemporary of Stesichorus. All accounts about him are undeserving of credit, except, perhaps, the one of the manner in which he deceived and subdued the Himeraeans." Whether he was actually the monster he is represented to have been in the traditions and in the declamations of sophists, cannot be ascertained; much has been said for and against it, and to the discussions about it we are indebted for the immortal work of Bentley,[5] the most perfect specimen of criticism that has been produced since the revival of letters. Phalaris, in the letters ascribed to him, appears as mild and as tender hearted as Napoleon in the " Mémoires de St. Hélène." If the opponents of Bentley had not been so extremely weak, they might, perhaps, have caused him much annoyance on this account. Phalaris afterwards disappears, and we only know that he made himself master of western Sicily.

Hippocrates, the tyrant of Gela, was murdered, and Gelon, one of his officers, undertook the government, at first as the guardian of the sons of Hippocrates. All the Doric settlements, no doubt, began with a kingly government, such as we find at Tarentum as late as the Persian war, and hence those monarchs are not surprising. Gelon inherited the power, and acted towards his wards in the manner in which it was often done during the middle ages, especially in Italy, as in the case of Ludovico Moro — the wards were got out of the way. Morality at that time was not particularly high, and such a murder was not much thought of. Hence Gelon, not-

---

[5] " Dissertatio de Phalaridis, Themistoclis, Socratis, Euripidis aliorumque Epistolis et de Fabulis Aesopi."

withstanding this crime, is regarded as a very virtuous man. He strengthened the power he had received from Hippocrates, and now aimed at making himself master of Syracuse, which his predecessors had not been able to accomplish. With this object in view, he declared himself in favour of the gentes at Syracuse; and thus paved the way for himself. The nobles opened the gates to him, but, after having got possession of the city, he acted differently from what he had promised : he assumed the government, and settled everything according to his own discretion, without consulting the nobles.

At the same time, Theron became monarch at Agrigentum, which formed the centre of another Greek part of the island. " All the towns, with the exception of Zancle, belonged either to Gelon or to Theron," and under these two rulers the Greek portion of Sicily was extremely prosperous.

The history of Gelon, however, is still very obscure ;[6] it is still so fabulous, that there is nothing more doubtful than the expedition of the Carthaginians against the island, and the destruction of their army, under Hamilcar, in the neighbourhood of Himera. The statement, that this battle was fought on the same day as that of Salamis, is a regular falsehood ; for if this were true, the battle ought to be placed several years earlier. But it is of more importance to know, that the whole affair is fabulous. The story that Hamilcar came with an army of three hundred thousand men has already been pointed out by many as fabulous, and I need not, therefore dwell upon its incorrectness. The number betrays itself as fictitious, and no man in his senses will believe it.. Nor need we look upon it with surprise ; for it is a general number to express a very great force, and intended to indicate something enormous. The Orientals, Greeks, and Italians, when asked how many inhabitants a town has, never mention a definite number, nor do they say, " I do not know," but they prefer mentioning any number that comes into their heads ; these are generally certain round numbers, which are constantly repeated, such as, a million, two hundred thousand, and the like. My father often heard this, and often put the question in joke, in order to learn how those people ought to be asked, and how far they might be trusted, A person in the East pronounces such a number without any concern, nor does he wish that

* See Vol. I. p. 352.

you should take it very strictly, for he only wants to mention a number like μύριοι. Travellers take such numbers in sober earnest, and thus they pass into scientific works on geography; but my father did not act in this way. Such also is the case with the number three hundred thousand; three hundred thousand and one hundred thousand are fundamental numbers. Other things also, which ought never to have been introduced into history, are related with serious gravity in historical works published at the end of the last century. Thus we find the inconceivable statement from Diodrous, that the army of Hamilcar crossed over in an enormous fleet of two thousand galleys; and the whole account of the course of the battle in Diodorus is full of incredible stories. The statement that Hamilcar was cut down near the altar by the Greek cavalry, which had unobserved entered the camp—that, in consequence of this, his army was defeated—and that, during the battle, the ships of the Carthaginians were set on fire in their rear—all these things are mere fables. " The statement that Gelon, in his peace with the Carthaginians, forbade them to offer human sacrifices, is equally fabulous." The same has been the case with some eastern tales, where fabulous traditions have often been childishly related as true, even by men of talent and judgment. Thus Ockley, the most ingenious orientalist of his time, and even Gibbon, have adopted some unfounded stories from the fabulous history of the conquest of Syria, by the Arabs under their first khalifs. The ancient history of Greece, down to the Persian wars, and even after them, is of the same kind; some of the stories which occur in it are beautiful, but others are foolish and childish. The Carthaginians may have undertaken an expedition against Sicily, " for it is evident that, during this period, the power of Carthage was increasing, in consequence of the decay of the Phoenician navy from the time of Amasis," but it cannot, at any rate, have been of great importance. " Certain it is, that, for a long time afterwards, Carthage was satisfied with the possession of a few points in the island."

Gelon reigned at least eleven years (?) (the duration of his reign is uncertain),[7] and towards the end of that period he resided at Syracuse and assumed the title of king, under which he exercised a beneficial rule until his end; and even after his death

[7] Comp. *Hist. of Rome*, vol. ii. note 201.

his memory was blessed by the Sicilians, who had had in him a most excellent ruler. The happiness which they enjoyed during his latter years, after the serious trials of the first, and his conduct during that period, endeared him in the remembrance of his countrymen; and the flexible nature of tradition has thrown many of his earlier acts of violence into oblivion. For he had indulged in monstrous cruelty, and, like an oriental despot, he often transplanted whole peoples to mix them; he destroyed towns, which he suspected of disaffection, and built others; but when all this was over, his government was a blessing to the island.

From him the government descended to his brother Hiero, who, in the Doric dialect, is called Hiaron. His most brilliant feat was a victory over the Etruscans (Olymp. 77, 4); but the Epinician Odes, in which Pindar celebrated his victories in the chariot race at Olympia, are a still more splendid monument of his reign. But however great the splendour may be with which this circumstance has surrounded his name, and will surround it as long as Greek literature exists, yet it must be owned, that Hiero's reign was by no means beneficial. He had all the faults of his brother, such as violence, etc., while he lacked his brilliant qualities; when he transplanted, for example, the Catanaeans to a place in the interior, he was guilty of Gelon's tyranny, without his great objects: he merely satisfied his personal feelings of anger and hostility. Nor had his government anything else which could make up for these things. He was succeeded by his brother Thrasybulus, who was to have acted as the guardian either of the children of Hiero or of those of Gelon. He had not the courage to despatch his wards, but endeavoured to keep them down, and thus gradually to change his office of guardian into that of king. This induced the friends of the boys to form a party against him, and the result was that he himself was expelled. But the citizens, who had in the meantime become acquainted with their own strength, and among whom the demos was by far the most numerous, the ancient circumstances having been forgotten, were now determined in due form to constitute a republic, and forthwith established a democracy. The family of Hiero and Gelon, the sons of Dinomenes, disappeared. It was probably nothing but flattery that traced the family of the second Hiero, who lived about two hundred years later, to that of the first Hiero.

After these times, the Syracusans had to maintain a hard struggle against the Siculi, among whom there had sprung up a great man, Deucetius, in Oscan probably Lucetius. He pressed the Greek cities hard for a considerable time, and founded Trinacria as the capital of Sicily. But his countrymen rewarded him with ingratitude, just as the Germans did Arminius; and he had no choice but to escape from the treachery of his nation to the Greeks, merely to save his life from their murderous hands. The Siculi, however, had to repent their conduct, for with him they lost their independence; and Trinacria disappears, being probably destroyed by the Greeks. Such was the reward of ingratitude.

LECTURE LI.

THE period from the death of Deucetius down to the outbreak of the Peloponnesian war[1] embraces about thirty years, during which the Greek towns in Sicily rose to an almost incredible degree of prosperity. The Carthaginians must have given up their claims to their conquests in the island, but for what reasons I am unable to say. In the first treaty which they concluded with Rome, we find them in possession of a part of Sicily; but in the time of the Peloponnesian war this is no longer the case, for they then only possessed the small towns of Motye, Soloeis, and Panormus on the western coast, but had no province as they had had before. The bond which kept the Greek towns together was broken by the fall of the monarchy; all of them, great and small, were αὐτόνομοι, and all had democratic institutions, for the Doric oligarchy, which in the mother country was peculiar to the race, because in Peloponnesus it ruled over the ancient subdued population, did not exist in Sicily, but had ceased every-

---

[1] So it is in the MS. notes; Niebuhr, perhaps, meant to say, " down to the expedition to Sicily."—ED.

where. All the towns, the Doric as well as the Chalcidian ones, were democracies. The influence of all external circumstances upon this constitution must have been uncommonly favourable. The island was extremely prosperous, but it was not rich in great men. The cities lived on in the greatest carelessness, imagining themselves to be safe against the attacks of every one. Hence they had not even a shadow of a federative constitution, by which they might have been kept together, nor a federal law, whereby, in cases of dispute, the decision by arms might have been prevented.

Under these circumstances, the Syracusans, whose city was incomparably the most flourishing, aimed at subduing the other places: Syracuse and Agrigentum gained a decided ascendancy, for they were more prosperous than any other, but especially Syracuse, where Achradina was filling with houses, and where the two great suburbs of Tycha and Neapolis were already beginning to rise. During these hostilities, the supposed rather than real difference of race between the Dorians and Chalcidians (for the populations were very much mixed) still continued to exercise its influence. The Chalcidians, being the weaker of the two, were somewhat more closely united together, though without forming a real confederacy, and looked for support to the Athenians, as being akin to the race to which they considered themselves to belong. The Dorians, moreover, were disunited among themselves, and the Syracusans and Camarinaeans, in particular, were hostile to each other.

The first opportunity for the Athenians to interfere in the internal affairs of Sicily, which they had so long desired, was furnished by the disputes between the Chalcidian Leontini and Syracuse. I have already remarked in my Lectures on Ethnography and Chorography, that we ought not to speak of an ancient town Leontium. The town of the Leontini is called Leontium in all modern maps and in books on geography and history, and if there existed such a name, we might, indeed, derive from it the form Leontini; but there is no proof anywhere of the name of Leontium having ever been in use. It is possible that the Greeks may have called the town $\Lambda\epsilon o\hat{\upsilon}\varsigma$, the Siculi Leontum, just as Taras, Tarentum. Leontini is only the name of the citizens, who were in possession of the most fertile district of the plain. Cicero, in his Verrine orations, speaks in high terms of the *Campi Leontini*. Gelon had once expelled them, and annexed the plain to Syracuse. Subsequently, however, they returned, either being restored by the descendants of Gelon, or they had come back after the expulsion of the tyrants, when the monarchy was abolished. Being now pressed again by the avarice of the Syracusans, they applied to Athens, whither they sent the celebrated Gorgias. This first support which the Athenians sent them during the first period of the Peloponnesian war, was insignificant; for twenty galleys were despatched, which nowhere decided anything, though they might have done much. The Doric Camarina was united with the Chalcidians in the war against Syracuse. After the third campaign, the Syracusans and the other Siceliots became reconciled, for they had discovered that the interference of strangers was the most dangerous of all things.

But if this wise determination was to bear its fruits for the good of the island, and if no more opportunities were to be offered to strangers for interfering, the Syracusans ought not to have allowed themselves to annoy the Greeks with fresh acts of oppression. They had, indeed, preached the truth, and had met with obedient followers; but soon after they abused this obedience, became more arrogant, and again interfered in the affairs of the Leontini, who, to their own and their country's misfortune, had become involved in quarrels with one another, and whose parties waged war against one another with great exasperation.

The Selinuntians, on the other hand, were at war with the neighbouring Egestaeans, both of whom occupied the western coast of Sicily. It is surprising to find that Thucydides unhesitatingly regards these Egestaeans, or Segestaeans, as descendants of the Trojans, that is, as Elymians. But this tradition is as deficient in internal probability as that of the settlement of the Trojans on the coast of Latium. I have, I think, satisfactorily explained how it could come to pass, that the Tyrrhenians on the coast of Latium considered themselves to be Trojans. My conjecture is, that the Tyrrhenians from the coasts of Latium and Etruria founded a settlement on the coast of Sicily, in the same manner as there existed a Pelasgo-Tyrrhenian colony in Sardinia; and that, as the Trojan tradition existed among them, and as they considered themselves more closely connected with the Trojans and Samothracians than the Oenotrians, the same tradition was adopted by their colonists in Sicily, and that hence arose the opinion that the Elymians were Trojans, but not the Siculian inhabitants of the eastern parts, who were undoubtedly of the same race as the Oenotrians, and had immigrated from Oenotria. "The Egestaeans were evidently quite different from the Sicani, among whom they dwelt; the Sicani never became hellenised, and there is not a single Greek coin belonging to a Sicanian town, whereas the Egestaeans had adopted altogether a Greek civilisation and Greek customs." These Elymians were called by the Greeks, with their usual incivility, barbarians, though not in the sense in which we employ the word, but only in that wide sense in which it denoted all those who were not Greeks, and which does not imply that they were devoid of intellectual culture or refined humanity. Even the most civilised people, such as the Lydians, Carians, and Pamphylians, are called barbarians, merely because they were not Greeks; for if we examine their coins and other works of art, we find that they have the same degree of beauty as those of the Greeks. Those nations, especially the ancient Lydians, as well as the Tyrrhenians in Italy, were not inferior to the Greeks, particularly in matters of art: but what they were deficient in was literature. There is no trace of any of the nations, whom the Greeks designate as barbarians, having had a literature of their own: this was the peculiar glory of the Greeks, which distinguished them above all other nations.

The Egestaeans, to return to our subject, were harassed and oppressed by the wealthy and powerful Selinuntians with unjust demands. Selinus, whose gigantic ruins still attest its ancient greatness, was at that time possessed of such wealth and power, as clearly prove that the Carthaginians had no influence in Sicily, and that they had only a few landing-places, to keep up their commerce with the interior. The Athenians traded no less with the so-called barbarians than with Greeks, for we know from a passage in Aristophanes, that they carried on commerce with Epirot tribes, and hence it is not surprising that the envoys of the Egestaeans met with a favourable reception at Athens (Olymp. 91, 1).

Athens was then in the enjoyment of peace; the attempt to overthrow the Spartan dominion in Peloponnesus had failed, and the Athenians now looked to other quarters for occupation and a more extended sphere of action; for Athens was in the condition of a military prince, whose whole activity consists in extending his dominion and territory. It has often struck me, in the history of Rome, that the Romans could have no other system, but that of either conquering till they had subdued the whole world, or being themselves crushed by others. Such also was the case of the Athenians, but with this difference, that at the same time they tried, and understood how to enjoy life, and could be happy and comfortable at home even without undertaking anything, which was impossible for the Romans, who soon wearied when they had no war, or internal disputes. The Athenians had their great festivals; they had their poets, and their taste for everything beautiful. If there have ever been men that exercised a beneficial influence, it is the poets of Athens: it was the tunes of Amphion's lyre which soothed and engaged the wild passions of the multitude. When the mind of the Athenian was fed with the sublime thoughts of tragedy and the melodies of song, he was happy and satisfied; he did not feel his poverty, and required no violent excitements. Notwithstanding this, however, there always existed a desire to undertake something new and great, and when the Athenians thought of the preceding year, when there had been such an anxious expectation of success and victory, they felt uneasy in the actual circumstances of the time, and longed for fresh activity. This feeling of uneasiness must be regarded as the chief reason, why the Athenian people were so easily persuaded to undertake the expedition which they had to carry on at their own cost, and which ultimately threw them into a condition of extreme danger. It is true, the Egestaeans deceived the Athenians, and made them believe that they possessed great riches, and the means of furnishing large subsidies; but even if the Athenians had not believed this, the prospect of the possibility of subduing Sicily would have tempted them. Alcibiades in particular insisted upon it, that he might have an opportunity of doing something most brilliant. " He was at the commencement of his career, and the propensity to hazard everything, which impels the most active minds, and which led Napoleon to his ruin, induced him to stake everything for the purpose of winning his game. All that was near at hand, was too little for him; he wanted a gigantic undertaking, to accomplish great and unprecedented things, and through them to place Athens at the head of Greece."

It is evidently the opinion of Thucydides, the most keen-sighted and unbiassed judge, that the undertaking might have been successful; that it failed only through the faults of the Athenians; and that Alcibiades, even in his apparently fantastic schemes, clearly saw that the subjugation of Sicily was feasible, and might be accomplished at no very distant time. And if Sicily had been subdued, we cannot say at all how far the Athenians would have extended their power, and to what this would have led. The Peloponnesians, and especially the Corinthians, received their supplies of corn chiefly from Sicily; and had the island fallen into the hands of the Athenians, the difficulties in which the Corinthians and others would have been involved, would have obliged them to change their policy towards Athens, and to recognise her greatness. " Sparta would then have necessarily succumbed." Nor would the Athenians have stopped short there: they themselves were already thinking of the conquest of Sardinia, and even the subjugation of Curthage was engaging their minds. To me it is quite clear, that Sicily might have been conquered, and no one can predict where such a continued career of conquest would have ended. If we consider how unwarlike the Carthaginians in reality were, how easily they were frightened by misfortunes, how they were terrified by Dionysius, Agathocles, and Regulus; how they did not trust even their own kinsmen, it is certainly possible that even the Carthaginians might have submitted to the Athenians. But, as the Athenians never modified their constitution, and would never have consented to admit their subjects to the enjoyment of the franchise, whereby the Romans formed a basis for themselves, it cannot be doubted that, sooner or later, the Athenian empire would have fallen to pieces with as great a crash as it now did in Sicily.

Alcibiades exercised at that time an extraordinary influence upon his country, but in a very different way from Pericles. For while the latter had been regarded as the leader, who, like a father, presided equally over the whole community, Alcibiades always interfered only in a transient manner, in particular events, while the republic as a whole had no guide at all.

Hitherto his influence had not been of a salutary nature. He had indeed brought about the alliance with the Argives, and if it had not been hastened too much, it might have been followed by very fair and happy consequences ; but the Athenians lost them by too quickly bringing about the unfortunate war, which they ought to have delayed, until more allies in Peloponnesus had joined the Argives. But his influence was particularly deplorable in the fearful decrees of the Athenians against the revolted and re-conquered towns in Pallene, Scione, and Mende, which are an everlasting disgrace to the Athenian name : in order to induce other places to remain faithful, the men were butchered, and the women and children were sold into slavery. They were indeed small towns, but their πάθη were remembered by orators and poets as a stain on the memory of Athens.[2] His influence upon the conduct of the Athenians towards the Melians (Olymp. 91, 1) was still more direct, and that, too, on grounds which are still less excusable. The Melians were an ancient Lacedaemonian colony, which, with a correct feeling, had always remained neutral. Until then the Athenians had respected this neutrality, and this is one of the noble and humane features which reflect honour upon the Athenian people. But now they became unfaithful to themselves ; and Alcibiades, " who endeavoured to violate the peace in every possible way," persuaded them to demand of the Melians, openly to join them, to submit to them, and to fight against the Lacedaemonians. When, on account of the moral impossibility, the Melians refused compliance with the demand, the Athenians sent an army against them, as if they were revolted subjects, to chastise them as faithless rebels, and carried on an internecine war against them. Alcibiades is responsible for this inhuman decree.

" His influence now also determined the Athenians to accept the proposals which were made to them by the Sicilians, and to undertake the expedition against Syracuse. It was decreed without inquiring after any security as to the reinforcements which they might expect in Sicily, and without having formed a clear idea of what they wanted, as if they could do anything they pleased. They confidently calculated upon the accession

[2] So it stands in all the MSS.; so that Alcibiades seems to be confounded here with Cleon.— ED.

of many allies from the Chalcidians, Siculians and Sicanians: all this Alcibiades had described in glowing colours.

At this time Alcibiades was guilty of an act of frivolity, which created general indignation." In the midst of the democracy, he indulged in the feeling that he was above all laws, and by this feeling he prepared his own downfall. He not only disregarded the duties of a citizen, and offended individuals, but with equal levity he scorned and violated all regard for established customs and religion. I do not know what was taught in the Eleusinian mysteries, nor whether they were something really venerable or not; but whatever they may have been, they were recognised by the state as a hallowed institution, and were regarded by many individuals with a feeling of reverence, and whoever treated them with ridicule was a bad citizen and a frivolous person. The Athenians at that time were very easily excited by popular orators, to whose advantage it was to be very zealous about anything relating to the established worship of the Gods; as we see from the fact that Aspasia and Anaxagoras were brought to trial, and that Diagoras of Melos was declared guilty of a capital offence for having denied the existence of the Hellenic gods, and a prize was offered for his head. Thus the people, who were on the whole already annoyed at the audacity and frivolity of Alcibiades, and distrusted him, seem to have been ready to listen to the charge preferred against him, that, in conjunction with initiated and uninitiated persons, he had acted the mysteries in the form of a comedy or masquerade, in the house of the wealthy Polytion, one of the most magnificent private houses, and perhaps the only one of its kind at Athens. He and Polytion, it was said, disguised themselves, and acted the mystic initiation into the mysteries, whereby, it was argued, the mysteries were betrayed to the uninitiated who were present. It would have been the greatest blessing for Athens and all the world, as well as for Alcibiades himself, if the wise, though terrible law of the ostracism had been applied against him, and if by it he had been removed from Athens for a while.

Even before this time, matters had once come to that point, that it seemed necessary to ex-ostracise either Nicias or Alcibiades, who were opposed to one another. To send Nicias into exile, would have been an act of glaring injustice; for he was a man of limited powers, and very harmless; he never acted against the interests of the republic, and certainly made no bad use of his wealth. But if ever there was a man whose removal was needed, that man was Alcibiades; at least so long as he continued to live in the same reckless way, and while his youthful impetuosity lasted. His youth, and his personal character and influence were really dangerous, so that it would have been best both for himself and for the republic, if he had been sent into exile for ten years, which the Athenians might have done without making him their enemy. He would not then have gone to the Lacedaemonians, however indignant he might have been; but he would, no doubt, have proceeded to Argos, where he would probably have been useful to the interests of Athens. During his absence, he would have become a stranger to Athens, and would have returned in the end considerably older, more thoughtful, and sobered down. The Sicilian expedition would never have been undertaken, the happiness of Athens would not have been hazarded, and he himself would not have been involved in that succession of unfortunate enterprises which he had afterwards to repent; but he might have been the salvation of Athens. In his later years he saw all this; and if the ostracism had been employed against him, he would not have lost his life in the ignominious manner he did. But man does not foresee such things; he looks only to that which is immediately before him, either to repel or to seize it. Alcibiades now reconciled himself with Nicias, for there existed a third party of contemptible demagogues, who might decide matters either in favour of Nicias or of Alcibiades; whereas now these two being united were more powerful than that other party. It was headed by a demagogue, Hyperbolus, whom Thucydides does not even honour so far as to mention his name, and in comparison with whom Cleon himself appears in a favourable light and as a respectable patriot; Hyperbolus was an infamous and detestable man, who had irritated in the highest degree the wit and sarcasm of the comic poets. It was against him that Nicias now united himself with Alcibiades, in order to make him a scapegoat. All the votes of their friends were given against him; and instead of either of them, Hyperbolus, to the surprise of all, was banished from Athens. During his exile, he was murdered by some one. The Athenians thought the ostracism, by its application to so unworthy a person, so thoroughly profaned, that they abolished it; for hitherto it had been an honour and a distinction, though a very sad one, but now it had become a degradation. In this, as in all other things, the Athenians showed their refined and correct feeling.

———◆———

LECTURE LII.

BESIDES the profanation of the mysteries, another event happened, with which public opinion charged Acibiades, and which roused the indignation of the Athenians in the highest degree against him, namely, the mutilation of the Hermae. This was a most singular occurrence. There existed, from the earliest times, half-statues, consisting of a bust upon a square basis of stone, of about the height of a man. They were at first, like all statues, dressed, whence it was thought unnecessary to sculpture the bodies. In the time of the Pisistratids, a great number of these old fashioned statues had been set up in Attica, in front of buildings, and at the corners of streets. All of these were mutilated in one night, with the exception of the one standing before the house of the orator Andocides. It is to me quite unaccountable, how this mutilation could have such a great political influence; and I have never been able to understand how it could be regarded as evidence of a political conspiracy with a definite purpose; or how they could have been conceived as naturally and directly connected; it was, indeed, a justifiable conclusion, that, as a crime of such extent had been committed, a great number of persons must have been concerned in it; but how they arrived at the further conclusions, that those persons designed to overthrow the democracy, and how it was that this was regarded as certain—these are questions which I cannot explain to myself. But I must mention to you here, that there existed at Athens a number of small societies—a necessary consequence of the anarchy after the death of Pericles—which we cannot designate by any other name than that of *clubs*, in which the men of the different parties met and agreed upon their mode of action. Such societies had existed from early times, not only at Athens, but in all the republics of Greece, under the name of ἑταιρίαι, resembling the *sodalitia* at Rome. They are formed in every republic, and are natural to every democratic state, especially one like that of Athens, which, down to the time of Demosthenes, became more and more anarchical. The more the democratic principle was carried to extremes, the more central points were formed, from which it was intended to control the whole unbridled multitude. These centres were called συνωμοσίαι ἐπὶ δίκαις καὶ ἀρχαῖς, especially at the time we are now speaking of. Although no author gives us any particular information about these συνωμοσίαι, yet it is self-evident, that they agreed among themselves as to the course to be adopted at elections, and what candidates they were to vote for. For although the archons, the senate, and many other magistrates, were ἀρχαὶ κληρωταί, there yet remained a large number of offices which were filled up by election. There never was a state in which there was such a variety of offices and places as at that time at Athens; and if an official calendar had then been written, it would have been as bulky a volume as that of a great monarchy. In these συνωμοσίαι, then, the men agreed as to how these offices were to be disposed of, to whom they were to give their votes at the election of strategi, etc. At elections, therefore, these societies voted for men belonging to them. The same clubs also exercised their influence upon the courts of justice. If a person belonging to such a club was a member of a popular court, he was instructed beforehand how he was to work upon the minds of his colleagues, and how he was to vote in order to gain his object. The factions had thus reached their highest pitch. Afterwards, in the time of Demosthenes, the Athenian democracy had, in many respects, acquired a far more regular organisation. Investigations and researches into these changes of the Attic constitution might still be made, which, though they would perhaps not lead to satisfactory results, might yet lead us to form a clear idea of the state of affairs : such investigations have not yet been undertaken.

We must, perhaps, take those societies into consideration, in order to understand the impression produced by the mutilation of the Hermae. It is possible that, just because such clubs existed, people thought that the crime must be an attempt to see how far the secresy of the members of a society might be relied upon, and that the leaders wished to try how far they could calculate upon the readiness and unconditional obedience of the inferior members in such an undertaking, by ordering them to destroy the objects of ancient art and veneration, an act which was contrary to all established order.

After much conjecturing, it became the general opinion, that Alcibiades was the guilty man, and that he was aiming at the tyrannis. Many were arrested and tried. At first, it was intended to arrest Alcibiades also; and, even now, if he had been seized and tried, it would have been better for Athens, than his subsequent persecution. But his opponents, who had witnessed how he, united with Nicias, had withstood Hyperbolus, did not venture openly to attack him. " They allowed the fleet to sail without any steps being taken against him."

As the expedition had been decreed on the most urgent advice of Alcibiades, while Nicias had as urgently opposed it, the people had come to the unfortunate determination to appoint both of them commanders of the undertaking. Whoever has taken part in the management of state affairs can perfectly understand the logic of such a resolution; but it is, nevertheless, a most perverse mode of reasoning. They ought to have given the command either to the one or to the other, but not to both, who had united only against a third party, but were by no means reconciled. The people thought that they were neutralising the opposition of the two by adding the brave Lamachus as the third commander, who was to overcome the timidity and hesitation of Nicias, and at the same time, by his great age and experience, bridle the folly and rashness of Alcibiades. Thus the matter was decided; but a right understanding of the circumstances shows, that this mode of reasoning was absurd, and that the means taken were quite unsuitable,

The expedition was enormous: it was undertaken by the Athenians not only with the greatest efforts on their own part, but the allies also were summoned, and even those over whom the Athenians, properly speaking, had no right of supremacy. Cities connected with Athens by friendship, and which were under no obligations, were called upon to furnish their contingents; thus, one thousand volunteers from Argos enlisted, and publicly declared that they joined the expedition to please

Alcibiades, and to serve under him.[1]   This excited the suspicion and jealousy of his fellow-citizens more and more.   A hundred galleys, perfectly equipped, sailed out with five thousand one hundred Athenian hoplites,[2] four hundred and eighty archers, many hoplites from other Greek states, a number of horsemen, several hundred transports for troops and provisions: in short, an expedition of such a magnitude and extent as never had yet sailed from any Grecian port, set out for Sicily (Olymp. 91, 1): according to the notions then entertained, an invincible armada.   As if in mockery of the Spartans, it sailed round the coasts of Laconia, coasting along the shores, as galleys were always obliged to do, because they could not so easily weather a storm as merchant vessels.   The galleys were very long and narrow, and not going deep into the water, they might easily be upset and wrecked, as soon as the force of a storm surpassed the power of the rowers.   Accordingly, they were obliged to sail along the coast, in order that, in case of a storm, they might quickly land on some flat beach.   Merchant vessels could much better stand the high waves of the open sea and the violence of storms.

In this manner they reached Corcyra, whence they cut across to Iapygia, a Greek country, which was then not yet regarded as a part of Italy.   At Tarentum they found the people ill disposed towards them: as this was a thoroughly Doric city, it closed its gates and harbour against them. Thurii, however, acted differently, for this colony had been established on principles quite different from those of all previous Greek colonies.   It was not a settlement of any one particular Greek city, nor did it represent one particular branch of the Greeks, but it was a colony of all Greece.   This was, in fact, the meaning of the Delphic oracle, which commanded them to regard Apollo as their οἰκιστής, and to look upon themselves as a colony of all Greece.   Hence, also, the colony had twelve phylae, twelve being the multiple of the Doric three and the Ionic four, just as at Rome twelve is the multiple of the Latin three and the Sabine four.   Those twelve phylae

[1] This number, in opposition to Thucyd. vi. 43, is taken from Plutarch (*Alcib.* 19), who states, that the number of the Argive *and Mantinean* hoplites together was 1,000.—ED.

[2] Niebuhr was here thinking either of the sum total of the Athenians, who from time to time were sent to Sicily, or the sum total of the hoplites belonging to the first expedition, embracing not only the Athenians, but also their allies.—ED.

were named after the different parts of Greece. At Thurii, then, the Athenians met with a friendly reception, but that was the only city where they were so received; the Achaean Croton, further south, was not indeed hostile, but being afraid of admitting them, its inhabitants closed their gates and harbour against them. Even Rhegium and the Chalcidian towns, which, during the first expedition, had been friendly towards the Athenians, now showed great mistrust and apprehension; they were well aware that their kinsmen, the Ionian allies of Athens, the Samians, Chians, and others, were, in reality, the subjects of Athens, and they dreaded a similar fate, if the undertaking of the Athenians should succeed. In this manner the Athenians were disappointed from the first, and felt that they were not received as they had anticipated. This, however, was a matter which could decide nothing. They then proceeded to Catana.

The nearer they approached Syracuse the more favourably were the people disposed towards them, for there the antipathy against the mighty neighbour naturally prevailed, and Leontini would have gladly received them, if it had been situated on the coast. Thus, even at Catana, a considerable party was decidedly in favour of Athens, and Alcibiades was enabled by a stratagem to cause the gates to be thrown open to him, and to make himself master of the place with an appearance of force which was required for honour's sake, and which Alcibiades did not object to employ. Thus they had at least one stronghold in Sicily: Catana had then a good harbour, which, however, was in danger of the lava from Mount Aetna.

The island itself was very much divided and distracted: few of the Greek towns had declared themselves in favour of Syracuse, most of them remaining neutral, which was greatly to the advantage of the Athenians. Very few, however, declared for the Athenians, who found most favour among the Siculian towns, which cherished a bitter national antipathy against the Sicilian Greeks, or Siceliots, and especially against Syracuse. It was, moreover, soon discovered that the Egestaeans had deceived them by their promises of large treasures and resources; they had imposed on the Athenian envoys with the appearance of great wealth; and now, when they were to pay the Athenians, it was found that they were unable, and that very little could be expected of them. The Athenian commanders now deliberated what was to be done. The best plan, no doubt, would have been to march straightway to Syracuse and attack it: partizans of Athens, indeed, could not be expected there; but the most terrible consternation and the greatest uneasiness prevailed in the city, and its inhabitants might possibly have been seized with such a panic, that during the first surprise the Athenians might have made themselves masters of the place. At any rate, they ought immediately to have established themselves close by the city, and if the Syracusans had sallied forth and been driven back, such circumstances might always have furnished excellent opportunities for fresh undertakings. " This was, in fact, the advice of Lamachus, but the timid Nicias opposed it; and, strange to say, Alcibiades, also, did not agree with him." The plan, therefore, was given up, the decisive moment was lost, and the Athenians remained at Catana, while every day that the enemy was allowed to pass undisturbed, made a fresh addition to his strength. Most unfortunately, there arrived at this very moment the trireme Salaminia, with commissioners to summon Alcibiades and some of his friends before the popular court, to answer to the charge of having profaned the mysteries and mutilated the Hermae.

Ever since the departure of the fleet, the mistrust at Athens had become greater and greater, and the number of persons arrested had increased every day. As was formerly the case at the trials for witchcraft, one arrest led to another. When a person had been seized upon suspicion, the suspicion in a few days became certainty, and his friends were suspected as his accomplices. Thus all the prisons were crowded with persons apprehended on suspicion ; and every one that was imprisoned was at once regarded as convicted and guilty. This state of things was so fearful, that people longed for some decisive trial, even if some innocent persons should be sacrificed, in order that matters might at length be cleared up, and the general mistrust might cease. It was believed that a clue to the mystery had really been found. Those who were apprehended were principally members of the noble families, which still existed as before ; and though they no longer enjoyed any privileges, yet, among themselves, they still displayed the same pride as their ancestors had done a hundred years before, when they were invested with all the high offices. Now these families agreed among themselves to make disclosures, and to come forward as informers; it was especially Andocides who had recourse to this expedient. But, before coming forward as an informer, he had stipulated for an amnesty for himself, and he now made disclosures which led to the condemnation and execution of many. The consequence of his denunciations was, that Alcibiades was believed to be decidedly guilty, and his condemnation was determined upon. When the Salaminia appeared among the Athenian ships, he could not do otherwise than follow her. He was treated with respect and distinction, and was even allowed to follow the Salaminia in his own galley. Thus he escaped to the coast of Italy, and thence fled to Elis, which was neutral, so that his first step was evidently such as not to make himself an enemy to his country. But when he was condemned in his absence, and his friends were persecuted in every possible way, he proceeded to Sparta, an unfortunate step, which, however, considering the circumstances of the case, we must not judge too harshly.

" Thus the Athenians brought ruin upon themselves through their own folly. They had made the most dangerous of all men their enemy; and in him the army in Sicily lost its hope of success. It also made a very bad impression upon the Siceliots, to see the first commander of the Athenians called away like a criminal." Nicias and Lamachus had now to bear a burden which was above their strength. The first moment having been neglected, it was difficult to say what should be done. It was evident, that it was very difficult to take a city of the size of Syracuse, if it was willing to defend itself, by a regular siege; it would, at least, have required a succession of fortunate circumstances which could not be expected, and the actual forces of the Athenians were insufficient for such an undertaking. Nicias, therefore, attempted a *coup de main* upon Syracuse (Olymp. 91, 2). By a celebrated stratagem, he drew the Syracusans towards Catana, and then landed himself near Syracuse; there he fought a successful battle against them as they returned from Catana; but, notwithstanding this, he himself went back to Catana. The object of his expedition had, no doubt, been no other than to take the city by surprise; and having failed in this, he retreated, although he had been successful in the battle. If

Syracuse had, at that time, had an oligarchical constitution,
so that the Athenians could have offered them democratic
ones instead, the Athenians might, perhaps, have found a party
in the city, and a revolution in their favour might have
broken out; but the Syracusans had already a democratic
constitution; and their only apprehension was, lest the
Spartans should introduce an oligarchy, as they did everywhere; but these apprehensions were then not general. The
good genius of Syracuse, moreover, raised among the Syracusans themselves an eminent man, Hermocrates, who showed
a superiority of intellect and talent, which for a long time was
acknowledged by his fellow-citizens without jealousy, though,
unfortunately, not to the end of his life. He did not, however, experience their ingratitude until he had saved his
country. He, together with two colleagues, were entrusted
with absolute power to defend the city, and he made his preparations with the greatest prudence.

Meanwhile, Nicias, after his return from Syracuse, endeavoured to extend the influence of Athens more and more over
the island, as well as to increase his forces. In this attempt
he was successful; he drew more and more places into the
interest of the Athenians, and strengthened himself with
auxiliaries, so that, in the end, he thought himself sufficiently
prepared and strong enough to undertake that for which he
had been sent out, and appeared with his fleet before Syracuse
in order to blockade it. It was now the sixteenth year since
the beginning of the Peloponnesian war (Olymp. 91, 2), six of
which had passed in peace with Sparta.

When Nicias had landed, all his hopes were based upon the
results of a blockade. After the first unexpected attack, he
ought not to have gone back again, but to have attempted
even then to surround the city as much as possible; for there
can be no doubt that, when he appeared, the city was not yet
prepared, nor sufficiently provided with stores of provisions.
But the Syracusans had now received a warning, and, of
course, had collected as great a quantity of provisions as they
could. The whole country about Syracuse is rocky, with a
very thin crust of soil; the district is in many parts torn by
chasms in the ground, so that it forms a number of *plateaux*,
rather than hills, which are separated from one another by
deep chasms, and upon these *plateaux* the several quarters of

Syracuse had been gradually built.   At a distance of about three English miles from the sea, there runs a chain of hills nearly parallel with the sea coast; that chain of hills is nearly three miles long, and then sinks down into the plain at both ends.   These are the 'Επιπολαὶ, which are so often mentioned in Syracusan history.   The *Vorgebirge* here, in the neighbourhood of Bonn, may give you some idea of what they were, only you must not conceive Epipolae to be as long, and at both ends it slopes down into the plain.   On those heights the Syracusans had built a fort in order to compel the Athenians to give to their circumvallation so great an extent, that it was impossible for them to surround the city.   The first undertaking of the Athenians, therefore, was naturally directed against Epipolae, and it was perfectly successful : they made themselves masters of the height, and used it as the centre of their operations.   From this centre, regarding it as the head of a triangle, they formed two straight lines extending to the bay, in order to cut off the importation of provisions. It was impossible to surround Syracuse on all sides; but they cut off the greater part of the supplies.   They had taken possession of a port near Syracuse, where they had fortified themselves, and thence they stopped the communication between Syracuse and the sea.   Everything now depended upon the completion of the lines between the city and Epipolae. But this was frustrated by Hermocrates, who formed a line against the Athenians from the city, which intersected the straight lines which the Athenians intended to construct.   The best way of defending a fortress consists in placing, during the siege, a number of new difficulties in the way of the enemy, as was done, for example, by Carnot, when, in 1814, he was blockaded at Antwerp, and when he built new ramparts outside the city, and directed all the strength of the enemy to that point; or as General Gneisenau did in his defence of Kolberg.   We must conceive the works of Hermocrates to have been of the same kind; and they were perfectly successful. The attempt of the Athenians to form their lines for the purpose of surrounding the city was frustrated, and they were obliged to give it up.

But although the Athenians were not very successful, the condition of Syracuse was anything but comfortable.   Very great dissatisfaction was manifested in the city, and this would perhaps have led to an insurrection, and the regents would have been forced to make overtures to the Athenians, which would have been very gladly accepted by them and by Nicias. Syracuse might have obtained a peace on tolerable terms, and the Athenians would have been glad to get out of their disagreeable position. The Syracusans would have been obliged to renounce their alliance with the Peloponnesians, the Leontini would have been restored, and would have recovered their territory ; and the other towns, at least the Chalcidian ones, would now have recognised the supremacy of Athens. This would have been a fortunate issue for the Athenians, and it was the more necessary for them to make peace, as the Spartans, stirred up by Alcibiades, had renewed the war.

Alcibiades, enraged at the ignominy with which his native city had treated him, had thrown himself entirely into the arms of the Spartans: he urged them on to renew the war, and convinced them, that their want of success in it was only the result of their unskilfulness. He pointed out to them a new and destructive method of carrying on the war, and showed that they must be successful, if they would take a permanent post in some fortified place in Attica itself, and would not, as they had done before, invade the country anew every year. They were advised to build a fortress in Attica (which was called in Greek ἐπιτειχισμός), from which they might continually ravage the country around. This plan was adopted. War was again declared; King Agis invaded Attica with a Peloponnesian army, and the Athenians, as before, took care not to meet him in the field. He accordingly took possession of the little town of Decelea (Olymp. 91, 3), about fifteen miles from Athens. The Spartans fortified the place as carefully as they could, and left Agis there with a strong corps as a permanent garrison. From this time the Spartans naturally demanded contributions in money from their allies, for it was impossible to keep that garrison without pay.

. This is the beginning of the second half of the Peloponnesian war. The new war which now commences, is called by the ancients, the Decelean war (πόλεμος Δεκελεικός), as the first is called the Archidamian (πόλεμος 'Αρχεδάμιος); the name "Peloponnesian war," did not come into use until later times. Those who lived at the time, distinguished the two wars as different. How far this opinion prevailed, is clear from

Thucydides, who thinks it necessary expressly to demonstrate, that, after all, it was but one and the same war.

Events now happened at Syracuse, which changed the course of the history of the world. I allude to the arrival of Gylippus from Sparta, and the first auxiliary force from Corinth.

LECTURE LIII.

THE arrival of Gylippus at Syracuse (Olymp. 91, 3) is one of those events, in which one moment decides the fate of the whole world for centuries to come. One would have thought, that the communication between Syracuse and Greece was quite cut off by the blockade, and it seemed impossible to introduce succour into the city. But an event happened, such as occurs frequently during a blockade: a Corinthian galley reached Syracuse, and its commander brought tidings, that Gylippus was on his way to Syracuse. This news produced a sensation, which at once caused a change in the minds of the people; but if Gylippus himself had not arrived soon, the excitement would have been fruitless. However, he did arrive soon after. He had sailed to Italy, whence he succeeded in crossing over to Sicily. Had the Athenians more carefully watched the passage between Rhegium and Messana, his crossing over might have been prevented; but he arrived in the island without difficulty. This event was as decisive as Napoleon's return from Egypt to France: had the latter been captured by the English, the fate of France and the world in general would have been determined in a very different way; or the fall of the Directory would have given quite a different turn to things, and France, without Napoleon, would have been conquered. In like manner, had it not been for the arrival of Gylippus, Syracuse would have concluded a peace which would have satisfied the Athenians. Gylippus was obliged to take a very round-about way: he proceeded along the northern coast of the island to Himera, whose inhabitants, though they were Chalcidians, he found favourably disposed towards the Syracusans.

He showed, from the very commencement, great adroitness and skill. From Himera he commenced negotiations with the Selinuntians and other towns, and there formed a force for the relief of Syracuse. In this he would not have succeeded, although the circumvallation of Syracuse was not yet completed, if Nicias had been more enterprising. Nicias ought to have gone to meet Gylippus and repel him; but, it seems, he did not venture to do so, and thus Gylippus, under the very eyes of the Athenians, entered Syracuse. Then he marched out against the Athenians, and with perfect confidence in his success, he immediately made to them one of those proposals which make a terrific impression upon the mind: he offered them a truce, on condition that they should forthwith quit Sicily. The more intelligent among the Athenians assuredly did not look upon this proposal as a mere piece of boasting, but as an indication of his being conscious of his strength, and they recognised the threatening danger.

By a sally, he soon recovered the forts which the Athenians had taken on the heights of Epipolae, and as soon as they were in his hands, the plan of completing the circumvallation round the city was entirely frustrated. After this success, he built several other forts, and the communication between Syracuse and the interior of the island was quite free, while the Athenians were confined to the line of operation on the south-western side of the city.

The Athenians now built a fort on the Plemmyrium, at the entrance of the harbour, in order to keep open the entrance into it. The great harbour of Syracuse formed a considerable curve, at the one extremity of which was an island, and at the other the Plemmyrium. It has a great resemblance to the bay of Toulon, and the loss of the Plemmyrium produced the same consequences to the Athenians which the English experienced when General Dugommier drove them from the height. The account of the several engagements, one after another, by which the Athenian expedition was destroyed, must be read in Thucydides: few events in history are related in a manner so painfully interesting as those occurrences in Thucydides. To enumerate all the particular engagements by which the Athenians were ruined, would take too much time. Although I have been rather minute in my account of the Peloponnesian war, because of its decisive importance, still this minuteness affects only the most important groups of events. You cannot read Thucydides too often upon these events; I can lay before you only the most momentous among the occurrences that took place under the walls of Syracuse. One of them is, that after the first success, the Syracusans were not only encouraged by the skill and valour of Gylippus, but from that time fortune also favoured them more, and their courage increased. At the same time, the Athenians seem to have relaxed their watchfulness the more they lost their hopes and their courage. The Athenian army and fleet were in a demoralised condition, that is, a condition in which the law of subordination, and the feeling of honour and military duty, lose their power, when the soldier forgets that he is only a part of a whole, loses sight of the common object, and thinks only of himself, is bent upon taking revenge, plundering, and escaping from danger. This demoralisation had spread both in the fleet and in the army of Nicias; the troops had no discipline, and their minds were fixed upon plunder and other secondary things. At the same time, the imperfection of a democratic constitution became visible—an imperfection, which, in particular great resolutions, can be remedied only by good feeling: the expedition had been prepared with great exertions, but it was now left to its fate, and the Athenians allowed it to become more and more reduced, without sending any reinforcements.

Owing to this carelessness, the Peloponnesians, especially through the exertion of the Corinthians, succeeded in introducing a squadron into the harbour of Syracuse; and the Syracusans, led on by their excellent commander, Hermocrates, and the great general Gylippus, now hastened with all their might to get ready for striking a decisive blow at sea, before the Athenians could receive reinforcements. The ships of the Athenians were not built of dry wood, hence they easily began to rot, and could be saved only by being drawn on land and placed under shelter; and as they had been obliged always to be out in the harbour, they were greatly injured. The crews were extremely demoralised; many of them were slaves, and most of the latter had run away. But the Syracusans nevertheless perceived that they could not cope with the naval tactics of the Athenians and their skill in manoeuvring, and hence they endeavoured to arrange their ships in a manner suited to a simple and rude sea-fight, by making them much stronger, and adapting them only to violent collision. After some trifling attempts, in which they were unsuccessful, they now made (Olymp. 91, 4) a sudden attack on the Athenian fleet in the great bay, and in this they succeeded so well, that the Athenians, to their greatest consternation, lost a considerable number of their ships. Even before this (Olymp. 91, 3), Gylippus had taken possession of the fort of the Athenians at the entrance of the harbour, so that the Syracusans were now masters of both points at the entrance; and as the camp of the Athenians was within the bay, they were surrounded by the enemy.

Their situation was, in point of fact, already quite desperate, and it was high time to depart. Nicias was in a sad predicament; his health was very much affected, and he was in the greatest alarm (which can be understood, though it may not be justifiable), lest the demagogues should make him responsible for the unfortunate issue of the undertaking, especially as he had thwarted the plans of Lamachus. Up to this time he had always been favoured by fortune, and now superstitiously believed that his good fortune would extricate him from his difficulties. He wrote a letter to Athens, representing to the people his melancholy situation; his despatches were honest, and he begged of the people to recall him if they distrusted him, and drew their attention to the bad state of his health; but he demanded, at any rate, strong reinforcements. These last actually came, under the command of Demosthenes, the most distinguished general that Athens then possessed. He was the son of Alcisthenes, and had for some time lived in exile; he now arrived with Eurymedon, his colleague, and with a force of seventy-three galleys, a large number of transports, four or five thousand hoplites, and very many light-armed troops.

When Demosthenes arrived (Olymp. 91, 4), he sailed into the bay without being prevented by the fleet of the Syracusans, and thus restored the superiority of the Athenians at sea; but he at once perceived the hopelessness of the undertaking, and advised to raise the siege, and to lead the army back, while it could yet be done without loss of honour. Nicias, however, voted decidedly against this proposal; he hoped, in the long run, to be successful after all, and to render matters more favourable by delay; he also reckoned upon forming connexions in the city, and founded his hopes more especially upon dissensions at Syracuse, a numerous party being already opposed to Hermocrates. Nicias trusted too much to the possibility of envy and jealousy rising against the stranger, who on many occasions, no doubt, acted in an imperious manner. Nicias thus felt sure of success; and in this feeling, he unhesitatingly voted against the proposal of Demosthenes, who saw more clearly the precarious position in which they were. Demosthenes now advised that they should make a bold attack upon Epipolae, which, though it proved a a failure, was yet the only right way of proceeding. I must also agree with him, that there was no other choice, except either to raise the siege, or, if that was not to be done, to make every effort to recover the possession of Epipolae. As the undertaking proved unsuccessful, Demosthenes is generally blamed for having attempted it; but I should like to know, what else ought to have been done, seeing that the Athenians would not retreat? In addition to this, it must be borne in mind, that the neighbourhood of Syracuse is very unhealthy, and now, during the summer, the malaria was already making fearful havoc among the Athenians. There was accordingly no other choice.

The attack upon Epipolae had nearly succeeded; the most important point was already taken, and the entire position would have been conquered, had not the Athenians been thrown into confusion through their ignorance of the locality, and deceived by the light of the moon. The moon was shining, but the light of the moon is sometimes as illusive as darkness itself. When they had already advanced from point to point, they experienced the same thing as king Frederick, at Kunersdorf, who likewise continued to advance, and, after taking all points, came to one which he was unable to conquer, and then ordered his men to retreat when it was no longer possible, but when there was no choice between a complete flight and a total defeat. In like manner, Demosthenes continued his attacks upon one strong point which was guarded by the Boeotians, until his troops, after several unsuccessful assaults, were seized with a panic. The Boeotians offered a brave resistance, and repelled the Athenians; and while the latter renewed their attacks, troops from the city arrived, and assisted the Boeotians in their defence. " The Athenians were terror-stricken ; many fell into abysses ; the Argive allies, being Dorians, were mistaken for enemies : the most fearful confusion arose, and" the Athenians were completely defeated. They lost a few thousand men, which, at that time, was an immense blow, and a great number were entirely dispersed. The remainder re-assembled, as fugitives, in the fortified camp.

After this misfortune, the necessity of giving up the undertaking, and of quitting the island, could no longer be questioned ; and Nicias himself was now of opinion that they ought to withdraw. But, unfortunately for the Athenians, during the night preceding the day on which they intended to depart, an eclipse of the moon occurred, and the superstitious Nicias was almost in despair : he conceived it to be so unfortunate an omen, that he could not be induced to give his consent to the embarkation. According to the opinion of the soothsayers, they had to wait thrice nine days, that the influence of the evil sign might pass away. The Syracusans employed this time in blocking up the harbour of Syracuse, from the Plemmyrium to the Nasos, with blockships (*vaisseaux amarrés*), that is, ships fixed upon blocks, and connected together by chains, but in such a manner as to leave, in the middle, a narrow passage, through which their fleet might pass in a long line. By this contrivance they were enabled to fight with the Athenians, and then to retreat. Unfortunately for the Athenians, reinforcements of Peloponnesians had also arrived. Modern critics have wondered, why they had sailed from Peloponnesus to Cyrenaica, on the coast of Africa, and thence proceeded to Sicily. It has been asked, why they committed the folly of taking such a roundabout way ? But it was no folly at all; the nature of the galleys required them to sail along the coast, and if they had sailed along the coasts of Epirus and Italy, they would have fallen into the hands of the Corcyraean and Athenian ships, near Naupactus and Corcyra. Hence they cut across to the African coast to deceive the Athenians, just as Napoleon, on his return from Egypt to France, compelled the admiral, Gantheaume, to keep close to the coast of Africa, being convinced that the English would not be looking out for him there. There was, indeed, some risk in taking that course, but they exposed themselves only to the elements, not to the enemy, and the success was complete. From Cyrenaica they proceeded to Malta, and thence to Sicily. The Carthaginians, if they did anything, supported the expedition; for they looked with great jealousy upon the undertaking of the Athenians. As the Syracusans sailed with their ships through the narrow passage into the harbour, they could afterwards, with equal facility, sail out again through the same passage, and re-assemble in good order behind the block-ships.

At length, when the Athenians were allowed to break up, they attempted to force their way through the block-ships, and this formidable undertaking nearly succeeded; but their galleys suffered immensely, and the Syracusans, supported by the Corinthians, now attacked the Athenians with such resolution, that the latter, whose ships were greatly injured, and who had suffered so much from diseases, were unable to hold out against their enemies. In that sorrowful battle, the Athenian fleet was completely defeated, many ships were taken or sunk, and those which escaped, had to take refuge in a deplorable condition on the shore.

After this blow, there remained for the survivors nothing else, but to escape by land, and, if possible, to force their way to Catana, where they intended to establish themselves, in order to continue the war from that place against Syracuse; they hoped to keep up a desperate guerilla war, in order to sell their lives as dearly as possible, and perhaps also to bring about other events. It was, moreover, not improbable, that as the Athenians were in a condition to need assistance, many towns would declare in their favour, which were otherwise jealous of them. At all events, however, they ought to have broken up at once, and to have left behind whatever they could not immediately remove, as the Syracusans, intoxicated with victory, abandoned themselves during that night to rejoicings. This was, in fact, the proposal of Demosthenes, and it was quite natural; but Nicias allowed himself to be duped by a treacherous message from Hermocrates. This was probably not the first time that he was thus deceived, for all the pre-viously expected connections in the city were nothing but tricks, by which he allowed himself to be imposed upon. Hermocrates caused a message to be carried to him advising him not to break up in too great haste, but to prepare himself for his departure; for the Syracusans, he said, would allow twenty-four hours to pass before undertaking anything; and Nicias ought not to leave behind anything that could be saved. The Athenian, allowing himself to be misguided by this pretended friendly advice, waited, and when at length the Athenians broke up, they found the roads occupied, the passes blocked up, and other roads made impassable; and thus, after a succession of unfortunate engagements, in which their condition became more and more pitiable, their army was broken into two columns: the one under Demosthenes lost its way, and was obliged, on account of want of water, in a deplorable condition, to lay down its arms. The Syracusans assured them that their lives would be spared. Soon afterwards the army of Nicias also was forced to surrender.

The leaders of the Syracusans now showed, by the most brutal cruelty, how unworthy they were of such a victory. Notwithstanding all the promises that their lives should be spared, Demosthenes and Nicias were stoned to death, on the advice of Diocles, in opposition to the urgent entreaties of Hermocrates, who preserved his character of a great man even as conqueror. Gylippus did not like this measure either, for he would have preferred to save the commanders, and to send them to Sparta, partly as a means of commencing negotiations, and partly as trophies. The allies and slaves of the Athenians were sold into slavery; the Athenian citizens were thrown into the quarries, where they were treated in the most barbarous manner, and most of them perished miserably. A small number only was saved by humane Syracusans, who employed them as tutors to their children, and as domestic slaves.

Syracuse and Sparta were indebted for this great victory to two distinguished men of very different characters. Gylippus was the son of Cleandridas, a man who in his time had greatly distinguished himself as a general, but was in ill-repute on account of his dishonesty, because in the earlier Attic wars he had sold himself; and having frustrated the expedition, he was afterwards brought to trial and condemned. He spent the remainder of his life in exile at Thurii. His son Gylippus was equally distinguished as a general, and certainly one of the greatest that Greek history can boast of; but he was influenced by the same vulgar avarice as his father. This he showed at a later time, when Lysander, after the taking of

Athens, entrusted to him the treasures which formed part of the booty, and which were to be carried to Sparta. On that occasion, Gylippus actually stole a portion of them in a base and vulgar manner. He was brought to trial for it, and condemned without mercy: he was banished, and ended his life in exile like his father.

Hermocrates, on the other hand, was likewise a great general, but at the same time an estimable and excellent man, who strongly opposed the cruel treatment of the Athenian prisoners. Afterwards, when commanding the galleys, which the Syracusans sent to Asia Minor to assist the Peloponnesians, he displayed his skill as a general, and neglected none of the duties of a conscientious commander. But his opponents, the leaders of the blood-thirsty party, caused him to be recalled and condemned. Conscious of his own power, he withdrew, and showed his greatness in his misfortune, for he took no revenge on his country, but acted so nobly that his fellow-citizens felt ashamed of their conduct, and longed to see him again among them.

The catastrophe had taken place at the beginning of the 4th year of the 91st Olympiad, and in the very next Olympiad the Carthaginians landed in Sicily, took and destroyed Selinus, Himera, and Agrigentum, and appeared before Syracuse. The opponents of Hermocrates, who were now at the head of affairs in Syracuse, behaved in such a foolish manner, that misfortune followed upon misfortune. Hermocrates then came to their assistance, in a similar manner as Marcellinus did, who was one of the few distinguished men in the western empire during the fifth century, and who, as an exile, came forward in Sicily, and from thence defended Italy, which had exiled him, as long as he lived, against the undertakings of the Vandals. In the same manner, Hermocrates now collected a few ships and soldiers, and appeared with them at Himera, which the Carthaginians had reduced to ashes. In the rear of the hostile army, he ventured upon the boldest undertakings, did incredible injury to the Carthaginians, and having collected the unburied remains of the unhappy victims of Carthaginian cruelty, he buried them, which, with the Greeks, was not only a praiseworthy act and a sign of good feeling, but an act of religious piety. His whole ambition was to induce his country to recall him, but in this he was unsuccessful, notwithstanding the miserable way in which his opponents governed the state. He continued the war against the Carthaginians, and when, at length, an undertaking against them brought him to the very walls of Syracuse, some friends, indeed, got one of the gates opened to him, and he entered the city; but all pretended to dread his ambition, and all took up arms against him who alone had saved them.   In the fight, he fell in the agora of the very city for whose service he had lived and fought (Olymp. 93, 1). Such was the conduct of the Syracusans, who immediately afterwards, readily elected Dionysius στρατηγὸς αὐτοκράτωρ, a man who was not indeed without talent, but a detestable tyrant.   It is possible that Hermocrates may have claimed the sovereignty; but he was a very different man from Dionysius. Such is the envy which never spares truly great men.

At Athens, where, even before this, every one had been in the most anxious suspense, the news of the loss of the expedition, produced a consternation, which was certainly greater than that at Rome after the battle of Cannae, or that in our own days, after the battle of Jena.   And a defeat like this, after which absolutely nothing remains to check the rapid course of overpowering misfortune, and when there is nothing to retard the conqueror's progress, is really the most fearful condition in which men can be placed.   "At least 40,000 citizens, allies, and slaves, had perished; and among them there may easily have been 10,000 Athenian citizens, most of whom belonged to the wealthier and higher classes.   The flower of the Athenian people was destroyed, as at the time of the plague. It is impossible to say what amount of public property may have been lost; the whole fleet was gone."

The consequences of the disaster soon shewed themselves. It was to be foreseen that Chios, which had long been wavering, and whose disposition could not be trusted, would avail itself of this moment to revolt; and the cities in Asia, from which Athens derived her large revenues, were expected to do the same.   It was, in fact, to be foreseen, that the four islands of Lesbos, Chios, Samos, and Rhodes, would instantly revolt. The Spartans were established at Decelea, in Attica itself, and thence ravaged the country far and wide: so that it was impossible to venture to go to the coast without a strong escort. Although there were many districts in which no Spartan was seen from one year's end to the other, yet there was no safety anywhere, except in fortified places, "and the Athenians were constantly obliged to guard the walls of their city; and this state of things had already been going on for the last twelve months." In this fearful situation, the Athenian people showed the same firmness as the Romans after the battle of Cannae. Had they but had one great man among them, to whom the state could have been intrusted, even more might perhaps have been done; but it is astonishing that, although there was no such man, and although the leading men were only second or third-rate persons, yet so many useful arrangements were made to meet the necessities of the case. The small number of ships, which the Athenians still possessed, scattered in various parts, were quickly drawn together; for everything depended upon Athens keeping her allies in submission, and if they revolted, all was lost.

The most unfortunate circumstance for the Athenians was, that Alcibiades, now an enemy of his country, was living among the Spartans; for he introduced into the undertakings of the Spartans the very element which before they had been altogether deficient in, namely energy and elasticity: he urged them on to undertakings, and induced them now to send a fleet to Ionia. This first fleet, on account of awkwardness, failed in its object; it was obliged to run into port, and the whole undertaking seemed to be on the point of breaking down. But Alcibiades made this first failure quite harmless. With a few ships, he himself sailed to Chios and Ionia (Olymp. 91, 4) and there proclaimed that these galleys were only the forerunners of a larger Peloponnesian fleet, which would soon follow; and that, therefore, they might now rise against Athens. The Chians, believing this, actually revolted, and united their own important fleet with that of the Peloponnesians, whereby the latter acquired a naval force at once sufficient to meet the Athenian galleys. The Peloponnesians now proceeded to the continent of Ionia, where they were joined by many places, which were in the strange relation of dependence both on the Athenians and the Persians. Although the tributes of those towns were regularly entered in the account-books of the Persians as belonging to the king, yet most of them gave nothing to Persia, but paid their tribute to Athens. Thus Erythrae, Teos, and Miletus, one after another, revolted to the Peloponnesians, who now concluded treaties with Tissaphernes in the name of the king of Persia—Darius was then king—and in his own name as satrap; and in this manner they sacrificed to him the Asiatic Greeks.

LECTURE LIV.

THE thing which, under the present circumstances, was most dangerous to the Athenians, was the connection which Sparta formed with the Persian satraps, Tissaphernes and Pharnabazus, and through them, with the court of Susa. The Athenians were an object of antipathy and implacable hatred to the Persians; they had never doubted that the Athenians were their real opponents in Greece, and were afraid of them; but they did not fear the Spartans. They knew that the Athenians would take from them not only the islands, but the towns on the main land, and were in great fear of their maritime power. Hence they joined the Spartans; and the latter were not ashamed of negotiating a treaty of subsidies with the Persians, in which Tissaphernes, in the king's name, promised the assistance of the Phoenician fleet, and large subsidies, as pay for the army; so that the Spartans, with Persian money, could sail in all the Greek seas. In return for this, they renounced, in the name of the Greeks, all claims to independence for the Greek cities in Asia. This treaty was very comprehensive, for all the countries which had belonged to the great king, or his ancestors, were made over and secured to him. It is not only the peace of Antalcidas, which is so much blamed by rhetoricians, that deserves censure, for it was not worse than these first treaties, which show the morality of the Spartans. By these treaties they gave the death-blow to the supremacy of Athens; and when they had broken down her power, and when, after the Peloponnesian war, they had recovered the supremacy for themselves, they indulged in their habitual faithlessness also towards the Persians. There does not exist a more faithless and unjust war than that of Agesilaus against the Persians, considering the treaties which had been concluded. The Spartans had given up all those countries, but as soon as they felt powerful enough to extend their empire, they violated their former treaties.

Alcibiades had led the Spartans to Ionia, and when he had done this, his revenge had become cool. The vengeance he took on his country, was like the murder committed in a fit of jealousy, which the perpetrator himself does not survive. He wanted to avenge himself, but it was not his intention to annihilate Athens; and he soon repented of his cruelty. The Spartans, who noticed the change in his feelings, had, according to their ordinary morality, no scruples, and gave orders to their commander to cause him to be assassinated. But Alcibiades could not be deceived by Spartan clumsiness; and seeing his life in danger, escaped, under some pretext, to the continent of Asia, and went to Tissaphernes (Olymp. 92, 1). He immediately won the confidence of the satrap, who like every one else that came in contact with him, was completely charmed by the personal influence of his character. Alcibiades convinced him, that it would be foolish to go further than he had already done; he showed to him how immoderate the claims of the Spartans were in regard to the subsidies, for that they demanded sums altogether exorbitant as pay for their sailors; he advised him not to take upon himself this responsibility towards the great king, and showed him that his true policy ought to be to allow the two cities to destroy each other. In this manner he completely paralysed Tissaphernes, and repaid the Spartans for their base designs against him.

His heart was bent on returning to Athens; and the Athenians, too, soon perceived in what manner he used his influence with the Persian satraps, and how useful he might be to them. Hence arose the thought, first among the army in Samos, of recalling him, because ever since his exile everything had gone wrong. He himself promoted these sentiments in every possible way, and exerted his whole influence to mitigate the misfortune of Athens. A great Phoenician fleet of one hundred and sixty ships, had appeared on the coast of Pamphylia, ready to sail into the Greek seas. If they succeeded in reaching Greece, the power of Athens would have been destroyed. He accordingly induced the Persians to allow the fleet to return, under the pretext that it must sail to Syria, which was threatened by the rebellious Egyptians. The Spartans could not alter this resolution, whereby the greatest service was done to Athens.

" He now applied to the commanders of the Athenian army, to effect his recall, and for this purpose, he proposed to change the constitution into an oligarchy.   This appeared very tempting, especially as he also promised to draw Tissaphernes away from the Spartans; and if he could not win him over as an ally, to cause him, at least, to remain neutral."

The Athenians now generally entertained the opinion—which frequently shows itself after great misfortunes, and arises from the tendency of human nature to hope for better things—the opinion that the cause of our misfortunes lies in ourselves, and that we ourselves must bring about a better state of things. We often seek the improvement where it is not to be found, and imagine that it is in the power of man, and that he can help us.   In this manner it was believed, that by changes in the constitution and in the institutions of the country, a different turn might be given to fortune, and the course of the war might become more favourable.   These sentiments are manifest in the plays of Aristophanes, not indeed as his own, but as the prevailing feeling of the Athenians manifesting itself in various ways: that all things might be altered, if all things were but taken differently.   " The democracy was in a state of perfect dissolution; the people were guided by the worst demagogues, and not a single great man was at the head of the state.   All men of talent belonged to the aristocracy, and parties had already been formed at Athens, with a view to change the constitution."

Samos was the principal point of the Athenian power in those parts which were the seat of the war, while the Spartans were masters of Chios and Rhodes. Samos, which had formerly carried on a most obstinate war against the Athenians, was now very much attached to them, because an entirely democratic revolution had taken place in the island, and the aristocracy had been completely put down.   There, as well as in Chios, a demos existed, consisting of the inhabitants of the country, who were ruled by the townsmen.   The Athenians had transferred the power of government to the country population, which, for this reason, was decidedly in favour of Athens; just as the new cantons of Switzerland thought their own safety to consist in the fact, that the ancient thirteen places were not restored.[1]   Samos remained faithful even after the fall

[1] The sentence here given occurs only in one MS.   There must be some mis-

of Athens. " With a little more exertion, the Athenians might, in Chios, also have called forth a revolution in their own favour."

Samos, as I said before, was the head-quarters of the Athenian power; but the war was carried on with little spirit. Now, all at once (Olymp. 92, 1), a year after the destruction of the fleet in Sicily, Samos became the seat of an endless complication of intrigues; such as we find again, for example, in the Italian states of the fifteenth and sixteenth centuries, where it requires the greatest attention to comprehend them, and not to be misguided, because they often have a tendency very different from that which the contemporaries themselves saw in them. In order to understand those intrigues, it is necessary to make oneself acquainted with the men who then exercised the greatest influence, and with their personal characters.

The two most eminent men at Athens were, at this time, Antiphon, of Rhamnus, and Theramenes. Antiphon was the father of what may be called the really perfect form of oratory in Greece; at least, he was the first who wrote perfect orations. Before his time orators had, indeed, meditated on what they intended to say, but they had not committed their speeches to writing, and spoke, in a great measure, extempore: Antiphon was the first who made oratory a part of literature. We have two orations by him which are unquestionably genuine, that on the death of Choreutes, and that on the murder of Herodes; several others, which are ascribed to him, are certainly spurious. The former two give us an excellent picture of the character of oratory at that time. His eloquence forms the basis of the style of Thucydides. At first it appears harsh and severe, and, according to our feeling, it is too stern; it requires to become familiarised with it, and when you have done this, you will find it quite beautiful, like the style of Thucydides. The oratory of Antiphon and Thucydides stands, to that of Demosthenes, in the same relation as Doric architecture to that of the Ionians; and that of Demos-

---

take here, but it is impossible to propose any plausible emendation. In 1826, Niebuhr (following Thucydides) considered the demos in Samos and Chios as serfs, as is also assumed by the grammarians, and he, therefore, referred to Ruhnken's notes on Timaeus, *Lex. Plat.* s. v. πενέσται, to Alberti on Hesychius, and to Steph. Byz. s. v. Χίος.—ED.

thenes, again, bears the same relation to that of Demetrius
Phalereus as the Ionian architecture does to that of the
Corinthians; nay, we may go even further, and compare the
degeneracies of the later rhetoricians with the further degeneracy of architecture. Of the first two, neither can be unconditionally preferred. We may also compare the earlier art
with that of Polygnotus and Phidias, as contrasted with that
of Praxiteles. The more ancient art is, the more vigorous
and joyous, because it could yet take a step in advance,
and had yet space for development; while the other has
already reached its goal, and can only advance beyond perfection. Beyond the perfection of Demosthenes, orators fell
into a faulty mannerism; beyond the style of the matchless
Praxiteles, art took a false direction; and so architecture
also fell into decay as soon as it went beyond the Ionic style.

Antiphon was an Athenian of distinguished condition and
good family, who made use of the talents with which nature
had endowed him for the purpose of making money by
writing speeches for others who were unable to make them
for themselves, and who thus availed themselves of the charms
of his eloquence. He was, in all his relations, distrustful and
averse to the democratic constitution; he was inclined to
change, but was one of those men who, when institutions
have grown obsolete, in their desire for innovation, act with
an unreasonable expectation of success, while others aim at
the same things from impure motives. It was the misfortune
of Antiphon that he did not at all mingle in state affairs, but
was far removed from real life and actual circumstances. He
had no proper idea of a state, and seems to have lost himself
in dreams about the good old times. I shall, hereafter, have
occasion to mention what strange dreams were then going
on in the heads of some, and how others took advantage of
them.

Theramenes, who afterwards fell a victim to the tyranny of
the Thirty, whose institution he had himself promoted, was a
man of quite a different kind; he was far more able to act a
part in the state, and possessed eminent talents, but was wanting in conscientiousness. He is one of the most remarkable
characters in ancient history, and I intend one day to publish
my opinion upon him. He was a distinguished general,
successful, indefatigable, and clever; he was uncommonly

eloquent, perhaps not according to the strict rules of the art, but very powerful. With all this, though we should scarcely expect it, he was a thoroughly benevolent and equitable man, who was provoked by perverseness and unfairness wherever they occurred, but who was altogether under the influence of the moment, caring neither about the past nor about the future. In this manner it was possible for him suddenly to join the opponents of the party to which he had, until then, belonged, because it no longer pleased him, or was unfair enough not to listen to him. He thus went over to the other party; and when this one, in its turn, no longer pleased him, or when his former party made fresh overtures to him, he returned to it. Owing to this inconstancy, he was nicknamed κόθορνος,[2] for he changed his party very often. Much has been said and written about him; and the few moderns who have seriously occupied themselves with him, do not know what to make of him. I comprehend his character perfectly, and believe that it can be quite satisfactorily described. Notwithstanding all his faults and misdeeds, I cannot help loving him; he has paid dearly for his sins. He was one of those sinners of whom we read in Scripture: "joy shall be in heaven over one sinner that repenteth, more than over ninety and nine just persons who need no repentance." Whoever is in danger of falling, and is made to fall by laudable motives, is better than he who is guiltless from mere incapacity, or from the absence of temptation. Viewing him in this light, I find nothing repulsive in him; and I have the feeling which the ancients generally manifest towards him. Cicero loved Theramenes,[3] although assuredly he had rightly estimated the several acts of his life, and did not intend to defend them. Theramenes certainly did things which are altogether unjustifiable; but they may be excused, for immediately after them we always find him nobly retracing his steps, and attempting to make amends. He was the most open-hearted creature in the world; he was never afraid of confessing his guilt, and always showed the greatest zeal to make amends for what he had done.

He was one of those who saw in the degenerate condition

---

[2] "Sandals were made for only one foot, but the cothurnus was made to fit both feet, so that it might be used for either foot."

[3] *Tuscul.* ii. 40.

of the Athenian democracy a state of things that could not possibly continue, and who were accordingly inclined to bring about some change; he also looked upon a change of the constitution, as a means of restoring the general peace of Greece.

These were the two most eminent among those who at Athens were in favour of a revolution. In the camp at Samos, on the other hand, there were among the generals, two distinguished men of quite a different kind. Pisander, one of them, was a very practical man, of whose moral worth, however, we cannot form as accurate an estimate as of that of Antiphon and Theramenes. I have an unfavourable opinion of him. He was an immense intriguer, and was the first in the camp that conceived the idea of an oligarchical revolution. He was very dexterous and cunning, possessed great influence, and an uncommon degree of recklessness and boldness. It was he who went to Athens, made preparations for the revolution, and carried it out with the greatest zeal. But Phrynichus, the real commander-in-chief, was far worse, and, in fact, the very worst of the men of that time. From his connections, as well as from inclination, he belonged to the democratic party, and seems to have risen by demagogic artifices. "He was a man of great talent, but perfectly unprincipled, and without a trace of conscientiousness. Under a monarchy, or in a strict aristocracy, he might have become very useful; but in the circumstances in which he lived, he became a real demon. Similar men occur not unfrequently in the Italian republics during the sixteenth century; and I may here remark, that the study of the history of those republics, is an excellent preparation for the study of ancient history."

In order to gain favour for his revolutionary scheme, he made his friends believe that Alcibiades would win over Persia to the interests of Athens. Alcibiades had been exiled in the most solemn and awful manner; and it was now thought, that if a revolution took place, he might be recalled, and that he would transfer the treaty of subsidies of the Spartans with Persia, to the Athenians. But Phrynichus was greatly opposed to it, for he was decidedly and personally envious of Alcibiades: he could not help fearing lest Alcibiades, if he returned, would quite eclipse him; and he may also have shared the opinion that Alcibiades would then in some way or another, either openly or secretly, exercise a kind of dictatorship at Athens. I do

not believe that Alcibiades actually aimed at making himself
tyrant, for such a thing had then become quite foreign to the
minds of the Greeks.   Things, moreover, depend very much
upon the circumstances of the times and what is possible at
one time, is at another utterly impossible.   Thus in the earlier
times, and down to the seventieth Olympiad, nothing was more
natural in Greece than for an eminent man to set himself up
as tyrant; and again after the Peloponnesian war (after Olymp.
100), when all states kept mercenaries, nothing was more
natural, than that those mercenaries in the cities revolted and
gave rise to tyrannies; but during the intervening one hundred and twenty years a tyrannis was something unnatural.
Whoever, therefore, frightened the people by speaking of such
a scheme, was either a simpleton or an impostor.   Alcibiades
no doubt believed that without any *doryphoria*, and through
his personal character alone, he would be able to exercise the
same influence as his guardian Pericles, only a much stronger
one, inasmuch as he himself was a stronger man.

When, therefore, Alcibiades made the first proposal and
was supported by Pisander, Phrynichus opposed it, and represented it as a most dangerous scheme; he advised them to give
up all thoughts of it, that it would lead to nothing, and only
make bad worse.   " He very justly observed, that according
to his personal character, Alcibiades could not seriously wish
for an oligarchy; that what he required was a democracy."
For the purpose of thwarting his enemies, he now entered
into a treacherous correspondence with the Spartans, revealing
to them how matters stood, and advising them to make an
attack upon the Athenians.   The letters were intercepted,
and brought to Alcibiades, who sent them to the Athenians.   When Phrynichus found himself betrayed, he made a
fresh attempt, which, as he foresaw, could not but be likewise
betrayed, and now pretended that he had intended to deceive
the Spartans, and to tempt them to make an inconsiderate
attack.   He played the same game which Wallenstein played
in his latter years, and which was thoroughly dishonest, being a
mixture of treason and counter-treason. In this manner, Phrynichus informed the Athenians beforehand of his correspondence.   But as he thought himself after all highly compromised
by the information given by Alcibiades, he now, in order to
save himself, entered into the proposals of Pisander; and from

this moment the most serious opponent of the revolution became its most active and skilful promoter.

Pisander now went to Athens, and on his arrival, all the various clubs (συνωμοσίαι), which I have already noticed, began to exert their influence to further his plan, partly to intimidate people, and partly to win them over. To their own amazement they now discovered how many, and what men, were disposed to overthrow the constitution: many who had been considered to be thorough democrats, and to be attached to the constitution, were found ready to join the conspirators. "There are certain words and ideas which can often create parties, because they have a wide meaning, so that every one sees in them something different, and just that which suits his purpose. Such party cries are, for example, "liberty and equality;" and such was then the case at Athens with the term *oligarchy*. It comprised the most different interests: some were tired of the rule of the demagogues and sycophants; others hoped to acquire greater influence; and others again even imagined that the ancient aristocracy might be restored. All thus united for what they believed to be their common object;" and there now arose that state of feeling, in which alone a revolution is possible, and in which those who are at the head of the government say to themselves, "It is all over, the revolution must come; matters may yet go on for a week or a fortnight, but it must come, and we must succumb." Those who wish for the revolution under such circumstances, likewise feel that it is coming. This is the only state of things in which a revolution is unavoidable; and if it does not exist, a government childishly betrays itself, if the revolution does break out. Such was the state of feeling at that time, and every one must have owned to himself, that the ancient constitution was gone, that a new one must come; but no one knew what it was to be. An assembly of the people was summoned, and a resolution was passed, that nomothetae should be appointed to draw up a constitution.

On that occasion, it became thoroughly manifest, that the great mass of the people was completely powerless. The multitude who had hitherto taken part in the government, remained silent, and allowed anything to be done, although they lost their great advantages. All pay for public services was abolished, everything was to be arranged in the most economical way; and the principle was established that no one should be paid either for attending the popular assembly or the courts of justice. A decree was then passed, making it lawful to bring forward any of the proposals which until then had been regarded as illegal; for certain proposals had been forbidden under the severest penalties (γραφαὶ παρανόμων), and men were very much on their guard. These penalties were now abolished, and any one was at liberty to make proposals respecting the new constitution. The psephisma of Pisander was then passed, enacting that a council should be formed by an ever-increasing system of *cooptatio*. Three men were to be appointed: each of these was to select others up to the number of one hundred; and each of these hundred was to select three others; and this board of Four Hundred was to form the sovereign council, which should have the whole government in its hands. At the same time five thousand of the most respectable and most worthy were to be selected from the whole body of citizens; and these five thousand were to have the sovereign power as an extended council: they were to elect men for public offices, and if necessary to consult with the smaller council of Four Hundred. This constitution completed the revolution. The council, down to the time of Cleisthenes, had consisted of Four Hundred, each of the ancient phylae contributing one hundred members. Now when the admirers of the ancient institutions, who were anxious to restore the good old times in the shortest possible way, were told that the senate was restored in the same form as that in which it had existed in the days of Solon, they were quite satisfied. For, thought they, as we now have a council of four hundred, we have recovered the good old times, when everything went on regularly and in an orderly manner, without revolutions: five hundred is a bad number. And this logic was quite decisive.

The way in which this revolution was brought about, the means by which the clubs made the revolution possible without foreign aid, and how the democracy was induced to annihilate itself—all this is indescribably interesting in the narrative of Thucydides. The leaders of the clubs had recourse to intimidation, committed several murders, as if they had been decreed by a secret court, and the opinion became prevalent, that whoever opposed the clubs, forfeited his life. No person trusted another even within his own party. The supporters of the old government also distrusted one another; when it was discovered that a man was not favourable to the revolution, he became an object of fear, and no one seemed to know to what party he belonged.

Critias, the elegiac poet, and grand-uncle of Plato, was even then of some consequence among the leading men of the time. He belonged to the ancient Attic aristocracy, and was a man of the highest talent and education, whose productions, if they had come down to us, would no doubt belong to the most distinguished works of the old school of Greek literature. But he was a thoroughly bad man, without a conscience, and of inexorable cruelty; nay, he was bloodthirsty in the real sense of the word. At that time, however, this side of his character cannot yet have been known, and his talents and intellectual culture secured to him great influence. On the opposite side there stood only Thrasybulus—afterwards the deliverer of Athens from the tyrants—and Thrasyllus. The latter was not of great personal importance; but the former was a man of great practical ability, of character, earnestness, and excellent sentiments ; but he was anything but distinguished for talent and mental culture. He is one of those men who have become great through their character and practical skill.

LECTURE LV.

It cannot be believed, that the authors of the revolution, with the exception of a few, were not in any secret understanding with the Spartans. At least many who had believed it, "and had joined the oligarchs in the hope of obtaining an honourable peace," found themselves bitterly disappointed in their expectations. They had imagined, that the Spartans would make no difficulties in negotiating with the Athenians, as soon as they had a moral security for the continuance of peace. Hence proposals of peace were made to them soon after the change of the constitution; but they were received as ill and as contemptuously by the Spartans, as if they had been made by the most determined party of the democrats. In short, the Four Hundred found, to their great consternation, that they could not get out of the previous situation.

In this manner the revolution had made the condition of Athens considerably worse; the leaders had to direct their attention to two quarters, as they had to keep their eyes upon those also who wished to see the former state of things restored. Hitherto the power of Athens had been founded upon its attachment to democratic principles, and had had a security in the democratic government of its allies; but now the leaders saw no security except in abolishing the democratic government in the states which were dependent upon Athens, and in introducing in its stead a moderate aristocracy. But this step was followed by consequences so unavoidable, that we should be able to supply them at once, even if not a word about them had come down to us. The revolution which had now been made, satisfied no party, just because it was moderate, and the oligarchs were not pleased at all; the latter, therefore, went a step farther: they made a second revolution, drew up an entirely oligarchical constitution, and at last threw themselves into the arms of Sparta. Athens thus lost many of her allies.

It cannot, however, be said of the Four Hundred, that they ruled Athens tyrannically. Even Pisander and Phrynichus, although they were not men of honour, and although their names are not favourably known to posterity, yet did not commit any crimes, and no such charges are brought against them as against the Thirty. But matters went on very badly: the army at Samos refused obedience to them; and within their own body, there was now formed a much worse party, which was thoroughly aristocratic, though it was headed by Pisander and Phrynichus, and by many of the eupatrids. Among others we also find a Miltiades, probably a descendant of the great man of that name. We must console ourselves with the knowledge, that another descendant of Miltiades, at the time of the decay of Athens, was one of the bravest opponents of Macedonia, and conducted himself manfully and excellently.

Fortunately the army and fleet at Samos were enjoying a period of tranquillity, owing to the inactivity and indescribable indolence of the Lacedaemonians. Brasidas and Lysander were the only true generals that Sparta had during that period;

they were the only men that bestirred themselves and carried on the war with spirit. With these exceptions, all the Spartan commanders were unspeakably drowsy, and this was very fortunate for the Athenians; for had the Spartans, under these circumstances, carried on the war with vigour, Athens would have been lost. The army at Samos, which regarded itself as the soul of the Athenian people, now passed decrees, as if it had been the people of Athens; and it was resolved, especially on the advice of Thrasybulus and Thrasyllus, to recall Alcibiades, " who had never been in earnest about the oligarchy;" the supreme command, with unlimited power, was now entrusted to him conjointly with Thrasybulus and Thrasyllus. The conduct of Thrasybulus on that occasion, was the first act by which he deserved well of his country; and Alcibiades saved his own Athens. For the exasperation in the army was so great, that all were unanimous in their determination to sail to Athens and bring about a counter-revolution; but Alcibiades prevented it, and bade them trust in the good sense and good-will of their countrymen at home. Matters there, he said, would soon change without any violence; they themselves must protect their country abroad, and hold out against the enemy; and that so long as they were there, war would be kept away from Athens. This high-minded advice was followed, and they acted like Sulla, when he carried on the war against Mithridates, leaving his enemies at Rome to do as they pleased. Alcibiades foresaw that the rulers at Athens, pressed by the Spartans, would, in their distress, apply to them, and that divisions would arise among them. "Meantime, however, the fleet resolutely continued the war against the Spartans; Alcibiades himself went to Tissaphernes, and once more averted the arrival of the Phoenician fleet."

The army in Samos was daily increased by the arrival of men who sided with it; and in the city it soon became clear, that the rulers would come to the resolution to submit unconditionally to the Spartans, as they had neither an army nor a fleet. At the same time, as Alcibiades had foreseen, divisions arose among the rulers themselves, for their leaders were men of no ability, and the negotiations with the Spartans completely failed. Theramenes was the first who proposed and urged the abolition of the new constitution, and he possessed the confidence of the citizens. It had been resolved that the number of citizens should be reduced to 5000; the Four Hundred had never yet chosen these 5000, who were to have been the great council, and it was now demanded that they should forthwith make the selection. But the circumstances which determined the outbreak of the counter-revolution are obscure to us. At the entrance of the harbour of Piraeeus, apparently on the pier of the harbour itself, the oligarchs built a fort. It is not very difficult to determine the localities of ancient Rome; but those of Piraeeus are very difficult, because its natural features are so much changed: nearly the whole is filled up with deposits; the small harbours have become almost entirely changed into sandy meadows and fields, which cannot be distinguished from the ancient shore. The walls and the port of Piraeeus might easily be discovered by excavations, but it would be difficult to find out the pier. The mole of the port of Claudius at Rome[1] can be more easily discovered. A report now spread at Athens, that the fort which the oligarchs were building, was intended treacherously to open to the Spartans the entrance into Piraeeus. Theramenes opposed the fortification and stirred up suspicion against it. Then all at once the revolution broke out, the first acts being that Phrynichus was slain, and Pisander, who was sent on some embassy abroad, was arrested.[2] As the oligarchical party had thus lost its two leaders, Theramenes found no difficulty in bringing about a change, by which the old constitution was so far restored, that the number of sovereign citizens remained limited to 5000. After this, the reconciliation with the army, which behaved very reasonably, was not a matter of much difficulty, for they allowed this measure about the 5000 to pass as a matter of indifference.[3] According to Harpocration, on the authority of Aristotle, the rule of the Four Hundred lasted only four months.

For a time this limitation of the citizens continued, and matters went on satisfactorily. This, however, must probably

[1] What Niebuhr here means, is the port of Claudius near Porto, the mole of which is very distinct in the alluvial ground north-east of the basin of Trajan.—ED.

[2] There seems to be some mistake here, for Pisander remained at Athens, and afterwards escaped. See Thucyd. viii. 98.—ED.

[3] " Many citizens had fallen in Sicily, and the remaining old citizens formed a natural opposition to the many new ones, and looked upon themselves in a spirit of exclusiveness."—1826.

be explained by the fact, that a very bad state of things followed, when the ancient democracy, which was nothing but anarchy, was unconditionally restored. This must be the meaning of Thucydides, who describes that period as a happy one ; he does so only with reference to the later period, which was the real time of sycophancy at Athens, when, through men like Cleophon, Epitedeus, Nicastratus, and others, it acquired its greatest power and exercised its most injurious influence. That worst period of sycophancy, which left the most fearful recollections on the minds of the Athenians, coincides with the last period of the Peloponnesian war. Afterwards, I mean after the archonship of Eucleides, the evil never again rose to the fearful height which it had reached before. At a still later period, also, it never became again what it had been before ; in the time of Demosthenes, sycophancy was not nearly so bad as we see it pictured in Aristophanes. There were, it is true, people like Aristogiton ; but still the state of things then cannot be compared with what it had been, during the latter years of the Peloponnesian war, when it was quite unbearable. I direct your attention to this as an example, how, in the study of ancient as well as modern history, you must be prepared to find, even when the constitution is apparently the same, that, through the influence of a variety of circumstances, the state of things is at one time quite different from what it is at another, and that at one time evils exist which at another do not appear at all. The chief cause of that fearful system of sycophancy was, probably, the recollection of the occurrences of the time, and of the revolution of the Four Hundred. Even five years later (Olymp. 93, 3), we meet with constant annoyances and accusations for things which happened under the Four Hundred ; nay, even during the time of the Thirty, persons were accused of having been partisans of Pisander and Phrynichus. From the Frogs of Aristophanes, and the scholiasts, we see, that most of those who had taken a part in the government of the Four Hundred were branded with *atimia*, i. e., they were deprived of the active franchise, and some of them were even sent into exile. They ought not, however, to be called tyrants. Some were afterwards brought to trial, not immediately, but probably when the moderate democracy of the Five Thousand had come to an end, and when the whole body of citizens, the ancient assembly of the people, had been restored. It was not till then that Antiphon was tried, and, after delivering his splendid. speech, as Thucydides attests, was put to death.

Thus ended this revolution at Athens; everything returned to its former condition, but matters became worse, and there arose still greater lawlessness. Another great misfortune was, the circumstance that the power of Athens was extremely and irremediably weakened, and this was felt very painfully after the restoration of internal tranquillity. The four months during which the Four Hundred had been at the head of affairs had been a period big with misfortunes. Many places, in which the oligarchs had just newly set up the aristocracy, declared in favour of Sparta; this was the case in the important island of Thasos, and in several of the Cyclades. But the severest blow, the loss of Euboea, was yet to come. While the Four Hundred were in power, and while the Athenians had neither fleet nor troops, but at the same time dreaded to commit arms to those whom they distrusted, news reached Athens that Euboea was on the point of revolting, " and a Spartan fleet was sailing unmolested along the coast of Attica." The Athenians did, indeed, equip a fleet, but a mutiny soon broke out in it, and the mistrust prevailing in it was so great, that it arrived too late, and all Euboea renounced its connexion with Athens. The Athenian squadron not only came too late, but it was defeated by the Peloponnesians, and many ships were lost. Euboea, with the exception of the Athenian colony of Oreus, was thus gone. This was a fearful blow to Athens, and was felt the more painfully, because, until then, Euboea had supplied the loss of Attica, and had provided for the wants of the Athenians in times of need. Private persons also were great losers in consequence of these events; for there existed, both in Thasos and in Euboea, many cleruchiae, from which the Athenian citizens received a rent; many also had private property in those islands, and all this was now lost.

The remaining period of the Peloponnesian war may be treated of according to the following divisions: 1. The war on the Hellespont, whither it was transferred soon after the revolution of the Four Hundred; 2. From the Hellespont it was transferred to Ionia; 3. From Ionia to Lesbos; and, 4. Again to the Hellespont, where it was decided. It is necessary to divide such wars into periods, or to make the division according to the countries in which they are carried on. In like manner, it is impossible to remember the thirty years' war, unless you classify the events according to different epochs. The same must be done here also.

I will relate the first occurrences very briefly. On the Hellespont (Olymp. 92. 2) there were three great days, or, if you will, four battles, for there were two in one day, one by sea and the other by land; but I cannot possibly enter into the detail of them, and I shall give you only a brief survey. Alcibiades, having been confirmed by the people in his office of strategus, had acquired almost absolute power, partly by the commissions he received, and partly by the superiority of his genius. It was the Spartans who transferred the war to the Hellespont, almost the whole of which had revolted to them; for they had been joined by Byzantium, Chalcedon, and most of the towns in Chersonesus (where likewise the Athenians had cleruchiae) and on the Asiatic side of the Hellespont, as well as by those on the Propontis and on the coasts of the Bosporus. When, in these accounts, the ancients mention only the Hellespont, the expression is quite correct, according to Greek usage, for Hellespont has two meanings, the one a narrow and the other a more extended one; in the latter it also comprised the Propontis, and, no doubt, the Bosporus also. I have nothing to prove the latter; but that the Propontis is comprised in the name is attested by many circumstances. It is in the latter or wider sense that the war on the Hellespont is to be understood. To those quarters the Spartans were followed by the Athenian fleet, which was commanded by Alcibiades with all his energy. Mindarus, the commander of the Spartans, was one of their best, and deserves to be mentioned after Brasidas and Lysander. The Athenians fought two naval battles in the Hellespont itself, and, to the great astonishment of all Greece, gained the upper hand. While the Spartans received subsidies from the great king, while most of the Athenian allies had joined them, and while the Athenians were confined to Attica, Samos, and a few other islands, it appeared that this limited state had acquired an immensely increased power, merely because a great man was at the head of affairs, and because the people had confidence in themselves. A third decisive naval victory was gained off

Cyzicus (Olymp. 92, 3); after the fight a landing was effected, and the Peloponnesian land army was defeated and routed. The Athenians thus recovered the whole of the Hellespont; Abydos alone, unfortunately for Athens, could not be conquered, and remained in the hands of the Spartans. It was difficult to take the towns on the Asiatic coast, which were supported by the Persian satraps; and if an Athenian army had landed there, on the Persian territory, and attempted to besiege a place, Tissaphernes and Pharnabazus would have advanced with all their forces to meet them. This is the cause of the unfortunate issue of the war.

" The contest was carried on in those parts for several years." The great importance of the Hellespont consisted in its commanding the navigation of the Euxine. Hence the Athenians made every effort to recover possession of the Bosporus also. They first conquered Chalcedon (Olymp. 92, 4), which was an easy undertaking, because the Bithynian Thracians who dwelt there were, in reality, independent of Persia, nor did the Persian satraps take the trouble to keep them in submission. These satraps were bound to pay to the great king a certain sum of talents, the full amount of which they were obliged to furnish: whatever was required for war and the administration, they had to provide themselves as well as they could. When possible, they extorted the necessary sums; but if not, they were obliged to apply to this purpose the revenues that were assigned to them for their own use. But those satraps rarely practised sufficient self-denial to do this, nor were they very scrupulous about honour; when, therefore, a people revolted, they did not concern themselves about it, if it required too much exertion to subdue it; and they rather extorted the necessary sum selsewhere. In this manner, they were indifferent about the independence of the Thracians, who paid a tax in return for their freedom. Those oriental despots were insensible to honour, and were as unconcerned about the independence of certain tribes, as the Turkish pashas in the eighteenth century were in regard to the Albanese tribes. Such people as the Bithynians would not submit to seeing Persians in their own country, but did not hesitate to pay tribute, just as the Suliots paid such a tribute, and as the Servians still do; but woe to the spahi who should venture among them.

After the taking of Chalcedon, Alcibiades directed his arms against Byzantium, and conquered it by a stratagem which is often mentioned by the ancient writers on stratagems. He deceived the inhabitants by pretending to go away and raise the siege; but suddenly he returned, and made a false attack on the side of the harbour, while the city was taken on the land side, in the same manner as Constantinople was taken by Mahomed II. This conquest was an immense advantage to Athens; for they there levied customs duties, which enabled them to cover the expenses of the war; they levied ten per cent. on the value of all merchandise and cargoes which passed into the Euxine or came out of it, and this impost produced an immense revenue. They seem to have made use of the same licences as Napoleon did against England. The possession of Byzantium was of the highest importance to them, and Alcibiades now returned in triumph to Athens (Olymp. 93, 1).

This was the most glorious day that not only Alcibiades, but Athens herself, had seen since the beginning of this unfortunate war. Whatever losses had been sustained, the people now felt elevated and comforted for their previous reverses; and however much Athens had grown old and weak, in comparison with her youthful vigour of former times, yet everything was now revived. On that day, the walls and gates were guarded against Decelea only by as many as were absolutely needed, all the rest of the population crowded to Piraeeus, to receive the fleet and to welcome the returning Alcibiades. He was reconciled to the people as they were to him; and it is no more than strict justice to say, that, whatever tyrannical inclinations may have existed in his mind before, from the moment he came to Samos he was not only a good and unpretending citizen, but a beneficial one, that he exerted himself only for good purposes, and that he was of such service to his country as but few men have ever had it in their power to be. Every one at Athens was full of the brightest hopes, and of the joy of victory, although, perhaps, no one had formed any definite idea of the issue of the war; and it seems that they were only impressed with the feeling, that, with the assistance of the gods, they must take courage and go on. But it was unfortunate, that the proposals of peace which had been made by the Spartans after the victory of Cyzicus were rejected by the Athenians. Endius, a Spartan ephor, had himself appeared at Athens with proposals of peace, which would, no doubt, have found favour with every sensible man, and which, though disadvantageous to Athens, were yet such as might have been accepted; namely, according to the basis *ut possidetis*, that is, that each should retain what they had conquered. Such a peace would, indeed, have been sad for Athens; but a better one was not to be had, and they ought to have accepted it, in order to gain time for strengthening themselves. It is inconceivable how Athens, confined as its dominion was, could find the resources which it opened for itself after the Sicilian war; but as it did find them, and satisfied all its wants without contracting debts, there can be no doubt that, if peace had been then concluded, it would have recovered with immense rapidity, and regained its ancient prosperity. Considering the indolence of the Spartans, who were already hated by many of their allies, the Athenians might, during the peace, have gained over many allies who were disgusted with the Spartan yoke. But the dictates of reason were not listened to, because Cleophon and his party absolutely demanded the continuance of the war. This Cleophon is known to us more particularly from the later plays of Aristophanes, and from the instructive scholia upon them. He was an ingenious man, possessed of great intelligence and talent, just as Cicero says of L. Apuleius Saturninus. It is quite an erroneous opinion, entertained by those who look at history only through a telescope, that those men who gave bad advice, and are mentioned with detestation, were in reality low and contemptible persons. Apuleius was not such a person, and Cleophon too was a man of talent and wit, and not only warlike with his mouth, like the foolish Cleon, but he was probably a man of courage and firmness; for he remained consistent to the last day of his life, never yielding to the Spartans, though he lived in fearful circumstances. He was by trade a λυχνοποιὸς, which has been interpreted to mean a candle-maker; but this he was not; he was the proprietor of a manufactory of lamps, and as bronze lamps belonged to the finest works of art—even those found at Herculaneum are very beautiful, and those of Athens certainly were much more so—his establishment was a workshop for artists. This Cleophon, however, was the ruin of

Athens, and the most unfortunate adviser for the republic
under the circumstances of the time.   His advice was pregnant
with misery.

Alcibiades probably did not leave Athens with exactly the
same feelings, and in the same relation to the republic, as
when he returned to it; and it is quite in accordance with
human nature, that he who has been so received, does not
stand to his fellow citizens, on the day of his departure, in
the same position as he did on the day of his arrival. It would
have been better if he had deferred his triumph until the end
of the war.   Unlimited power had been intrusted to him, and
abuse of it was a natural consequence.   In addition to this,
he had his favorites, as men of great personal power generally
have some whom they indulge too much, though they may be
otherwise strict and severe.   Many of his companions may
deserve the blame which is cast upon them, and he himself
may have committed many arbitrary actions; and it was in
the circle of his own friends that most disagreeable reports
were afloat.   Thus the republic saw him depart, in point of
fact, not without some degree of mistrust.

One of the favourites of Alcibiades was Antiochus, who, in
the absence of Alcibiades, supplied his place in the fleet, and
is called his κυβερνήτης, a term which we may translate by
lieutenant-general. He was an able man, but had never before
been intrusted with the command; Alcibiades connived too much
at his actions, and trusting to this indulgence, Antiochus once,
while Alcibiades was absent, ventured upon an engagement,
in order that he too might win a victory (Olymp. 93, 1); but
he was overpowered, and when Alcibiades returned, he found
his fleet completely defeated. He was, moreover, now opposed
by the Spartan ναύαρχος Lysander, the greatest general of
Sparta, who had in the mean time arrived in Ionia, and transferred the war to that quarter.   The *nauarchia* was a new
dignity at Sparta, the beginning of which cannot be determined; it may, however, have arisen during the Persian
war, or perhaps somewhat later; " but it did not acquire any
importance until the time of the Peloponnesian war."   This
much is certain, that it was a magistracy with more than
kingly power; for kings were controlled by the ephors, while
the nauarchos was not subject to the superintendence of the
ephors; but he was invested with his office for only one year.

This dignity was accessible also to the Lacedaemonians or Spartan plebeians; and Lysander himself did not belong to any of the Spartan families. He was by descent a Lacedaemonian, a *Mothax*, belonging to those who were half Spartans, but could never become full citizens of Sparta.[*] Hence he was filled with hatred against the Heracleids and the whole Spartan oligarchy, and was altogether dissatisfied with the constitution. He intended to bring about a revolution; and these party divisions give us some insight into many of the circumstances of those times. Lysander had obtained the office of nauarchos, because the Spartans probably began to think the war troublesome, and because they must have owned to themselves that there was no one to equal him.

Fortune seemed to have deserted Alcibiades: he undertook several things, but in most of them he did not succeed. He was in great difficulty about money, and the means he was obliged to adopt for the purpose of raising it, were odious and lamentable. This furnished the sycophants with opportunities of accusing and calumniating him, although the state left him without money; while Sparta received her subsidies from Persia. Alcibiades thus seeing himself threatened, and without means, and his powers being at the same time limited, withdrew to Thrace (Olymp. 93, 2), where he possessed castles and estates. The climate and the country there is as beautiful as in Greece, but he still continued to turn his eyes towards his native land; ever wishing her well, and preparing assistance, and watching what turn the war would take.

———◆———

LECTURE LVI.

AFTER the withdrawal of Alcibiades to Thrace, the Spartans again transferred their operations to the north of the Aegean

---

[*] " The divisions of the Laconians are very obscure, and the difficulties seem to be insurmountable. Thucydides and Xenophon contradict each other in such a manner that they cannot be reconciled, which seems to be owing to the fact that the *usus*, which had gradually been established, was different from the objects of the constitution itself. There existed, to mention one example, means of raising one's self from the commonalty to the ranks of the oligarchs."
—1826.

and against Lesbos. This island had taken no part in the revolt of the Chians; and it is remarkable, that Mitylene, after having been subdued by the Athenians, honestly adhered to their cause until the end of the war. When Lysander's year of office had terminated, Callicratidas had obtained the command of the Spartan fleet; he was a distinguished man among the Spartans of that time, and his honesty and valour reminds one of Brasidas. He undertook the conquest of Lesbos, and succeeded in taking Methymna by surprise; and then, with his greatly superior fleet, he drove that of the Athenians into the port of Mitylene. I must here pass over the repeated and indecisive naval engagements in front of that port. Conon, the commander of the Athenians, after having discharged all the duties of a great general, found himself in extreme difficulties. After several unsuccessful engagements, the city was surrounded by land and by sea, and the port was blockaded. The city would have been unable to hold out, and would have surrendered, had not the Mytileneans remained thoroughly faithful to the Athenians. Great consternation prevailed at Athens, for every one knew that the fleet would be lost, if it were not speedily relieved. Hence preparations were made with the greatest exertions: all free men, and even metoeci and slaves, were called upon to take up arms, and all those promises were made to them, which, in extraordinary circumstances, are so readily suggested: the metoeci who were ready to take up arms, were promised the franchise, and slaves their liberty. This latter point is not quite intelligible; it is possible that masters, under such circumstances, were compelled to restore their slaves to freedom. In this manner a considerable fleet was equipped, and strengthened by the Samians and some other allies; the Athenians, with a fleet of 150 galleys, sailed against Callicratidas, whose fleet was somewhat weaker in numbers. Theramenes and Thrasybulus (or Thrasyllus) were among the Athenian generals.

The two fleets met each other near the Arginusae, a group of islands near the coast of Lesbos, containing an Aeolian town. There now ensued a great sea fight, the greatest of all the battles that had hitherto been fought between two Greek fleets; for never had two Greek armaments of such power faced each other. Victory was certain on the part of the Athenians, and remained so throughout, although the Peloponnesian fleet, in its long service, had been well trained, and was very unlike the former motley armaments of the Peloponnesians. The battle thus ended with perfect success for the Athenians; Callicratidas himself was slain, and a great number of ships fell into the hands of the conquerors; but many of the Athenian galleys also were destroyed, and, in consequence of a storm, they were obliged to bring the fight to a speedy termination.

Had it not been for that tempest, this victory would have done the Athenians nothing but unmixed good; but unfortunately a violent gale arose during the battle, which, towards the end of it, became a perfect storm. Hitherto it had always been the first business of a victorious fleet, after the battle, to collect the wrecks and corpses, to give to the dead a quiet resting-place, and also, a circumstance which is here overlooked, to save the living, whether whole or wounded, from the water and the wrecks. On that occasion in particular, the object was to save the many living citizens who were clinging to the wrecks. This was a matter of humanity, and not merely the pious superstition that thought it necessary to bury the dead. Immediately after the battle, the generals were not agreed what was to be done, whether they should collect the wrecks, or immediately sail to Mitylene, and avail themselves of the victory for the purpose of there destroying the remnant of the Spartan forces. They ought to have divided the fleet, and sent a part of it to Lesbos; but they were inclined to sail thither in a body, although it was a painful thing to leave the dead uncared for. The storm, however, became so violent, that, from the fear of losing more ships, they neither collected the wrecks nor undertook the voyage to Mitylene. The siege of this city was indeed raised by the Spartans, but without their suffering that loss which they might have suffered; for they after all saved a part of their fleet. Had the generals agreed among themselves, the misfortune of being obliged to leave the wrecked to their fate, would have had no evil consequences. But unfortunately the discord among them continued, and some charged Theramenes and Thrasybulus, who had urged them to sail to Mitylene, with having neglected to collect the wrecks with the men, and to bury the dead, although they had been commissioned to do so. This accusation was untrue,

and was its own punishment; and it was an absurdity to
regard the neglect as a political offence; but the sycophant
Callixenus took up the accusation and brought it before a
popular court.   Everything that now happened shows the
state of the demoralisation of the time.   Theramenes and
Thrasybulus, on being summoned before the court, defended
themselves by clearly proving that they had received no
orders; and it now began to be suspected that the neglect had
arisen from some evil intention.   The accusation was then
directed against the other generals, who were summoned to
take their trial as criminals.   Two of them made their escape,
Theramenes and Thrasybulus were acquitted, and the remaining
six were brought to trial and condemned.   On that occasion,
Socrates, who was then a member of the council, was bold
enough to speak against so severe a judgment, and exerted
himself to the utmost to save the unfortunate men, but in vain.
In order to obtain their acquittal, it was proposed to judge them
one by one, but the votes were taken upon them in a body, and
all were sentenced at once to drink the hemlock.   It was on that
occasion that Diomedon, when he was led away into prison to
drink the poison, said to the people in the agora, " We pardon
you; may that which you have done to us, not turn out to
your own misfortune; but the vows of gratitude which we
have made to the gods for the victory, you must perform,
because we cannot."   A noble trait !   The man who spoke
thus, did not harbour the desire to take vengeance on his
country, as Camillus is said to have done.

The year after this, matters were again, according to all
appearance, extremely favourable to the Athenians.   The
greater part of Lesbos was again in their hands, they had a
fleet of 200 galleys, and the time seemed to approach more
and more, when the tyranny of the Spartans was to be followed
by the revolt of their allies.   The Spartans were excessively
hard masters everywhere, as is clear, for example, from the
attempt to murder the inhabitants of Chios, in order to make
themselves masters of the town.   " Cheerfulness once more
revived at Athens; the Frogs of Aristophanes, the most ingenious and most refined of all his plays, is a proof of the
hopeful disposition after the battle of Arginusae : such a
piece cannot be produced at a time of mental depression."
But, unfortunately for Greece, Darius of Persia was now dead;

his younger son, Cyrus, who, through the influence of his mother, had become governor of Asia Minor, and there ruled with greater power than was customary with a Persian prince, was harbouring ambitious schemes against his brother, and trying to make himself king of Persia.   He endeavoured to win the Spartans over as his allies, hoping with their assistance to deprive his brother of his throne; but he deferred his expedition against Artaxerxes, until the Spartans should have brought their own war to a close.   In order to accelerate this event, he offered to Lysander all the treasures which he had at his disposal, in so extravagant a manner, that Lysander was enabled to send great sums to Sparta, and to offer such large pay to the soldiers, that desertion in the Athenian army became very prevalent.   Many of the slaves, especially, who had acquired their freedom, went over to the Spartans, so that a considerable army was formed.

Lysander now again, for various reasons, transferred the war to the Hellespont (Olymp. 93, 4).   It is possible, that misunderstandings between Pharnabazus and Cyrus existed as early as that time, and Lysander feared lest the prince should form connections with Athens, and support it; but his intention also was to recover the Hellespont, to destroy the commerce with the Euxine, and to deprive the Athenians of their revenues from transits, and of the supplies which came from that quarter.   Abydos, unfortunately, was in the hands of the Spartans: there he took his station with his fleet, and thence he attacked and conquered the wealthy town of Lampsacus, which was closely allied with the Athenians.   The latter commanded by their new generals, among whom Philocles seems with the greatest justice to be branded in history as a traitor,[1] now hastened to meet their enemy.   " Conon was the only able man among them; the ancient race of Athenians had been destroyed in the Sicilian war."   The Athenians took their position in the neighbourhood of Sestos, opposite to Lampsacus, near the river Aegospotami, where not long before the Peloponnesian war, the celebrated large meteor had fallen from heaven, which Anaxagoras has described, and which no doubt exists there still.   I cannot understand why it has not

---

[1] All the MSS. here and afterwards call this traitor Philocles, so that there can be no doubt that it is the name mentioned by Niebuhr.   In 1826, he mentioned Adimantus, who was the real traitor. See Xenoph. *Hellen.* ii. 1, § 31.—ED.

yet been searched after, as in modern times so many Europeans have visited those parts. We should thereby be enabled also to determine the river Aegospotami, which is as yet doubtful. On that river, I say, the Athenians took their post on a flat beach, fitted for their galleys; but they were far from the nearest town, and there was no possibility of obtaining provisions except from Sestos, which was more than two miles distant. For the purpose of collecting supplies, the men accordingly dispersed, carelessly foraging in all directions; there seems to have been no discipline at all. Alcibiades, perceiving the danger of their situation, appeared among them, and earnestly cautioned them: he advised and implored them to transfer their camp to Sestos, in order not to be exposed to a sudden attack; he offered to induce the Thracian princes connected with him by friendship, to come to their assistance, and proposed himself to lead them over to Asia to attack the Spartans near Lampsacus. The advice was excellent, for Lysander would then have been forced to give battle; and if he had been conquered, it would have been easy to inflict a second and fatal blow upon the Spartans. But it was all in vain: the Athenian generals rejected his offers in an unfriendly manner, Adimantus and Tydeus perhaps from pride, and Philocles from treacherous motives, and they intimated to him, that being an exile, he had no business to press his advice upon them.

The Athenians usually tried every day to provoke the Spartans to a battle; every morning they embarked, proceeded to the Asiatic coast, and manoeuvred against the Spartan fleet; the latter declining to fight, the Athenians returned to their station, and when the Spartans landed, the Athenians also left their ships and dispersed over the coast as far as Sestos. This was no doubt betrayed to Lysander by Philocles, who contrived to induce the soldiers to wander about. It was probably according to a design preconcerted with Philocles, that Lysander formed the plan of an attack, and on the fifth day, after these movements had been repeated, Lysander ordered his troops not to quit their ships, but to keep themselves in readiness to cross the Hellespont with the greatest expedition, and attack the Athenian fleet. This was done: he fell upon the Athenians quite unexpectedly, and the manoeuvre was fearfully successful. The Athenians had no time left to man their ships: with the exception of ten galleys, which, under the command of Conon, formed a kind of advanced outpost, not a single ship escaped.   Conon fled to Evagoras in Cyprus, and sent the galley, Paralos, to Athens, to convey the news of the disaster.   The other ships were found by Lysander partly unmanned and empty, and partly insufficiently manned; and thus, within a few minutes, the whole Athenian fleet, of 200 ships, was in the hands of the Spartans, and the whole army was routed.   Many Athenians were taken in the fleet, and those who had escaped were captured one after another on land, and in the interior of the Chersonesus.   All the Athenians were put to death: such was the inhuman character which the war had assumed!   The Spartans did this, alleging that the Athenians had passed a psephisma, that all the free Peloponnesian prisoners should have the thumb of their right hand chopped off, and then be dismissed.   Under this pretext, the Athenians were put to the sword; the same was the fate of the generals, with the exception of Adimantus, who had been opposed to the war, and Philocles, who was thus rewarded for his treachery.[2]

We are told by an author who is altogether unpoetical,[3] that when the galley Paralos arrived in Piraeeus, the mournful news spread through the city, one proclaiming it to another; and cries of lamentation were heard in every part of the city.   All was now lost; the Athenians could do nothing, all their strength was exhausted, all the world was against them, and there was no help anywhere.   It was now expected that Athens would be besieged; and there was nothing to be done, but to defend themselves until they might succeed in obtaining peace on tolerable terms.

After the victory, Lysander was busy in taking the towns which espoused the cause of Athens, and capturing the Athenian garrisons; for this purpose he sent out ships in all directions, and himself slowly sailed from place to place.   He made no other stipulation with the Athenian garrisons, except that they were to return to Athens; it being his object to overcrowd the city with human beings, in order that they might the sooner begin to suffer from famine. In like manner, he sent all the Athenian cleruchi from the islands which he visited, as well as the colonists of Lemnos, Imbros, and Scyros,

---

to Athens, in order to reduce the crowded population to extremes. Gylippus, who, on this occasion, was sent to Sparta with a part of the captured treasures, embezzled a portion of them. Meanwhile, the Athenians, who had no means of obtaining supplies from any quarter, felt the terrors of a famine approaching, and beheld the most fearful destruction staring them in the face. There was at that time no one among them fit to take the lead; they prepared, however, to defend themselves as well as they could. The Spartans were everywhere sure of success.

In this condition, Athens was surrounded by Lysander with his fleet, while the kings, Agis and Pausanias, blockaded it on the land side most effectually; they proclaimed that they would throw into the sea the crew of any ship which should attempt to introduce provisions into the city. "Salamis was occupied by Lysander." The Athenians stopped up the entrance into their ports in order to prevent the enemies forcing them; "The Spartans, however, were enabled quietly to wait until famine should compel the city to surrender. How long the blockade lasted cannot be accurately ascertained; but it is evident from several statements of Lysias, that it was continued for a considerable time. Even at an early stage," the Athenians sent to king Agis to negotiate with him, declaring themselves ready to acknowledge the supremacy of the Spartans, and to obey them by land and by sea; but they stipulated that their walls should not be demolished, and that they should be allowed to retain the yet remaining ships. But Agis rejected the proposal, saying that he had no authority, that they must send an embassy to Sparta to negotiate there; and as a preliminary condition, he proposed that the Athenians should pull down the long walls on each side to a distance of ten stadia,—whether he also desired the walls of Piraeeus on the land side to be destroyed, is not clear from the accounts,—and that then they should send envoys to Sparta, and await her final decision. Ambassadors accordingly were despatched to Sparta. The first embassy was stopped on the Spartan frontier, and asked whether it had full power, and although the envoys answered, that they should lay their terms before the government of Sparta, they were sent back in order to protract the matter still longer; for the Spartans knew that famine was already raging at Athens. Theramenes now offered to conclude a peace with the enemy; and he, together with others, was accordingly sent to Sparta with unlimited powers; but these envoys too were detained until the fourth month, with the view of increasing the famine, so that even the most humiliating terms might be accepted in the city. " During this time the famine at Athens was ever increasing; many men died daily of starvation; and the people had recourse to the most fearful means to escape from it. A veil is thrown over that period. Thucydides would have placed everything in its true light, and in all its fearfulness; but Xenophon's partiality conceals the horrible deeds of the Spartans. Whether Theramenes deserves censure for this embassy, God alone knows, but Lysias, I think, judges him too harshly."

At length (Olymp. 93, 4) Theramenes and his companions appeared, announcing to the Athenians the will and commands of Sparta, which were, that they should demolish the long walls, and the walls round Piraeeus. The walls round the city remained untouched, although it is commonly believed, and is expressly stated by some authors, that they, too, were destroyed; but I state it with full conviction, and after a careful comparison of all the passages, that the walls round the city remained uninjured, while those of Piraeeus, and the long walls, as far as was thought necessary, were completely demolished. The Athenians, moreover, had to surrender to the Spartans all their ships, with the exception of ten or twelve, and to follow the conquerors whithersoever they might direct them. Lastly, the Spartans, with their artful ambiguity, commanded that the Athenians should adopt the constitution of their ancestors (κατὰ τὰ πάτρια πολιτεύεσθαι).

This expression was altogether equivocal, and no one knew whether the constitution of Solon, or what constitution was meant. But about this the Spartans did not concern themselves, if they could but form in the city a party favourable to themselves; and they determined that thirty law-givers should be appointed to make out this ancient constitution. As the Four Hundred had renewed the ancient Ionic council, so these Thirty evidently represented the Doric character, or the Doric senate of twenty-eight members with the two kings. Ten of these Thirty were to be appointed by the Spartans, ten by the ephors (the societies, or revolutionary clubs, at Athens were regularly organised, and had a government directing them in all their movements, just like the United Irishmen about the close of the last century, and the members of this government, called ἔφοροι, were now recognised by the Spartans as lawful authorities), and the remaining ten were to be elected by the people. But the first twenty, being in the Spartan interest, formed, under all circumstances, the great majority; and it is clear that the poor people, on the very brink of starvation, appointed no others but such as were agreeable to and proposed by the Spartans.

On these terms the lives of the Athenians were spared, for this was the utmost they obtained; and the destruction of their ancient splendour was accompanied by the scorn which is even more painful than misery and subjugation itself; for Lysander ordered the walls to be pulled down to the accompaniment of music; and music was playing while the surrendered ships were taken out of the harbour and burned. The Athenians, no doubt, were in a state of perfect consternation and stupor: *curae leves loquuntur, ingentes stupent.*

These thirty were commissioned to draw up a constitution and laws, which, however, they never accomplished; for instead of making laws, they ruled like the Roman decemvirs. They had full power to appoint all magistrates, and accordingly they now elected according to their own discretion a council and magistrates from among their own partisans. They then drew up a list of three thousand citizens, to whom they limited the franchise; three hundred being taken from every phyle, perhaps in imitation of Doric institutions; it is not impossible they may have wished to divide Athens into three phylae. These three thousand were the real citizens, "and were to form the assembly, but they were citizens only in name, and in reality they had no power." Besides the Thirty, two local magistracies were appointed, which formed a sort of police, eleven men for the city and ten for Piraeeus, one of whom was Charmides, the cousin of Plato: these police officers were subordinate to the Thirty.

"The Thirty were for the most part exiles who returned to their country with anger and exasperation in their hearts. To their disgrace it must be said, that most of them belonged to the most ancient and best Attic families, descendants of Neleus,

Solon, etc , who had acted a prominent part at the time of the Four Hundred. They were people who looked upon the whole state as a prey given up to them."

They commenced their rule by putting to death some of the worst men, who had previously committed crimes, and indeed deserved to suffer; Cleophon had already been executed by the people themselves. The period preceding these events had been an unhappy time of sycophancy, and accordingly there were many who were universally execrated, and whose death was regarded as a general blessing. The Thirty enacted two laws: the council alone had to decide upon the lives of those enrolled in the catalogue of the three thousand citizens; while the Thirty disposed of the lives of all the others not contained in that list. This state of affairs, therefore, somewhat resembles the convention under Robespierre and the committee of public safety. The sycophants, who were first seized upon, were no doubt sentenced to death by the council in a summary manner, and without minute enquiries. But imprisonments and executions were gradually more and more extended. At first, no one regretted this, but it was soon discovered what the Thirty were really aiming at. "When those who had deserved it had been put to death without a trial," the Thirty began to imprison and execute whomsoever they pleased; and the Athenians perceived that, if a person was rich, this alone was a sufficient reason for condemning him, and that wealth was a crime—perhaps from hatred of the ὄχλος! But when, owing to the increase of the executions, discontent became more general, the terrorists began to be alarmed, and as they discovered that even men of their own party were beginning to hesitate, they requested the Spartans to send a harmost with a Spartan garrison to the Acropolis. This garrison was their ready tool on every occasion, and whenever a murder was to be committed, the harmost sent forth his men to do the bloody deed. "The Athenians were disarmed, and even the three thousand were scarcely trusted to bear arms."

Critias and Charicles were at the head of the Thirty, whom they ruled in the same manner as Robespierre ruled and dictated to the committee of public safety. Aristotle justly calls them demagogues among the Thirty. Critias was a peculiar being, a man of talent and rare intellectual culture, and a graceful poet, who was very fond of playing the man of rank; and yet, during his exile in Thessaly, he there excited the serfs against a nobleman, who wanted to set himself up as ruler. These dark tyrants were opposed by Theramenes, with that peculiarity of temperament which I have before described, and he rose against their measures in the same manner, as in the national convention so many who had before entered very deeply into the schemes of the terrorists, rose against the furious tyranny of Robespierre and his associates.

Critias at first endeavoured to pacify him by flattery, and pointed out to him how much better it would be if they would agree among themselves. But Theramenes felt that the state of things was unbearable, and endeavoured to bring about a decision; he either did not fully estimate the circumstances, and believed in the possibility of success; or life was insupportable to him, and he wished to die, a wish which is quite accountable in a character like his. He carried his opposition so far, that Critias and his followers summoned him before the court of the council, consisting of their own creatures, and accused him of harbouring revolutionary schemes. Armed men were posted in the council-room to influence the decision. Theramenes defended himself most brilliantly, in a memorial which was much read at Athens for many years, but is now lost; Lysias has preserved some genuine passages from it.[4] The defence which Xenophon assigns to him does not appear to be genuine, and is no doubt of his own composition. With him all speeches are variations of the same tune, for, whoever is introduced speaking, Thracians, Persians, Athenians, men of all parties, great or little, spirited or dull, all have the same style of speaking, the peculiarly trivial and somewhat loose manner of Xenophon himself. If he had omitted these speeches, his history would not have been so bad as it is. In the speeches of Thucydides, the words and diction are his own; but still every one is made to speak in accordance with his own circumstances, and the intelligent reader feels the difference in every instance. The members of the council consisted of two classes of men, those who were real partisans of the tyrants, and those who, by some unfortunate accident, had been thrown into that position, and were now longing to get out of it, but were no longer able to do so, and looked upon the fate of Greece as decided. This

[4] *Contra Eratosth.* p. 127, Reiske.

feeling, as well as the opposite one, of taking things too lightly, leads to unhappy consequences; but both are very common. The former of these feelings was entertained by the majority of the council, which certainly ought not to be named along with the Thirty, for there were among them, no doubt, a great many good men, who had got into their position by unfortunate circumstances. It is an erroneous statement of Diodorus, that Socrates was a member of the council; he confounds him with Isocrates, who, then a young man, was in the council, and behaved more nobly than he did in all the rest of his long life. He was younger than Theramenes, and rose to speak in his favour; but Theramenes dissuaded him from it, because after all he could not save him. The council, although otherwise dependent on the Thirty, refused to condemn Theramenes: the feeling that they ought not to deprive the country of such a man, rendered his condemnation impossible. Then Critias declared: " Since the law does not declare it to be necessary, there is no need for the council to vote, as we ourselves can decide upon those who do not belong to the Three Thousand. We have the right to draw up the list, and consequently we have also the right to expunge any one from it; we shall, therefore, now exclude Theramenes from the list of citizens, and decide ourselves on his fate." This was done, and Theramenes being condemned to drink the hemlock, was led to death. When he was crossing the market-place, and exhorted the people not to endure this tyranny any longer, one of the Thirty said to him, " You will be a lost man if you do not hold your tongue." He replied, with a smile, " Am I not a lost man, even though I am silent?" The cheerfulness with which he emptied the poisonous cup to the health of Critias, shews the composure of a man of unusual moral strength, but who was heartily tired of life, as of a long burthen, from which he was at length to be delivered.

LECTURE LVII.

THE accounts of the various inhuman cruelties of the Thirty tyrants would lead me too far: I refer you to the classical

emancipated and free.   All were thus to be free, and bound to obey and follow none but the Spartans, as the head of the Greek confederacy.   These demands, which the king of Persia guaranteed in the peace of Antalcidas, were the cause which afterwards led to the war of the Thebans against Sparta.   According to such principles, the Spartans acted even as early as that time; and this, no doubt, was the main cause of distrust and hatred of the Thebans against them. The Thebans, moreover, saw that the Spartans formed the closest possible connection with the Thirty at Athens, and may have feared, lest they should completely establish themselves in Attica, and change it into a second Laconia out of Peloponnesus, from which they might extend their dominion farther beyond the Isthmus. Their eyes were thus opened to these schemes, and it was for these reasons that they afforded shelter to the Athenian exiles. The thought of the destruction of the Spartan power at Athens was therefore gratifying to them, and the more so, if it could be brought about by the blood of others.   This connection of events is generally overlooked in manuals of Greek history; and I here explain these causes, because it would otherwise be inconceivable, how the Thebans, who six or nine months before, had proposed to destroy Athens, could now follow so very opposite a policy, as to side with Athens against Sparta.

When thus the Spartans had proclaimed throughout Greece, that whoever received or concealed an Athenian exile in his house, should have to pay a fine of five talents, the Thebans made known, that any one who injured an Athenian exile should be punished, and that no one should take any notice of it, if any of the exiles should go armed from Boeotia to Attica. This was a happy event, and Providence kindly interfered, in making the unworthy Thebans the means of the restoration of Athens, so far, at least, as it could be restored.

Thrasybulus, the son of Lycus, of the demos Stiria, and by far the most distinguished among the exiles, had settled, with many others, at Thebes, and in conjunction with only a few others (their number at first amounted only to thirty) he formed the determination to attempt the liberation of Athens (Olymp. 94, 1). All were desperate, and bent upon making the attempt, even if they should perish in it.   Thrasybulus gathered several more around him, and in the winter, when he took possession of the fort of Phyle, one hundred stadia (about twelve miles) from Athens, their number had already increased to seventy. The rulers at Athens had left all fortified places without garrisons, and thought of nothing but murder and rapine. The number of the exiles at Phyle continued to increase, and the Thirty at length sent a detachment against them, which, however, set out with little spirit in the bad cause, and was overtaken at its post by an unusually heavy storm of snow and wind, which affects southern nations much more than us; the Greeks are not, indeed, unaccustomed to snow, but it is, nevertheless, very disagreeable to them. Thrasybulus availed himself of the opportunity, attacked, and routed them. Several little engagements took place on that occasion, the accounts of which differ from each other, and which I must here pass over. But I will mention, as a point of history, that Phyle can still be perfectly recognised, and that its walls are in perfect preservation, as if it had been the will of heaven to preserve that venerable place! I will also introduce here a grammatical observation, about a peculiarity which occurs in the accounts of this enterprise. Thrasybulus and his fellow-exiles, before their return to Piraeeus, and so long as they were assembled at Phyle, are called οἱ ἐπὶ Φυλῇ, and not οἱ ἐπὶ Φυλῆς; and Thrasybulus himself is described as ἐπὶ Φυλὴν στρατηγήσας, as if the expedition had been made against Phyle, which is not the case.

" It seems inconceivable that the Thirty still found people ready to shed their blood for them; but it arose partly from the want of principle in men, and partly from the malignant cunning of the tyrants; for we know from the apology of Socrates, that they sent orders to persons not belonging to their party to apprehend others, so that a number of persons, in spite of themselves, were drawn into the party of the Thirty."

The tyrants went so far in their measures to secure themselves, as to oblige all persons not contained in the catalogue of the 3000 to quit Athens and to dwell outside the city, in the unprotected Piraeeus, and in the space between the two long walls. Hence the distinction between οἱ ἐν ἄστει and οἱ ἐν Πειραιεῖ. Piraeeus was inhabited by sailors and merchants, who naturally formed a democratic element, and now their number was swelled by all those who were suspected, the city being inhabited by the partizans of the tyrants alone. When therefore Thrasybulus arrived in Piraeeus, he was received with open arms. But before matters came to this, the tyrants had sent envoys to him inviting him to return; they had even proposed to make him one of their number in the place of Theramenes, and offered to allow him to bring back with him ten of the exiles in perfect safety. Thrasybulus justly rejected such a base proposal as it deserved. Had the Spartans not demolished the walls of Piraeeus, a small garrison might have repelled the returning exiles; but it now was an open place, and the exiles entering without opposition, were joyfully received by the inhabitants. "Thrasybulus established himself in Munychia, and the population of Piraeeus uniting with him, armed themselves in any way they could. All the people, who formerly had gained their bread by being employed in the navy, the arsenal, and in commerce, and who were now without occupation, flocked to them." In Piraeeus, we know not how long after Thrasybulus' arrival, a battle was fought; the Spartan garrison withdrew, the exiles, though badly armed, manfully defended themselves in the streets, and repelled the enemy. Critias very fortunately fell during the engagement, and with him fell all the strength of the Thirty. In Theramenes they had destroyed their brightest ornament; in Critias their soul was lost; the rest were mere miscreants.

On returning from Piraeeus, they could no longer maintain themselves even among their own party—the 3000 contained in the catalogue. Those who are seduced into things that are worse than their hearts, are silent so long as fortune favours them; but when fortune forsakes them, they rise with all their indignation against the seducers. Hence the general feeling of the 3000 was against the Thirty: they, it is said, were the cause of all the misfortunes; they had carried matters too far, and ought to resign their power. This demand they complied with, and ten men, one from every phyle, were appointed to bring about a peace and reconciliation with the exiles. But these Ten did not answer the expectations of the people; they were not indeed as blood-thirsty as the Thirty, but equally hard-hearted and insensible to the honour and liberty of their country; they were equally ready to keep Athens under the Spartan yoke, but were not so prudent. They frustrated all negotiations with the exiles, and Thrasybulus and his men were obliged to make an attack upon the city. Proceeding from

Piraeeus, they blockaded it, and committed acts of hostility, by burning down houses and cutting down trees, while the people of the city, and the Ten, were equally determined not to yield. The Decemvirs now sent two men to Sparta praying for support against the common enemy. The Spartans actually advanced them a sum of money to enable them to engage mercenaries. Thus the decisive moment seemed again removed to the distant future; and if the Spartans had acted with energy, Athens would have been lost for ever. At Sparta it was even decreed, that king Pausanias,—" Agis, the mortal enemy of Athens, fortunately was old and weak, and had no influence,"—should lead an army against Athens to protect the lawful government against the rebels.

If things had now proceeded in their natural course, the exiled Athenians would evidently have been lost, for they were confined to the unfortified Piraeeus, while their opponents were in possession of the fortified city, and were supported by an army. But heaven willed it otherwise; the jealousy and personal animosity among the enemies served to save the good cause. The first thing, was the great aversion and the general distrust which the Greeks felt against the Spartans: the Boeotians did not join in the undertaking at all, and the others did it very reluctantly, loudly demanding that Sparta should conclude a fair peace, and not disgrace them by fighting for tyrants. King Pausanias listened with pleasure to such things, and resolutely exerted himself to bring about a reconciliation; for he was an opponent of Lysander, and saw that the government of Athens formed a strong support of his adversary, who had made the revolution and instituted the tyrants. Both Pausanias and others, moreover, feared Lysander as a revolutionary person—and such he actually was, for he was strongly suspected even during the conspiracy of Cinadon —who intended to abolish their oligarchy, to make the kingly dignity elective, or perhaps even to abolish it, and to appoint annual elective generals in the place of the kings. In all he did, they saw strongholds which he was building for himself out of Lacedaemon, for the purpose of carrying his plans into effect. All this fortunately induced Pausanias thoroughly to make up his mind to save Athens and restore the exiles: these circumstances explain what is otherwise unaccountable. He did advance indeed, and appeared before Piraeeus; but although

two ephors, as usual, accompanied the king (just as commissioners of the national convention accompanied the French
generals), he contrived to give matters a different turn.   He
not only undertook nothing against the exiles, but even
cautioned and advised Thrasybulus and his party, to trust him
and commit no hostilities against him.   It would certainly
have been a bold thing to trust a Spartan, but it would have
been well, if Thrasybulus had, on that occasion, done so at
once.   But he did not do so until he had been once defeated by
Pausanias.   An engagement took place, in which the Peloponnesians were at first repulsed, and many fell: one would imagine
that Pausanias was now provoked, and would have commenced
in implacable war, but he was content with driving the
Athenians back, and again admonished them to be quiet, and
entreated them to act rationally and trust him.

A reconciliation was now actually brought about (Olymp.
94, 1); whether he secretly communicated his plans to the
exiles, is unknown; but he fulfilled the duties of a mediator,
and did not disappoint the hopes of the exiles.   The Spartan
garrison was withdrawn; a general amnesty was decreed, and
the constitution of Athens was restored, with the proviso that
it should be amended.   It was then arranged, that the Thirty
should withdraw to Eleusis, and that any one who did not feel
safe at Athens should remove thither; for the massacre of the
Eleusinians had annihilated the population of that town.

On these terms peace was unexpectedly concluded, and kept
most faithfully.   This, and all other conciliatory measures, were
this time honestly carried into effect, and the peace was not
disturbed by sycophants, who are not often mentioned during
this period.   Severe measures must have been adopted against
them, and a change must have taken place in the δίκαι δημόσιαι,
in consequence of which, such accusations became impossible.
Henceforth, and down to the end of his life, Thrasybulus was
the first citizen of Athens; the gratitude of his fellow-citizens
was as great during his lifetime as it was afterwards.

The history of these events shows, that we ought not to
judge of the moral worth of a man from the party colour of
his politics; and that we ought not to say: " This man belongs
to this or that party, and therefore he is a bad or a good man."
It is a most convenient method of judging a man in this way,
but it is a bad one.   History teaches us a better method: the

very worst men often fight under the colours of the best cause, and in a bad party we often find the best men, imagining that they are doing good, while they are doing what is wrong and evil, because they are short-sighted and mistaken in their aim. Such also was the case here. Thrasybulus was an excellent citizen, and a man free from all reproach; but Anytus, the subsequent accuser of Socrates, belonged with Thrasybulus to the supporters of the good cause: he was one of the first who undertook to restore the ancient constitution, and was himself one of the leaders. But it can hardly be doubted, that he who accused Socrates, and brought about his condemnation, was a bad man: he was a religious hypocrite. In like manner, there may have been very excellent men among those ἐν ἄστει; Socrates himself was then ἐν ἄστει, and so were no doubt most of his friends. I for my part would certainly have joined the party in Piraeeus and Phyle; but I do not on that account cast a stone at those who were in the city, I only pity them. I must here add the remark, that the joining a bad party often has an injurious influence upon the whole life of a man; impressions are made which can never be effaced. In this case also, something of this kind clung to the persons throughout their lives; for the people who then were in the city, showed ever after a feeling of hatred to those who had been in Piraeeus. Thus Lysias, as good a man as ever lived, though he was only a metoecus, had been in Piraeeus, and was judged of unfairly by Plato, who was in unfavorable circumstances, for it cannot be anything but party spirit that led Plato, in his Phaedrus, to raise Isocrates so high at the expense of Lysias. Isocrates had openly sided with the party of the tyrants; he did not indeed belong to the faction of Critias, " the party of the mountain," but to that of Theramenes, which may be compared to the Girondists; but he was after all of the party of the Thirty, and one of the βουλευταὶ at the time of the tyrants. There can be no doubt that the schools of Lysias and Isocrates stood in hostile opposition to each other. To me it is inconceivable, that any one should lower Lysias for the purpose of raising Isocrates: the former is a man of infinitely greater intelligence and ability; he is a practical, active man, and immensely superior to Isocrates. He showed his noble character by sacrificing his whole property

to the cause of the exiles and to the city of Athens, though
he belonged to it not as a citizen, but only as a metoecus, and
lived in it in the condition of a child. I have never discovered
the slightest trace of Isocrates having sacrificed a single drachma
to his country; but it is well known that he was in the receipt
of large sums. I mention this, in order to explain fully, what
notions I entertain of the great men of that period.

The amnesty was decreed at Athens, and honestly kept.
The thirty tyrants lived for a time at Eleusis, but they harboured
treacherous designs, attempting to effect their return to Athens;
but when this happened we do not know. The attempt, however, failed, and the tyrants were abandoned by their own
followers and killed. Their death propitiated the republic; no
one else was put to death, and all that had passed was honestly
and truly forgiven.

"Athens had thus unexpectedly recovered her autonomy;
but for ten years longer, until Olymp. 96, 3, she lay prostrate
in the greatest weakness, like a sick person who has escaped
from death only by his strong and healthy constitution."

Let us now turn our attention to the condition of the other
parts of Greece, which were under the supremacy of Sparta.
"The Spartans now threw off the mask entirely, and no one
could any longer be mistaken about their plans. They now
took vengeance for every offence that had been committed
against them during the war," and as far as their arms could
reach, they subdued the Greek cities.

In all the places which had been allied with Athens, and
had surrendered to the Spartans, or had been captured by
them, they abolished the constitution, and established δεκαδαρ-
χίαι, that is, they appointed ten men, who were sovereigns of
the cities, and intrusted with full authority. We do not know
whether they left to those cities a shadow of their council and
demos. The Ten men who were appointed at Athens after the
removal of the Thirty, were just such a decadarchia; and the
same form of government was instituted by the Spartans at
Chios, in the towns of Lesbos, and in many other places. In
each of these towns they also appointed a commissioner, with
the title of harmost (ἁρμοστής) who was a Spartan, and was
not only permitted, but ordered to enrich himself there as
much as he could. The name, ἁρμοστής, is connected with an

expression which occurs in a writer of that period; I do not recollect this moment whether it is in Xenophon or Lysias;[a] namely, the nomothetae, who constituted, arranged, and settled the affairs of the towns, are said ἁρμόζειν, whence ἁρμοστὴς is he who has to arrange and settle the constitution of a city. But matters were managed as in France in the year 1793. The Spartans did not trouble themselves about establishing a constitution; and the regular constitution remained always suspended, wherever there was a harmost and a decadarchy.

In the other states which had not been subdued by the Spartans, but had been allied with them before, the Spartans could not at once introduce such a change, except in those cases where they had effected a revolution; as for example, when they, as the phrase was, had freed a country town from the dominion of a ruling city. In such a case, they immediately sent a harmost as its protector, and instituted a decadarchy, "under the pretext of protecting the weak, and freeing the perioeci from the tyranny of the powerful." And the Spartans were excessively zealous in finding out such opportunities: they were extremely watchful and indefatigable in making enquiries wherever a territory had complaints to make against the ruling city; and when the discovery was made, they immediately interfered, even though they were not invited to do so by the discontented. In this manner, they also took vengeance on the Eleans, by demanding of them to renounce their dominion over their perioeci. When the Eleans refused to comply, they sent an army, as the protector of general liberty, compelled the Eleans to give up their sovereignty, and then constituted the Elean territory, Triphylia and Cyllene, according to their own fashion, and under their immediate protection.

"Thus the result of the war was universal slavery in Greece; the power of the Spartans extended nearly over the whole country; the distant Aetolia, Acarnania, and Thessaly, against which an unsuccessful expedition was undertaken, being the only exceptions. In the islands, their tyranny was worst. It had been made a subject of reproach to the Athenians, that they had disarmed their allies; but history does not record a single instance in which the Athenians did so without being provoked by insurrection, rebellion, and the like. Sparta, on the

---

[a] Xenoph. de Republ. Laced. 14, § 2.

other hand, without the least cause, now compelled Lesbos to deliver up its fleet, although that island, by its revolt, had greatly contributed to bring the war to its issue. Besides Chios, it was more particularly Lesbos and Samos, that were severely oppressed. Samos, which had remained faithful to Athens to the last, escaped from utter destruction only with great difficulty; for its citizens had to capitulate for a free departure, and abandon their island without taking with them any of their property."

In this way things were managed in Greece itself, and on the coasts of Asia Minor, as far as was practicable; for in the latter country the Spartans did less, since they gave up most of the cities there to prince Cyrus of Persia.

LECTURE LVIII.

"DARIUS had promised the throne to Xerxes, who, accordingly, succeeded on the demise of Darius. Darius had sons from two marriages—the one with the daughter of Gobryas, and the other with Atossa, a daughter of Cyrus. The succession was disputed between the sons of these two mothers. Xerxes rested his claims upon the fact of his being, through his mother Atossa, descended from Cyrus, and of his being *in purpura natus;* but Ariobarzanes was the elder. Darius appointed Xerxes his successor, in order to connect his dynasty with that of Cyrus.

Xerxes is known from Herodotus as a foolish and boastful man." [1] After the battle of Salamis, he gave himself up to sensual lusts, without any concern about his empire, and continued to reign for about fifteen years, without anything of importance happening during that period. His empire does not seem to have been shaken through that defeat; but it is historically certain that he did not die a natural death.

Our knowledge of the history of Persia is extremely scanty; our real authorities are the excerpts from Ctesias in Photius, and some isolated statements from Dinon; and for the later

[1] " Ahasuerus is not to be taken for Xerxes, as is done by some authors, but for Cambyses."—1826.

times, to which Herodotus does not extend, these are our only sources. It is impossible to say what is the value of Dinon's authority, because it does not appear to us of such a nature as to induce belief in the author's statements. About Ctesias I have already expressed my opinion. I do not reject his testimony for the later times; for concerning these he is always a little more trustworthy than in regard to the earlier ones. But although I admit, that for these later times he had every opportunity of knowing the truth, yet he was incapable of making critical researches, and had no inclination to make them; whence we must, after all, look upon his history as highly uncertain. The Alexandrian grammarians had certain critical marks to distinguish what they considered spurious passages, and I would that we had similar ones to distinguish in history that which can be strictly called historical, and that of the kind to which the accounts of Ctesias belong, which we cannot indeed regard as absolute romances or fictions, but which are yet not quite authentic.

To return to our subject: it is indeed an established fact, that fifteen years after the battle of Salamis (Olymp. 78, 4), Xerxes was murdered by an Hyrcanian Artabanus or Artabanes, who had great influence at the court; but the circumstances of the murder are described in very different ways. His death and that of his second son, Darius (some call him the elder), are connected in the traditions, but the details are different. There existed two traditions about it: the one was adopted by Aristotle,[2] a great opponent of Ctesias, who relates that Artabanes murdered Xerxes from fear of punishment, because, without the king's knowledge, he had caused his son Darius to be put to death. The account of Ctesias states, that Artabanes murdered Xerxes, and, "in order to destroy the whole royal house of Persia through its own members," threw the guilt upon Darius, and charged him with the murder before Artaxerxes, just as Macbeth imputes the murder of Duncan to the prince. Artaxerxes, then, it is said, ordered his innocent brother to be put to death.[3] This account is the reverse of the other. A third tradition makes Artabanes take

---

[2] *Polit.* v. 8. § 14, perhaps from Dinon.

[3] "On such occasions we still see some traces of the ancient Persian liberty, and of a high aristocracy; even under Darius Nothus, judges are mentioned in the royal house."—1826.

possession of the throne and rule for a time as a usurper over Persia; " in many canons he is mentioned as king with a reign of seven months." But however uncertain this history is, it is agreed on all hands, that Artabanes was the murderer of the king, and that Artaxerxes avenged the blood of his father on him.

Xerxes was now succeeded by Artaxerxes, surnamed Macrocheir (long-hand), who reigned thirty-six years.[*] His reign was disturbed by the revolt of Egypt, which I have mentioned before, and in which Achaemenes lost his life. The Athenians interfering, supported king Inarus against the Persians, until, through the skilful management of Megabyzus, they sustained that fearful loss, which, as far as the ships were concerned, was almost as great as the disaster in Sicily. Egypt was indeed soon recovered by the Persians; but there now followed a succession of other storms and convulsions in the Persian empire. From Ctesias, it is evident that the empire was already experiencing the fate of all great oriental empires, which are governed by satraps: such a satrap, even though he paid tribute, was yet, in point of fact, independent, and any occasion might lead him to rebellion. Thus Megabyzus, the conqueror of Egypt, himself revolted. The interference of the royal ladies manifested itself as early as that time: the queen was exasperated against Megabyzus, but afterwards, when he married one of the princesses, she became reconciled to him in a very extraordinary manner. The accounts of these occurrences are so completely in accordance with the unvarying character of eastern despotism, that it is as if we were reading the history of the Mongoles in India or other eastern nations.

In the reign of Artaxerxes, a state of peace was restored between the Greeks and Persians in a somewhat unaccountable manner, which I have already mentioned in discussing the peace of Cimon. An actual peace with the great king is out of the question; the Greeks continued their undertakings on the coast of Pamphylia and against Cyprus, " where the Greek towns had evidently solicited their assistance."

After the death of Artaxerxes I., the throne was occupied by Darius called Nothus, because his mother was not a genuine

---

[*] In 1826, Niebuhr assigned forty-one years to the reign of Artaxerxes, from Olymp. 78, 4, to Olymp. 89, 1. As all authorities mention forty years, it seems that our text contains an error.—ED.

Persian, the Persians regarding every other marriage but that between genuine Persians as concubinage. This Darius, however, did not succeed Artaxerxes at once, for Xerxes II., the only one among the sons of Artaxerxes whose mother was a Persian, reigned for the short period of forty-five days, when he was murdered by his younger brother, likewise a Nothus, though it was pretended that he had died in some accidental but incredible manner. He was succeeded by his murderer, whose real name is perhaps altogether unknown. It is mentioned in two different ways: according to the statement of Ctesias, in Photius, he was called Secundianus, which looks like Latin, and is quite improbable; I suspect that Photius, who often misquotes Ctesias, has corrupted the name; others call him Sogdianus, which is likewise rather improbable. This fratricide, whatever his name may have been, reigned in a manner which might have been anticipated after such a crime: his object was to get his other brothers into his power and to despatch them. The most enterprising among them was Ochus, afterwards Darius II., who was then governor of some province. The king tried to entice him, but he did not allow himself to be entrapped; and the king was in such fear of him, that he entered into a negotiation with him, according to which Ochus, too, was to assume the royal tiara, and both were to reign in common. This they did for a time, but then the one ensnared the other; Ochus deceiving his wicked brother induced him to put his whole trust in him. Cunning as the Orientals are, yet nothing is more common than for them to allow themselves to be cheated by those whose designs lie perfectly clear before their eyes; as, for example, Ali Pasha of Janina, allowed himself to be deceived by Curshid Pasha, although every one could see through his scheme. They are almost justified in their belief in fatality, because it so often displays itself among them. Ochus, therefore, seized the person of his brother and caused him to be murdered. On this occasion we hear of a mode of inflicting the punishment of death, which has existed in the East from the earliest times: it also occurs in Egypt, and in several instances among the Persian kings, and it is strange that it is no longer mentioned among modern nations. Something similar, however, does occur in Turkey, where the Mufti is a sacred person, whom the Sultan is neither allowed to behead nor to strangle, but Murad II. or Mahomet IV. contrived to evade the law by ordering his Mufti to be pounded in a mortar.   Thus it was sinful among the Persians to shed royal blood; nor was it allowed to pollute the elements by drowning or burning a member of the royal family.   When, therefore, any member of the royal house was to be put to death, they filled a large space, of great depth, with ashes, into which they threw and suffocated the culprit; for ashes are not an element which might be polluted by royal blood, nor was any blood shed, so that the king remained perfectly pure.   Such horrors frequently occur.   The Persians were not very ingenious inventors in other arts, but displayed incredible ingenuity in inventing instruments of death and torture. There is a magnificent work on Chinese tortures; but the Persians were not much inferior to them.

After this, Darius reigned with a perfectly easy mind, for such is the character of the Orientals; his reign lasted thirty years,[5] but the Furies after all visited him in his own family. The history of Persia, henceforth, becomes more and more a history of the palace; the empire was, even at this period, sinking fast.   This is, indeed, the period during which Persian influence became established in Greece; but it is at the same time probable, that, even in his reign, many parts of the empire were lost.

In the fifth or sixth year of his reign Egypt again revolted, and now completely emancipated itself.   " The particular circumstances are not exactly known, but the Persians were driven from all the country," and, for about sixty years, Egypt remained a perfectly independent and powerful state; " it was, indeed, never recognised by the Persians, but, in point of fact, it was thoroughly independent.   In comparison with ancient Egypt, it was but a small state; but" when Egypt, under the Fatimids, emancipated herself from the Abassids, she was also comparatively not a large state, but yet, considering what those times were, wealthy and respected.

Bactria also revolted : it is said to have been reduced again, but I believe that this is the time in which the Indian provinces permanently emancipated themselves, and were lost to

* This date is apparently a *lapsus memoriae.*—ED.

the Persian monarchy; for under Alexander they were already independent and consolidated empires; "Alexander found Indian princes even from Candahar."

But the greatest misfortune for Darius arose out of his own family, through the "hands of worthless women." It arose from the marriage of his eldest son, who was then called Arsaces, and afterwards assumed the name of Artaxerxes, with Statira, the daughter of Hydarnes, governor of western Asia, and a noble Persian, who was probably a grandson of one of the great Persians under Darius Hystaspis. This man had two children, a son and a daughter; between his daughter, Statira, and Artaxerxes, the king brought about a marriage, and the son was married to one of the king's own daughters, named Amestris. Darius himself was married to his natural sister, Parysatis; for marriages between brothers and sisters were lawful among the Persians. Parysatis is a genuine Persian name, signifying *child of a fairy*, "or *child of a peri*;[6] the masculine, Perisades, occurs as the name of a king of Bosporus." This Parysatis ruled her husband entirely; we are elsewhere told what chamberlains ruled the king, but, in the case of Darius Nothus, the authority of the queen was much greater. The son of Hydarnes, the king's son-in-law, now murdered his wife, the princess, and this brought upon him well-deserved punishment; he, together with his father and son, were put to death: whoever interfered in the feuds of that house had to bear the unfortunate consequences. Statira, the wife of the prince Artaxerxes, vowed vengeance on him who had killed her father and brother. Darius left it to Parysatis as to whether it would not be better to kill Statira likewise; but she then disdained such a measure, and thought Statira harmless, although he cautioned her, and told her that it would be better to get rid of her.

During the latter period of his reign, his governors in western Asia, first Pissuthnes, and then Tissaphernes and

---

[6] " It has been supposed that *fairy* is derived from *Peri*, but *fairy* is rather connected with *Fata*, a term applied to everything in which the interference of supernatural powers is perceived. Hence, in the third century, a sorcerer was called *fatuus*, and *fatuus* and *fatuellus* are ancient Italian words. The fairies were no doubt imported into Europe at the time of the Crusades; and our fairies in the tales of chivalry arose from a mixture of eastern traditions with those of Scandinavia and those which were yet current in the south from the time of the Romans."—1826.

Pharnabazus, interfered in the affairs of Greece.   When the
end of his life approached, he sent thither his younger son,
Cyrus, as viceroy of Asia Minor, with great powers (Olymp.
93, 1).   This was done through the influence of his mother,
who preferred Cyrus to her elder son, and was anxious to
secure the throne to him who had been born after the accession
of his father.   It is an eastern notion, which also occurs in the
middle ages, that a son born before the accession of his father
has no title to the succession, but that the succession belongs
to him who has been born during his father's reign.   This
dispute about primogeniture has shewn its effects also among the
Turks, and led to fearful crimes, the object being to prevent a
prince having children before his accession, and thereby to
avert civil wars.   Opinions upon this point have differed at
all times, one considering justice to be on one side, and another
on the other side.

In the account of Xenophon, Cyrus appears as an interesting character; but, if we judge of him without bias, we have
no reason for believing him to have been a better man than
any other Eastern prince of the ordinary kind; his revolt
against his brother is, after all, nothing but a rebellion, and
has something particularly revolting in it; because, among
the Persian kings of whom we know anything, Artaxerxes II.
is the best; nay, in his conduct towards his brother, he shews
a frankness and generosity which are unusual in a king of
Persia.

Darius died before the end of the Peloponnesian war
(Olymp. 93, 4); and although Cyrus had already been accused
of cherishing hostile plans against his brother, and although
nothing was more evident than this to any one who had his
eyes open, yet Artaxerxes, who is surnamed Mnemon, honestly
invited him to come to Persia, at the time when he solemnly
assumed the kingly dignity at Pasargadae or Persepolis.[7]   On
that occasion, Cyrus was charged with having intended, during
the solemnities, to get his brother assassinated.   Whether the
charge was well founded or not, no one can say; but the conduct of Artaxerxes was at any rate generous.   According to
some accounts, he did not imprison him at all, but merely

[7] " This was a kind of consecration called μνῆσις by the Greeks.   It is possible
that the kings of Persia at their coronation entered the order of the Magi, which
conferred upon them a higher dignity."—1826.

reproached him; according to another statement, he ordered him to be arrested, and according to the Persian ceremonial, to be kept in golden chains; but at the request of his mother, and from a natural kindness of disposition, he soon set him free again. He then even allowed him to return as viceroy to Asia Minor, on his oath that he would not undertake anything against him. Cyrus, however, setting out with a fixed determination not to keep this oath, immediately renewed his connections with the Spartans, the Peloponnesian war having, in the meantime, been decided by his pecuniary support, and made known to them his design of raising himself to the throne by main force. Cyrus was on tolerable terms with Pharnabazus, the governor of Phrygia and Mysia; but Tissaphernes, the satrap of Lydia and Caria, was his mortal enemy, and cautioned the great king.

It was about this time that Alcibiades arrived in Asia. After the subjugation of Athens, the Spartans, and the Thirty persecuted him and drove him out of Thrace. He knew that assassins were tracking his steps; he felt that his life was threatened, and that he could not be safe in Thrace: accordingly leaving his treasures behind, he went to Asia, and entered the dominion of Pharnabazus. His real intention, however, was to go up to Susa, in order to open the eyes of king Artaxerxes to the plans of Cyrus; and he thus hoped to inspire the king with confidence in himself, and to induce him to entrust to him the command against Cyrus: an office which he might use for the good of his country, and perhaps for the restoration of Athens. But whether it was that the Spartan commanders cautioned Pharnabazus, and advised him to kill Alcibiades, or that he acted in the interest of Cyrus to prevent his going to Susa—in short, Alcibiades, under some pretext, or without any, was surrounded in his house by the troops of Pharnabazus, the house was set on fire, and he himself was shot from a distance while attempting to escape through the flames.

The Spartans were thus at rest as far as Alcibiades was concerned, and now negotiated with Cyrus. They were not inclined to enter into an open alliance with him, because his enterprise might prove unsuccessful, and because they did not wish to offend the king of Persia. But as Cyrus promised them enormous advantages, they secretly supported him, and allowed Greek mercenaries to be enlisted for his army. Clearchus engaged for him the mercenaries known under the name of the Ten Thousand; and on the coast of Cilicia Cyrus also found a Spartan fleet with Spartan troops, which entered his service, but pretended to have landed there quite by accident, and without the command of the republic, in order that afterwards they might be able to deny that they had been sent by the government of Sparta.

Clearchus was a man of the worst description. He had been commander as early as the time of the Peloponnesian war, and was an able officer, but of the same class as the rapacious generals in the thirty years' war on both sides were—such as Pappenheim on the one side, and Banner on the other; men who, in strict justice, can be called neither more nor less than highway robbers and murderers. It is disgusting to find such men described as heroes—a sign of utter ignorance of real history. Banner, like Clearchus, had the talent of a great general; but he, as well as Pappenheim, was a monster such as, thank heaven, none has appeared throughout the whole of the revolutionary war. During the latter, some individuals were guilty of the worst actions; but what they did was no worse than what during the thirty years' war was done by the best among them. Gustavus Adolphus alone formed an exception. Bernard of Weimar may have done worse things than Vandamme, yet at the time he was one of the better men.[a] After the defeat of Aegospotami, when Byzantium had been obliged to surrender to the Spartans, Clearchus, who was sent thither as governor, raged in such a manner, that the Byzantians, in their distress, implored the protection of the Spartans. As Byzantium was a very strong place, the Spartans mistrusted him, and fearing lest his undertaking should become dangerous, they sent a strong detachment against him. He resisted, and they were obliged to force him to give up Byzantium. Although this was in fact rebellion, yet (for he was a Spartan) this, as well as his offences against other Greeks, were immediately pardoned, and he continued to enjoy the confidence of the rulers as much as before. Clearchus accordingly formed a corps of 13,000 Greek mercenaries; for in the course of the Peloponnesian war there had sprung up the great and unfortunate change by which the armies, instead of being formed of

[a] It is uncertain whether this sentence is correctly restored.—ED.

citizens, were composed of mercenaries; just as during the fourteenth century in Italy. It was the natural consequence of this change, that the lawful liberties of the cities could no longer be maintained. " Mercenary service had become quite customary among the Greeks, and thousands now had scarcely any other resources; wherever the drum was beaten—I say intentionally the drum, for it was used in Asia, and was perhaps an invention of the Lydians—mercenaries assembled in crowds." Clearchus became the commander of these 13,000 Greeks, and with them entered the service of Cyrus, who employed them as the principal soldiers in his undertakings, in order to over-awe the Asiatics who served under him, consisting of the militia of Asia Minor and Persians—for every satrap had a body-guard consisting of genuine Persians. Most of these mercenaries were attached to him because he paid them, or because they expected rich plunder; some, however, joined him from pure enthusiasm; and among these was Xenophon, a sad anomaly in the Hellenic world! If he had gone to Cyrus as a rude mercenary, with the view of collecting wealth and plunder in the country of the barbarians, I should not blame him, but he joined Cyrus from enthusiasm!"

The history of this war is, as every one knows, the subject of his celebrated Anabasis. It is unquestionably by far the best of Xenophon's works: it is indeed wanting in historical dignity; it is wanting in that which Xenophon could not give, because he did not possess it—a great and noble spirit. He also passes over many things lightly which a thinking reader requires to know; and its beginning in particular is composed with too great haste. But from the point at which the retreat begins, the work is written with animation, and becomes a very valuable book, which we can read with great interest. It must, however, be observed, that as a piece of historical composition, it cannot be mentioned along with the great artistic works of Thucydides, Tacitus, and Sallust. But, nevertheless, it is a book which one likes, and from which much may be learned. If at that time almanacs had been published, it ought to have appeared as an almanac, with coloured maps: for this is its form. Notwithstanding great carelessness, and much that is foolish, it is written with great liveliness: it could, in fact, not be otherwise, considering the character of the author. Every one should read it. From it we may form an idea of the weakness and the deplorable condition of the Persian empire; of the extreme feebleness of the government, and the merely nominal dependence of the satrapies. The condition resembled that of the Subadars in India under the Mongoles and in the feudal times. Some satrapies had already become hereditary, just like the great fiefs in the middle ages. The satrapy in Pontus, for example, was a real hereditary fief.

Cyrus marched into Upper Asia (Olymp. 94, ⅔); the troops, both Greeks and barbarians, were several times upon the point of revolting, because they found themselves deceived; and twice they were on the point of abandoning Cyrus altogether; but by immense promises he prevailed on them to accompany him as far as Babylon. There he was met by his brother, who had come from Upper Asia with all his forces, and a decisive battle was fought in the neighbourhood of Cunaxa. " It is certain that the course of the battle was not quite as it is described. It is evident, that the 13,000 Greeks on the one wing chased the Persians without opposition; but when we are told that they slew 10,000 Persians, while they themselves had only one man wounded, it is more than we can be expected to believe. The struggle seems to have been fiercest in the centre, where the two brothers fought against each other in person; Artaxerxes was wounded by Cyrus, but was saved. Clearchus, by a slight manoeuvre, might now have attacked the Persian centre; but he was afraid of venturing upon such a movement, as he might easily have been surrounded by the superior number of the Persians. Both armies were thus in confusion, but that of the king was most so; it was already nearly dispersed. Artaxerxes was severely wounded, and was almost dying with thirst, when Cyrus, at the fall of evening, was killed." His death decided the battle.

If Cyrus had not fallen, he would have won the battle, and strange circumstances would have been the consequence. The Greek mercenaries would have remained with Cyrus as a bodyguard; and in this manner the Persian empire would perhaps have acquired much greater stability than it otherwise had. The dynasty of Psammetichus maintained itself through Greek mercenaries, and the same would have been the case in Persia. The Greeks would have become the noblest in the Persian empire; their numbers would have increased, and it is possible, that they might have prevented the overthrow of the empire by Alexander, or at least, he would not have overthrown it so easily; or they would very probably have dethroned the dynasty of the Achemenidae, and established a Greek empire, just as the Turkish guards made themselves masters of the empire of the Khaliphs, and as the Mamelukian guards overthrew the dynasty in Egypt, and other dynasties in Mosul and Aleppo. But as it was, there remained for the Greeks nothing but to return; and it is owing to this retreat, that they have a great and brilliant name in history; for they were in reality no better than robbers, and would have been mentioned as such in history only with disgrace.

LECTURE LIX.

WHEN, after the battle of Cunaxa, the Greek corps found that they themselves were victorious, but that it was impossible to continue the war, they joined the surviving Persians of Cyrus under their commander Ariaeus. But this man contemplated to betray them, as a means to make his peace with the great king, and could not be trusted. "Negotiations into which they entered with the Persians, led to no results, and thus they formed the desperate determination to fight their way back. There were two roads; the one along the Euphrates through Mesopotamia, was the nearest, and would have led them by the shortest line to the sea; the northern road ran across the Tigris and the hills of Armenia." It seemed impossible to them to take the road along the Euphrates, which they had come. Opposite they Euphrates a desert extends as far as the mount Sindjar in Armenia, which is quite of the same nature as the Arabian desert, and is inhabited by Arabs. Only the banks of the Euphrates itself form a narrow stripe of inhabitable and fertile land, and the army, on its march through it, had conveyed provisions with them in boats on the Euphrates. But in marching up the river this was impracticable, nor could they be certain that they would find provisions along the river. Moreover, in the plain they would

have been much exposed to the attacks of the Persian cavalry,
"for they themselves had no horse." In short, there remained
for them nothing but to take the road across the hills towards
the Black Sea. This is the brilliant retreat of the Ten
Thousand.

"In this manner they arrived on the river Zab, across
which there was no bridge." There they were met by
Tissaphernes, who, by the command of Artaxerxes, followed
them with a large army, and offered to enter into negotiations
with them. Their leaders were imprudent enough to accept
his offers. Ariaeus made his peace with the king, and sacrificed
the Greeks; the Greek commanders allowed themselves to be
persuaded to have an interview with the Persians, at which,
they were told, a free departure would be granted to them;
but they were treacherously seized and murdered. "The only
one that was spared was Menon, the grandfather of Menon of
Pharsalus, who was the brave commander of the Greeks at
Lamia, and the great grandfather of Pyrrhus. To him the
king granted his life for reasons unknown to us, but all the
other commanders were beheaded." The Persians now believed
that they had the whole army in their power; but the soldiers,
although deprived of their leaders, remained together, shewed
great determination, and did not allow themselves to be
deceived. It cannot be doubted, although we have only his
own word for it, that Xenophon on that occasion behaved in
a praiseworthy manner; "under his guidance the Greeks
continued their march, and with great danger they fought
their way across the Zab, one of the most rapid rivers, in
which my father nearly lost his life. It was there they had
to encounter the greatest danger."

The further retreat was facilitated by the circumstance of
Tissaphernes hastening to Asia Minor, to take possession of
the new satrapy which he had received as a reward; and
because the rude Asiatics gave up the pursuit without reason,
imagining that the Greeks would run into their own destruction in the impassable mountainous countries. The Greeks
accordingly continued their march across the mountains of
Kurdistan and Armenia without being pursued by the
Persians.

"But although they were not pursued, they met with immense difficulties. There were no bridges across the rapid

rivers; and in the mountains they had to encounter nations which were independent of Persia, but all the more warlike, and determined to admit neither the one nor the other enemy into their country.

In Kurdistan they met with the first of these independent tribes, the Carduchi, who would not allow them to pass, so that they had to force their way with great loss. They suffered still more from the cold in Armenia. There the peculiar circumstances of the disorganisation of Persia already shewed themselves. The satrap of Armenia was satisfied with concluding a truce with them, just as the Pasha of Egypt at present acts as an independent prince; he promised to supply them with provisions on condition that they should pass through his territory as quickly as possible, and commit no act of hostility : they might attack other satraps if they pleased. Xenophon's description of Armenia is remarkable. It must be observed, that Armenia with the Greeks, and especially with Herodotus, ought not to be regarded as corresponding with the modern Armenia or the Armenia of the Romans; according to the Greek writers, it is much less extensive, and is situated further south. The northern districts in Mesopotamia, in Herodotus and Xenophon's Anabasis, belong indeed to Armenia, but it does not by any means extend so far north as at a later period. The accuracy of Xenophon's description of this march through Armenia has been doubted ; but it has been proved to be correct by modern travellers, and especially by the late Russian campaign, through which that country has become infinitely better known than through all the books of travel together: Tournefort's description, however, is excellent. In the same manner as Ovid has been blamed because he speaks of the frozen Danube, Xenophon's description of the fearful cold in Armenia has been thought incorrect; but this very point has been most thoroughly confirmed during the Russian campaign. The mountains of Armenia are far higher than has been hitherto believed; and Armenia is a very cold country, as is manifest even from Tournefort's account, who, on his journey from Erzeroum to Tabris, met with snow even about the end of June. It is, in fact, now generally known, that the fearful cold of which Xenophon speaks, and by which many Greeks had their hands and feet frozen, is faithfully described.

But another circumstance, I mean Xenophon's account of the subterraneous habitations of those tribes, has not yet been so well attested; but it is, nevertheless, perfectly true, and is still quite customary in those as well as in the adjacent countries. Men dwell in caves, especially from want of timber, and partly perhaps also on account of the intense cold: an Armenian village is scarcely visible at all, the habitations being cut into the mountains. The description of the Armenian villages in Xenophon exactly corresponds with what they are at the present day.

They then continued their march, " forcing their way through the midst of the barbarous mountaineers; probably the modern Caucasian tribes of the Lesghi, Ossetes, etc." But there occurs here a great confusion in Xenophon's geography, for he is in error about the Phasis. They came to a river, which was no doubt the Araxes; and as Alexander's soldiers confounded the Jaxartes with the Tanais, so now the soldiers of Xenophon believed the Araxes to be the Phasis. The cause of it was this : the Colchians, who now dwell about Trebizond (they are the Lases), must, at that time, have occupied a much larger extent of country, and dwelt as far as the Armenian mountains; as, therefore, the soldiers found Colchians and a broad river, they concluded they were on the Phasis. They then at length crossed an immense mountain, and at a little distance to the east of Trebizond they reached the Euxine, and thence proceeded to Trebizond. They now marched from one Greek city on the Pontus to another; these places were all tolerably independent, although their names stood in the lists of the Persian dominions, for beyond Armenia there were no Persian armies. In order not to be obliged to proceed by land they embarked, and thus the remainder, about six thousand, arrived in Thrace, where they made fresh engagements, and served as mercenaries under the Spartan commanders who were carrying on war in Asia (Olymp. 95, 1).

Meantime, the fact, that the Spartans had supported Cyrus, was followed by consequences which might have been anticipated; for Greece thereby became involved in war with the great king. But, as the mere touch of the spear of Achilles healed Philoctetes, so this war delivered Greece from the misfortune into which it had fallen.

" The support given by the Spartans had not remained

unknown to the Persian court.   The Lacedaemonians, indeed, denied that it had been done with the consent of the government; but, in the camp of Clearchus, letters were found which shewed that Cyrus had been in correspondence with the Spartan commanders."

As soon as Tissaphernes returned, after the death of Cyrus, he treated all the excuses of the Spartans as mere pretences. The Persians could not undertake anything against the Spartans themselves, but attacked the Greek cities (Olymp. 94, 4) which paid tribute to Sparta, and were now under her protection, " although, in the previous treaties, she had completely sacrificed the rights of those cities in order to obtain money from Persia."   It was, moreover, to be expected, that the Persians would equip a fleet, and thus Sparta was obliged in self-defence to send an army into Asia Minor.

During the first years, this army was very badly commanded, at first by Thimbron, and then by Dercyllidas; it did, indeed, greatly increase, so as to enable Dercyllidas to make incursions even into the satrapies of the interior, but both generals carried on the war very sluggishly.   " They had been sent to protect the cities, but were, in reality, contemptible robbers, who thought of nothing but enriching themselves."   The survivors of the ten thousand Greeks who had returned, now diffused a general feeling of contempt for the Persians, who, in the few engagements, really shewed themselves so wretched, that the Greeks began to think that, in one resolute attack, they might, if not deprive the Persians of the whole of Western Asia, yet make great conquests and obtain much booty.   Hence the Spartans entrusted the supreme command in this war to their king, Agesilaus (Olymp. 96, 1); they sent him into Asia, and with him only thirty Spartans.   The valour of the Spartans is indubitable, but the great care they took of themselves is equally certain; there existed at the time not more than one thousand Spartan citizens, and the experience of the Peloponnesian war had taught them to act as they did.   The Spartans accompanied the armies only as officers, and all the other troops levied in their country consisted of hired perioeci and emancipated helots, both of whom are mentioned under the mysterious name of νεοδαμώδεις; the war of Leuctra alone was of a different kind.

Agesilaus had not been long on the throne of Sparta; he was a younger brother of king Agis, and a son of Archidamus, who, at the beginning of the Peloponnesian war, had commanded the Spartan armies; Agis had conducted the Decelean war. Agesilaus ascended the throne because the legitimate birth of his nephew, Leotychides, the alleged son of king Agis, was disputed. It had not been anticipated that Agesilaus would succeed to the throne, and he had therefore received that Spartan education, from which, otherwise, the eldest son of the king was always exempted. Agesilaus is one of those characters to whom the lustre in which they appear is injurious, as soon as we proceed to examine them more closely. If a man is raised higher than he deserves, it is clear that an enquiry into his reputation damages it, for the natural consequence is, that people are inclined to pull him down, and he thus loses more than he would have lost if he had not been unduly praised. This may easily be the case with Agesilaus. The qualities for which Agesilaus is set up as an extraordinary man are, seriously considered, actually of a kind that we cannot help smiling at, and asking whether such things can constitute a great man. Very many trifles are related of him with a kind of unction and admiration. " Xenophon wishes him to appear as a genuine Greek aristocrat and Heracleid, and as a champion of liberty." If we judge of the man from his actions, there is in Agesilaus very little that deserves praise.

He was, it is true, a good general; no man denies this, although I, if there still are admirers of Xenophon, would ask them, What extraordinary action Agesilaus ever did? But there were, probably, few men, except the thoroughly bad, who were farther removed from justice than Agesilaus. This is owned by Plutarch, who otherwise writes a real panegyric on Agesilaus, without perceiving how much he thereby lowers himself. He had made it altogether his maxim, to meet his friends as a friend, and his enemies as an enemy, without enquiring what they were worth; this is related by Plutarch, who has no idea of the force of these words. He protected the most unworthy persons if they belonged to his party, he gave them appointments, and if such a person was guilty of any crime he was sure of impunity. Hence the command of Agesilaus, although he was personally not a robber, but an honest man, called forth the same exasperation against the Spartans as that of the worst general, or of an avowed robber among the Spartan kings would have done. His government not only failed in its attempt to allay the hatred against Sparta, but extended and increased it. I knew a French general who was, in reality, a good man; but, where he commanded, the discipline was bad, and the country suffered more than if an odious and bad man had had the command, and that merely because he had an infamous person among his staff, of whom he said, "*C'est un bon garçon;*" he wanted to be friendly and kind towards every one, but his promises were not kept, and crimes were left unpunished. Similar things are recorded of Agesilaus; thus he patronised a certain Nicias, and when this man was imprisoned in Caria, Agesilaus wrote, " If Nicias is innocent, set him free; if he is guilty, set him free for my sake; at any rate, you must set him free." When he was angry with any one, he oppressed, dishonoured, and injured him in every possible way. Such a character is assuredly not that of a great man. In a similar manner he also behaved towards Lysander, who accompanied him into Asia. The latter was a far greater general, and was looked up to by a large party. Whoever enjoyed the patronage of Lysander was sure not to receive justice at the hands of Agesilaus; and whoever was recommended or favoured by Lysander, was sure of being slighted. Agesilaus carried his insults so far as to appoint Lysander κρεωδαίτης, that is, provision-master of the head-quarters, which was quite a low office that they might have given to any ordinary man, and to say, " I want to see whether they will still court him." In all this conduct, I see nothing but that of a very ordinary man. " His policy was as abominable as that of any Spartan had ever been. The most disgraceful act of the Spartans, the occupation of Thebes by Phoebidas, was probably known to him; certain it is, that he afterwards approved of it, and, among the apophthegms ascribed to him, there are words of which a Greek ought to be ashamed, and which shew how little feeling the Spartans had for a common Greek country." His character seems to me to be sufficiently indicated by the fact, that, subsequently to the fall of Sparta's greatness, he went to Egypt and did not blush to command an army under the barbarian king of Egypt, merely for the purpose of

obtaining rich pay : the end of his life proved the worth of
the whole.   These are the bad sides of his character, on
account of which it is utterly impossible to regard him as a
hero.   It cannot, however, be denied, that he was personally
free from the cruelty and bitter harshness of Lysander ; he
was a man of a friendly and cheerful disposition, and remained
faithful to his country.

Agesilaus made about three campaigns, partly against
Tissaphernes and partly against Pharnabazus.   These expeditions afterwards acquired great celebrity; and Isocrates, the
patriarch of all rhetorical declaimers, in several speeches ex-
horting the Greeks to wage war against the Persians, again
and again reverts to the campaigns of Agesilaus; and from
the manner in which he speaks, it might seem as if Agesilaus
had conquered all Asia west of the Halys.   But there is not a
word of truth in this; he advanced into Lydia and Phrygia,
but in the interior he did not take a single town, " which
certainly was doing little enough, seeing that but very few
towns had any fortifications; for the Persians, like the Lom-
bards, allowed no castle or fortress to exist in a conquered
country. .Sardes alone was fortified, and this city ought to
have been taken if Ionia was to be free, but his expeditions
were only ravaging and predatory excursions, and it was
extremely easy to make such enterprises against the Persians."
Wherever he fell in with Tissaphernes, he defeated his enemy,
but it was only once or twice that a regular battle was fought;
on the whole, the engagements were only skirmishes.   The
Persians conducted the war in a truly ridiculous manner: as
soon as Agesilaus advanced a little, they concluded a truce,
paid him large sums of money, and assigned quarters to him,
or one satrap paid him and sent him into the territory of
another.   Thus Tissaphernes paid him to attack the territory
of Pharnabazus, and the latter acted in the same way.   Tissa-
phernès conducted himself altogether very wretchedly, in
consequence of which he was recalled, and, as it seems, put to
death.   Tithraustes was appointed in his place.   The campaigns were, in truth, conducted in a miserable way, " and
Agesilaus did in reality no more than his predecessors."

The war might have continued for a long time, for the
Spartans found this kind of warfare very agreeable; the army
cost them nothing, and the repeated victories could not but

gratify them. But in the meantime a far more formidable enemy was quietly rising against the Spartans. This was Conon, who, after the defeat of Aegospotami, had fled to Evagoras, prince of Salamis, in Cyprus. Evagoras was of Greek descent, master of a great Greek city in Cyprus, and a wealthy Persian feudal prince, but a Greek in feeling. He recommended Conon to the great king, in order to punish the Spartans for what they had done against Athens and Greece in the Peloponnesian war. Conon accordingly proceeded to the court of Artaxerxes Mnemon, and advised him to attack the Spartans by sea. He asked for money and the power to form a fleet, in order to seek the Spartans in Greece itself. He was authorised to equip the Phoenician fleet, but the undertaking was delayed for several years. Meantime, however, the general feeling in Greece had risen against the Spartans, and an alliance had been formed against them as early as the beginning of Olymp. 96. Some voices, especially that of the Thebans, had been raised against them even before. We have seen how, at the end of the Peloponnesian war, the Boeotians and Corinthians were exasperated against them, because they had been refused their share in the booty. The fact that, on the presents which, after the victory, the Spartans sent to Delphi, they inscribed only their own name as victors, and refused to add the names of their allies, exasperated the Greeks still more. Such things created bad blood, and were regarded in Greece as a mortal offence. The angry feeling of the Thebans manifested itself at Thebes even at the time when Agesilaus embarked to cross over to Asia; for as he refused to observe their rites in their territory, when offering sacrifice, they not only disturbed the sacrifice, but refused to furnish him with auxiliaries for his Asiatic expedition. There existed accordingly between the Thebans and Spartans a feeling of irritation, and both parties were quite aware that they hated each other cordially, although no acts of hostility were committed. "The Corinthians, too, had determined to rise against Sparta."

It is not quite clear, as to what was the first occasion of the outbreak of the Boeotian war; the ancients give various accounts of it. According to some, the Boeotians instigated the Locrians to levy the taxes in a district which was disputed between them and the Phocians, and if they should be refused, to compel the inhabitants by force to pay them. The Phocians, provoked at this, invaded Locris, whereupon the Boeotians, for the purpose of assisting the Locrians, invaded Phocis. This is the statement of those who favour the cause of Sparta. Others deny this course of events, and declare that the interference of the Boeotians arose from accidental circumstances, and not from design. But however this may be, the Spartans were much pleased with the pretext for a war against the Boeotians; and no one denies that Lysander stirred up the feelings of the Spartans against them.

A corps under Lysander was then sent across the Crissaean gulf (Olymp. 96, 2); he was there to assemble the Phocians and other neighbouring tribes, and invade Boeotia from the west. At the same time, another army under Pausanias, was to advance from the south across the Isthmus towards Plataeae. Pausanias commanded all the Peloponnesians, with the exception of the Corinthians, who refused to join him, and the Argives.

The Boeotians applied to the Athenians who lay then as prostrate and as helpless as they possibly could be. They had not been allowed to restore their navy, and possessed no more than twelve ships; Piraeeus lay quite open, and the long walls were demolished. Athens, therefore, might be surrounded on all sides, and all supplies from the sea might be cut off, without any prospect of compelling the besiegers, by succour from abroad, to raise the siege. But the Athenians, under the guidance of Thrasybulus, determined to forget, that, during the Peloponnesian war, the Thebans had been their bitterest enemies; they only remembered that the Thebans had sheltered their exiles, without thinking of their motives, and that the Spartans were their mortal foes. Thus they resolved to try their fortune, and to support every one who declared against Sparta: the Thebans, the king of Persia, all were their natural allies, until their independence was restored. In this manner, although the Athenians were extremely weak, a corps of Athenian hoplites, under Iphicrates, who was then only twenty-four years old, went to the assistance of Thebes. The Thebans and Boeotians were then on good terms.

Lysander came down from Phocis, took Orchomenos, and appeared before Haliartus with a large army, intending to lay siege to it. There the Boeotians and Athenians were encamped for the purpose of protecting the town.   Under these circumstances, Lysander ought to have waited until Pausanias, who was already on his march, arrived by way of Plataeae.   But there is an account, which seems to be true, that a letter sent by Lysander to Pausanias, advising him to hasten his march, did not reach its destination, but was intercepted.   Hence the Thebans and their allies, knowing that Pausanias would soon arrive, were the more inclined to risk a battle.   An engagement thus ensued, in which Lysander fell; and his death decided the defeat of his army, which sustained great loss and was obliged to retreat.   Two days afterwards, Pausanias arrived, and no longer found Lysander's army.   The ephors who were with him, now ordered him to attack the allies, but he, justly or unjustly, refused to obey them to his own ruin. A capital charge was raised against him at Sparta, because he had allowed the demos to be restored at Athens, and had neglected to destroy Athens; and also because he had now acted carelessly, having come too late, and refused to attack the enemy.   He seems to have acted with true Spartan sloth.

This was the first defeat sustained by the Spartans since the battle of the Arginusae, and on land the first since the loss of Pylos.   It made a powerful impression on their minds. They now sent orders to Agesilaus to appoint, in Asia, another commander, who was to continue the war there only on the defensive, and himself to return with his army to Europe, through Thrace, Macedonia, and Thessaly.   This he accomplished with great skill (Olymp. 96, 3).   In the neighbourhood of Coronea, the Boeotians wished to obstruct his passage, and opposed him, but were defeated.   The whole result of the engagement was, however, no more than that the road to Peloponnesus was now open for Agesilaus, although he could not return by the Isthmus, Corinth being hostile. He accordingly led his army through Phocis, and embarked in the Gulf of Crissa.   The victory yielded no other advantages.

About the same time, though somewhat earlier, another event had occurred of infinitely greater importance.   Agesilaus had learned, even on his march, that the Spartan fleet had been defeated near Cnidus.   Conon had employed the treasures of the king in forming an excellent fleet.   The Phoenician navy, from causes which we cannot explain, seems to have fallen into decay; but Conon restored it with great care, increased the fleet with Greek vessels, manned it with Greek sailors, and thus formed an armament with which, though it was not very great, he might still venture to oppose that of the Spartans.   It is owned by Plutarch himself, that the defeat of the Spartans was owing to Agesilaus.   Sparta still had a fleet of seventy sail, consisting of the contingents of cities, which were anything but cordially attached to her; but they nevertheless fought and did their duty; the contingents, moreover, were very well trained.   But Agesilaus had appointed Pisander, his wife's brother, commander of the fleet, contrary to the advice of all who knew him.   Pisander was a good man, but imprudent; he could only fight and stake his own life, but was utterly incapable of commanding.   Conon and Pharnabazus now appeared off Cnidus with their fleet of Phoenician and Greek vessels.   Pisander sailed out to meet them, and the battle was easily won by Conon; Pisander was completely defeated, and lost his life.   This memorable battle of Cnidus was fought Olymp. 96, 3.

The consequence was, that the allies of the Spartans, the Chians, Rhodians, and the towns on the main land, declared for Conon and the king of Persia.   Conon sailed among the Cyclades, everywhere expelled the harmosts and the Spartan decadarchies; he then first went to Corinth, which also was delighted at his success, and then sailed to the port of his native city.

LECTURE LX.

CONON (Olymp. 96, 4) had, with great skill and prudence, induced Pharnabazus to furnish money for the support of Athens, and brought with him considerable sums as Persian subsidies.   The same Persia which, ten years before, had given subsidies to the Spartans in order to break the power of Athens, now gave those subsidies to restore it!   But what could be done there, was, after all, but a very slight commencement of restoration, for Athens never recovered from the wounds of the Peloponnesian war.   Conon found the long walls and those of Piraeeus razed to the ground.   He now gave a large sum of money towards the restoration of the former ; and the Athenians, on their part, added whatever their activity and their good will enabled them, to promote the work with all vigour.   Other Greek nations also had their eyes now opened to the truth, that their freedom was secure only through the existence of Athens ; and even the Thebans sent workmen and money to restore the same walls, at the demolition of which, ten years before, they had triumphed. The work was executed with the greatest exertion and rapidity, in a manner suited to the wants of the moment ; afterwards it was completed and improved.   " The ancient fortifications were then not quite restored ; Conon rebuilt the demolished fortifications of Piraeeus on the sea-side only, and more was not needed, as the long walls were restored."[1]   When Sulla besieged Athens, the walls of Piraeeus must have been restored to their full ancient extent.   The long walls continued to exist even in the Macedonian period : they were destroyed by Antigonus Gonatas, and were never after rebuilt.

The Athenians now also restored their fleet with the same energy which they had displayed in the Peloponnesian war; it is inconceivable, how such a single city, after such immense losses of capital, and whole fleets and armies, could obtain the means of her recovery.   " She must evidently have been raised by commerce, but we do not know what kind of commerce it was that was so particularly drawn towards Athens; that which was carried on between Athens and the Euxine, provided the Athenians only with their necessaries, and could not enrich them."   It is probable that Conon supplied them with timber for building their fleet, and other needful things from his friend Evagoras, in Cyprus;   for otherwise the rapid formation of their fleet is unaccountable.

" Athens thus revived in the feeling of her independence. But here we may apply the passage of Nehemiah, in which it is said, that those who had seen the magnificence of the first Temple wept at the sight of the second.   They wept for joy, because they were again permitted to worship Jehovah in his

[1] " When Themistocles fortified Piraeeus on the land side, no one as yet thought of the long walls; but when the latter were added, the fortifications of Piraeeus were, to some extent, superfluous."—1826.

temple; and for sadness, when they compared it with the former temple.   Such also was the feeling of the Athenians at the sight of Piraeeus and the walls.   Every thing was changed at Athens, and sank down into lifeless learning; and lyric poetry disappeared everywhere."

The newly-built fleet was sent towards the coast of Ionia, where the towns were now just as anxious to remove the Spartan dominion, whose benefits they had experienced, as they had been before to cast off that of Athens.   Chios, which in the Peloponnesian war had in reality decided the fate of Athens, was now the first to emancipate itself from Sparta and join Athens; and the same thing happened everywhere on the continent of Asia, as well as in the islands.   Mitylene in Lesbos declared for the Athenians; while the other towns were in the hands of the Spartan party, which under its harmosts had used its power for the purpose of murdering or expelling the leading men of the opposite party.   Rhodes and Samos likewise returned to the Athenians, and Samos did so although its ancient inhabitants, the real supporters of the Athenians, had been expelled by the Spartans from the island.

We here see a very remarkable instance of a revolution, in which the fickleness of men displays itself most manifestly at Rhodes, which now declared in favour of Athens.   Another party afterwards gained the upper-hand, which overpowered the leaders of the Athenians.   There are times when men cling to fixed and distinct recollections; and there are others when everything ancient has become rotten, when men have no other support but the present, and when the circumstances of the moment decide everything.   When the former sentiment prevails, everything is positive: men, whether right or wrong, cling to definite forms, a definite order of things, a definite constitution, or a partiality for foreign nations.   But when these illusions are exhausted and worn out, the steadiness perishes by which those ancient prejudices were fostered, and whence they derived their real power; men are then independent of such feelings, and judge of things from their direct influence upon themselves; they are then in reality negative, have become old and wise enough not to be deceived about actual circumstances; they no longer feel attachments, but have antipathies, and these too are often not lasting.   Such was now the case with the allies of Athens.   That party among them which had formerly admired the Spartans as an extraordinary people, had now become intimately acquainted with them, and found that they were robbers and impostors and that they had themselves laboured under a delusion; wearied of the incessant robberies, they now regarded those as benefactors, who rescued them from their position. Hence the Athenians were again heartily welcomed by them. Had the Athenians possessed ample financial resources, and had they not been obliged to make great demands upon the efforts and purses of their allies, all would have been well; but Athens had become poor, had to make great efforts, and could not do so without the help of her allies. The Athenians accordingly again introduced the system of tribute, and demanded of the allies to serve in their armies; in addition to this, they established cleruchiae in the sense of the *coloniae civium Romanorum*, in some refractory places which they had taken by force. The tyranny of the Spartans was over; but the Rhodians and the others were now to pay money, exert themselves, and take the field. This was disagreeable to their effeminacy, and their egotism; and those who had shortly before exulted at having got rid of the Spartans, now quickly became tired of the Athenians; and if there had been a third party, they would have thrown themselves into its arms; but as it was, Rhodes and other cities again joined Sparta. Thus the whole was thrown into confusion: there were no longer any decisive parties opposed to one another, and a mutual want of confidence prevailed everywhere.

Under these circumstances, Thrasybulus (Olymp. 97, 2) appeared in Ionia with an Athenian squadron; he did the same thing which Alcibiades had done before: he proceeded to the Hellespont, made himself master, with the exception of Abydos, of all the places which had formely been subject to Athens, and again introduced the δεκατευτήριον, the toll of ten per cent. in the Bosporus for the benefit of Athens. It must be remarked in general, that the Athenians had everywhere to adopt means of providing themselves with money; and this necessity led their generals to many measures and undertakings, which on the whole were directly opposed to their policy.

It ought to have been their endeavour to keep up a favorable relation with the king of Persia, and to obtain subsidies from him; but in the midst of the war the Spartans contrived to insinuate themselves into the Persian court, and to prevent this. They represented to the king his own danger, saying that the Persians were fools if they supported the Athenians, who were most dangerous to them, since the Greeks could endanger Persia only by means of a fleet, and that by such a support they were forging arms against themselves. The Persians accordingly gave the Athenians nothing. But Evagoras, Conon's friend, still sent them support, though he was then not yet in open enmity with the king of Persia. He was king of nearly all Cyprus, but paid tribute to the great king, and an Oriental monarch is not very scrupulous in such matters, so long as they can be concealed.

The Persians were, in fact, already so hostile to the Athenians, that Conon (Olymp. 96, 4) was seized by the satrap Tithraustes, and thrown into prison. Although there is a statement, that he died in captivity, yet it is more probable that he escaped from prison to his friend Evagoras, and there died. His family was at Athens. Conon was one of the most excellent citizens that ancient history knows of; his conduct towards his country was not only thoroughly blameless, and in the highest degree disinterested, but so salutary and useful, as, perhaps, no other individual citizen has ever had it in his power to be. " We cannot blame him for serving the barbarians, for he served them only with his body, for the purpose of benefiting his country." He left behind a son, Timotheus, who, in his disposition, was worthy of his father, and who afterwards greatly distinguished himself. Thrasybulus, who had the unfortunate duty of collecting means from the Greek allies, and was obliged to sail with his fleet from place to place in order to raise the contributions, was slain during this odious business by the Aspendians, while landing in Pamphylia (Olymp. 97, 3). The history of Thrasybulus has not yet been satisfactorily made out, and the materials for it are very defective. Woe to him who pretends to write Greek history when we have Thucydides; but to write it from the point where he ends is a grateful task. This is a history which does not require researches into constitutions, but a knowledge of the world and of men. In this portion of Greek history, many laurels are yet to be gained, and many heads must be stripped of those which they already wear. Conon, for example, must be treated with still more respect than is usually done.

During this period, the Spartans were in constant negotiations with the Persians, for the purpose of restoring a peace that might suit their own purposes. Antalcidas negotiated twice; the first time without success, but the second time (Olymp. 98, 2), he was but too successful. "Artaxerxes abandoned the cause of Athens, and came forward in Greece as mediator: a triumph of the worst policy for Sparta."

In the mean time, the war in Greece continued; the so-called Corinthian war had broken out, which was, properly speaking, only a continuation of the former war, that had commenced with the expedition of the Phocians into Boeotia, and in which Lysander had fallen near Haliartus; the allied states were the same, but the scene of the war was transferred from Boeotia into the territory of Corinth. The ancient friends, Argos and Athens, were allied with Corinth and Boeotia; the Boeotians are named, but they stood under the supremacy of Thebes. The war was transferred to Corinth, because Boeotia had become free, and the Athenians and Boeotians exerted all their powers to close the Isthmus against the Spartans. The Argives were connected with Athens by friendship, but had yet another object in view.

For at Corinth a revolution had broken out, which had the singular effect, that Corinth united with Argos into one state, —one of those phenomena which commenced in the Peloponnesian war, and now decidedly shewed that the Greeks felt the want of uniting into larger states. "While the Spartans broke up the whole, in order to subdue them one by one, an instinctive feeling impelled those who were isolated to form unions, because in this manner alone independence could be secured." It was this feeling which led the Corinthians to unite themselves with the Argives into one state, so that both became Argives: τὴν Κόρινθον Ἄργος ἐποίησαν, and the peace of Antalcidas afterwards effected ὥστε μηκέτι Ἀργείαν τὴν Κόρινθον εἶναι. In what form this arrangement was made we are not told by our authorities; but it is probable that the Argives increased the number of their tribes, and that Corinth entered into the state with a definite number of tribes. To the same period also belongs the revolution in Elis, in which the Eleans admitted the ancient inhabitants, their former perioeci, to the franchise, and thus increased their tribes from three to twelve.[2] This revolution overcame the little municipal prejudices of those who found great happiness in their own separate existence, and those notions which counteracted the advantage of union in greater masses. Many circumstances are quite different at different times; those of Corinth, for example, had in earlier times been of such a nature, that it could exist by itself; but this was no longer the case; it was now obliged to have allies; and as it could no longer maintain itself alone, the best thing was to join Argos, just as it was wise on the part of the Eleans to grant the franchise to their perioeci. Let no one here assign to me a meaning which is not my own. In my last year's lectures, I have frankly expressed my opinions upon the state of our country.[3] If in great countries the federative constitution is of such a kind as not to be unjust towards the great states, and that the smaller ones can neither outvote the great, nor the great ones the smaller, and that further, fair justice cannot be violated by intrigues and factions in all its interests, that confederation is based on fair principles. In such a case, the smaller states are protected by justice and equity, and a closer union is not necessary. This sad necessity, however, shews itself when small states, which contribute least, and take a delight in insisting on their vote, acquire too great an influence. This is a bad state of things, which cannot but be followed by evil consequences. Among the Greeks there did not exist any common bond for the whole nation; when the dissolution commenced, there was no alternative but to unite in larger masses, as ought to have been done in Italy after the

[2] In 1825, Niebuhr placed this event expressly in Olymp. 96.

[3] The Lectures contained in this volume, from XLIV. onward, were delivered in the year 1830. Hence, Niebuhr here refers to the Lectures on the French Revolution delivered in the summer of 1829, and probably alludes to the concluding words, which, according to Niebuhr's own statements made in his letters, contained the most pressing exhortations to the Germans to maintain union among themselves. It was impossible to give those words complete in the published edition of those Lectures; but what he there said on the German confederacy, cannot be matter of doubt to any one acquainted with Niebuhr's sentiments. He regretted extremely, that the small states had the same vote as the larger ones, because thereby chance and intrigue were all powerful, and the smaller states had a preponderance, as soon as a second-rate state adopting an ambitious policy opposed the great powers, and rallied the little ones around itself.—ED.

dissolution of the empire. Afterwards, the movements in which the Arcadians attempted to form a state, the establishment of the Achaean league, and the whole political restoration of Greece at that time, shewed an instinctive desire to draw the smaller states together into greater masses. Those Corinthians who voted for the union with Argos were good patriots; but those who, clinging to a name, lamented that Corinth lost its sovereignty, and shared it with Argos, were idle dreamers. This is one of those cases, in which we must keep our own judgment independent of that of ignorant historians. Even Diodorus, bad as he is, and although he has no notion of all these circumstances, judges correctly, because he follows Ephorus.

This revolution at Corinth might have been followed by very advantageous consequences, if it had been carried through, and had produced lasting results. It is possible that an unsuitable constitution was drawn up, and that its form was not the most agreeable or most convenient; but if carried out it might have been of great importance for the whole of Peloponnesus, as well as for the separate states. It might have formed a beginning of what was subsequently effected for Peloponnesus by the Achaean league. Phlius and Mantinea, which had to suffer so fearfully at the hands of Sparta, ought likewise to have joined Argos. That city had this advantage, that every Greek, from reading the Homeric poems, knew it as the centre of Greece; but unfortunately it produced no great characters, and did not possess a constitution upon which anything great could be raised.

The innovations in tactics introduced by Iphicrates, which appeared in Greece about the same time, might likewise have been followed by important consequences, but produced no effect. He was one of those men who are destined at an early period of their life to engage in great actions, and who have not to discover the right way through many and unsuccessful experiments, but to whom things are clear from the first and at once; and whatever he clearly saw, he carried into execution. He was only in his twenty-fourth year when he became the author of a new system of tactics. His system was similar to one which was devised at the same time by a man in Italy, though the latter was on a larger scale. As in Greece, the combination of several states into larger unions began at that time to be felt as a necessity, out of which severe conflicts must ensue, so the Romans also were convinced that the ancient tactics of the phalanx could lead to nothing. The phalanx could be made to decide an engagement only by increasing its depth, and by lengthening the long spears still more, or else it was necessary to invent an entirely new system of tactics, in which individual training might be set against the power of the masses. The latter was done most successfully by the Romans about this time, perhaps somewhat later, according to the example of the Samnites; and they contrived in an admirable manner to give to the old phalanx more individuality. Something similar was now attempted by Iphicrates in the formation of the πελτασταί. These peltasts were light troops armed with swords. The phalanx was armed with spears and shorter swords, resembling the knives of the Albanese, which were at most one foot long, and had been used by the Greeks from the earliest times. Their form remained unchanged for the peltasts, but Iphicrates doubled their size. All the ancients, moreover, are unanimous in saying that he increased the length of the spears by one half. This however must not, as is usually done, be referred to the peltasts. The historians of that period are so utterly uncritical, and on the whole such unpractical men, that one merely copies such things from the other without insight, and without knowing what he is speaking about. In this manner the notion has also passed into the work of Cornelius Nepos; according to whom we ought to believe, that the peltasts received both longer swords and longer spears. But in the accounts of military operations, we find the peltasts armed with javelins (ἀκόντια); though it is impossible that that they should have carried at once spears and javelins. They were, moreover, very light skirmishers, who could disperse and easily assemble again; and they are mentioned by the ancients between the ψιλοὶ and ὁπλῖται. But it is nevertheless not erroneous to say, that Iphicrates increased the length of the spears by one half; only we must separate those statements which have been incorrectly combined. Iphicrates was thus, no doubt, the first to lengthen the not very long spears of the phalanx, an innovation which was afterwards carried much further by Philip, by introducing the σάρισσαι, whereby the hinder ranks were enabled act. When Arnold Winkelried broke through the ranks of the enemy, the spears were of the same length as the modern Greek lances. By this means the phalanx acquired much greater strength, for now the men stationed in the third and fourth ranks were also enabled to use the iron points of their spears with effect. This is a separate matter. But that was a different arrangement by which Iphicrates armed the peltasts, according to the Thracian fashion, with small light shields and javelins:—the Thracians had such light armed troops with light shields, whereas the ψιλοὶ had neither shields nor swords. Such light troops, every man of whom was trained separately in throwing the javelin and fighting with the sword, formed an important element in an army. This great advance of the military art, however, was applicable only to mercenaries, whom Iphicrates himself had enlisted, and whom he drilled both in peace and in war, since to them alone he could give the necessary training. The Athenians, however, and other citizens continued to serve as hoplites, and fought only in the phalanx; they formed a simple militia, and were accustomed to nothing else but to exert their strength; they learned to make evolutions and to attack, but otherwise they had nothing to do but to advance as a mass. When such a mass was checked, or fell into disorder, it was lost.

The peltasts, in later times, are no longer mentioned, but the Agrianians, under Philip and Alexander, were probably peltasts. I cannot convince myself that the ἄγημα of the Macedonians was the phalanx; the phalanx was the militia, and the real strength of the Macedonian army were peltasts.

The new tactics of Iphicrates were extremely successful in the Corinthian war; but the system was nevertheless not thoroughly developed, and, in point of fact, it produced nothing new in the mode of Greek warfare, nor had it those permanent consequences, which the changes probably introduced by Camillus effected in the military affairs of the Romans; who by this means advanced from one improvement to another until they reached the highest point of perfection. The Greeks continued their old system without saying wherefore.

The Corinthian war lasted a long time, and its course was indescribably tedious; it was conducted feebly, and in a petty spirit; and not a single occurrence is worth relating excepting the end, the peace of Antalcidas. " There are, properly speaking, only two great events which occurred during the war, namely, the taking of Lechaeum by the Spartans through treachery, and the cutting to pieces of a Spartan mora by the peltasts of Iphicrates."[4]

LECTURE LXI.

THE oligarchs at Corinth, who had been expelled in the revolution, had taken refuge among the Lacedaemonians, and opened Lechaeum to the Spartans, so that Corinth was cut off from the Crissaean gulf. A Spartan garrison occupied Lechaeum, while the principal corps of the Spartans was encamped at Sicyon; the Athenians, under Iphicrates, were at Corinth. When the garrison of Lechaeum was changed, and the morae stationed there made room for new ones (for, as the Roman legions were formed every year anew, so also fresh Lacedaemonian morae were sent into the field, and took the place of their predecessors), the former returned to Sicyon; and Iphicrates, seizing the opportunity, attacked the departing Lacedaemonians on their road with his peltasts, routed them, and almost destroyed one entire mora. This was a serious blow, but yet not to be compared with the blockade of their troops in Sphacteria, since only few real Spartans seem to have been among them. We have no distinct testimony as to the proportion in which the Spartans served in the morae, and no conjecture of any degree of probability has yet been advanced. My belief, in the meantime, is, that the Spartans were distributed in the morae according to a certain propor-

[4] " The Spartan infantry was divided into six morae (μόραι), which at different times had a different organisation and numbers. A mora in Polybius necessarily consisted of a very different number from that in Ephorus and the earlier writers, as the constitution of Sparta had already sunk. It is very possible that, as a Roman legion, though commonly consisting of 4,200 men, was sometimes more numerous, so also the morae may, under particular circumstances, have been increased, but the normal number seems at that time to have 500. These morae in the later writers are the same division which the more ancient ones call λόχοι; in the time of Xenophon, lochos already signifies something different."

tion; we may assert, without hesitation, that, after the Peloponnesian war, they were distributed among the morae, but it is not quite clear whether previously they served in a different manner; our accounts on this point are highly unsatisfactory. The destruction of the mora is, in our eyes, an event at which we cannot help smiling, when it is described as a matter of the highest importance; but it was one of those subjects to which the Attic rhetoricians always reverted, when they wished to praise Athens, and has furnished them with endless materials for declamation: it is perpetually mentioned, from the time of the author of Menexenus, who forgets that Socrates did not live to see it, down to the later rhetoricians, Aristides the sophist, and others of the same kind.

This war was to no one more injurious than to the Corinthians; the Athenians were not much injured by it, if we do not take into account some slight disturbances in their reviving commerce by petty acts of piracy. Attica was not ravaged, the war was carried on at a distance from its frontiers, and, as the husbandman in southern countries, if not oppressed by taxes and feudal relations, very easily recovers, the peasantry of Attica very quickly rose again to comparative prosperity; it was easy for them to build a house, and to restore their establishments. The Athenians would not so soon have thought of terminating the war, had not at the moment the peace of Antalcidas brought about a complete dissolution of the confederacy, as it had hitherto existed (Olymp. 98, 2). We must, however, conceive the Athenians as placed on an equality with the others, the Boeotians, Corinthians, and Argives, and without any kind of privilege in the deliberations and in the confederacy.

While the war was carried on in this manner, without any great events, the Spartans, through Antalcidas, concluded with the king of Persia the well-known unfortunate peace. In it they renounced, in the name of the Greeks, all claims to independence on the part of the cities on the coasts of Asia Minor, including Clazomenae; they handed them over as unconditional property to the Persians, and declared that those towns had no further claims to their protection, as they had already said before to Tissaphernes and Cyrus; the supremacy of Cyprus was likewise fully conceded to the Persians, and Evagoras, who aimed at independence, was sacrificed to the Persian king.   Painful as this peace was to the feelings of the Greeks, who were obliged to leave the dominion over their countrymen to barbarians, yet the hypocrisy of the Spartans, who, by this peace, allowed the Persians to interfere in the internal affairs of Greece, was worse.

For it was stipulated, that all Greek cities should be αὐτό-νομοι, and that all municipal towns should receive full freedom and independence; the Athenians alone were allowed to remain masters of Lemnos, Imbros, and Scyros, " in order to draw them into the peace.   These islands had been taken from them by Lysander, but the Athenians had recovered them, and many citizens had property there."   Boeotia was to be broken up; all the districts and the individual towns were, at the utmost, to be allowed to form a loose confederacy; but they were not to form one state, with one supreme government, but, at best, to be in a condition like that of modern Switzerland.   The consequence was, that all confederacies were broken up; and the great king, moreover, declared that he would assist the Spartans in carrying the terms of the peace into effect, if any Greek cities should refuse to comply with this beneficial law.

This was announced to the Greeks by the Spartans, and no one, of course, could resist.   " At Corinth, the faction of vanity, which felt hurt that their city should form only a part of Argos, decided to accept the terms."   The Athenians not being then in a position to carry on war against the king of Persia and against Sparta, allowed themselves to be enticed to give their consent, by the promise that they should retain Lemnos, Imbros, and Scyros.   Thus they submitted to the peace, and nearly all the Greek states did the same.   It was concluded in Olymp. 98, 2, the nineteenth year after the battle of Aegospotami.

" In this manner all Greece was to be free; but Persia and Sparta had guaranteed the peace; and this circumstance produced the same consequences as those which in Germany followed the peace of Westphalia, for which Sweden and France became securities.   This was the point from which the Spartans were enabled to continue their intrigues and pretensions."

It now became evident what profound hypocrites the

Spartans had been. Although nearly all the other states were broken up, the Spartans continued to insist upon their claims to the supremacy, and placed themselves at the head of a confederacy, in whose name they alone acted. They no longer convened the assemblies of the allies, but did everything by themselves, and acted in a perfectly arbitrary manner. It was, perhaps, this very absence of all forms, which they brought forward as an argument to justify their mode of acting; for although the allies were nominally independent, they were not so in reality.

In every town, the Spartans restored their partisans, who had been expelled in former times; these men alone were now invested with power, and the Spartans aided them in taking revenge upon their fellow-citizens. " They again sent out harmosts, and even garrisons, ostensibly for the purpose of seeing that the terms of the peace were carried into effect, and of protecting the smaller towns against the more powerful ones. In this manner, they extended their dominion over all Greece, and carried it to the highest pitch. Deceived and intimidated, Greece was for several years in a state of stupor, and knew not what to do. Had the Spartans shown only a little moderation in the exercise of their power, its end would not have come so soon; but they were deaf to every advice of prudence; they would not listen to what was required by circumstances, and they rushed into their own destruction."

The tendency by which the weak states subordinated themselves to, and formed part, of the more powerful ones, showed itself also in Arcadia. By συνοικισμὸς, that is, by uniting five little towns into one, the Mantineans had become strong, and had been rising greatly for some time. Their city had become powerful in Arcadia. But unfortunately jealousy was at work there: Tegea, which from early times had been the first city in Arcadia, was ill-disposed towards Mantinea; and although the Tegeatans had hitherto been always hostile to the Lacedaemonians, they now were led by jealousy to stir up Sparta against the Mantineans, thinking it better to be the slaves of the Spartans than the friends of the Mantineans. There is an excellent pamphlet written about the beginning of the Thirty Years' war, I believe, by the Bohemian, Theobald. The style and typography support my conjecture. It contains a collection of wise saws; and, as far as I know, I possess the only copy that is extant. Among its maxims there is one to the effect, that it is better to clean a countryman's shoes, than to kiss the feet of a foreigner.[1] This truth ought to have been borne in mind by the Tegeatans. Such was the state of Greece; and this is the cause of its downfall. The later history of Greece is extremely painful; but it is at the same time very instructive to those who wish to know the course of the history of the world and acquire real knowledge, and not to draw up a mere speculative philosophy of history.

A Spartan army now appeared before Mantinea: the servile Xenophon, even on a former occasion, remarked that Mantinea had secretly rejoiced at the destruction of the Spartan mora; and this, although he himself speaks only of a secret joy, is to his mind a sufficient justification for destroying Mantinea by force of arms. The Spartans declared that there were too many ill-disposed persons among the Mantineans, that they were always disturbing the peace, and that for the tranquillity of Greece, and for their own good, it would be better if their state were broken up, and the city, which was only a gathering-place of rebellious people, were destroyed. The Mantineans manfully defended themselves; but the Spartans succeeded in leading the river against the walls, which were not well built, and therefore easily destroyed by the water. The Mantineans, then, were obliged to surrender (Olymp. 98, 3). The Spartans distributed the inhabitants of the city among five villages, and sent the opponents of the oligarchy into exile; the city itself was destroyed.

It is here, if any where, that we see a characteristic example of the servile manner in which Xenophon, in his partiality to Sparta, wrote his history. Afterwards, says he, the Mantineans themselves saw, that the Spartans had been right in doing as they did, and that they had really acted with the best intentions; for after that time the Mantineans, tilled their fields in peace, and abstained from all foolish undertakings.

This base act was followed throughout Greece by universal detestation and hatred of the Spartans; and there followed

[1] The title of this pamphlet is " Wahrhaffte neue Zeitungen von unter-schiedlichen Orten und Landen d. i. Die alte Wahrheit mit einem neuen Titul. Gedruckt in der Parnassischen Druckerei," 1620, 4to.—Ed.

another undertaking at a great distance from home, which was very imprudent on the part of the Spartans. It involved them in enterprises which they were not sure of being able to carry out without a fleet; and this undertaking cannot be accounted for in any other way, than by supposing that Amyntas of Macedonia offered money to the powers that were to decide the question.

Macedonia had risen gradually, and even under Amyntas II. it reached a considerable height, until it became involved in an unfortunate war with the Illyrians. During that war, he sought the assistance of Olynthus; when he had lost everything, he was extremely liberal with a portion of his kingdom; just like the people who imagined they saw the day of the last judgment approaching and gave away everything, he gave to the Olynthians an extensive tract of country, on condition that they should come to his assistance. But when the war took a more favourable turn for him, he repented of his generosity, like those who saw that in the year 1000 the day of judgment had not come, and had given away everything; he now refused to give to the Olynthians what he had promised them. Hence fresh hostilities and a war arose between him and Olynthus, which was more powerful than he. That city had arisen out of the union of the small Chalcidian and Bottiaean towns, between Potidaea and the Thermaean gulf, into one city and forming a sympolity ($\sigma \nu \mu \pi o \lambda \iota \tau \epsilon \iota a$): this had been done by the advice, and with the support of Perdiccas. During the Peloponnesian war, the city was not yet of any great importance, but it very soon acquired power, and afterwards it was equal to any of the large cities in Greece, either because it had a large number of inhabitants (it is called a $\pi \delta \lambda \iota s$ $\mu \nu \rho \iota a \nu \delta \rho o s$), or because it was the centre of the other towns. Olynthus had now become a new power, and was beyond the connection with Greece proper.

Against this city Amyntas (Olymp. 99, 2) invoked the assistance of the Spartans, and they sent an army to his support. The war lasted four years; great losses were sustained on both sides, the brother of Agesilaus fell, and the Spartans were often seriously beaten. But in the end the power of Sparta and Macedonia necessarily gained the upper-hand, for all the rest of Greece was stupified and silent, and was unable move. The Olynthians were accordingly obliged to join the Spartan league (Olymp. 101, 1); but this was not followed by any consequences. This war is, on the whole, important only because it led to the treacherous seizure of the Cadmea, which gave quite a different turn to the affairs of Greece.

The Spartans (Olymp. 99, 3) sent fresh troops, either to relieve or strengthen the army at Olynthus, under the command of a certain Phoebidas. His road to Macedonia lay through Boeotia and Thessaly. When he arrived on his march in the neighbourhood of Thebes, he halted, either because he had come to Thebes with the intention of serving his country by a breach of peace, or, as is commonly said, because Archias and Leontiadas, the leaders of the Spartan party at Thebes (the grandfather of the latter had betrayed Greece to the Persians, and his father had invaded Plataeae in time of peace), had made overtures to him. No man can say with certainty which of the two was the case; but the fact itself is the main thing. We may, however, ask, why did he halt at Thebes if he did not want anything? I will readily admit that he had not formed the plan, for this is to me a matter of no consequence: in regard to forms of laws, we can guess the truth with certainty from internal evidence, but not so with regard to particular occurrences, where the improbable is often true. But however this may be, Phoebidas united with Leontiadas and Archias, and in conjunction with them he surprised the city and took possession of the citadel.

Sparta had even before broken up the Boeotian state and confined Thebes to itself, whereas before it had stood to Boeotia in the same relation in which Rome at one time stood to Latium. It is uncertain whether there were eleven or twelve boeotarchs, but Thebes appointed five or six. Leontiadas, it is said, opened the gates, and Phoebidas overawed the Thebans, as, in the beginning of the Peninsular war, the French officers did near Barcelona and Figueras. While they were playing at ball near Mont Juick, all on a sudden, a signal being given, they ran and disarmed the Spanish sentinels; so, in like manner, and with equal treachery, the Spartans slowly advanced towards the posts and overpowered them; a part of the troops advanced to the strongly-fortified Cadmea. As no one suspected their design, as no one gave any orders, and as the traitors were invested with most of the principal offices, nothing could be done ; the Cadmea was surrendered without resistance, and the Spartans entered.

Ismenias and Leontiadas were the first men in Thebes; they were opposed to each other, and Ismenias resisted the treacherous proceedings. He was the same man who, in the time of the Thirty Tyrants, had caused the decree to be passed whereby protection was afforded to the exiled Athenians, and who had provided the returning patriots, Thrasybulus among others, with arms. The Spartans had never forgotten this, and, although more than twenty years had now elapsed, Leontiadas, as soon as the Spartans were in the city and the citadel, declared that, by virtue of his office of polemarchus, he charged his colleague with high treason, and would bring him to trial. Ismenias accordingly was sent to Sparta, and there condemned to death. We find none but such traits as these in the character of the Spartans, and they must be known in order to judge of that people; they must also be our guide in estimating and judging of the comedy about Sparta. Phoebidas, too, was, for the sake of appearances, put upon his trial, because he had presumed to commit such an act without orders, and he, again for the sake of appearances, was sentenced to pay a fine. Old Agesilaus, who spoke for him, said, that they must examine as to whether it was useful to the republic, and that in war sometimes things must be done without premeditation. That Phoebidas was condemned only for the sake of form, may be seen from the fact, that he was afterwards again entrusted with a military command, and was neither made ἄτιμος nor exiled; for those who were *bona fide* condemned, were ἄτιμοι, but this case had been a mere farce. The Spartan garrison also remained for three years in the Cadmea, as if it had been taken by fair means. Under its protection, the supreme power at Thebes was in the hands of a party, which was not indeed so bloody as the Thirty had once been at Athens, but morally it was still more abject, as on the whole the Boeotians were a much more ignoble people than the Athenians. A great number of the best Thebans were at that time sent into exile, and others were thrown into prison; many also, no doubt, were executed, as a matter of course, and, therefore, no importance was attached to this fact; but, after all, that period was not as terrible for Thebes as that of the Thirty Tyrants had been for Athens.

In consequence of the unfortunate divisions generally prevailing in the Greek cities, disturbances about the same time also broke out at Phlius; part of the citizens were expelled, and the condition of the city resembled that of the Italian cities in the middle ages; our German cities furnish fewer examples of the kind. The exiles belonging to the oligarchical party applied to Sparta, and Agesilaus led the whole Spartan army against the place. He demanded of the Phliasians to surrender to him, and if they had done so he would, perhaps, have treated them more gently; but they applied to the government of Sparta. He and his friends now contrived to induce the ephors and the council to declare, that they would not interfere in the matter, and would leave it entirely to him; and hence the Phliasians were informed that Agesilaus had full power to decide upon their fate. He now took revenge for the slight offered to him, and pressed the city to the utmost, until, compelled by famine, it was obliged to surrender at discretion (Olymp. 100, 1). When Phlius was thus taken, he not only brought back the exiles; but mark how he settled the affairs of the city! He appointed a council of fifty, selected from the exiles, to whom he added fifty of those who had remained in the city, and who, of course, all belonged to the same party. Now, what was the commission of that council? Xenophon tells us, with a smile worthy of a cannibal, that they were to decide "which of those who had been in the city were to live and which were to die." Such is the language of a disciple of Socrates! It is the language of an old juryman of the revolutionary tribunal, picturing to himself the time of Robespierre as the happy period when he and his friends might send to the guillotine whomsoever they pleased. If it were only for this single feature, the history of Xenophon would be not only a wretched but a branded production; but it is not the only feature, though perhaps the worst.

We now come to the period of the greatness of Thebes, and to the two great men through whom it attained that greatness. We here find, side by side, two men living at the same time, who are both deserving of great admiration, though both were not of the same greatness; the younger and less gifted cheerfully joins the elder and greater without envy and jealousy, as is always the case in great and noble souls; and, as we see, in the correspondence of Schiller and Goethe. Pelopidas felt no envy of Epaminondas, who was by far the greater man of the two.

If we trace the course of the history of Greece, it is impossible to rejoice at the turn of affairs, which placed the supremacy of Greece in the hands of the Boeotians, for they unquestionably deserved their reputation for rudeness and want of cultivation; they were, on the whole, inaccessible to noble ideas, and cannot in the remotest degree be compared to the Athenians. But their cause against the Spartans was most just; it is one of those points, which in reality it is hardly necessary to touch upon, and where yet the victory of the just cause is followed by terrible consequences. Nothing could have been more just than if Pisa had revolted against Florence; but it would have been deplorable if Florence had been overpowered. There are circumstances in which there is undeniable injustice, and in which it must nevertheless be owned, that, if this injustice is punished, the misery becomes still greater: injustice is sometimes better than its punishment. This was the case with Thebes. Who would not rejoice at Thebes recovering her freedom and Sparta being punished? He who does not rejoice must be a man of perverse feeling; but every one must at the same time wish that matters had rested there, and that the second peace before the battle of Leuctra had been firmly established and lasting. This would have been fortunate for Greece, for it was then advancing towards a suitable condition. "The ancient idea, that no state but Athens or Sparta should have the supremacy in Greece, had been from early times the *arcanum imperii*, as Tacitus says; and when the thought arose, that another people might exercise the same supremacy, Greece completely decayed. When a third state stepped in, no one could accustom himself to the idea of regarding it as the head, and the Thebans themselves did not know how to conduct themselves in their position. Misfortune thus came on irresistibly."

This opinion regarding the Thebans must not prevent us from acknowledging that Epaminondas truly and fully deserves the praise which antiquity bestows upon him; and it would be the greatest injustice not to admit this.   For it is quite possible that, among an ignoble people, there may rise up a man who stands higher than his contemporaries in a far nobler state: this is the work of providence.

Epaminondas is distinguished among his fellow citizens first of all by his thoroughly developed character as a Greek, for while the Thebans were vulgar and rude, he was refined like a Greek of the best kind. With this mental culture he combined the greatest talent as a general, the warmest patriotism, the purest disinterestedness, and the most faithful feeling of friendship; he was perfectly free from all vanity and the other weaknesses, which so often lead a great man into sad errors. His character as a general he shewed at Leuctra and at Mantinea, and he displayed his statesmanship in the attempt to unite the Arcadians in one state, though he did not quite succeed, and in the restoration of the Messenians, in which he was perfectly successful. All antiquity is in reality unanimous about Epaminondas; the judgment of Ephorus may be seen from Diodorus and Polybius, and the later Greeks express the same opinions; what the Romans thought of him, may be seen from Cicero.   Xenophon is the only one who endeavours to diminish his fame, for throughout his history he ignores him; he never mentions him in his accounts of the greatest exploits of the Thebans, and that in the childish belief, as if through this act of ignoring him he could politically annihilate him.[2] This is one feature among many, which sufficiently shows the unworthy sentiments of Xenophon, and his utter inability to appreciate pure greatness and virtue. The same man who makes the unjust Agesilaus his Achilles, does not even once mention the great, pure, and altogether excellent man!   Such sentiments sometimes manifest themselves in national prejudices; but this is, thank God, not the case with us Germans, even though we may have sustained serious injuries at the hands of such a man as, for example, Carnot.

[2] It is well known, however, that this ignoring refers only to the first actions of Epaminondas.—ED.

LECTURE LXII.

IT is impossible for two men to present more striking diffe-rences than Pelopidas and Epaminondas; and yet they lived in perfect harmony with each other.   Epaminondas was poor, and Pelopidas wealthy and of a great family, which is not known to have been the case with Epaminondas.   In gentle-ness of disposition, Pelopidas cannot be compared with Epaminondas, nor was he so thoroughly and absolutely just; for he did not shrink from acts of violence, when he thought them necessary.   Pelopidas, moreover, was not the man to change the fate of the world or of his country, in the manner in which this was done by Epaminondas.   But although he was unequal to his friend, yet he is deserving of the highest esteem and praise.   He was a distinguished general, though not one of the first order; but among those of the second rank he is certainly one of the most eminent.   He was more-over quite as disinterested and quite as good a citizen as Epaminondas, and what more particularly reflects honour upon him, is the brotherly, nay filial attachment, with which he clung to Epaminondas, and his cheerful submission to his friend, whom he acknowledged to be greater than himself. The co-operation of these two great men produced an immense change in the affairs of Thebes.

The tyranny of the polemarchs appointed by the Spartans—the office of boeotarch had ceased to exist since the Spartans had broken up the Boeotian state, and the Theban praetors were now called polemarchs—has already been described. A Spartan garrison of fifteen hundred men was in the Cadmea. During this state of things, Epaminondas was living quietly at Thebes, for he had not been expelled.   But Pelopidas was among the exiles; and, with his friends in misfortune, he undertook the deliverance of Thebes under circumstances as difficult as those under which Thrasybulus had delivered Athens.

"The exiles had been received by the Athenians, who now repaid Thebes for what she had done to their fellow-citizens under Thrasybulus; and when the Spartans demanded their

surrender, the Athenians, though standing quite alone, answered, that, from early times, it had been their custom to
protect suppliants, even though they should thereby bring
suffering upon themselves." It now happened fortunately for
the exiles, that Phyllidas, one of the notaries of the polemarchs, was favourable to their cause. He was an honorable
and well-meaning man, for it generally happens that, among
the persons employed by a bad party, there are honorable men,
who have been drawn into their position often by timidity,
sometimes by the necessity of providing bread for themselves
and their families, and sometimes also by a caprice of fortune.
When Jerome was king of Westphalia, the Germans filling
the highest offices were, for the most part, thoroughly bad
men; there were among them, at the best, only a few honest
men who did not stain their characters by base actions; but
in the inferior offices — for example, those connected with the
levying of taxes, and with the administration of justice—the
greater number of the *employés* were good men, who performed their duties conscientiously, and with as much delicacy
towards their fellow-citizens as possible. Such also was the
case in France during the reign of terror; and I had an
excellent friend, who was *chef de division* under Carnot, and
made his reports to Robespierre, but was otherwise a man of
unimpeachable character. We must conceive the same to
have been the case at Thebes, and Phyllidas, whom the
polemarchs had taken into their service, seems to have been a
perfectly honourable man. Having gone to Athens on public
business, he made many important revelations to the exiles;
he offered them his assistance, and met them with the proposal to make use of his situation to restore them to their
country.

The day of a festival (Olymp. 100, 2) was chosen, on which
Archias and Philip, two of the polemarchs of Thebes, gave a
banquet; the young conspirators were concealed in the house
of Charon, a respectable citizen. From this point, the accounts
differ from one another; but the following is the more probable, because it is the less theatrical. According to a strange
Greek custom, a number of *commissantes*, intoxicated with
wine, ran from one banquet to another, as in Xenophon's
Symposium; and, in the guise of such young men, the conspirators, in a riotous procession, as κωμασταὶ, rushed into the

hall where the polemarchs were assembled; there they drew
their hidden swords, and cut down the polemarchs. This
account seems to be infinitely more probable than that in
Plutarch and Xenophon, according to which they came disguised as abandoned women. But however this may be, they
found the polemarchs intoxicated, and murdered them. The
plan had been nearly discovered, as a relation of the polemarch
Archias, the hierophant Archias of Athens, had reported the
matter to him; but the polemarch had put away the letter
without reading it, as Caesar is said to have done, and had
said, that important business must be left for ordinary days.
Meantime other conspirators, guided by Pelopidas, entered
the house of Leontiadas, the most powerful of the polemarchs,
and, after a severe struggle, succeeded in killing him. The
conspirators then liberated the prisoners, and spread the joyous
tidings throughout the city.

All the people exulted at their deliverance from the tyrants,
and took up arms, although the citadel was in the centre
of the city. As circumstances then were, it was quite a
reasonable supposition that the garrison of the citadel would
not be able to crush them; but if there had existed artillery,
which might have been used against the city, the undertaking
of the Thebans would have been impossible.

Epaminondas took no part in this enterprise; even the
most distant semblance of assassination seems to have been
opposed to his nature. He was engaged in devising measures
for stirring up the people, and for putting the city in a state
of defence, in case the harmosts should make a sally. But
here, too, the sloth of the Spartans was the salvation of their
opponents: the Spartan garrison did nothing; the streets
were quickly barricaded, and the Spartans, blockaded in the
Cadmea, suffered from want of provisions, because they had
not thought of so sudden a change of circumstances, and had
therefore neglected to supply themselves. The other exiles
now returned; a part of the emigrants had assembled in the
Thriasian plain in Attica, in order to advance on the first
signal. An embassy from Thebes went to Athens with a
request for assistance, and, notwithstanding the great danger,
the strategus Demophon, having summoned all who were
capable of bearing arms, led a band of Athenians to Thebes.

The garrison of the Cadmea was suffering severely from

famine.   When the news reached Sparta, an expedition was
prepared, but could not arrive in time, for the garrison had
been obliged to surrender before the succour reached Thebes.
The Spartan commanders, foreseeing their fate, had refused to
surrender, but the other Peloponnesians and allies would not
hold out, and capitulated for themselves; and after their
departure, the harmosts, with the small number of real
Spartans who remained behind, were incapable of maintaining
themselves any longer; they too were accordingly forced to
surrender, and departed.   Here again the Spartans displayed
their hypocrisy: they had, as I have already remarked, punished Phoebidas for the sake of appearances, and he was now
again stationed as harmost at Thespiae; but the commanders
who now evacuated the Cadmea were put upon their trial. Two
were executed, and the third, whose life was spared, was sent
into exile, leaving his property behind.

.   This was a fearful blow; but Sparta, still unwilling to
abandon her scheme, determined to carry it out.   Agesilaus
was to lead an army into Boeotia, and to try to recover the
city; but his mind was already impaired.

.   The undertaking of the Athenian strategus, Demophon, was
an irregularity, for he had made the expedition in the midst
of peace, without a decree of the people; nay, perhaps even
without a resolution of the senate.   As the Persian king was
still closely allied with Sparta, and as no other city revolted,
the Athenians allowing themselves to be intimidated by the
great danger of a war with Sparta, listened to the accusation
against those, who on their own responsibility had undertaken
the expedition to Thebes, and condemned them.   The guilty
escaped by flight, at least most of them.   Athens had become
pusillanimous, as is often the case in times of excitement, when
people first show courage and then timidity, as we ourselves
have seen in 1809, and to some extent also in 1813.   When
the power of the oppressors seems to be firmly established,
and when the attempts of the first excitement are not crowned
with success, they afterwards appear culpable, because all has
been risked by them.   For these reasons, Athens would
probably have continued the peace with Sparta, and no blood
would have been shed, had not Sphodrias, a Spartan harmost
in the part of Boeotia still faithful to Sparta, in the hope
of being supported, attempted to make himself master of

Piraeeus; he imagined that he might surprise the place, as the Athenians, trusting to the peace, guarded their gates carelessly; he no doubt thought this to be an undertaking as glorious as that of Phoebidas against the Cadmea had been. The undertaking would perhaps have succeeded had he not come from too great a distance; but as it was, a report had reached Athens, so that the gates could be closed in time, and the plan was foiled. This undertaking, in which the Spartans had advanced as far as Piraeeus, now determined the Athenians to ally themselves with the Thebans against Sparta. This gave to the war quite a different turn, and the undertaking was followed by such unfortunate consequences for Sparta, that Xenophon thinks Sphodrias to have been led into it by the cunning and bribes of the Thebans. But how are we then to account for the fact that Sphodrias was acquitted at his trial? It is curious to see how senselessly and detestably Xenophon treats this matter, by stating that the Spartan commander was bribed to take from the Athenians their harbour and their fortress, while the Athenians, trusting to the peace, suspected nothing. But the fact that a Spartan commander could be bribed is indulgently passed over by him. When afterwards this general was acquitted, as he himself admits, through the mediation of Agesilaus, Xenophon again has this excuse, that the son of Agesilaus affectionately entreated his father because the son of Sphodrias was his bosom friend. This evil deed turned out for the Spartans as they deserved.

Agesilaus now (Olymp. 100, 3) invaded Boeotia. The Athenians sent thither a detachment under Chabrias, and in the ensuing engagements with Agesilaus, the troops of Chabrias overawed the Spartans by their excellent discipline, and compelled Agesilaus to retreat. The Spartans, however, retained some strong points in Boeotia, especially Thespiae; and until the peace before the battle of Leuctra, they invaded Boeotia every year with their Peloponnesian allies. Thebes, which had protected its territory in a manner unaccountable to us, suffered scarcely anything, and the Peloponnesians only wore themselves out. Meantime the Boeotians, under Epaminondas and Pelopidas developed their strength more and more. Epaminondas remained boeotarch almost without interruption, and Pelopidas was elected year after year. But the war was protracted.

Under these circumstances, the Athenians again built a fleet, and sent ships to the coast of Asia; the islands of Chios, Rhodes, Samos, Mitylene, and even the Hellespont, again joined the Athenians. The expedition was commanded by Timotheus, a son of Conon, a general who is particularly renowned for his good luck, but must at the same time have had great skill in winning over the minds of others, and bringing every one to be on his side. His good luck is particularly celebrated; and hence an artist painted him sleeping, with a net into which the cities slipped of their own accord. The Spartans also made preparations and got together a small fleet from their allies, with which they blockaded Athens.

How low Athens had sunk, may be seen from the smallness of the preparations they then made. In the time of Demosthenes its population and financial resources must have been immensely increased, and it also displayed quite a different material strength; but how this had grown we are not informed. When Chabrias was sent out to besiege Naxos, the resources of Athens must evidently have been very small, for they could not get together more than eighty galleys, and some of these were not even Athenian ones. Pollis, the Spartan admiral, followed him to relieve the town, and this led to the celebrated naval engagement near Naxos, the first which the Athenians fought since the Peloponnesian war, and they gained it. The result is differently stated. In Diodorus and Ephorus the number of ships taken by Chabrias is smaller than in Demosthenes (against Leptines) who mentions forty-nine captured galleys. I am not fond of harmonising different statements; in the mythical ages I reject this method altogether, but in historical times a harmony may often be found. My belief is, that the forty-nine galleys mentioned by Demosthenes comprise all the ships which Chabrias captured during the entire campaign, while Diodorus is speaking only of the ships taken in the battle itself. Xenophon does not describe this battle at all, and mentions the engagement of Naxos only *en passant* as one in which Pollis died as a brave soldier.

This victory caused the general desertion of the Spartan

allies to Athens; and the Athenians now showed great prudence, such as could scarcely have been expected from the many-headed monster of a democracy; for they offered to these cities a share in their deliberation, as had been the case in the time of Aristides, and they summoned all their allies to a general diet at Athens. This synedrium was joined also by the Thebans, and for a time there existed a lively connection and good understanding between Athens and Thebes. But in this synedrium of seventy towns, the mistake was committed, that even the smallest places, such as Paros, obtained equal rights and an equal vote with Athens. No confederation could be permanent on such terms, and this disproportion necessarily soon led to the opposite extreme, the dependence of these places upon Athens; and we accordingly afterwards find, that they lost their independence. At first too much was conceded to them, and at last too little was left them. They ought to have remained free, but their share in the government ought to have been determined by what they were able to do for the confederacy.

The Athenians at that time shewed their desire to be fair in all they did, and perhaps even went too far; for it is unfair to concede to a small state the same rights as to a large one. Callistratus, who was then the real leader of the Athenian republic, was a very worthy man; Cephalus also was much respected, but not as much as the former. It was a particularly favourable circumstance, that the strategi at that period enjoyed the full confidence of the people, and took a very prominent part in public affairs. I need only remind you of such men as Thrasybulus, Chabrias, Iphicrates, and Timotheus. " This is a beautiful period in Athenian history, though it had no really great men of the first order." The Athenians showed their desire to act fairly, more particularly by their spontaneously withdrawing their cleruchiae from the places which had formerly been subject to them, and to which they had sent citizens as cleruchi ; they now even passed a decree that no Athenian should possess land out of Attica. This measure greatly restored the confidence of the allies, and the Athenians retained it for a time. But owing to the common weakness of human nature, it was soon destroyed, and in some cases by extremely trifling circumstances.

Euboea (Olymp. 101, 1) also joined the general confederacy.

Timotheus undertook with his fleet a celebrated expedition round Peloponnesus to the islands of Cephallene and Zacynthus, during which he ravaged the coast of Laconia. The Athenians at that time advanced as far as Corcyra, and although they did not exactly rule everywhere, yet they exercised an influence.

But both parties were soon exhausted by the war, and under these circumstances, Athens applied to the court of Persia, soliciting its mediation. After many negotiations, a decision came (Olymp. 101, 2) in the form of a proposal for a peace (you may read the detail in Diodorus), which was an exposition of the peace of Antalcidas, and in which it was settled, that all towns should be really and truly αὐτόνομοι, and that accordingly the Spartans should renounce all claims to the supremacy, and that all the garrisons should be withdrawn. This peace stood to that of Antalcidas nearly in the same relation in which the executionary measures stood to the peace of Westphalia. These proposals were partly carried into effect, but only very imperfectly. The Spartan garrisons were withdrawn from many places, and Corinth, Sicyon, and Phlius became free; but in other towns the garrisons remained. If the Spartans had honestly wished to carry the terms of the peace into effect, tranquillity might have been restored in Greece, and they would have been spared their humiliation. But they demanded, that Thebes should be separated from the rest of Boeotia, and that the Boeotian towns should be made independent of Thebes. Thebes resisted this demand, and the Boeotian towns themselves were divided. By far the greater number, however, were satisfied with their alliance with Thebes, and remained faithful to her; and a few only were ambitious to maintain their little independence. This is the reason why the Thebans did not sign the peace, although all the rest of Greece had agreed to it. This period after the peace is a very sad one in Greek history, although freedom was restored.

LECTURE LXIII.

THE condition of Greece at that time shows, that during the long convulsions, all the old sentiments and associations had been lost, and that Greece had now come to a point at which most of the states could not exist without a protector. It required that fearful training which the Greeks had to submit to for nearly a whole century, before they became capable of living under a really free federal constitution like that of the Achaean league: a firm union into one whole, when the isolated existence of the separate states had become a matter of impossibility. The state of Greece was indescribably sad, and the most atrocious scenes occurred everywhere. The Spartans had forced their form of government upon others, and could maintain it only by armed force. Now when the Spartans had withdrawn their troops, the exiles everywhere returned, and reactions of the wildest kind ensued. And such reactions took place, even in towns such as Argos which had not been dependent upon Sparta. The returning exiles took vengeance, and in some cases they were again expelled; blood flowed everywhere in torrents, and the greatness of the misfortunes of that period can hardly be estimated. According to the account which mentions the smallest number, no less than 1200 persons are said to have perished during the frightful period of scytalism at Argos; other accounts, which are deserving of credit, mention 1500. As if there had been a general madness, the most illustrious citizens, on the mere denunciation of wretched demagogues, were seized upon as guilty of high treason and conspiracy against the state, and some were even subjected to the torture. When the latter confessed that they were guilty of conspiracy, not only they themselves were put to death, but a great number of others, whom they had denounced during the torture, were, on the ground of a mere suspicion, arrested and executed. Suspicion was everywhere raging. The massacre was as great as during the most fearful period of the French revolution; and Argos suffered as much as Lyons or any other town can have suffered in the time of the revolution. When in the end the informers who had commenced the movement, wished to check it, they too were considered as guilty accomplices; they were tried and put to death.   Such was the case in a great many other cities of Greece; but Athens formed an exception.

If we were to ask the detractors of Athens, at what time murder was there indulged in, so long as the lawful constitution was in force, it would be difficult for them to answer; but such murders were perpetrated in other places, which were not more democratical than Athens.   The cause of this lay in the mild and humane character of the Athenian people, and in their high state of education. Although the Athenians cannot be called a reading people (every person in Greece, and more especially at Athens, however, could read and write, which is at present the case in very few countries[1]), yet they were constantly passing through a course of mental training in their theatre, which then still existed in all its lofty greatness and excellence; and to my mind, that uninterrupted intercourse with the muses sufficiently accounts for their mild disposition. The enjoyment of the theatre, poetry and music, in the sense of the ancients, was the highest delight of the Athenians of all ranks; the great performances, either of new pieces brought out at the great festivals, or of the old splendid dramas of the great masters, furnished them the highest enjoyments, in which even the humblest Athenian partook.   The refinement of their feelings thus acquired was the cause of their mild and humane conduct.

Intellectual culture had spread more and more among many Greek tribes.   The remark of Polybius (iv. 20), that in his time the Cynaethians were the rudest and most uncivilised among the Arcadians, because they did not practise music, must not be understood to apply so much to music in our sense of the term, as to their not maintaining any intellectual intercourse with other minds through the occupation with poetry; for with the Greeks a poem was more than a melody. The nations who took no part in this life of poetry, were barbarians, even though they spoke Greek. We cannot wonder that at Sparta everything was rude and barbarous, for the stiff and obstinate clinging to the old forms excluded all elasticity of thought.   If man must always think and do the same

---

[1] " Even now the number of the people in the Morea that are able to read and write is incredibly great."

things, he ceases in reality to think and to act; and when such a stagnation of his thinking faculties has taken place, he seeks all his happiness in brutal pleasures. Hence harshness and cruelty, and delight in brutal amusements became prevalent at Sparta. But even people like the Argives had scarcely a faint shadow of the life of Athenians; and we cannot therefore be surprised at finding that they fell into a state of brutality to which the history of Athens presents nothing analogous.

The condition of Greece exhibited a state of hopelessness resembling that at present existing in Spanish America, where there is nothing good, nothing cheering, nothing hopeful. Such a barbarous state of things was then prevalent in Greece; its only safety would have been, if the Athenians could have obtained the supremacy of the whole nation; but under the circumstances this was impossible. This was the condition of Greece during the period of three years preceding the outbreak of the war of Leuctra.

The peace had not yet lasted long when Athens and Sparta again came into collision in the poor island of Corcyra. The Spartans soon regretted having evacuated the towns, and were seeking (Olymp. 101, $\frac{4}{3}$) fresh opportunities of extending their dominion and of recovering possession of those towns. It so happened that disturbances broke out in Corcyra, and availing themselves of the opportunity, they sent out a squadron to take possession of the island. Corcyra was allied with Athens, and the ruling party applied to the Athenians for assistance. The latter sent an expedition under Timotheus, Chabrias, Callistratus, and Iphicrates, which did its duty, and liberated Corcyra. The difficulty which Athens felt in equipping this fleet, and the weakness which Corcyra then showed, are characteristic of the great exhaustion. The miseries of the time are quite manifest during the siege of Corcyra; if we compare it with the Corcyra of Thucydides, it appears like Magdeburg before and after the thirty years' war: this was a punishment for the crimes and horrors which had been perpetrated there. Corcyra then had only seven galleys, four of them were taken, and three had been destroyed or thrown upon the coast; and that same state at the beginning of the Peloponnesian war had had 120 galleys. This shows how much Greece had worn herself out, and into what misery she had fallen. She was, on the whole, in a condition similar to that of Germany after the thirty years' war, when the latter country, at the utmost, had but one-fifth of the population it had had at the beginning of the war. Würtemberg, which before had had a population of half a million, was reduced after the battle of Nördlingen to 46,000: such had been the havoc made by the leaguers; thousands had been strangled.

The Athenians, as I said before, relieved Corcyra, and this expedition gave rise to a fresh war between Athens and Sparta. But Athens had at the same time fallen out with Thebes. Plataeae, which had been restored in consequence of the peace of Antalcidas, and had been in the relation of isopolity with Athens ever since the time of the Pisistratids, refused to join Boeotia. The Thebans now overpowered the weak little community; all its inhabitants were expelled and fled to Athens, where they were received and obtained the franchise according to the law of their ancestors. Athens therefore became exasperated against Thebes, and was ready to become reconciled to Sparta. Under these circumstances (Olymp. 102, ½) a peace—the third effected through the mediation of Persia—was concluded. Greece had, through her own sins, fallen into the necessity of looking upon the king of the barbarians as her deliverer: the greatest of all humilitions, but unavoidable. This peace was concluded immediately before the battle of Leuctra, either at the end of the first year of Olymp. 102, or at the beginning of the second. It was a complete and still more explicit confirmation of the earlier treaties, and reinforced the obligation of withdrawing the garrisons from all places, and to give them their independence.

The Spartans might now have enjoyed peace; but they were still incorrigible. When pressed by great difficulties, they always signed the treaties; but when they were out of danger, and the treaties had to be carried into effect, they felt uneasy; they could never prevail upon themselves to exercise self-control, or to give up anything. The Thebans seemed to be ready to accede to the peace; but the Spartans still insisted upon the necessity of Thebes separating from Boeotia, although they had not undertaken the guarantee of the peace; in the peace of Antalcidas they had done so, but this was not the case now. King Cleombrotus was stationed with an army in Phocis; that army they ought now to have disbanded, and this was the opinion of a few sensible men ; but the majority thought that it should be employed in compelling the Thebans to set the Boeotians free. The ruling party at Sparta now hoped to be able to compel Thebes, which was forsaken by all the other Greeks, without any difficulty, especially as some of the Boeotian towns, such as Orchomenos, sided with Sparta. Orchomenos was still dreaming of her ancient splendour and glory, and of the mythical times when Thebes was separated from Boeotia, when Orchomenos was the most powerful city, and Thebes paid tribute to her. These recollections were cherished by the Orchomenians with great and fond partiality; just as if Amalfi wished at present to re-establish the claims of its ancient greatness.

Cleombrotus, therefore, full of hope, entered Boeotia, after the peace had been signed, demanding that Boeotia should carry the terms of the peace into effect, and renounce Thebes, and that every town should assert its independence. The other Boeotian towns, with the exception of Orchomenos and Thespiae, were reasonable enough to see that their dependence on Thebes, with extensive rights, was far better than independence; and Thebes was supported by far the greater number of the Boeotians. The Thebans, joined by their Boeotian allies, now took the field. I pass over the smaller engagements, and merely add, that only twenty days elapsed between the conclusion of the peace and the battle of Leuctra. If this account is correct, the battle, considering the circumstances of the case, was greatly accelerated; I believe that the twenty days is too short an interval.

Fortunately for Boeotia, Epaminondas was boeotarch at this time (Olymp. 102, 2). Pelopidas, likewise boeotarch, commanded the ἱερὸς λόχος, the *elite* of the citizens. If Epaminondas had been an ordinary man, he would have turned back again almost immediately after he had marched out ; for the omens, or οἰωνοὶ, to which the ancients attached so much importance, strangely accumulated to such a degree, that they might have shaken a firm mind which was not altogether proof against superstition. When the army passed out of the gate, for example, they met a herald bringing back a deserter, and uttering ominous words, " You ought not to be led out of the city." Then a high wind ·rose, carrying off ribbons with which they had adorned themselves for the sacrifice, and these ribbons clung round a pillar on a tomb. Hence an indescribable consternation arose, but Epaminondas recited the magnificent line from the Iliad —

εἷς οἰωνὸς ἄριστος ἀμύνεσθαι περὶ πάτρης !

and boldly marched out.   It is a pity that we have not got a life of Epaminondas by Plutarch; with his Boeotian patriotism, he would certainly have produced a pleasing biography; but how, with his superstitious notions, he would have managed it, I do not know. Every one of the Thebans knew, that they should have to fight a battle against the Spartans, and with heavy hearts they set out against an enemy who had never yet been conquered in the field. But the confidence of Epaminondas was unshaken. Although himself armed against all superstition, he willingly allowed his soldiers to fortify themselves with their belief in supernatural signs, and did not oppose the spreading of the rumour among his troops, that the armour of Heracles had disappeared from his temple at Thebes, the birthplace of the god, and that consequently the god himself had taken up his arms to fight for his fellow citizens. He made his preparations in full confidence, and did what was best under the circumstances. He foresaw that the Spartans would have the belief in their favour that their tactics were superior; for it was the general opinion that their tactics of deep masses were unconquerable, just as it was believed of the drilling regulations of Frederic II. after the seven years' war, when all the states ordered their troops to be trained according to it, imagining that thereby they could gain battles as he had done. Epaminondas, moreover, had to overcome the pride of the Spartans. Now, in order to meet their tactics and break their pride, he made an excellent disposition, " employing the system of defeating masses by still greater masses." The Spartans were drawn up together with their allies; Epaminondas advanced in an oblique line, sending forward the left wing and keeping back the right; but he then ordered the left wing gradually to withdraw to the left, and thus formed on that wing an immense mass. With this he now made a most vigorous attack upon the right wing of the enemy, where the Spartans themselves were stationed. An ordinary general would have done the contrary, directing his force against the part from which no such powerful resistance was to be expected. Pelopidas conducted the attack, and ordered the mass to advance with immense rapidity. I do not know whether the statement is true, that the Thebans advanced fifty men deep. We have only the testimony of Xenophon, but I see no reason for denying it. His troops must have been excellently trained, for notwithstanding the dense mass, they advanced with an alacrity as if they had been light troops, just as at present troops advance in an attack with the bayonet, and not according to the fashion of pha-langites, who otherwise advanced with deliberate solemnity. The Spartans made a skilful move: in order not to be out-flanked, they turned to the right, intending to throw their cavalry upon the right wing of the Boeotians. But the Boeotians made the attack with such precision and quickness, that being beforehand, they routed the Lacedaemonians and Spartans. There Cleombrotus fell, and the Spartans were as decidedly beaten as they well could be. The army did not indeed disperse, but it was absolutely impossible to find any pretext for saying, that they had been victorious at any one point, a matter in which the Greeks were otherwise extremely inventive. " It requires the partiality of a Xenophon, to leave it undecided as to whether the Spartans were defeated."

After the battle, they appear to have remained together for a time, but there was no one among them able to undertake the command. Meantime, as a report had reached Sparta, that the Boeotians offered resistance, another Spartan army, under Archidamus, a son of Agesilaus, had marched across the Isthmus, and was now approaching, but found the Spartans already defeated. All he could do was to collect the remains of the defeated army and to return with them. They seem to have effected their retreat under the protection of a truce.

The only auxiliaries of the Thebans in the battle of Leuctra, had been the Thessalian troops of prince Jason of Pherae: one of the phenomena of an age, when the old order of things has disappeared, and new institutions have been formed.

If we believe Diodorus, the battle of Leuctra was the direct punishment for perjury; for Cleombrotus, it is said, had con-cluded a truce with the Thebans, but on the arrival of reinforcements from Peloponnesus, he broke it. One of the narratives must be untrue, either his or that of Xenophon; if the reinforcements under Archidamus arrived before the

battle, Xenophon's account must necessarily be given up.   I
believe that Cleombrotus may have had the peculiar misfortune,
which happens to many a one who has been unsuccessful; all
that is bad and disgraceful is attributed to such a man, and it is,
I think, quite unfair, after his misfortune, to charge him with
having broken a truce.   If there was an interval of only twenty
days between the peace and the battle of Leuctra, it seems to me
impossible, that in that time a second army should have arrived
from Sparta, at least it is improbable.   What makes me still
more inclined to disbelieve the account of Diodorus, is, that if
Archidamus had been present at the battle, it could not have
been said, that after the battle, the Spartan army was without
a commander.   I believe, therefore, that Diodorus too eagerly
caught up an account which throws the blame upon the
Spartans: it was not invented by himself, but either by Ephorus
or by Callisthenes.

   The loss of the Spartans in the battle is very differently
stated.   According to one account, it amounted to 4,000 men,
which would include, besides the Lacedaemonians and Spartans,
all the other allies; others mention only 1000 slain, which
number would comprise the Lacedaemonians only ;   others
again estimate their number at 1700; but this last number is
erroneous, as has been correctly observed by Schneider in a
note on Xenophon,[2] and arose from a hasty glance at the
numbers written in the characters of the Greek alphabet. We
may take it for granted, that not less than 1000 Lacedaemonians fell in the battle ; but whether this number also
comprised the Spartans or not, is a question which cannot be
answered at all.   But it is a fact, that the number of the
Spartans was so extremely small, that the strength of the
Spartan citizens as a body was completely paralysed by the
loss of this battle.   At one time there had been 9000 citizens,
subsequently they are said to have amounted to 8000, but at
this time there cannot have been 1000 real citizens, and at a still
later time there were only 700.   At Leuctra several hundreds
of them fell.   The ancient Spartan citizens were certainly not
more numerous than the *nobili* of Venice.   They now had to
feel the consequences of their wretched selfish policy, which
had been so jealous in granting the franchise to the perioeci,
as to exclude a great many excellent men as unfit and

[2] *Hellen.* vi. 4, § 15.

unworthy, and had cut them off from every prospect of obtaining it.

All Greece was startled at the news of this victory; it seemed impossible that Sparta should have been beaten in the field. The Spartans themselves were quite dejected. Their allies turned their backs upon them, and in a moment all the states of Peloponnesus, which had hitherto followed their standards, threw up their connection with them, and declared themselves independent; the Phocians, Locrians, and other allies beyond the Isthmus, immediately concluded a peace and alliance with the Boeotians. Not eighteen months passed away, perhaps it was even in the very winter after the battle of Leuctra (the years of the Olympiads began with the new moon after the summer soltice), when the Boeotians invaded Peloponnesus. The Spartans were panic struck and retreated. The Boeotians announced themselves as the protectors of liberty, and there can be no doubt that the personal character and the eminent qualities of Epaminondas everywhere excited great confidence, while the national character of the Thebans would certainly have called forth the opposite feeling.

The Athenians kept at a distance, nay, they saw the greatness of the Thebans with uneasiness and alarm; but they also had another feeling, which is expressed in the sentiment, that Greece should not be allowed to lose one of its eyes. Athens was accustomed to see in Sparta a constant and natural opponent, but one who was honourable and worthy of her. And Sparta was now on the point of falling, for no man could expect that, left to itself, it would be able to stand against the attacks of the Argives, Arcadians, etc., the city itself was not even protected by walls. Under these circumstances the Spartans resolved to send an embassy to Athens to ask for support; and the Athenians forgot all they had suffered at the hands of the petitioners. They resolved to act with all vigour in order to save Sparta, and sent an army under Iphicrates to its assistance, to prevent the destruction of the city.

Meantime Epaminondas, invited by the Argives and Arcadians, had entered Peloponnesus (Olymp. 102, 3), without meeting with any resistance. He was accompanied by the Phocians and Locrians. His progress was not impeded anywhere; almost all the towns threw their gates open to him and openly joined him; "in Arcadia he was universally received

as a deliverer," and in reality he was joined by, all the Peloponnesians, except the Achaeans, and his army was increased
by them.   This army, including the allies, amounting to
70,000 men, entered Laconia at once by four different roads.
The Spartans were unable at any point to oppose an army to
the enemy; and where they attempted to protect the passes,
they were overpowered with little exertion.   The columns
thus united near Sparta, and the open city was attacked,
stormed and defended.   The distress was so great, that the
helots were called upon to fight, freedom being promised to
all those who should take up arms.   The helots had terrible
recollections; thousands did indeed come forward, but as soon
as they had received arms, a great many of them deserted to
the enemy.   " A part of the perioeci also revolted, such as
those of Sellasia and Carya, the Sciritae, who had been the
flower of the Spartan army; and the country round Sparta
was in a state of insurrection."   This is the moment when
Agesilaus distinguished himself as a brave man, for it was he
that defended and saved Sparta.   Epaminondas was in a
difficult situation: in the midst of winter he had to provide
for an immense army in the heart of the enemy's country.
The winter in Laconia is very severe, mount Taygetus is
covered every winter with snow, and there his army was
stationed in the open air.   Being thus pressed by the winter
and want of provisions, the army was obliged to retreat, after
having fearfully ravaged the territory round the city and
advanced as far as the sea coast.

But Epaminondas employed his stay in those parts as a great
man: he proclaimed the restoration of Messenia.   He fortified
the town of Messene, and called upon the Messenians scattered
in all parts of the world to return to their country, the safety
of which he guaranteed to them.   All the helots and perioeci
who had deserted to the Thebans, received settlements along
with the Messenians, and they united into one state around the
city of Messene.   In this manner the new Messenian nation
was composed of people of all kinds, among whom there was
comparatively only a small number of descendants of the ancient
Messenians.   This restoration is an imperishable monument to
Epaminondas.   The nation he thus newly created acquired
such consistency, that it was enabled to maintain itself even
after his departure.   The perioeci of the neighbouring towns

which had revolted from Sparta, were likewise added to
Messenia, and in this manner there arose an essentially democratic people by the side of the oligarchic Spartans, and became
the more formidable by setting free, not only the districts
of the Spartans, but even their own serfs.

LECTURE LXIV.

THE fortifications of Pylos in the Peloponnesian war had been
a small prelude to this. Messenia was at first only a very little
state, but increased more and more: " one town of the perioeci
after another, as Methone and Asine" (see Scylax) joined them,
and Messene again became what it had been of old, and as we
see it marked in our maps. " The Spartans afterwards succeeded in reconquering several of the towns of the perioeci in
Laconia proper, but they were unable to recover the west."

In the restoration of Messene, Epaminondas obeyed the dictates of prudence and of his own noble heart; and he could not
have acted otherwise even if he had foreseen the consequences.
It must be observed, that this is again one of those cases in
which the accomplishment of justice was not followed by happy
results. The restoration of Messene produced, at a later period
of Greek history, terrible consequences. The Messenians being,
by their peculiar situation, the implacable enemies of Sparta,
were obliged to seek support against her; and they preferred
doing so at the greatest distance, which made them the humble
servants of Macedonia, and the perpetual enemies and traitors
of Greece. There was no people so devoted body and soul
to king Philip, as the Messenians. The death of Philopoemen
is an example of the mischief which Messenia created in Greece,
an ineffaceable brand on the name of Messenia. Things which
every honest man must desire, are in the end often followed by
the saddest consequences.

When Messenia was restoring herself, a new creative spirit,
fostered by Lycomedes (or Lycophron) of Mantinea, began to
stir the Arcadians also (Olymp. 102, 3). Diodorus calls him
a Tegeatan, but this is a mere slip of the pen; we cannot

VOL. II.　　　　　　　R

suppose that the blunder arose with the copyists; but the author himself probably confounded the name. This Lycomedes, in concert with Epaminondas, formed the plan of uniting the Arcadians into one nation. For Mantinea this was a sacrifice. The plan is but imperfectly known, but can be made intelligible. A great city was to be built in Arcadia, a μεγάλη πόλις: the form Megalopolis does not occur till the time of the Romans and the later Greeks; the very names show the prosaic character of the age. This city was to be the centre of all Arcadia, and was to stand to the country in the same relation as Athens did to Attica, and all Arcadia was to form a commonalty (μύριοι) of 10,000 country people. They were not all to live at Megalopolis, but those of them who should each time happen to be present there for the purpose of voting, were to constitute the sovereign popular assembly. This idea was quite suited to the wants of the time; Diodorus and modern writers do not quite understand it. The plan was little more than half executed; and the real object was not attained. The city of Megalopolis was actually built; and in order to have a great city on the very borders of Laconia, the inhabitants of forty smaller places " of the Maenalians and Parrhasians" were compelled to settle there. The μύριοι also were formed; and the constitution was for a time in force. But to unite all Arcadia into one political community, was impracticable. The Tegeatans immediately opposed the scheme, and deranged the alliance among those tribes; the old divided state of the country continued. It must, however, be observed, that even before this the Tegeatans had been connected with Sparta by friendship, and remained so for a time; but afterwards the case was reversed, and for a while the Spartans were on terms of friendship with Megalopolis. After this, however, they were always hostile against each other, until Cleomenes destroyed Megalopolis. In this manner, the plan was scarcely half realised. The college of the μύριοι disappears soon afterwards, and the μεγάλη πόλις became only an Arcadian town like many others.

Not one of the eight years from the battle of Leuctra, from Olymp. 102, 2, until Olymp. 104, 2, passed away without acts of hostility. The feud was always continued, though nothing decisive was effected. Athens was indeed on terms of friendship with Sparta, but without being really at war with Thebes; the mutual boundaries must have been secured by a kind of neutrality. The Spartans recognised the Athenians as the chief maritime power ; the supremacy of Athens over the islands of the Aegean became again established, and was not disputed. The cities on the coast of Asia Minor are no longer spoken of, as they were then permanently under the dominion of Persia.

The most remarkable among the expeditions which Epaminondas undertook in the meantime, was a campaign against Peloponnesus (Olymp. 102, 4). The Athenians and Spartans had recovered Corinth and several other towns; the Thebans, moreover, had fallen out with the other Peloponnesians; and when the partisans of the Thebans in Arcadia called in their aid, and Epaminondas wanted to make another attack upon Sparta, he could not pass the Isthmus without great danger. But in order to get into Peloponnesus, the Thebans were obliged to pass the Isthmus, as the Athenian ships of war prevented their going by sea. The Spartans were encamped near Corinth, and so also was Chabrias with light-armed Athenian troops; the allies had fortified the Isthmus with lines. Some geographers have imagined, that there existed long walls between Corinth and Cenchreae, as between Athens and Piraeeus; but this is incorrect, for such walls existed only between Corinth and Lechaeum. Between Corinth and Cenchreae there never were any other than temporary lines. These lines were now attacked by Epaminondas, and he broke through them; he not only repelled the Lacedaemonians who defended them, but would even have made himself master of Corinth, had not Chabrias at the right moment thrown himself into it, garrisoned the walls and gates, and frustrated an attempt to betray the city. For Corinth was torn to pieces by factions, which had existed for the last thirty years. Epaminondas then took possession of several towns in Peloponnesus; and afterwards (Olymp. 103, $\frac{2}{3}$) he made yet another successful expedition into Peloponnesus. " A peace was then (Olymp. 103, 3) concluded with the Peloponnesians; but Sparta took no part in it, because she first wished to subdue the Messenians, and continued the war, although she had not the strength necessary for it."

The influence which Epaminondas exercised upon his cruel

and blood-thirsty fellow citizens, and by which he prevented
them from destroying Orchomenos, is still more glorious than
his great exploits: it was he alone 'that inspired them with a
sense of honour. But he was not always in office, and was
sometimes absent; once (Olymp. 103, 1) when he was engaged
in an expedition against Pherae, the Thebans carried out this
design: they took Orchomenos, massacred all the men, and
sold the women and children. No base act was ever committed
when he was in power.

The expedition on which Epaminondas was then absent, was
directed against Alexander, tyrant of Pherae. The name
Thessaly came into use for the ancient Aemonia proper, comprising the towns along the hills in Thessaly, at the time when
it was conquered by the Thesprotians. Barbarous oligarchs
established themselves in the country, and the old inhabitants
became serfs. After the Thesprotian conquest, ancient Aemonia
(now Thessaly, which was nothing else but a very wide-spread
Pelasgian name,) was for a time under common kings, and
formed one nation. But even before our history begins, it
was divided among several cities, in each of which certain
dynasties ruled over the city and its territory. This is the
designation of an oligarchy in which a single family is in
possession of the sovereignty and of all the offices. Pharsalus
was thus governed by the Scopadae, and Larissa by the
Aleuadae, a very numerous family which stood to the citizens
of Larissa in the same relation, in which the body of Laris-
saeans stood to the *penestae* of the country. Thessaly was a
completely barbarous country, and quite estranged from Greek
culture and literature: upon this point the Greeks have but
one opinion, and even its language does not seem to have
been genuine Greek. The Thessalian inscriptions are indeed
written in Greek, but they belong to a later period. It cannot
indeed be questioned, that the Thessalians adopted the Greek
language; but that their original language was Pelasgian and
could scarcely be called Greek, may be seen from a passage of
Dicaearchus, who mentions that even in the Macedonian period
subsequent to Alexander, the question was raised, whether
Thessaly was actually a Greek country.[1] The individual cities
were perfectly independent of one another; and every trace of
unity had disappeared. Larissa, Pherae, Pharsalus, and Crannon,

[1] " Apollo, for example, was there called 'Aπλοῦς."

were as foreign to each other as the Arcadian towns were at the time when the union of the ἔθνος in Arcadia was broken up. The only unity of the ἔθνος consisted in isopolity, that is, if a person moved from one city to another, he enjoyed the rights of a member of the commonalty, was regarded as a *popularis*, and possessed those civil rights, which were otherwise inseparable from the franchise.   The history of these Thessalian cities is involved in utter obscurity; and it is only on particular occasions that they appear in history, as in the Peloponnesian war, when Thucydides speaks of the δυναστεῖαι.

It was before this great shock[2] that Jason, a man of great eminence and of a noble race, rose at Pherae, the ancient city of Admetus and Alcestis. It was not difficult for him, during the confusion, to usurp supreme power, of which he made a just and fair use; and the people were satisfied with his government.   But he also aimed at subduing the rest of Thessaly, and in this he succeeded from city to city; for the people everywhere were so tired of the despotism and the anarchy of the dynasties, that they regarded such a dictatorship as a blessing.   A general Thessalian diet, which probably existed at all times, though only for religious purposes, made him the sovereign of the whole country with the title of Tagus. Τάγος is an ancient Greek word, signifying the kingly dignity, exclusive of its hereditary character, and refers especially to the command in war.   In ancient times, it does not seem to have been very unusual for the Thessalians to elect a Tagus, or dictator for the whole of the country.   Jason did not long survive the establishment of his government, being murdered soon after.   He was succeeded by a brother, who was perhaps not innocent of his death; he, at least, is known to have caused the murder of another brother, whose death was avenged by a nephew; this nephew again was murdered, whereupon the dignity passed into the hands of Alexander of Pherae, a brother or nephew of Jason. He may be said to have stepped into the place of Jason, though his dominion was not as extensive.   It had been the endeavour of Jason to gain for Thessaly the supremacy in Greece; and if he had lived longer, he would have succeeded; " but, Alexander was not prudent enough to develop such a delicate power."   The assistance of the Thebans against this Alexander was invoked

---

[2] This probably alludes to the battle of Leuctra.—ED.

by the Heracleans and the inhabitants of the country about the Malian gulf, whom he oppressed. The Thebans sent succour twice; the first time (Olymp. 102, 4, and 103, 1) without any success, but the second time (Olymp. 103, 4) they were very successful. But they had to pay dearly for their victory, for immediately after it, when Pelopidas led them back, he lost his life in a victorious engagement with the peltasts who followed him; and in him Epaminondas lost half his strength. The battle of Mantinea would perhaps have been much more decisively won, if Pelopidas had been alive, and the fruits of the battle would certainly not have perished with Epaminondas.

Meantime, the war with Sparta was conducted languidly on both sides. Among the great ideas of Epaminondas there is one which was, perhaps, a little fantastic, although it might have been carried out successfully. He roused among his countrymen the thought of claiming the supremacy by sea as well as by land. He actually drew Euboea away from its connexion with Athens, built a few galleys, and went himself with some ships across to the Ionian islands (Olymp. 104, 1), which were induced, at least for a time, to recognise the supremacy of Thebes;—the supremacy of a state without a navy may have been more agreeable to them than that of a great maritime power.

" But now the war blazed forth again in Peloponnesus. Division prevailed everywhere; the Arcadians and Eleans were quarrelling about the wretched Triphylia, a quarrel which commences with the beginning of our positive history, and continues down to the Macedonian and Roman periods. The Arcadians themselves were split up into parties, and these" internal divisions of the Arcadians led to the expedition into Peloponnesus, in which the battle of Mantinea was fought (Olymp. 104, 2).

The Mantineans and Tegeatans, who were always hostile to each other, were now more so than ever; and this time the Mantineans, from hatred of Tegea, sought to form an alliance with the Spartans, formerly their bitter enemies, who had dispersed them in villages. " The other Arcadians, however, united with the Messenians and Argives, called in the aid of the Thebans." Two armies were now formed in the interior of Peloponnesus. Epaminondas came with a Boeotian force to the assistance of the Tegeatans, and was joined by the

Sicyonians, a portion of the Arcadians, the Argives, and Messenians. He was opposed by the Mantineans, Eleans, a part of the Achaeans, the Athenians, and Spartans. In this campaign Epaminondas was deserted by his good fortune; even the very first undertaking showed that it had forsaken him. Formerly he had been favoured by fortune, although the most brilliant success was always owing to his own wisdom and character. Several marches he undertook were thwarted by unfavourable circumstances; he failed more particularly in one quick march, in which his object was, to take Sparta by surprise, while the Spartan troops were stationed near Mantinea. His plan was betrayed; the Spartan commander had time to send home a messenger and give information of the danger which was threatening the city, so that there was time for making the necessary preparations. When, therefore, Epaminondas arrived at sun-rise, he found all parts of the city guarded, his whole scheme betrayed, and learned that the Spartan army was approaching. He was repelled, and was obliged to depart without having effected anything. His taking vengeance by laying waste the country was a mere trifle. He set out in the hope of reaching Mantinea before the Spartans should have returned thither. But this plan was again betrayed; he was detained on his march, and the Spartans were already in their camp when he arrived with his worn-out troops. " Meantime, the Athenians also had arrived at Mantinea, and were united with the Spartans. Epaminondas, however, had a far more numerous army, and the Spartans must have been forced to accept the battle."

The battle of Mantinea may justly be regarded as the greatest that was ever fought by Greeks against Greeks; but it is at the same time one of those great battles which produced a most insignificant effect: no battle ever left matters so completely in the same state in which they had been before, as this battle of Mantinea. The Spartans faced the Boeotians, and the Athenians the Arcadian auxiliaries and Eleans; the cavalry was stationed on the wings, that of the Athenians facing that of the Thebans, which was reinforced by an immense number of skirmishers (ψιλοί). The Athenian cavalry was unable to maintain its ground against them; after heroic and glorious exertions, it was entirely defeated, and would have been annihilated, had not succour arrived. On the other wing the cavalry of

the allies was victorious.   On the wing occupied by the
Athenian infantry, its opponents were overpowered; the
Thebans and Boeotians, on the other hand, broke through
the lines of the Spartan infantry, and defeated it with their
tactics of greater masses.   But in this struggle Epaminondas
fell; and all that his heroism could effect was, that, after his
fall, the contest was continued as if he were still cheering his
men on, and that the ground already gained was maintained.
After this, no more regular commands were given, and the
battle on both sides was only a vigorous butchering.   The
Thebans could justly call themselves the conquerors, as they
maintained the ground on which they had advanced, and as
they had driven the Spartans so far back, and their cavalry
had beaten that of the Athenians.   On the right wing, on the
other hand, their cavalry was defeated, and so also had been
their left wing; but their loss was not as great as that of the
Spartans.   At the moment of his death, Epaminondas, seeing
that his two sub-commanders had fallen, advised his fellow-
citizens to make peace.   After his death, an arrangement was
made, that both parties should deliver up the dead; each
party buried its own, and thereby acknowledged the battle to
have been half won and half lost.   Both armies retreated and
dispersed.

After this battle (Olymp. 104, $\frac{2}{3}$) a general peace was concluded among the Greeks.   It seems that Epaminondas' last
words were as much taken to heart by his fellow-citizens as
those of Fra Paolo, in his dying hour, about the revolution of
the Venetians.   The peace was concluded after transactions of
which we know nothing.   From this time, peace was established between the Thebans, Athenians, and the other Greeks:
Sparta alone, with strange obstinacy, refused to sign it,
because Messene had signed it—an obstinacy like that of
the Spaniards, who refused to recognise the States in America.
In point of fact, Messene was generally recognised as a
state, but the Spartans could not make up their minds openly
to confess it.

The Archidamus,[3] a declamation of the rhetorician Isocrates,
refers to these circumstances; it is a remarkable instance of

─────────────
[3] In the Lectures of 1826, Niebuhr placed the Archidamus in the time of the
separate peace between the northern Peloponnesians and Thebes, Olymp. 103, 3.
—ED.

THE ARCHIDAMUS OF ISOCRATES.

the perverseness with which a rhetorician, a *homo umbratilis*, regards such an obstinate denial of a reality as something great. This is a view of matters which we find in many men; men of mediocrity, and a little warmth and liveliness, regard the ignoring of what really exists as something grand, as if thereby it actually ceased to exist. It is a foolish belief, that Isocrates wrote this oration with a view to its being read in the Spartan gerusia by Archidamus, the heir of Agesilaus; the whole oration is nothing but a declamation of the closet, and mere trash, without any further object. This perverseness is peculiar to the whole character of Isocrates, who had as poor a head as can well be imagined. It is quite inconceivable how such a man can have acquired so great a reputation, his whole skill consisting in making words and rounding periods which are thoroughly empty. His Areopagiticus, for example, in which he calls upon the Athenians, to restore the good old times, is quite silly; it is nothing else but the everlasting lamentation, O would that the good times of old might return! but he never makes a proposal, and we do not hear a word as to how the good old times are to be restored. I have read the Areopagiticus again and again, thinking there must be something in it which I did not see, because it is admired by ancients and moderns. The Panegyricus is a homage paid to Athens, which loses all its value if we recollect, that he laboured at it for thirty years. The Admonition to Philip to transfer the war to Asia, might be allowed to pass, as far as appearances go, but in a political point of view it is senseless. A statesman like Demosthenes knew well, that, at that time, the preservation of the Persian empire was a necessary evil for Greece, as that empire alone formed a counterpoise to the power of Macedonia; and he saw that, if Philip were master of Asia Minor, all would be lost; but the old rhetorician forgot that he wrote in the 109th Olympiad, he imagined that he was living about Olympiad 79, and knew not where he was. In like manner, his Archidamus is altogether foolish; it has found its admirers in antiquity and in modern times, because Sparta would rather perish than submit to the humiliation of recognising the independence of a country she had once subdued. Even a Philip of Spain recognised the liberty of the Netherlands! When Philip stood there with an overpowering army, Sparta was obliged to allow him to constitute

Messene without consulting her; but, a hundred years later, she became more reasonable, for then there existed a good understanding between Sparta and Messene.

"Thus the feud between the Spartans and Messenians continued, without any regular battles being fought; and Sparta thereby became weaker and weaker, while the Messenians extended their state more and more. The condition of Peloponnesus remained on the whole the same. The Arcadians, disunited among themselves, were always at war with each other; so-called aristocratic and democratic parties were constantly raging at Argos, but they wanted nothing but violence and bloodshed. In Phlius and Elis there also was a struggle between the aristocracy and the democracy. At Corinth Timophanes, the brother of the great Timoleon, set himself up as tyrant. The armies of mercenaries now gave rise to a new kind of tyrants. As all order was completely broken up, and the citizens were no longer accustomed to the use of arms, the commanders of the mercenaries, without any political motives usurped the supreme power; the people, still called the sovereign people, being without arms and means of defence, were subdued and oppressed. Such tyrants appear in many small towns of Peloponnesus, and its condition thus became more and more wretched, without there being any hope of deliverance.

The condition of Thebes, in a material point of view was still prosperous; but after the battle of Mantinea it again became powerless. The downfall of Greece was thus irresistibly approaching. Its existence against foreign enemies was possible only so long as the two leading states, Athens and Sparta, stood on firm ground. In the mean time, however, a state in the north which had hitherto been despised, rose through the energy of a man, whom we cannot help calling great; for no other man is great but he who produces great results with small means. This man is Philip of Macedonia."

LECTURE LXV.

THE origin of the Macedonians is as obscure, as their subsequent appearance in history is great and remarkable. The question as to whether they were Greeks or barbarians, is one which must have occurred to every one engaged in historical studies, but the answer to which is connected with the greatest difficulties.

Later writers, such as the Romans, certainly consider the Macedonians as Greeks; and who would not regard Alexander as a Greek? Greece herself considered Alexander and Philip as her sons, and in Herodotus, king Alexander claims to be an ἀνὴρ Ἕλλην, though he distinguishes himself from his people by the addition καὶ Μακεδόνων βασιλεύς. In Polybius there is no decisive expression to show whether he considered them as Greeks or not. This much, however, is certain, that the later Greeks regarded the Macedonians as so much hellenised, that they did not hesitate to treat them as Greeks. As early as the time of Philip, they took part in the Amphictyony as well as in the Olympian and other great contests of the Greeks. By these circumstances, their character as Greeks was recognised; for it was an ancient and strict maxim, that none but Greeks should be allowed to take part in those contests. During the times of decay the scrupulous exclusion of barbarians was more and more relaxed; subsequently, and even in the days of Cicero, the Romans regarded as Greeks all those who spoke Greek and carried on their business in the Greek language, such as the Carians, Mysians, and Lydians; although the Greeks themselves did not consider those nations as *sinceri Graeci* any more than Cicero did.

Strabo, on the other hand, seems to reckon the Macedonians partly among the Thracians and partly among the Illyrians; this, it is true, occurs in the seventh book, which is very much mutilated and corrupted, but Strabo at any rate does not regard them as Greeks.

" At the time when Greek philology was not studied seriously, the question as to the nationality of the Macedonians was treated very superficially, and in my youth they were generally considered as Greeks; and when an enlightened man like Palmerius observed that the ancients did not look at them in this light, the remark was met with shallow replies. But within the last thirty years, during which history has received a new life, it has become the general opinion that they were not Greeks. But to what race did they belong? Some maintain that they were Illyrians, while others deny it." In the second edition of my Roman History[1] I have touched upon this question only by the way, but afterwards C. O. Müller, of Göttingen, in a small treatise on Macedonia, has investigated the matter in a truly excellent manner. He does not, indeed, enter upon the one side of the question which is yet to be discussed; but the statement of Strabo, that the Macedonians were Thracians or Illyrians is most satisfactorily answered, and Müller has clearly proved, that the real Macedonians were neither the one nor the other; he has directed my attention to a passage in a fragment of Hesiod, which I had overlooked, and in which Macedon is called a brother of Magnes, so that the Macedonians and Magnetes were regarded as kindred tribes.

" The result at which I have arrived, and which on the whole agrees with that of Müller, is as follows:—In the time of Philip, a large portion of the Macedonians certainly was partly Thracian and partly Illyrian; some also were Greeks, Ionians, and Dardanians; but the Macedonians of later times must be well distinguished from those of the earliest ages." To what race, then, do the real Macedonians belong? are they a nation of quite a peculiar kind? I answer, no, they belonged to the race of Epirots, because " Strabo states, that in Upper Macedonia there were tribes which, in their mode of dressing the hair, and in other customs, agreed with the Epirots." Accordingly they are of the same Pelasgian race to which the Epirots belong, " that great race which extended from Italy to Asia, and though akin to the Greeks, was yet different from them." In a passage of Justin, which may be regarded as taken from Theopompus, the Macedonians are expressly treated as Pelasgians. " But the passage of Hesiod pointed out by Müller is decisive."[2]

[1] Vol. i. p. 31.

[2] " Hence the strange circumstance, that in southern Macedonia, the seat of the most ancient Macedonians, and in western Thessaly, the language is Wallachian, a dialect akin to the Latin, though it did not arise from Roman colonies, which never existed there. It has arisen from the Macedonian and

If we go further, the passage in Thucydides, where, in speaking of the invasion of Sitalces, he mentions the extension of the Macedonian state,[3] is sufficient to enable us to gain a clear notion of all those relations. The real seat of the Macedonians is in the centre and on the eastern slope of the Cambunian hills, a continuation of Pindus, uniting Pindus and Scardus in the north of Macedonia, where the Atintanians and Orestians of the genuine Epirot race dwelt. There also dwelt the Macedonians, whose name is sometimes written Μακηδόνες and sometimes Μακέδονες. This name seems to embrace especially three nations, the real Macedonians, the Elimiotae ('Ελιμειῶται), and the Lyncestians. These three nations, therefore, were Epirots: Pelasgians, Siculians, Tyrrhenians, or by whatever name you like to call them; but they were no more Hellenes than the other Epirots. But as the ruling γένος of the Pyrrhidae among the Molottians in Epirus, traced its origin to the ancient heroic families of Greece, so the rulers of Macedonia, in its narrower sense, traced their family to Heracles. There are two different accounts about this point: the one adopted by Herodotus[4] places their arrival in Macedonia in later times; it represents the archegetes Perdiccas as migrating with two brothers from Argos to Macedonia, where they were kindly received by a native prince. The other account, which I believe to be of native origin, occurred in Theopompus, and was adopted from him by Diodorus, Justin, and Velleius, and passed over also into the sketch of Dexippus, which is preserved in Syncellus.[5] According to this latter account, the kingdom of Macedonia was founded by Caranus, who is connected with Pheidon, the last prince of Argos, being called by some his brother, and by others his son; this Pheidon is described by some as the tenth, and by others as the twelfth, descendant of Heracles. The one as well as the other account, therefore, traces the origin of

Thessalian languages, just as the Italian has arisen from the Latin. The Albanese are not descendants of a Pelasgian people; they are Illyrians. This is clear from their language, and if we knew more Illyrian words, it would be still more evident. A hill, for example, is in Albanese *mal*, and *di* two; and Polybius informs us, that the town of Dimalos was situated on two ἄκραι."— 1826.

[3] Thucyd. ii. 99. [4] Herod. viii. 137.
[5] Diod. *Fragm.*; Justin, vii. 1; Vell. Pat. i. 6.; Syncell. i. 495. ed. Bonn.

the Macedonian kings to Argos; but I believe that we can shew, step by step, how this derivation from Argos arose from mere speculation. There was in Macedonia a royal race in the same manner as we find the government exercised by certain families among all the tribes akin to the Greeks. This royal race of the Macedonians, as we know from Theopompus, was called the Argeads, and nothing is more natural than to infer from the name of these Argeads, that they were descended from Argos. This, however, does not render it necessary to look to Peloponnesus, the Pelasgian Argos being nearer at hand; but after they were once traced to Peloponnesus, it was no longer a bold step to regard them as Temenids, and thus they at once became Heracleids: that they were then connected with Pheidon, the latest and most celebrated of the Argive Heracleids, is likewise no more than might be expected. " We cannot be surprised to find that the names of the kings are genuine Doric, as they had once declared themselves to be Heracleids, and as people everywhere felt a pride in representing everything as Greek."

The most ancient seat of these Macedonian kings, setting aside Lyncestus and Elimiotis, was in Lower Macedonia, " while the other tribes dwelt in the mountains." The ancient capital of this country was Aegeae, which had formerly been called Edessa, and was afterwards again so called. In like manner, ancient names reappear in Asia, as Edessa, for example, is still called Edessa.[6] Now where ancient cities have two different names, it is always a proof, that they have been inhabited by different nations: thus Terracina and Anxur, the former being the Tyrrhenian and the latter the Volscian name; the ancient name, New Amsterdam, has been obscured by that of New York. This double name of the Macedonian capital shews the truth of the ancient tradition, that Edessa was conquered by the advancing Macedonians. Hence it is altogether probable, that the Macedonians did not advance into Lower Macedonia at a later period, since Thucydides also supposed, that they had expelled other tribes; he represents the Thracians as driven from Aemathia, and the Pierians from Pieria, and as having thus descended into the plains.

" A part of the Macedonian tribes, therefore, had descended from the mountains, and taken possession of Aemathia and the

[6] Is not this perhaps a slip for Amida?—ED.

fertile Thracian districts about Salonichi." On that occasion, the place called Edessa was conquered, and received the name Αἴγειαι, although that of Edessa was never entirely lost. I repeat this name for the sake of philologers, because they have taken offence at its foreign appearance, and because it is one of those names of places which have always been ill-used by the editors of ancient authors. It has been imagined, without reason, that the true name was Αἰγαῖαι (which is the name of an Aeolian city), because Αἴγειαι looks strange; and Αἰγαί arose only as an abbreviation from Αἰγαῖαι. This erroneous name has been introduced into maps, and I believe that the correct name is found in no map at all.

That city was for a long time the residence of the Macedonian kings. The Lyncestians and Elimiotans, who had remained in the hills, were governed at the same time, and even during the Peloponnesian war, by princes of their own, and of the same race, it is said, as all the Pelasgian tribes originally had their own kings. Nothing is known of Macedonian history before the reign of Amyntas I., a contemporary of Darius. Under him, the Macedonians descended into the plain as far as the Axius; but on the sea coast they possessed only a small district of from five to ten miles, about the mouth of the Axius, whereby they were enabled to keep up intercourse with the Greeks. All the rest of the coast was occupied by Greek cities, excepting, perhaps, a place like Dium in Pieria, which belonged to the Macedonians. We can form a tolerable estimate of the Macedonian kingdom at that time: it was small and very narrow, and seems to have extended a little beyond the Axius. The common manuals erroneously describe the kingdom of Amyntas as extending as far as the river Nestus; but the Macedonians for a long time did not advance even as far as the Strymon. The gradual extension of the kingdom is very well described by Gatterer in two maps, in the transactions of the Society of Göttingen;[7] modern books are full of mistakes on this subject. We possess silver coins, with the name of Amyntas, of very ancient coinage, and it cannot be doubted that they belong to this Amyntas; the coinage is too antique to regard it as made under Amyntas II., the father of Philip.[8]

---

[7] *Comment. Goetting.* ann. 1781. tom. vi.

[8] " The coins of Sybaris are of very ancient date, the writing being still from the right to the left. They are more ancient than any Greek coin extant. The

We accordingly see that even as early as that time the Macedonians had coins with Greek inscriptions, as was, in fact, the
case with most of the barbarians within the reach of Greece.
Few only had a different mode of writing; in Pamphylia, *e.g.*,
very beautiful coins, with peculiar writing, were made; but
the rule is, that barbarians employed Greek writing. The fact
that the Macedonians at that time coined such money, shows
that they had Greek civilisation.

Amyntas, who was king of Macedonia in the reign of
Darius, was obliged to do homage to the king of Persia. An
insult committed by the Persian envoys at his court was
avenged by his son, Alexander, who murdered them; but
this I have already mentioned before. This crime had afterwards to be atoned for by the payment of a large sum of
money. Subsequently, however, when Alexander saw that
the affairs of the Persians turned out ill, he took his revenge ;
making it appear as if he were anxious to be of service to the
Greeks, he gave them information about the Persians, and
afterwards the Macedonians boasted, that he had destroyed
the remnants of the Persian army on its retreat after the battle
of Plataeae. Even Demosthenes[9] concedes this praise to the
hated Macedonians, but with a remarkable confusion of
persons, which shows that he was not accurate in his historical
knowledge. But the historians Herodotus and Thucydides
do not mention anything about it. It is possible that they
may have killed some Persians fleeing by themselves, and that
afterwards they converted such a base act into something for
which they claimed gratitude. This Alexander attached
great importance to his being a Heracleid, and to his belonging to the Greek race, and he endeavoured to hellenise his
people. He obtained for himself, though not for his people,
the right of admission to the Olympic games, because, according to his own statement, he was a Heracleid descended from
Argos; but there was, at the time, considerable opposition,
and the Hellanodicae in that case were certainly not over

---

fact that we have no ancient Athenian coins, probably arises from the circumstance that Solon reduced the ancient standard, and that then all the earlier
coinage was melted down." [This passage occurs in one MS. of the course of
1829-30, written in the margin, and is probably taken from the Lectures of
1826, but this is not quite certain.—Ed.]

[9] *De Ord. Rep.* p. 173; c. *Aristocr.* p. 687, ed. Reiske.

scrupulous. The part, however, which he plays in history is very obscure; and from Thucydides we only know, that the Macedonians extended their dominion, more and more, by driving the Illyrians and Thracians from the country, and settling in the parts which thus became evacuated. The boundaries of the Macedonian kingdom, however, were still extremely narrow; Upper Macedonia did not yet belong to it, and the whole of the coast, except the small district about the Axius, was Greek.

Shortly before the Peloponnesian war, and during the disturbances which led to it, Macedonia, under king Perdiccas, first appears in the history of Greece (Olymp. 81, 3). It then shows a state of weakness which is hardly conceivable; small as the kingdom is, its weakness cannot but excite our astonishment. Its cavalry was pretty considerable, but it had no regular infantry, or hoplites. "We see the Macedonian king just as powerless as the Epirot princes, without money and without authority." Perdiccas distinguished himself by his fickle and untrustworthy character; he hated and mistrusted the Athenians, and wanted to deprive them of the possession of the towns on the coast; but he did not trust the Chalcidian cities either, which, on his advice, had united into one Olynthian state. Afterwards, he fell out with Brasidas, became reconciled to the Athenians, and thenceforth remained on tolerable terms with them.

He was succeeded (Olymp. 91, 3) by Archelaus, his natural son, who is universally believed to have murdered his brother, the legitimate heir of the throne, or at least to have derived advantages from the murder. It cannot, however, be denied, that the murderer was useful to his country and nation. "Hitherto, the Macedonians had been protected against their neighbours, the Paeonians and Illyrians, only by their mountains, and by the deserted state of the frontiers." It was Archelaus, as Thucydides says,[10] that founded and fortified the Macedonian towns deserving of the name: he did for Macedonia what king Henry did for Germany. He was the first that built towns; the Pelasgian tribes having before lived in little open places, from a dislike of towns surrounded by walls. Archelaus already transferred his residence from Aegeae to Pella, which, in his reign, continued to increase, though, even

[10] Thucyd. ii. 100.

under Philip, it was only a small place. You must conceive all those Macedonian towns to have been extremely small, as, for example, Zürich at its beginning, or St. Gall, which, in the fourteenth century, contained only one hundred houses; or, like our Bonn, where, in the twelfth century, the Brücken-strasse formed the boundary, and only the -district round the minster was inhabited. Such also was the case with Pella; in the time of Herodotus, it was still a πολίχνη. Archelaus also drew Greeks towards his court, and endeavoured to enlighten the Macedonians. These attempts bear a remarkable resemblance to those of Peter the Great and his successors. Thus the Academy of Sciences, which was instituted at Peters-burg, consisted only of foreigners; and Peter's own barbarians were only honorary members. Archelaus likewise instituted something resembling an Academy of Sciences: he drew to his court Greek poets and philosophers, to whom he gave residences and the means of living, among whom I may mention Euripides, who ended his life there. These Greeks, moreover, were treated by the Macedonian grandees, who were yet fearfully rude, in the same brutal manner as the foreign savants were in Petersburg by the Russian courtiers of Peter the Great. Euripides also experienced such treat-ment at the hands of a noble Macedonian. They were obliged to accept the favours from a fratricide, and in addition to this, to bear the insolent pride of the Macedonian nobles. But notwithstanding all this, Archelaus did very much for his country, and his reign is the beginning of a new era.

The reign of Amyntas II., (Olymp. 96, 3), the father of Philip II., was altogether unfortunate. He has already been mentioned in the history of the war with the Olynthians, when he solicited the assistance of the Spartans against them.

In the vicinity of Macedonia, a state had been formed, of which historians take no notice, and which the ancients mention only in passing. I allude to the state of the Taulan-tians in Illyricum, which had been founded by one Bardylis.[11] "The Illyrians had from early times been in a very divided condition; every tribe formed a state by itself, without any strong point of union. But Bardylis began to draw the

[11] "Whether the name is to be pronounced Bardýlis or Bardýlis cannot be decided, as it does not occur in any poet; but it was probably Bardýlis, because several authors spell it Bardyllis."

separate tribes together. We know for certain, that " he began as a robber, like Ali Pasha, and all the celebrated Albanese of the eighteenth century, genuine and true descendants of the ancient Illyrians, " who enter upon their career as highway robbers, and then form a state by subduing their neighbours." Such a man was Bardylis: we must not, however, imagine that he lived with his companions as a common robber in the woods; but he was like the proprietor of a strong castle, who gradually assembled round himself a large number of followers, consisting both of men of his own race and of foreigners. " In those countries, the robbers are the admired class; and the exploits of these bandits are the great feats and wars which engage their interest, for they know nothing else. In this manner Bardylis also excited admiration, and he was especially celebrated for the extraordinary love of justice, with which he managed his band; and being the leader of a body of highwaymen, he was gradually recognised as king by the Illyrians and Taulantians, and established a real kingdom. I think it very probable, that the latter Illyrian kings were his descendants. History has decided otherwise; but personally he is certainly not less deserving of consideration than Philip. The natural tendency to unite in larger states, which was then so general among the Greeks, also drew together several Illyrian tribes. ". Thus united, Illyricum was too powerful for the Macedonians." Although the Illyrians fought in separate bands as robbers, yet they were then, as they are now, particularly fit for the strict service in the line, and were regularly organised. Bardylis thus formed for himself an army, with which he invaded Macedonia, overpowered king Amyntas, conquered a part of his kingdom, and rendered Amyntas tributary for the rest.

Amyntas had many sons, and the history of Macedonia after his death (Olymp. 102, 3) is a great chaos, the unravelling of which is perhaps impossible, and after all of little use. The immediate successor of Amyntas was probably Alexander; and it seems that it was he who, during the feud with Thessaly, sent his younger brother Philip as a hostage to Thebes. The account of Diodorus, that Philip was educated there in the same house with Epaminondas, is inconceivably absurd, and is made without any regard to the respective ages of the two men. Theopompus certainly did not make such a statement.

But it is probable that Philip was actually sent as a hostage to insure the protection demanded by the king of Macedonia; and it is very credible, that Epaminondas afforded him an entirely Greek education, so that Philip afterwards had every reason to bless the period spent at Thebes.[12]   Alexander was murdered (Olymp. 103, 1) with the knowledge of the queen-mother Eurydice; and her paramour ascended the throne as regent. After his death (Olymp. 103, 4) Perdiccas III. succeeded to the throne.   The question now is, whether Philip had then already returned to Macedonia, and lived there confined to a small district; or whether, until the murder of his brother, he remained at Thebes, and then made his escape, as Demetrius escaped from Rome to Syria.   I believe the former to be more probable—an opinion supported by a story of Speusippus in Athenaeus;[13] it is difficult to believe that Speusippus should at that time have boldly invented it, if there had not been some truth in it.   Perdiccas fell in a battle against the Illyrians (Olymp. 105, 1).

The condition of Macedonia after his death was one of the most complete dissolution. A certain Pausanias, whose connection with the royal family is unknown, claimed the throne, and was supported by the Thracians. Another pretender, Argaeus, a grandson of Archelaus, was supported by the Athenians with a fleet, and an army of three thousand men, under the command of Mantias.   Against these two pretenders, Philip came forward. That period too may be compared with several epochs in the history of Russia during the fourteenth and fifteenth centuries, when several pretenders fought against one another, and hordes of robbers traversed the country. Philip, therefore, had to contend with great difficulties.

———◆———

LECTURE LXVI.

WHEN Philip ascended the throne, Macedonia was pressed and threatened not only by the Illyrians, and the great kingdom of

---

[12] In 1826, Niebuhr doubted Philip's residence at Thebes altogether.—ED.
[13] Athen. xi. p. 506, e and f.

the Taulantians, but on the other side also, by the great Paeonian kingdom, the extent of which cannot now be determined, and the very situation of which is not accurately known. It is, indeed, stated, that the Paeonians dwelt about the Strymon above Aemathia; but whether all the Paeonian tribes formed one state, or whether many stood by themselves, these are points concerning which we can form no conjectures. Beyond the Paeonians, there was the Thracian kingdom of the Odrysians, of large extent, but with very varying boundaries; it did not, however, touch upon Macedonia. On the sea-coast, the Macedonian kings had as yet no possessions, except the narrow tract on the Thermaic gulf, and some points in Pieria.

Methone and Pydna being the most important cities in that part, governed, it would seem, the country of Pieria quite independently and without any connection with Olynthus. This last city exercised the supremacy over the towns on the Thermaic gulf, as far as the second bay between Sithonia and Athos, which separated the state of Torone from that of Olynthus. These towns, with the exception of a few places under the supremacy of Athens, especially Potidaea, formed the Olynthian state. Acanthus and Apollonia, further east, were not connected with Olynthus. The most distant Greek city towards Thrace was Amphipolis, which Sparta, in the last treaty of peace, had expressly conceded to Athens. But the city itself, though ceded by Sparta, was not on that account inclined to submit to the Athenian supremacy. "With the view of repelling the Athenians, it had even before thrown itself into the arms of Macedonia;" and it was the constant endeavour of the Athenians to recover their authority at Amphipolis. "Some places on the coast of Thrace and Macedonia, however, had submitted to Athens at the time of the *reconstitutio imperii* by Chabrias and Timotheus, and" she probably possessed also Potidaea and the surrounding country.

During that period, and even for some time after it, Athens was managed most sadly. It had no leading man; there were indeed some, comparatively speaking, not contemptible commanders, but in the first place, they were no statesmen, and secondly, the best among them, like Iphicrates and Chabrias, had become old, and the youthful vigour so necessary to a

military commander, had become extinct in them. But independently of this, they could not be compared with first-rate
generals ; they were distinguished only among second-rate
commanders, like those in Europe after the death of Frederick
the Great. The two old men, Iphicrates and Chabrias, were
setting stars; the brilliant period of Timotheus was likewise
past, although he was not so old as the former two. The
younger generals at Athens were not only men of the greatest
mediocrity, but some of them were undeserving of any confidence whatever. If Leosthenes had then been in the vigour of
life, the fate of Athens would have been decided differently. The
foremost among the young men at Athens was Chares, although
as a general he was of very inferior talent; he was, moreover,
altogether reckless, and his unprincipled character rendered
him worthless. " He was a common *condottiere*, who had no
other good quality but that the troops liked to be engaged by
him." The next was a stranger, Charidemus of Oreus, whom
the Athenians had taken into their service against their own
interest, as his native town was hostile to them. But he, too,
was altogether an unprincipled *condottiere*, as ready to serve
any one who engaged him, even for the most desperate undertakings, provided money was to be made, as he was ready to
desert the cause he had undertaken and to lend himself to
others. With the exception of the single Callistratus, the
commanders were worth nothing. He was an able and skilful
man, a good orator, and a man of principle, though not of
first-rate qualities. With this single exception, the statesmen
of that time cannot be spoken of with pleasure.

The warlike spirit of the republic had become quite extinct;
the mode of warfare now prevalent in Greece was the same as
that which Machiavelli, in his time, found at Florence. No
war was carried on except by hired mercenaries; the ancient
personal service of the citizens in the armies was altogether
out of the question. The wealth of the Athenians, compared
with what it had been during the period immediately preceding, had been immensely increased. Although, at the
beginning of Philip's reign, the city was still in a state of great
decay, as we see from the small treatise of Xenophon (περὶ
πόρων, ii. 6), who says, that within the walls there were a
great many places for building unoccupied, so that the popu-

lation must have greatly decreased, yet the state appears to have become extremely wealthy.   If we consider, that about Olymp. 100, the Athenians had great difficulty in equipping a small fleet, that afterwards great armaments were got ready with facility, and that Athens kept large fleets and armies, we can easily see to what an extraordinary degree she must have recovered her strength.   The causes of this increasing prosperity cannot be very distinctly stated, and we can only form conjectures about it.   My belief is, that the restoration of the commerce with Persia and Egypt contributed most to it; great advantages must have been gained by it, for there could be no navigation between Asia Minor and Egypt, and Athens, as a neutral power, mediated between the two countries, and carried on their commerce.   The trade with the Euxine also appears then to have been much more extensive than before. This much only is clear, that Athens had recovered; and fortunate commercial junctures were certainly the main cause which produced this recovery.

With these resources, Athens stood alone in Greece; Sparta was no longer spoken of, and was engaged only in feuds with her neighbours.   No one placed any confidence in her, and Thebes had lost her soul in Epaminondas.   But Philip united in his person every danger with which all the other states had formerly, each in its turn, threatened Athens.

It is well known, that the history of Philip was written by Theopompus with great minuteness, and with an immense number of digressions and episodes.   This history is no longer extant, but has formed the basis of all the accounts which we have of Philip; and its very minuteness may be the reason why we now have such a meagre history of him.   We know it only very imperfectly, and for the most part only from the passionate speeches of Demosthenes and his adversary.   The connected historical narrative in Diodorus is incredibly brief and wretched : he is not struck by the most glaring contradictions, and there are many works referring to this subject which he had not even read, such as the speech of Aeschines against Ctesiphon; many things are recorded by him without any meaning and at random.   The first period of the history of Philip down to the siege of Perinthus, had been written also by Ephorus.   " Some ascribe his last (the 30th) book, from the end of the Phocian war down to this period, to his

son Demophilus.[1]   But if he wrote it himself, why did he
leave off there? I answer, because he was a man, and a Greek
of the right sort ; for the relief of Perinthus was the last
successful effort of the free Greeks.   Here accordingly the
patriotic Greek closed his history, while the capricious Theopompus, dissatisfied with himself, wrote the history of the
subjugation of his country."

Polybius[2] charges Theopompus with contradicting himself,
because he said he had chosen an historical subject richer and
more interesting than any other, the greatest revolution of the
age effected by Philip (he wrote under Alexander), and afterwards spoke of Philip in the most derogatory manner, relating
of him acts of the greatest baseness, e. g., that his court was
the rallying point of the most abject creatures from all parts of
Greece, and that the baser they were, the more kindly were
they received by Philip.   I am surprised at Polybius attaching
so much importance to this contradiction; for it is not so great
as he thinks, and the two statements may be easily reconciled.
We must distinguish in Philip the natural phenomenon and
the moral being.

Philip was unquestionably an uncommon and extraordinary
man, and the opinion of several among the ancients, that by
the foundation of the Macedonian state he did something far
greater than Alexander by the application of the powers he
inherited, is quite correct.   If we consider the strength with
which, first as the guardian of his nephew, who soon disappears, and then as king, he took up the reins of government;
the firmness with which, under the circumstances, when the
kingdom was almost destroyed, he took the crown; how he
persuaded and soothed some enemies, and made war upon
others; how he secured his successful undertakings by the
establishment and improvement of standing armies, and by the
introduction of new tactics:—if we consider all this, and if
we read how Demosthenes himself describes his qualities with
horror, how he was unwearied in his endeavours to gain his
end, how he endured both in summer and in winter every
kind of hardship and illness, and how then again he came
forward in full vigour; how every success incited him only to

---

[1] In 1825, Niebuhr, with reference to Diodorus, xvi. 74, expressed himself in
favour of this opinion.
[2] viii. 11.

make greater efforts, and nothing deterred him; how every failure only served him as a lesson that the time had not yet come, but did not lead him to give up his plans: we cannot do otherwise than look with amazement at his extraordinary qualities. When we regard him as the creator of his state, by uniting the most different nations, Macedonians and Greeks; when we see with what discernment he contrived to discover and win over to his side the men of great talent; when we reflect what man he must have been, from whom proceeded the impulse to train such great generals, who surrounded himself with such a large number of distinguished commanders—to whom Alexander, it must be observed, did not add one, for all Alexander's generals proceeded from the school of Philip, and there is not one whom Alexander did not inherit from Philip; —when we perceive the skill with which he gained over nations and states for himself and his interests, and made them willing to serve him, and to forget the most ordinary rules of prudence in regard to themselves; when we see all these qualities, we cannot but acknowledge that he was an extraordinary man.

Whether he was a good and a noble-minded man, is another question; that he had some good traits cannot be denied, nor am I inclined to deny it. There are features in his character which show noble and genuine humanity: he was a friend to his friends, and knew how to show his kindness towards those who stood near him. But, on the other hand, the object he had in view was everything to him: never did any regard to faith, virtue, or conscience, deter him from the pursuit of an object. There is a characteristic saying which is ascribed to him, and I can see no reason why it should not be his: " We deceive children in play with dice, and men with oaths." No reliance could ever be placed in him: he never had honest intentions when he concluded a treaty. He did not despise even the basest means to win over those who were opposed to him; he everywhere had traitors in his pay, and did not scruple to own it; nay, he boasted of having taken more towns by means of silver than of iron! It is a fact that his immorality was the most detestable and boundless. In personal character Alexander is superior to him; and had he not been addicted to the odious vice of drinking, it would not be possible to find in his history acts similar to those of Philip. It is indeed very possible, and I readily believe it, that the good features in Alexander's character were artificial: he looked for glory and honour; but he would not have been able even to simulate generosity, if he had not had a clear perception of its nature, and if he had not been naturally generous. In addition to this, however, it must not be forgotten that Alexander had the invaluable advantage of an excellent education at the hands of Aristotle; the blessed effects of which were never completely obliterated, although he emancipated himself too much from its influence. Philip had not received such an education, in which the mind was directed to what was truly good and noble. He spent his early youth at a half barbarous court, where indulgence in vice was part of the ordinary life. There can be no doubt that he spoke Greek from his infancy, but he did not acquire the sentiments of a Greek. He had, it is true, been at Thebes; but the story that he was educated in the house of Epaminondas, must certainly be taken with the greatest limitation; and who can say, whether the unpretending and modest virtue of an Epaminondas was understood by the young prince?

But at all events Philip was an extraordinary man; he alone raised the kingdom of Macedonia, and without him it would have fallen to pieces. From the very first moment it was his unshaken plan to make himself master of Greece.

Philip divided his enemies; he first (Olymp. 105, 1) satisfied the Thracian king who supported the pretender, with a sum of money; he then easily defeated the small corps which the Athenians had sent to Argaeus, the other pretender. He did not trouble himself with the question, as to whether the voice of the nation was in his favour. He was extremely anxious to gain time; and in order to bring about a speedy reconciliation with the Athenians, he restored to them the prisoners he had made, "and withdrew from Amphipolis, thinking that he might afterwards take that city at any time. The Athenians apprehended nothing from the small kingdom of Macedonia, and concluded peace, believing that they might easily recover Amphipolis. Having thus purchased the neutrality of Athens, he attacked his other enemies with all his might." He always combined preparation and execution at the same time, so that he could strike blow after blow. He now (Olymp. 105, 2) subdued the kingdom of Paeonia, which was perhaps not very great—the detail is unknown—and then ventured on taking the field against the Illyrians, whom he had already once defeated. He demanded of them to give up the conquered part of Macedonia, that is probably Upper Macedonia, the small principalities of Elimiotis and Lyncestus, which had acknowledged the supremacy of Illyricum, whereas formerly they had been connected with Macedonia. In this war he was met by the Illyrians with immense forces, for their attention had already been directed to the ambitious young man. He was only twenty-four years old when he ascended the throne.

But Philip had already formed his army.[3] He required great numerical strength and strong physical masses, and these he got ready. It would have been mere loss of time, if he had attempted to organise his forces in the way in which the Romans afterwards formed their legions, and Iphicrates his peltasts, by the personal training of individual soldiers; he was obliged to rely upon masses for his victories; as Carnot, in the wars of the revolution, restored the tactics of masses —though on a smaller scale—because the national guards did not maintain their ground, and the cavalry was bad; and this system completely decided the campaign of 1793 and 94. " Philip thus adopted the Greek phalanx; but as most of his opponents were phalangites—all the Greeks and the Illyrians also fought in the phalanx, the Thracians alone were peltasts—he opposed them with a stronger phalanx, and improved it to the highest degree of perfection." Even Iphicrates had increased the masses, by arming the men with longer spears; " and Epaminondas had drawn up the phalanx fifty men deep; but this was only for pressing onward, the hindmost ranks being a mass which was driven onwards at random." Philip now went much further, by combining great depth with arms that could be used by the men stationed in the fifth and sixth ranks. He gave his troops the immensely long sarissae, whereby he effected so much, that the men even in the fifth and sixth lines, could reach the enemy with the iron points of their spears; " he drew up his phalanx from twelve to sixteen men deep, whereas the Greeks usually stood only eight men deep, and the points of only three spears could reach the enemy." By this deep phalanx, with its heavy arms, Philip defeated the weaker Greek masses, in the same way in which in the naval warfare of the Romans, where their ships rushed

[3] See *Hist. of Rome*, iii. p. 445, foll.

together with their *rostra*, a quinquereme overthrew a trireme with its ἔμβολον. " His phalanx could be broken only by skirmishers, and upon uneven ground.

In addition to this, it was suited to the thin population of Macedonia; for the country was as depopulated as Sweden after the reign of Charles XII. But every one accustomed to hard labour, and every peasant of strong bones and muscles, could find his place in the phalanx; in any other place, even on the flanks, he would have been of no use, but in the centre he was excellent. He could, moreover, be trained in three or four days; for the whole military art of the soldier with the sarissa, consisted in marching; and as nature has not neglected any man so much as not to have given him some sense of keeping time, he was enabled to learn his duties in a few days without difficulty.

The phalanx was first tested against the Illyrians, who did not think it possible that the Macedonians should defeat them, and " with it Philip gained a great and decisive victory over them, in which thousands of the enemy covered the field of battle. He took from them not only the part of Macedonia they had conquered, but continued his conquests as far as lake Lychnitis, the lake of Achrida beyond the mountains, so that all the passes of Illyricum were in his hands.

He next directed his arms against Amphipolis (Olym. 105, 4). After having first supported the Amphipolitans against the Athenians, he bribed a party in the city, and with their assistance he took the place by surprise. Through this conquest he gained access to the rich gold mines of Crenides, which yielded annually about £214,285.[4] These mines he took from the Thasians, and afterwards founded near them the colony of Philippi, to facilitate the working of the mines.

The circumstance that Athens was then engaged in a highly unfortunate and difficult war, the so-called social war, was particularly favourable to Philip's progress. Athens had derived her greatest advantages from her supremacy over the cities and islands which had a considerable navy, such as Chios, Rhodes, Mitylene, Samos, and Byzantium. But those states were always distrustful of Athens; and it is possible, that at

---

[4] " Gold then stood to silver in the relation of 10 to 1, whereas it is at present like 15 or 16 to 1, so that, according to the present ratio, the produce of the mines would be considerably more."

that time the Athenians did not honestly adhere to the principle of equality at the deliberations, and they may have given various causes for complaint and mistrust. In short the allies revolted, and Athens, instead of waiting, until those states should be led by their own interest to return to their former relation, forgot that her ancient power and dominion were gone, and began a war, endeavouring to reduce them by force. This war, which lasted three years (from Olymp. 105, 3, to Olymp. 106, 1.), cost the Athenians immense sums, and drew upon them several severe losses; but it was above all injurious to their confederacy. The island of Cos, which was then powerful, had likewise joined the allies. We scarcely know any details of these occurrences, except those of one day, namely an attack which the Athenians made upon the allies in the harbour of Chios, which turned out very unfortunately, and in which Chabrias lost his life. The Persians too had a hand in this war, though they did not come forward themselves; but their vassal Mausolus, dynast of Caria, who had his residence at Halicarnassus, and afterwards made himself master of Rhodes, supported the rebels, perhaps by the suggestion of the king of Persia, with money ships and troops. At the end of the three years, the Athenians were obliged to recognise the independence of their allies, and be contented to secure by a peace a tolerable relation of friendship. But the war must after all have been successful in one point, in the conquest of Samos. That island also appears to have joined the allies against Athens, for we find a cleruchia there, which belongs to this time; and this shows that at the commencement of the war Samos was against Athens, and that on being taken by the Athenians it received cleruchi. For surely that cleruchia can be the result only of a conquest. These cleruchi remained there till after the time of Alexander, when they were driven from the island. The Athenians regarded that possession as particularly valuable. No historian, as far as I know, has yet noticed this circumstance. Several writers think that Philip in the peace after the battle of Chaeronea ceded Samos to the Athenians; this, e. g., is the opinion of Barthélemy, founded on Plutarch's life of Alexander; but Philip did not conquer Samos, and one of the terms in this peace, as in that of Antalcidas, was, that all the smaller Greek states should be independent, so that Philip declared himself the protector of the smaller states against the great ones; but cleruchi had been sent from Athens to Samos as early as Olymp. 107, 1.

This war engaged the Athenians so much that they allowed Philip to carry on his operations unmolested. He, in the meantime, established himself in his state, and extended his power more and more. The details as to the manner in which he consolidated the interior of his empire are unfortunately unknown. Olynthus, the existence of which Philip would not tolerate any more than that of Methone and Pydna, ought naturally to have regarded him with still greater jealousy than Athens did; and there is no doubt that many Olynthians had that feeling, but they allowed themselves to be disgracefully deceived by Philip. He pretended to be their warmest and most disinterested friend, and aided them in extending their territory in a direction where it should afterwards be of use to him, when the time should come for him to take everything. The Athenian settlement at Potidaea, through which Athens was the mistress of Pallene, was a thorn in the side of the Olynthians, just as Gibraltar in the hands of the English is to the Spaniards; and Philip constantly urged them on to take Potidaea. The Olynthians, however, not being powerful enough to conquer it, Philip assisted in conquering it for them, without being actually at open war with Athens. But the Olynthians were now avowedly hostile to Athens, and were in a condition in which Philip could make many demands upon them, which they did not dare to refuse. No state was ever more wretchedly deceived by him. The real leaders of the Olynthians, Lasthenes and Euthycrates were bought by him out and out; and through them he cheated the unhappy people of Olynthus, who, from hatred and jealousy of Athens, trusted to their most dangerous enemy, and received the merited reward for their stupid credulity.

LECTURE LVII.

WHILE, on the one hand, this war diverted the attention of the Athenians, and the want of great men paralysed their undertakings, an event happened, on the other, which furnished Philip the means of extending his power over Greece, and of dividing the Greeks by party feuds among themselves. This was the Phocian (Olymp. 106, 1), or as it is very improperly called the Sacred war.

This war is a proof of the evil consequences which follow bad and wicked actions, though they may not appear immediately after the deed. All Greece was suffering from the effects of the occupation of the Cadmea, not merely because the Boeotian power raised itself above the others, but all Greece lost its independence through this war. The Amphictyons were not a federative authority, which might have exercised a beneficial influence. The ancient public law of the Greeks, indeed, contained the injunction, that they were to watch over the sacred observance of truces; but they had then no longer the power to maintain peace among the Greeks. Their influence, which in ancient times had certainly been salutary, and had introduced fair notions of public law among neighbouring nations, by preventing inhuman cruelty in war, and watching over the observance of truces, worked in the times in which we can trace their history, only for evil; for by hypocritical verdicts they gave rise to wars, which in the opinion of the Greeks were religious wars. The cause of the Phocian war was as follows.

The Thebans brought before the Amphictyons a hypocritical accusation against the Lacedaemonians, because their general, Phoebidas, had made himself master of the Cadmea in the midst of peace, "though these saintly Boeotians themselves had destroyed Plataea in violation of all Amphictyonic laws." This accusation ought to have been rejected as absurd, because war had long since decided the question, and the Spartans had been sufficiently punished for their offence by the defeat of Leuctra and the restoration of Messene. But it was no bad calculation for the Thebans, since in consequence of their connection with Thessaly, they had great influence upon the votes of the barbarous and rude tribes, which through the senseless distribution of votes exercised an undue influence in the Amphictyony. Athens had only one vote among the Ionians, while the Aenianians, Malians, Thessalians, Dolopians, and small and almost barbarous tribes, and not even accounted as Greeks, had likewise one vote each. These tribes now were either indifferent, or voted for the interest of the Thebans; and the example set by the Thessalians naturally determined the votes of the Perrhaebians, Magnetes, and Phthiotans. The Spartans accordingly were sentenced to pay a fine of 1000 talents for having taken possession of the Cadmea.

A similar verdict was now pronounced against the Phocians also—perhaps the price for which the Locrians, and other little tribes which were exasperated against Phocis, had sold their votes against Sparta. This was perhaps the reason why the Thebans raised the accusation, though the ancient eumity existing between the Boeotians and Phocians must have been one of the chief causes.

The cause of the condemnation of the Phocians is indeed mentioned; but there is something obscure in it which cannot be cleared up. If the accusation was directed against the Phocian state, it is perfectly intelligible; but if it refers to the acts of individual Phocians, I cannot understand the condemnation. When the ancients dedicated a district as property to a god or a temple, the idea was not that the land should be cultivated for the benefit of the temple, or be let out to farm for a definite period, but it was dedicated in such a manner that a tithe from it was given to the deity, as we see from Xenophon's Anabasis.[1] This idea was widely diffused in antiquity, and was the reason why the tribe of Levi received the tithe in Palestine, that country, in the Old Testament, being represented as the direct property of Jehovah, and the Levites as his representatives. When, in the ancient sacred war (Olymp. 40), the Amphictyons destroyed Crissa or Cirrha, and dedicated the territory to the temple of Delphi, the meaning, no doubt, was, that the proprietors were to pay a tithe to the god. Now it so happened, that the boundaries between Phocis and Delphi were from early times, perhaps, ill defined, which is by no means surprising, seeing that the frontiers between the Phocians and Locrians had to be determined by a remarkable decree of a Roman consul;[2] it cannot be matter of surprise, that it would afford opportunities for dispute. The Phocians, as a state, might assert their right to levy the tithes in certain districts for themselves, while the temple also

---

[1] *Anab.* v. 3, § 12.

[2] Niebuhr here alludes to the Propraetor G. Avidius Nigrinus. Comp. *Corpus Inscript. Graec.* No. 1711.—ED.

claimed it. But in the ordinary accounts, it is represented, as if that district ought to have remained uncultivated, and as if the sin of the Phocians had consisted in putting it under the plough, wherein Philomelus and his friends are said to have been particularly guilty. If the country had been allowed to lie waste, it would have yielded no benefit to the god; but if it was actually to remain uncultivated, the probable meaning is, that the district should serve as pasturage. If, therefore, the Phocians took a piece of it into cultivation, they had, it is true, no right to do so; but they had a right to think it vexatious that such beautiful soil should lie waste. But however this may be, all the Phocian towns were sentenced to pay a heavy fine for this sacrilege, which consisted either in their appropriating the tithes to themselves, or in taking sacred land into cultivation.

The Phocians protested against the injustice of the verdict, declaring that the fine was far beyond their means, and that the whole country would be ruined. They did not pay it; thereupon the hypocrites inflicted the double fine upon them, as well as upon the Spartans, who also refused to pay; and when this, too, remained unpaid, the Thebans and the Thessalians were commissioned to march into Phocis and to levy the sum by main force. The Phocians, greatly terrified, applied to the Spartans, who were in the same predicament with them; but they, weak and abandoned by the whole country, were unable to do anything. The Phocians then addressed themselves to the Athenians, who, either from hatred of the Thebans, or from a feeling of humanity, declared for them, and made preparations to send them some assistance.

Delphi was at that time completely separated from Phocis, though my suspicion is, that at one time it stood to the rest of Phocis in the same relation as Thebes stood to Boeotia, and Rome to Latium. The Delphians were quite a contemptible people, like the inhabitants of places frequented by pilgrims, such as Compostella; or like those in watering-places, where the people live upon strangers; they were a thoroughly bad people, and hated by the Greeks, but they were extremely wealthy. They cherished great hatred of the Phocians, and maliciously rejoiced at the punishment inflicted upon them, for they had their profits on all such occasions, because the gold was wrought into ornaments. They resembled the goldsmith of Ephesus in the Acts of the Apostles. A great many artists lived at Delphi.

When the Phocians saw themselves outlawed, and on the point of being attacked, they very naturally said, " Well, we must carry our arms first to the place where our nearest enemies are." They accordingly advanced against Delphi, and occupied the town. It may be inferred from Aristotle's Politics [3] that the Delphians themselves were then divided into parties, but I do not place much reliance upon that passage.[4] When they were masters of Delphi, the Phocians issued protests throughout Greece against the inhuman verdict of outlawry; having the temple in their power, they wished to spread terror, and warn the Greeks not to drive them to extremes, but to cancel the unjust verdict. But no one listened to them; and the consequence only was, that they were decried ten times more as polluters of the temple, and robbers of its treasures, even before they had taken one ounce of silver. At first they did not touch the temple; nay, Philomelus even caused an inventory of its treasures to be made, and the treasures to be put under seal; but he levied immense contributions on the Delphians themselves. With these he hired mercenaries, of whom countless numbers were ever ready in all parts of Greece; he raised the pay, which had been high even before, by one-half, and thus a numerous army flocked around him. The Thebans and Thessalians being now called upon to protect the Delphic Apollo, advanced to chastise the profaners of his sanctuary. Philomelus went out to meet them; he had money, while the Thebans were only trying to beg it of the king of Persia, and he accordingly beat them right and left, and made many prisoners. Although, as yet, no treasures had been taken from the temple, yet the Thebans had already declared the Phocians to be robbers of the sacred treasures, and ordered the prisoners to be killed with javelins (κατακοντισθῆναι). Philomelus repaid them for this by taking revenge on the greater number of his prisoners. The separate engagements are not worth being related. After a succession of petty fights, Philomelus in the end lost his life in a battle, being obliged to fling himself

[3] v. 3, 3.

[4] " The Phocian state consisted of more than twenty towns, which were united as one whole; but we are absolutely ignorant of the relation existing among them."

down a precipice, in order not to fall into the hands of his enemies (Olymp. 106, 3).

Towards the end of his life, he had been under the necessity of making use of the treasures of the temple; but Onomarchus, his brother, who succeeded him, continued the plunder with more audacity, for there was no other help. The brass and iron of the temple were wrought into arms, and the Rubicon being once passed, the gold and silver were coined into money. Onomarchus, by liberal pay, assembled a still larger army. The executionary troops did not fare much better than the last troops of the same kind in the holy Roman empire, in the years 1789 and 90, when troops of the elector Palatine, and others, were sent against the Liegois, who at first did not like to come forward, but when they did march out, the whole affair was finished in three days, and the aggressors fled back further than the point from which they had come; but more blood was shed. The Thebans and Locrians were completely defeated, and the Thessalians fared no better. The Phocians made themselves masters of the ruins of Orchomenos and Coronea, subdued the Locrians, and advanced into Thessaly.

The princes of Pherae now called upon them for assistance, for Philip had already commenced establishing himself in Thessaly. The Aleuadae had invited him to assist them against the citizens of Larissa; at the first call, he had appeared with troops, and in order to maintain the citadel he of course left a garrison in it. In this manner, he had already established himself in all Thessaly, with the exception of Pherae. The princes of that place now joined the Phocians, and offered resistance.[5] Philip advanced against the Phocians; and, at the request of the Thessalians, who were devoted to him, he availed himself of the opportunity, and declared his army the soldiers of the god; he carried on the affair with great hypocrisy, and pretended to be very zealous. He ordered his army to wear crowns of the laurel of the Pythian god at the commencement of a battle, as if the soldiers were going to perform some act of worship. In the first engagement he gained some advantage; but afterwards he lost two battles so completely, that he was obliged to retreat and evacuate Thessaly.

[5] In 1826, Niebuhr adopted the account that the Aleuadae invited Philip against the princes of Pherae.—ED.

This would have been the moment for rising and coming forward against him, if a better spirit had prevailed at Athens, and if the Olynthians had not waited until they were annihilated. But all remained quiet; and having thus been enabled to restore his forces, he again advanced against Pherae in Thessaly. Onomarchus went to its assistance, but was obliged to return, and during his retreat he was pushed by Philip towards the Malian gulf. There he was defeated, and the whole Phocian army was routed (Olymp. 106, 4): this was the greatest defeat which they had suffered during the whole war. An Athenian fleet had been very properly sent to those parts, in order to occupy Thermopylae, in case the Phocians should lose a battle. This foresight then saved Greece. Fear of being calumniated had prevented the Athenians from openly aiding the Phocians, and they contented themselves with anchoring near the coast. The Phocians endeavoured to escape to the Athenian ships, but most of them perished in the waves; Onomarchus himself fell on the coast, and Philip ordered his body to be nailed on a cross. But the Athenians now quickly guarded Thermopylae, so that Philip could not advance farther south.

The princes of Pherae now capitulated, and withdrew with their mercenaries to Phocis. Pherae thus fell into the hands of Philip; and immediately afterwards Pagasae also, the only large and real Thessalian town on the bay of Iolcos; there too Philip had had his traitors, who played everything into his hands.

It is possible, that it may have been as early as this time, that Philip, under the title of protector of Thessaly, regulated the affairs of that country. He did with Thessaly what Napoleon wanted to do with Poland: instead of restoring it as a great state, he cut it up into three small ones—an idea unworthy of his greatness, and one by which he injured himself exceedingly, and which was the principal cause of the failure of the Russian campaign. Thessaly had from early times been divided into four parts or cantons:—a division which tradition traced to Aleuas, a son of Pyrrhus, and grandson of Achilles. These cantons together formed one state, and the bond among them had become loosened very gradually.[6]

[6] " Even in the best maps, the whole of Thessaly, in its wider sense, is generally divided into four parts, Phthiotis, Hestiaeotis, Pelasgiotis, and Thessa-

Philip now instituted in each of the four districts a separate government, and thus formed four distinct states, tetrarchies, without any common bond among them. In this manner, he gained his end: the four different states, to the advantage of their conqueror, became jealous of one another; for such divisions always produce the effects desired by the enemy. He kept garrisons in the strong cities, and caused the important harbour of Pagasae, the common seaport of Thessaly, as well as, on account of its tolls, the common source of revenue of the country, to be entirely ceded to him, and levied there, according to his own discretion, whatever tolls he deemed necessary for the general wants of Thessaly; so anxious was he for the welfare of the country! The subject districts of Thessaly, Magnesia and Perrhaebia, had formerly been subject to Thessaly in general, and it would seem that these common territories were the only thing by which the state of Thessaly was kept together; just as, previous to the revolution, a common government was the only bond of union in Switzerland. Philip now caused those districts also to be given up to him, and he governed them completely as provinces.

liotis, so that the Magnetes, Phthiotans, and other tribes, appear contained in those districts. But that division affects only Thessaly proper, so that Phthiotis is the district about Pharsalus from mount Oeta; Hestiaeotis, the western country towards mount Pindus; Pelasgiotis is the country from Larissa to Pagasae, west of Magnesia and Thessaliotis, properly Thettaliotis, the plain. These names occur in Strabo (ix. p. 430, B. ed. Casaub.). The Scholiast on Apollonius Rhodius (iii. 1090) has some errors in the names; instead of Ἑστιαιῶτις, for example, he has Ἰωλκῖτις. The division of Strabo occurred also in Aristotle; and Theopompus, quoted by Harpocration, expressly says, that the division into four tetrarchies referred to the simple division of Thessaly. The passage of Demosthenes (*Philip.* iii. p. 117), in which he speaks of the arrangement of the tetrarchies, contains an expression which has its peculiar difficulty. He there mentions a Thessalian δεκαδαρχία, and afterwards a τετραρχία. The reading is as ancient as Harpocration, who is likewise struck by it, and endeavours to explain it. He says δεκαδαρχία is the government of ten, which the Lacedaemonians appointed in every town; and this he proves from Isocrates. But he adds: what the word δεκαδαρχία in Demosthenes means is a riddle to me, for Philip did not establish in Thessaly a δεκαδαρχία, but a τετραρχία. The reading, therefore, is ancient; δεκαρχία alone occurs as a variation. But we must bear in mind, that Δ in the ancient Greek numbers, especially at Athens, signified both 10 and 4. It has been proved beyond a doubt, that in the time of Demosthenes the cursive mode of writing was employed in MSS., and abbreviations also were used. The probable reading of the MS., therefore, was ΔΑΔΔΑΡΧΙΑ, which was afterwards, according to its usual meaning explained as δεκαδαρχία, but it must be read τετρααδρχία."—1825.

His dominion thus extended nearly as far as Thermopylae. It is not quite certain whether Phthiotis, as early as that time, fell into the state of dependence in which we afterwards find it.

Until now, there had been no πόλεμος ἄσπονδός between Athens and Philip; there was no open or avowed war, and the intercourse between the two countries was continued. When the two powers met each other, they fought; but there was, as yet, no direct war. Philip, however, fitted out pirate ships against Athens, interfered in everything, stirred up Euboea against Athens, sent troops from Thessaly to Euboea (Olymp. 106, 3), and there gained over a party by supporting the tyrants at Eretria and in other places. I have already remarked, that the tyrants which then rose in several cities, were quite different from those of earlier times.

It was not long before Philip became involved in a war with the Olynthians (Olymp. 107, 2). They had kindly received Philip's step-brother, who, not without reason, feared for his own life, because the other brothers of Philip had died, according to the fashion of eastern policy, and he too feared the same fate. He considered the atmosphere of Olynthus safer than that of Pella. Philip, regarding this as a hostile demonstration, demanded his surrender; but the Olynthians refused. Until then Olynthus had followed a policy which was as foolish as it was base: it had been the tool which enabled Philip to increase his power, to the detriment of Athens; and Philip had contrived to manage matters in such a way, that Olynthus had no allies, and was on terms of implacable enmity with Athens. In this condition it was attacked by Philip. Methone, the last Greek town on the coast of Pieria, and a very considerable place, had been taken by him shortly before (Olymp. 106, 4), on which occasion he lost one eye. He disarmed the town, and established a Macedonian colony in it. The Olynthians had hitherto been guided by those two demagogues, Lasthenes and Euthycrates, who were openly sold to Philip, and boasted of their prudence in having formed their profitable connexion with him.[7]   The

---

[7] " Olynthus is called πόλις μυρίανδρος, the body of citizens probably consisting of 10,000, though it does not follow that all of them must have lived within the walls. Many may have lived several miles off, though they were in the

Olynthians had looked upon Philip as their true ally, and upon themselves as his favourites; and now, when they found themselves deceived and attacked by their own idol, they were in great distress, and sued for peace. He answered, that they might have it on the same terms as Methone; that they must evacuate the city, but that their lives should be spared; that they might take their property with them, but that they must go and leave their city to him (Olymp. 107, 4). In their despair, they saw no other help but to apply to the Athenians, to whom they had, until then, done the greatest injuries.

The foolish among the Athenians rejoiced at the misfortunes of the Olynthians, and the less foolish were highly offended and annoyed at their proposal, saying, that it was the very height of impertinence. "The traitors, assuming the mask of patriots, advised the people to let the Olynthians suffer their well-deserved punishment, and to avail themselves of the opportunity of making peace with Philip, saying, that he would be sure to restore Amphipolis, and the like." The proposal of the Olynthians would have been rejected, had it not been for Demosthenes.

Demosthenes was then about thirty-four years old, and in the real vigour of manhood, when youthful vivacity is already tempered by experience and reflection. Much has been said and written about him, even in antiquity. Moderns read his speeches mostly on account of their merit as specimens of masterly oratory, and less with reference to the time in which he lived, and the personal character of Demosthenes; the importance of the last point, however, is far greater than the inquiry into the history of that miserable period. But by most moderns he is more named than known. In the case of great men like Cicero and Göthe, it is of much greater consequence thoroughly to know the men and their whole character, than to know their writings; because by means of the former we see how their whole nature differs in every respect from that of ordinary men, and we obtain a knowledge of the contrast existing between common characters and those who are in their inmost soul altogether of a higher species; letters of

---

relation of sympolity; for this relation is there mentioned for the first time in the history of the war, which Olynthus carried on against Amyntas and the Spartans."

such men are particularly instructive. It is my opinion, that in the speeches of Demosthenes we ought to study his personal character rather than anything else.[8]

If there is any tragic character in history, it is that of the man who, from the first, sees what should be done, recognises the wretched mistakes made all around him, sees how every thing is hurrying to ruin without his being able to make his fellow men see the truth, and has to suffer the pain of seeing destruction approaching long before it is actually felt, while all the others are still deceiving themselves with hopes, or live on heedlessly and thoughtlessly. This bitter cup, the foresight of evil, Demosthenes emptied with the purest patriotism. Such a man assuredly cannot be cheerful; and hence all his speeches are pervaded by a gloomy and serious melancholy, and are never hopeful. Cicero's speeches, especially those delivered immediately after his consulship, are very cheerful, and display a deeply-felt happiness; but this we never find in Demosthenes. His greatness, however, consists in this very circumstance, that he is nevertheless indefatigable, that he does not allow himself to be deterred by any misfortune or by any insult, and never swerves even when his sad advice has not been listened to, or has been so badly executed, that people afterwards, with some show of justice, could blame him for having pressed his advice upon them. Without ceasing, he keeps his eyes open, and sees at every moment what ought to be done, and is again ever ready to advise, urge on, and entreat his countrymen.

He found everything in a sad condition: the only moment when he could hope for better things, was that immediately before the battle of Chaeronea, when he had induced the Greeks to unite themselves with Athens. At that moment he enjoyed all the happiness of which he was capable. Greece was in a state of dissolution; Philip was powerful, and every-where parties were active in promoting his interest; in many cities there were hired traitors in the service of Philip; at Athens their number was indeed small, but the general corruption and degeneracy favoured Philip's plans. Many towns were wholly gained over by Philip. At home, Demosthenes found himself by the side of some men of talent and patriotism, but of an entirely different character from his own, "such as Lycurgus

---

* Comp. *Klein. Schrift.*, vol. i. p. 476, foll.

who was a thoroughly honest man, but not free from sycophancy, for *accusatorem factitavit*, as Cicero says of him; he was
of a soured temperament, which took pleasure in accusing. But
Demosthenes never accused in that way." Others, however, and
this was worse, were, though very honest men, perverse in
their judgment. Phocion, who is commonly called a model of
virtue, did nothing but injury to his country, and more injury
than any other man; except when matters had come to extremes, and his personal character made some impression; then,
however, it was not his virtue that saved Athens, but the fact
that Antipater recollected that he was the old opponent of Demosthenes, and of those whom Macedonia persecuted. He was
not a traitor, which we may say with probability of Aeschines,
and of Philocrates with certainty; he was not capable of such
baseness, but he had such an unfortunate conviction, of the
impossibility of conquering Philip, and was so firmly persuaded that the fate of Greece was decided, that he opposed
Demosthenes everywhere, and with all his might, because he conceived that resistance would not only be fruitless, but would only
make things worse. " He was in favour of Philip, from an irony
of life—to borrow an expression from a celebrated author—
with a constant smile at the folly, as it is thought, of undertaking great things with insufficient means." In such circumstances, in the midst of that dissolution of Greece, without any
support, in a state in which democracy had risen to its highest
point, amid such a fickle people, which had become wholly
unaccustomed to military service, with such inferior and
unfortunate generals, Demosthenes ventured to offer resistance
to Philip, who stood opposed to him in all his greatness and
with all his ability: it was truly the boldest enterprise ever
undertaken by an enthusiastic and extraordinary man, who
feels in himself a moral strength to bear everything.

Before Demosthenes came forward, Athens was in a perfectly
forlorn state. The superiority of the Athenians consisted in
their susceptibility; for never was a nation so susceptible to
the impressions of great men; and no spot on earth has ever
produced so many great men as Athens. But that time was
an unfortunate period. " The people had fallen into bad
hands, and its good fortune alone saved it from utter ruin."
Plato had unfortunately withdrawn from public life; his great
mind might have conferred unspeakable blessings on his

country, if he had approached nearer to the people, and had
not turned away with aversion from this susceptibility of his
countrymen.   But the people were not always susceptible, and
at that time they were greatly inferior to what they had been
in the Peloponnesian war, and much inferior, even, than afterwards under the general Demosthenes.   Through him the
Athenians had raised themselves again, and displayed a much
more vigorous and noble spirit.

  " When Demosthenes came forward in the public assembly,
he found a people corrupted by demagogues and seduced by
flatterers, with whom little could be effected.   By the gradual
progress which he made by dint of perseverance, by his talents
and patriotism, he soon gained the confidence of the whole
people, so that thousands of uneducated men followed him as
children follow a father.   He exercised this influence solely by
his oratory, his personal worth, the superiority of his talents,
and by his patriotism; and that too without occupying a
position in which he might have used authority, and in a state
the dissolution of which was so great that no one could
exercise any authority.   His personal influence effected more
than the most prudent decision of those who had the power of
commanding.   His oratory carried his audience with him,
and he guided them by the greatness of the talents with
which God had endowed him.   He was one of the greatest
administrative statesmen; to examine his plans and measures
is one of the highest enjoyments.   The greatest tendency at
Athens then, as in the French revolution, was, to change the
constitution, which is always the first idea of inferior minds,
who do not consider whether men are to be found capable of
working a new constitution.   Demosthenes never thought of
such a thing; he knew what could be effected with the actual
constitution, and that it was the best.

  He had to struggle against the most furious attacks of those
who were opposed to his principles, and against the vulgarest
interests of thousands.   And yet he inspired thousands of the
poorest to give up the support which, as sovereign members
of the state, they enjoyed, and to devote it to the good of their
country; the people, who had become unaccustomed to military
service, were inspired by him to take up arms, and to accustom
themselves to use them in the defence of their country.   This
truly is something greater than what Alexander did, when,

with an army of thirty thousand men, he traversed Asia as far as the Indus. The latter had full power of commanding, and full authority over his subjects; but Demosthenes produced the greatest self-denial by awakening the noblest feelings.

Under his training, the Athenians thus raised themselves more and more, and became more and more alive to everything that is great and noble. His enemies were not sparing of calumny; but the conduct of the Athenians was never nobler than towards Demosthenes. With this nation, regenerated by himself, he at last undertook what, indeed, proved unsuccessful; but, if the battle of Chaeronea could have been put off for two years, or if its issue had been different, which might very easily have been the case, Athens would have commenced a fresh and youthful career.

From Athens, his influence spread all over Greece, in a manner which was unparalleled in the history of his country. He saw that Athens could not rule over Greece; and thus endeavoured, with the greatest purity and disinterestedness, to concentrate all Greece in himself. If, as I said before, the battle of Chaeronea could have been put off for two years, he would have acquired an influence over Greece under which it would have been invincible; for he worked upon the other Greeks, as well as upon the Athenians, by travelling as Athenian ambassador from place to place. His reputation preceded him, and the people saw in him, not the Athenian, but the spotless Greek, although the bribed traitors left no means untried against him.

But the relation of Demosthenes to the Athenians never showed itself more beautifully than during the war of Philip against Olynthus.

----•----

LECTURE LXVIII.

FOR a period of eighty years, Olynthus had acted the part of an enemy towards Athens, and yet it now received its assistance against the common foe. It was one of the greatest triumphs ever celebrated by wisdom and excellence, that

Demosthenes inspired the thousands of Athenians who heard him with his own feelings, and persuaded them to succour the Olynthians.   But he was not able to induce them to make the succour as great and as extensive as he himself wished it to be.   His desire was, that the Athenians should exert all their powers, that they should embark themselves instead of sending mercenaries, and that with their fleet they should, by a variety of diversions, make the war oppressive to Philip, and draw him away from his main object.   " But it was still too early in the career of Demosthenes, and such resolution could not yet be expected of the Athenians."   They confined themselves to going to the assistance of the Olynthians with a few thousand men, and the command of this force was intrusted to wretched generals, such as Chares.   This could not produce any good.   But, even thus, the fate of Olynthus was delayed ; and the Olynthians might, perhaps, have saved themselves, had they been on their guard against internal treachery.   But they allowed themselves to be deceived by the same men who had formerly been sold to Philip ; and they were so imprudent as to intrust the supreme command to his most notorious partizans, Lasthenes and Euthycrates, who unhesitatingly betrayed them.   The detail of the capture of Olynthus is unknown; but it was taken by treachery (Olymp. 108, 1), and its fate was that of a city taken by storm.   The surviving inhabitants, women and children, were made slaves ; whole bands of them were given by the king as slaves to the traitors, others were sold, and others again were distributed in the provinces.   The taking of Olynthus completed the conquest of the Greek cities, from the Thessalian frontier as far as Thrace.

Philip treated the cities of that coast like a barbarian ; the inhabitants of many of them were made slaves ; but most of them were transplanted into other districts, to found new towns.   I have already compared the fate of Macedonia with that of the Muscovite empire under the Mongoles, and we here again have a resemblance between Philip and Peter I. Although Philip was not a barbarian like Peter, and although he was not as cruel, yet the internal arrangements of his empire greatly resemble those under Peter ; as, for example, the foundation of towns by transplanting entire populations. In this, both Philip and Peter took a delight ; and many

thousands were transferred from one place to another.   In the
Greek cities, he carried on this system on a large scale.   His
object was, to establish Macedonians on the coast, and to
transplant the Greeks to the interior of his kingdom.   But it
was not the Greeks only that he treated in this way, he also
transplanted and mixed the native tribes, in order to keep
them more easily in subjection ; thus, Paeonians, Macedonians,
Illyrians, and Thracians, were obliged, by his command, to
leave their native places, and settle at a great distance from
them.   Barbarous tribes feel the consequences of such measures
less painfully than civilised people; whence, in Macedonia, the
barbarous tribes, when mixed with one another, lost nothing
but a little of their nationality.

The destruction of Olynthus caused the Athenians afterwards
to regret that they had not completely adopted the advice of
Demosthenes, and had spoiled his plan in the manner of carrying it into effect.   His influence, therefore, continued to
increase; it was the very misfortunes of the time that then
called forth at Athens more and more men of eminence.   It is
quite striking to see so many more men of sterling character
appear during that unhappy period than there had been before.
But although the influence of Demosthenes was now on the
increase, yet the first step which was taken after the capture of
Olynthus was very unfortunate, and is imputed to Demosthenes
as a crime, by those who presume to judge of him.   I allude
to the peace with Philip, "which from the greatest traitor is
called the peace of Philocrates" (Olymp. 108, 2).   But this
unfortunate event ought not to be laid to the charge of Demosthenes; he could not prevent it.   Men of the ripest judgment
are least obstinate.   Demosthenes took the peace for what it
was—for a great misfortune; and if the Athenians had been
willing to follow his advice, he would have urged them to
continue the war under all circumstances; but as he saw that the
Athenians were only on the road to wisdom, and were as yet
but half wise, he comprehended the necessity of waiting until
there should be manifested among the Greeks a desire to come
to the assistance of the distressed.   Athens alone could not
possibly hold out in the unequal contest.

For the present Philip's influence prevailed all over Greece;
his shameless followers went so far as to boast of being his
servants.   Demosthenes, therefore, might say to himself, as he

actually does say in his speeches: we are now in a condition in which the continuation of the war will lead us only from one loss to another, and a coalition may be easily formed, against which it will be utterly impossible to contend, and then all is lost.   For these reasons, he agreed to the peace, but only on condition that it should be a general peace—that the Thracian princes whose empire Philip tried to destroy, and the Phocians, should be included in it.   Could this have been obtained, the peace, considering the circumstances of the time, would have been perfectly satisfactory.   Demosthenes knew that if Philip concluded such a peace, Athens would have a long time of rest and recovery; and that Philip's restlessness would drive him to make enemies among those who were then his friends. The Athenians, moreover, were greatly interested in retaining Chersonnesus, where they had established a cleruchia.

But the misfortune was, that the majority of the ambassadors were traitors.   Philocrates certainly was one, and Aeschines cannot be justified; all his excuses are worthless, just as his speeches in general are when compared with those of Demosthenes: they are, according to a Greek proverb, like the cricket compared with the nightingale.   They either allowed themselves to be deceived by Philip, or had sold themselves to him.   Thrice he delayed the negotiations under the most detestable pretexts, until he had made such progress that his objects were accomplished, and that he could march through Thessaly into Phocis.   " For until then the Athenians, in conjunction with the Phocians, had rendered it impossible for him to penetrate into Greece; " but after the peace, Athens was obliged to withdraw her fleet from Thermopylae.   " By this means the Phocians were thrown upon their own resources, and their ruin was inevitable."

The Phocians had become very formidable to the Thebans. They had conquered several places, were established in Boeotia, and ravaged the country.   After the death of Onomarchus, they were commanded by Phayllus, who had undertaken the administration for Phalaecus, the son of his brother Onomarchus.   These three brothers are justly called by Aeschines tyrants.   The ancient constitution of the Phocians lay dormant, and those strategi reigned with absolute power.   By the most glaring injustice the Phocians had been driven to despair; but despair generally produces moral depravity, which showed itself among them also. Their rulers were unprincipled and infamous men. We do not indeed regard the gifts in the temple of Delphi as sacred, but those men were, in their own eyes, guilty of sacrilege; and what was to be excused at first by necessity, could no longer be excused, when they rolled in the wealth of those treasures.[1] At first those treasures had been taken from the temple to satisfy the wants of the moment, but soon after the rulers robbed without necessity, giving away the sacred treasures to their wives or concubines, and dividing the ready money among themselves. Matters were thus in a bad state, and the system of robbery became worse and worse, while the unhappy people sank deeper and deeper into servitude.

After the death of Phayllus, Phalaecus, the son of Onomarchus, who was still quite a young man, undertook the command himself. At the head of his mercenaries he kept possession of the passes of Thessaly, thinking that it would thus be impossible for Philip to advance. Meantime, a sort of civil government had been formed in Phocis, with which he began to quarrel, because it commenced making inquiries into the system of peculation which had been carried on. Many of the robbers were condemned and put to death, and a part of the money was demanded back. This measure was taken very ill by Phalaecus; he felt still more affronted by the appointment of persons who were quite independent of him to the highest offices; and there can be no doubt that he betrayed the unhappy country to Philip. He capitulated for a free departure for himself and his friends, and surrendered the whole country. Soon afterwards he met in Crete with a disgraceful and well-merited death.

While the Athenian embassy was detained in the most shameless manner, and even Demosthenes, who was one of the ambassadors, could not help seeing how his colleagues betrayed their country without his being able to prevent it, Philip advanced into Phocis, Olymp. 108, 3. He was now in the heart of Greece, and Athens was completely deceived. Philip

[1] " The plunder of the treasures, however, cannot have been quite general, for Pausanias still saw many anathemata in the temple. But many things were no doubt taken away. If we bear in mind, that, as Appian says, the Gauls also plundered the temple, the Phocians must have left many treasures untouched. They are, nevertheless, said to have robbed 10,000 talents, more than £2,000,000, which is impossible."—1826.

appeared as one intrusted with a holy commission, and all
Phocis experienced the fate of a city taken by the sword. His
favorite excuse was, that all Phocians were sacrilegious persons:
every peasant was treated as guilty of sacrilege, and the whole
country was given up to the wildest licentiousness of the
soldiers. Countless numbers of human beings were recklessly
murdered, and many thousands were dragged away into
slavery. Few men are so absolutely bad as to be incapable of
one good act; and I do believe that Aeschines may be right in
claiming the merit of having prevented the total extinction of
the Phocians. The Amphictyonic council was then summoned;
the Lacedaemonians, as outlaws, being excluded. The Thebans
and Thessalians formed the majority, and it was agreed that
the Phocians should be declared unworthy of the right of
voting in the Amphictyony, and that they should be deprived
of the presidency of the Pythian games, and all other honorary
privileges. The vote of the Phocians, their share in the
Pythian games, and the other privileges, were now conferred
upon Philip. After this it was resolved to raze all the towns to
the ground, and to distribute the Phocians into villages. But
this decree does not appear to have been carried out completely,
for soon afterwards we find the town of Elatea still existing.
The Phocians, moreover, were not to be allowed to keep horses
and arms, the soil was to be left to them, but they were to pay
to the god of Delphi every year sixty talents, as an indemni-
fication for the robberies committed in his temple. The whole
of this sentence remained in force for sixty-eight years, down
to Olymp. 125, after the invasion of the Gauls, when the
rights of a nation were restored to the Phocians.

Their fate not only terrified the Athenians, but many
other Greeks now had their eyes opened. One good effect
in particular was, that the Thebans were very much exasperated against Philip: they had hoped, after the conquest
of Phocis, to receive an increase of territory and population,
but Philip kept everything for himself, and told them, that
they ought to be satisfied with Orchomenos, Coronea, etc.,
which he had restored to them.   Thus the Thebans, with the
appearance of gratitude, became his bitter enemies.   Demosthenes perceived this change, and knew how to make use
of it.

Philip now turned his attention northward against Thrace.

Even before this, he had extended his dominion in the direction of Epirus. His restless activity was successful. We cannot divide all his campaigns according to years; we only know, that in Olymp. 109, he was already in possession of Ambracia. He was married to an Epirot princess, of a younger branch which was not on the throne. He had founded in Cassopia, in Epirus, a small principality for his brother-in-law, Alexander, at the time when the aged Arybas was still reigning over the Molottians; and after the death of Arybas, he gave him the Molottian kingdom, and placed him on the throne of Epirus (Olymp. 109, 3). But with the same policy which Napoleon observed towards his brothers, to prevent their feeling themselves independent, he took possession of Ambracia, and stationed there a strong Macedonian garrison. Alexander, therefore, could not venture to move, being altogether in Philip's power.[2]

" In Thrace he was completely successful against the Odrysians. Previously to the Peloponnesian war all the Thracian tribes were independent; subsequently the king of the Odrysians had become king of Thrace, and the Thracians ruled from the Danube to the Aegean, and from Byzantium to Macedonia. But this was altogether a barbarous empire without any close bond of union; and even under Cotys, the son of the first king, it was in a state of dissolution." After his death the Odrysian empire was disputed by several pretenders. " Philip's assistance was called in, and when a reconciliation was brought about, he had already established himself from the Hebrus and Rhodope as far as the sea coast;" he had reduced a part of Thrace completely under his own dominion, and made the Thracian princes quite dependent upon himself, so that they were in a condition similar to that of the native princes of India.

Philip's first care now was to put himself in possession of the entrance to the Euxine; and there the cleruchiae of the Athenians in Chersonnesus were a stumbling-block in his way. Notwithstanding the peace, Athens was disturbed and annoyed in those possessions, sometimes directly and sometimes

---

[2] " An attempt to subdue the very strong city of Ambracia, where Philip's bribery had created a party for himself, had been thwarted by the activity of Demosthenes. But after Philip's death we find a Macedonian garrison there."
—1825. (Comp. *Hist. of Rome*, vol. iii. p. 165.)

indirectly. Not only was Byzantium an important city in those parts, but also Perinthus, afterwards called Heraclea; and the two cities were allied with each other, standing in the relation of sympolity. Now in order to extend his sway over all Thrace, and to deprive the Athenians of their navigation to the Euxine, which they kept up under the protection of Persia, and by which they greatly enriched themselves, Philip directed all his forces against Byzantium and Perinthus.

The siege of Perinthus (Olymp. 109, 4) is remarkable in the history of ancient warfare on account of the manly defence of its inhabitants, and the enormous exertions of Philip: "it is the siege during which the art of engineering rose from its infancy." Perinthus (now Erekli) was situated on a promontory, which had only one narrow access on the land side, and the town rose up on the side of the mountain. With an abundance of machinery which was unprecedented, Philip attacked the strong walls facing the main land. The Athenians sent a fleet to its relief; Demosthenes had persuaded them to do so, "although those cities had for the last fifteen years been at enmity with Athens; and it was not without difficulty that his advice prevailed over the traitors." The Persian satraps also sent provisions and ammunition from the opposite coast of Asia. At length Demosthenes had inspired the other Greeks also with so much confidence in Athens, that the Rhodians, Mityleneans, and Chians, who until then had been foolishly opposed to Athens, now likewise sent succour. Perinthus was thus supported and provided on the sea side, where Philip was unable to undertake anything. He confined himself to attacks on the land side. The first wall was indeed taken; but as the city rose on the hill side with high and massive houses, the Perinthians walled up the streets, and fortified their houses, so that a new wall was formed. In this manner he advanced a few times; but the power opposed to him was so strong, that after the greatest efforts he was obliged to raise the siege. His attempt upon Byzantium (Olymp. 110, 1) was likewise unsuccessful, "and Philip was obliged to withdraw his troops.

The failure of this undertaking produced among the Greeks the same sensation as Napoleon's unfortunate catastrophe in Spain; it was believed that Philip's good fortune had reache its turning point." He probably felt that his glory was beginning to fade; and in order to make the world speak of him, he entered upon fresh undertakings (Olymp. 110, 2) against the king of the Scythians in Bessarabia, north of the Danube, where he hoped to effect something grand and brilliant. He conquered the king, and brought back considerable booty, consisting of cattle and prisoners, but lost them on his way back, being attacked by the Triballi in the passes of mount Haemus.

The year thus passed very unfortunately for Philip. The influence of Demosthenes increased more and more, " for the younger and more susceptible generation became attached to him, and the number of his followers became daily greater." His influence gradually extended over everything; he introduced reforms in all directions and in all public affairs, especially in the Athenian system of taxation, and that too without any intention of sparing himself, for he was very wealthy, and his measures were calculated to make the burdens bearable to the whole, by making the greatest demands upon those possessed of property. " It was now easy for him to guide a great number of men who had heard him when they were young, and who had been trained by him; with older people he had indeed less influence, but every one of his actions greatly increased it."

He persuaded the Athenians to make the greatest efforts, and to make sacrifices which were large in proportion to the limited means they then possessed. It was at this period, about Olymp. 109, that the burdens of the trierarchy were so immensely increased for the wealthy, " and that the poor renounced their share in the public property." A considerable part of the revenues from subject countries and the mines, was distributed among the citizens at festivals; this money was not given to them, as has been said, to pay for their admission to the theatre—it would have been much easier to make the admission free—but it was pocket-money for holydays, to enable even the poorest to give himself a treat for once, and to celebrate the festival. Those poor people, however, had a vote in the state. The θεωρικὸν had frequently drained the treasury, and this circumstance had often led to discussions about its abolition. But on the proposal of flattering demagogues, a decree had been passed that no one, who did not wish to make himself liable to the γραφὴ παρανόμων and pay his offence with his life, should propose to apply that money to any other purpose.

But Demosthenes, disregarding everything, inspired even the populace with patriotism, and it was not in a moment of imminent danger, but at a time when it was only threatening at a distance, that those poor people willingly sacrificed their holiday-money, and resolved to apply the θεωρικὸν to military preparations. It must, however, be observed, that Athens at that time rose through commerce, and through commerce alone, as we see from the administration of the orator Lycurgus, during which so many new galleys were built, arsenals restored, timber for ship-building and arms were purchased, that we must infer that Athens was very wealthy.

The influence of Demosthenes thus grew from day to day; and the exasperation between Athens and Philip increased at the same rate.

The people of many other parts of Greece also began to repent, and to wish to undo that which had been done; but no one wanted to lose what he had got, and no one was willing openly to declare his sentiments. " Demosthenes had travelled wherever he thought the people susceptible to his ideas; he had agitated and stirred up the people; but his advice, not to engage mercenaries, but to fight themselves for their wives and children, fell heavily upon them." In Peloponnesus, Philip's influence was predominant, especially among the Messenians, Arcadians, and Argives, to whom he appeared as a natural ally against the Spartans, although the latter were so much weakened, that they could make no pretensions, and had ceased to be formidable. All they could do, if, in their weakness and prostration, they wished to continue their existence, was altogether to turn over a new leaf, and to confer the franchise upon the inhabitants of the country around them. This was afterwards seen very clearly in the case of Cleomenes and those who succeeded him as usurpers, Machanidas and Nabis, who, by overthrowing the ancient forms, and by conferring the franchise upon the perioeci and many helots, raised Sparta to such power that it could again rule over the whole of Peloponnesus. But they still remained in their misfortunes, and were just as narrow-minded as before. Archidamus, who was then king, was the very opposite of Cleomenes: he disdained to be king of a distressed state, but never thought of curing its disease. No one thought of making any change; what was hallowed by time was not to be touched.

Elis had been one of the first places that threw itself into the arms of Philip, and was closely allied with him. After the Sacred war, an aristocracy of wealth seems to have established itself there, and that aristocracy offered to co-operate with Philip. A great many citizens were expelled on that occasion; the exiles took the remnants of the mercenaries from the Sacred war into their pay, and returned to their country arms in hand. But the Eleans allied themselves with the Arcadians, defeated the exiles and mercenaries, and murdered their prisoners.[3] In Peloponnesus, therefore, there were but few inclined to listen to the voice of truth; but the Thebans, whom Demosthenes had brought to their senses, did listen to it. " Byzantium and Perinthus now warmly embraced the alliance with Athens, for it would have required incredible perverseness not to join those who, disregarding all previous enmity, afforded them help in the hour of need. But in Greece proper, Athens still stood alone against Philip."

————•————

LECTURE LXIX.

As the irritation increased, Philip tried by unexpected steps to overawe the Athenians. He suddenly advanced with a small corps through Thermopylae into Phocis (Olymp. 110, $\frac{4}{3}$), and took possession of Elatea. The accesses to Greece remained in his hands; but he had evacuated the country itself. When the news of this invasion reached Athens, it created a sensation as tremendous, as if it had been expected that the Macedonians would appear before the walls of the city with the same rapidity with which they had come upon Elatea. This was followed by the scenes which are described in so masterly a manner by Demosthenes in his speech on the crown. When the tidings arrived in the evening, the assembly of the people was immediately convened; but no one ventured to speak;

[3] " Diodorus, it is true, speaks only of the murder of the mercenaries; but there are many indications in Demosthenes, *Olynth.* iii, and iv., and also in the oration περὶ παραπρεσβείας, p. 424, 425, that the exiles also were murdered."— 1825.

all the demagogues, who had before been most ready with their advice, were now silent and concealed themselves. Demosthenes alone came forward, entreating the people not to be desponding, and to do their part to prevent the misfortune, to take up arms, and to guard every post. This was done. When Philip learned that the Athenians had not lost their courage, but were making preparations and sending ambassadors to all the Greek towns on which they placed any hope, and more especially that Demosthenes had gone to Thebes, he paused and reflected. His object had been to take them by surprise ; but with his small force he could for the moment do nothing; the main body of his troops was coming after him.

This is the time to which the great embassy of Demosthenes belongs. He had often been ambassador; " he had travelled to all the tribes of Greece which he believed capable of being roused ; but this was his greatest triumph." He went as ambassador for his own country, and not as in modern states, where business is transacted in the cabinet of ministers; but he spoke as the representative of his nation before a people whom he was to persuade, and whose minds he had to move and guide. His commission was one of the highest problems. He was to influence a people which was hostile to the Athenians and faithless, which had shown itself insolent under all circumstances, which had brought about the misfortune of Greece, " which was so sullied that he could not apply to it the most powerful means of incitement, lest he should offend it;" a people with which the Athenians, during the last thirty-five years, had scarcely once been on tolerable terms, and often at open war—such a people he was to induce heartily to ally itself with Athens; and, as the Thebans dwelt north of Attica, the object of the alliance was to have them as a strong bulwark, because they were more immediately threatened than Athens. Philip sent Python, an eloquent Byzantian, to Thebes, who, however, could effect nothing against Demosthenes; the great Athenian thwarted all his efforts. As we afterwards hear of so many Theban exiles, it is probable, that many of the bribed partizans of Philip were already expelled, and that the Thebans were ready to adopt the advice of Demosthenes; but the success with which his efforts were crowned is not on that account less glorious, and shows the man in all his greatness. His influence was so overwhelming, that the Boeotarchs admitted him to their meetings as assessor; and Theopompus and other enemies,[1] with the intention of blaming him, relate that his voice was more weighty in Boeotia than that of the Boeotarchs themselves. On the other hand, some contemptible persons, men to whom the honour of Athens was nothing, did not blush—an Aeschines could hardly blush—to charge him with high treason, for not having insisted on the precedence of Athens in concluding the alliance, and for permitting perfect equality to the Thebans and all other Greeks who joined them; although this had been the only way of gaining them over. In this manner, he at length succeeded in bringing about a great Greek confederacy; but it was unfortunately too late to exert all its powers.

We do not know the whole extent of the confederacy, but there can be no doubt that, besides the Athenians and Thebans, Megara, Corinth, and the Achaeans, perhaps also the Euboeans and other small states, were members of the league.[2]   " Other

[1] Plutarch, *Demosth.* 18.

[2] Diodorus mentions the Thebans along with the Athenians, as if the Boeotians had taken no part in it. It is however certain, that the Corinthians, mentioned by Strabo (ix. p.414), were among them. Demosthenes, *de Coron.* p. 306, Reiske, when relating what tribes he had united with the Athenians against Philip, mentions besides the Thebans and Corinthians, also the Megarians, Leucadians, Corcyraeans, Achaeans, and Euboeans. It is clear from Plutarch's life of Phocion, that Megara soon became reconciled to the Athenians, and was in alliance with them. The Leucadians and Corcyraeans and the Corinthian colony of Ambracia must be supposed to have belonged to the confederacy; because, as we know from the third and fourth Philippic of Demosthenes, they stood under the protection of Corinth, and accordingly were obliged to join that city. Corcyra, which had formerly been powerful, was then politically quite a feeble state; and the Achaeans were entirely opposed to Philip even after the battle of Chaeronea. In regard to the Euboeans, nothing is known. Plutarch, in his lives of the ten orators, mentions a psephisma, which had been passed in favour of Demosthenes on the proposal of Demochares. In it we read, that he had gained all those people for Athens; and the Locrians, Messenians, and Byzantians, of whom otherwise nothing is known, are added to them. The last of these three could not well send assistance from their great distance; and the former two must, it would seem, be referred to a different time, perhaps to the period after the death of Alexander. Aelian, *Var. Hist.* vi. 1, mentions the same tribes as are named in the speech of Demosthenes, and says that they surrendered after the battle; the Leucadians alone are excepted. But he mentions along with them also the Eleans and οἱ ἐν τῇ ἀκτῇ πάντες, i.e. the Epidaurians, Troezenians, and Halians, where Perizonius is mistaken, Wesseling on Diodorus (xii. 11?) must be compared. It is not impossible that the Eleans may have fought in the battle of Chaeronea, since it is not unlikely that the popular party may shortly before have recovered the upper hand among

states, such as the Arcadians, Messenians, and Argives, were
led astray by an intriguing and obstinate opposition fostered
by bribery ; the Spartans kept aloof from foolish narrow-
mindedness, because they were engaged in disputes with the
Messenian and other towns, and they also prevented others
from joining the confederacy.

The interval between the occupation of Elatea and the
breaking out of hostilities also cannot be accurately determined.   The battle of Chaeronea is said to have been fought on
the second of August, that of Cannae on the third of the same
month, " while the taking of Elatea has been assigned to the
end of June."   But all these identifications of days of the
Greek months with those of the modern calendar are very
uncertain, and you cannot rely upon them.   The calculations
have indeed been made with a vast amount of accurate mathematical learning, and those of Dodwell, for example, may be
very accurate calculations, but they are based on the assump-
tion of cycles, which are by no means certain.   In like
manner, the date of the occupation of Elatea has been calculated by French savans, who were certainly not deficient in
historical criticism, but who, in reducing the Attic calendar to
our own, were mistaken in believing that the days of the
cycle of Meton accurately agreed with those of the Athenian
state calendar.   The interval between the occupation of Elatea
and the battle of Chaeronea, must be much greater than is
usually supposed."

The course of the battle and all its details are likewise little
known to us.   Diodorus alone has some account, but a very
bad one; Plutarch and Justin furnish still less information.
It is as if the muse of Greece had grown dumb on the death-
day of Greek liberty, and had thrown her veil over the
death-blow.

While Philip was making vigorous preparations, and as-
sembling the best troops from his vast empire, an army of
Greek allies was formed.   " The Athenians did not take the
field merely with mercenaries, but most of them consisted of

---

them; but if this were the case, we should find traces of it in Demosthenes and
other writers; and it would, therefore, seem that Aelian is mistaken   Diodoru
(xvi. 86), however, says, that the Athenians drew up the army κατ᾽ ἔθνος, but
reserved the command for themselves, so that, even according to him, more
nations than the Athenians and Thebans were engaged in the battle."—1825.

their own militia, and the other allies also sent forth their own citizens." The Athenian citizens who took up arms, consisted of the younger generation of men, before whom Demosthenes had for the last twelve years always spoken upon important public matters. Some few speeches on public affairs had been delivered by him as early as Olymp. 106. His private orations commence at a much earlier date, and some were written by him when he was very young; but his real public orations (λόγοι δημόσιοι) begin in Olymp. 106; from Olymp. 108, and even from the end of 107, they become more connected, and show his fully-developed system of opposition to Philip. " But it was too late when the Athenians listened to the advice of Demosthenes, that they themselves ought to take the field; they were animated by the best spirit, but were deficient in military training." The misfortune in this general rising was, that the Athenians had inferior generals, such as Lysicles and the same wretched Chares who had been tried and found unlucky on so many occasions, and whom Demosthenes could not get rid of. The case was the same as that of the Austrian generals in the war of the revolution, when a first, second, and third general having been beaten, the first came forward again. Even Demades said to Philip, when speaking of Chares, " What enthusiasm would the Athenians have shown, if thou hadst been their commander, and Chares the commander of the Macedonians!" " Lysicles was a spirited general, but had no experience; there was, moreover, no one to undertake the supreme command. The Macedonian army, on the other hand, was commanded by experienced generals; it was accustomed to victory, had grown up in war, and had all possible advantages of armour and tactics, which rendered it superior to the mixed and untrained army of the Greeks." Nor can it be doubted, that in this battle the Macedonians were far superior in numbers to the allied Greeks; 30,000 are said to have been arrayed against 20,000. Their peculiar advantage was, that their cavalry was four or five times more numerous than that of the Greeks, and of a much better kind.

The Macedonian cavalry, commanded by Alexander, decided the battle (Olymp. 110, 3). The Athenians, as well as the Thebans, fought bravely,[3] and the contest, the decision of which,

---

[3] " In the λόγος ἐπιτάφιος (p. 1395), wrongly ascribed to Demosthenes, the

considering the forces of the belligerents, might have been
expected in a couple of hours, continued nearly the whole day,
until at length they were overpowered by the numerical
superiority and the cavalry.   The Athenian wing had at first
even gained some advantages: it had advanced, the Macedonian
infantry was defeated, and Philip nearly lost his presence of
mind, when the victory of his cavalry restored the day; "the
other Greek wing was completely defeated, and now the
victorious wing of the Athenians, which through the recklessness of Lysicles had advanced too far, was attacked in
its flank, and defeated with great loss."   The Athenians had
1000 dead and 2000 prisoners; but this was not all, for
the Boeotians and other Greeks sustained, no doubt, still
greater losses.

On that day Demosthenes, like every other Athenian, fought
in the ranks of the militia.   In the wretched anecdotes about
the lives of great men, we are told again and again, that
Demosthenes lost his shield, and fled with the rest.   I will
readily believe that he fled with the rest; heroic generals have
often been carried away by the current in a general rout.
Whoever has formed any close acquaintance with war, knows
this; even an Achilles cannot resist, if he is in the midst of a
routed and fleeing mass, and is carried along with it.   In
Greek history it is not sufficiently remembered, that the
materials used by Plutarch for his biographies, are for the most
part altogether wretched.   During the Alexandrine period a
vast deal of miserable stuff was written, especially in the form
of anecdotes and biographies; and such works he took for his
basis, although he himself wrote infinitely better.   His stories
are taken from collections of anecdotes, which have no claim
to authenticity, and partly originated from hearsay, partly
with writers of the greatest κακοήθεια; in addition to this,
Plutarch himself is altogether uncritical.   There was a time
when he was looked upon as one of the brightest ornaments
of ancient literature; and as far as his personal character and
his sentiments are concerned, he certainly is one of the most
amiable authors.   He shares this amiable character with
Montaigne, whom he resembles in the highest degree; to me

loss of the battle is ascribed to the conduct of the Theban commanders; but
this statement, not being supported by any other testimony, is suspicious."—
1825.

he appears even more amiable, and of a nobler disposition than Montaigne.[4]   But both are uncritical, and would have smiled at criticism, because in reality they were convinced, that after all, history could not be fathomed, and that therefore the problem of an historian was to make history pleasing and and attractive, and this latter was Plutarch's main object. Hence the historian, who reads his works with the seriousness of a matured judgment, will be vexed at him a hundred times, if he takes him for what he is usually taken, an historical authority. But this he is not by any means: it is inconceivable what silly stories he relates with the greatest composure! But notwithstanding all this, I like to read him, and every scholar must read not only his biographies but his moral treatises: he is a real store-house of information. As pleasing as Montaigne, but not so strict a philosopher, he resembles a good-natured old man who has read a vast amount of books, and is inde-fatigable in telling what he knows.   The first who twenty years ago directed my attention to the fact that Plutarch must be viewed in this light—which then startled me very much— was William von Humboldt, who said: "I do not mind what people say, if they will but cease to regard Plutarch as an historian." I was then a young man, but I have often thought of these words.   Plutarch, moreover, wrote with extreme haste, and is careless about contradictions.   Hence all those strange things! For the same reason, he did not scruple in his life of Demosthenes, to relate the most silly stories, which force us to ask, how it was possible for him to speak with admiration of the man if he believed them all?   It is he who relates the story of the flight of Demosthenes, in the same manner as he tells the absurd nonsense about Harpalus, which he has more widely diffused than any other writer. He did not know whether it was possible to hold out or not; he knew not what war is; he had only read in books that a man must die for his country, but he had never experienced that when a multitude flees, he must either flee with them or be crushed under its feet.   There is a sepulchral epigram on Demosthenes, from which it has been injudiciously inferred, that his want of

---

[4] " There is no greater resemblance than that between him and Montaigne; it is possible that, if Plutarch had lived in a different age, he would have been just such a sceptic as Montaigne, and have followed the fashion of the day. But as he lived in an age of superstition, he was himself biassed by it; nay, he is at the greatest trouble to be superstitious, in which he is more or less successful."

courage was the cause of the servitude of Greece; and Plutarch actually did understand it in this sense.[5]

Εἴπερ ἴσην ῥώμην γνώμῃ, Δημόσθενες, εἶχες,
Οὔποτ' ἂν Ἑλλήνων ἦρξεν Ἄρης Μακεδών.

" Hadst thou been as powerful as thou wert wise, Philip would not have ruled over Greece." What else can ῥώμη here mean but power ? The poet does not say, " as strong," as, for example, nine times nine men, but, " powerful," that is, " if thou hadst had as much power to command others."

During the banquet with which Philip celebrated his victory, he gave himself up to intoxication, to which he was generally very much addicted; the victory, however, made him quite insolent, and he ridiculed the Athenians. Dancing about on the field of battle, he recited verses on Demosthenes.[6] It is well known, that Demades, who was one of the Athenian prisoners, drew his attention to the impropriety of his conduct, by saying, " Fate has assigned to thee the part of Agamemnon, but thou actest that of Thersites," and thereby brought him to his senses. This shows the strange and peculiar character of Demades, who, with all his baseness, and though he allowed himself to be bribed, and sold himself to Antipater, yet was not servile. He was a Cleon in a fallen republic, and his greatest propensity was insolence; this accounts for his παῤῥησία before Philip. The king took the hint, and his conduct towards Athens after the victory, under the appearance of generosity, was extremely prudent. His object was, to separate the Thebans from the Athenians, and he at once advanced against the former. The Athenian prisoners he sent home, free and clothed, accompanied by Antipater; he ordered the dead bodies to be burned, and their ashes to be conveyed to Athens, while the Thebans had to purchase their dead from him. He then entered Thebes, which he seems to have taken without any resistance, placed a Macedonian garrison in the Cadmea, and, with the same policy which Sparta had followed at Athens after the Peloponnesian war, he established an oligarchy of three hundred of his partizans, who were for the most part returned exiles, and

[5] Plut. Demosth. 20, 30.

[6] " Even now the Greeks, in their dances, sing songs in iambic catalectic trimeters, like the verse of Philip. Justin, probably following Theopompus, relates that after the battle of Chaeronea, Philip conducted himself in a very dignified manner; but the other account was much more commonly received."—1825.

who now, under the protection of the garrison in the Cadmea, ruled like tyrants, and raged in a fearful manner. But, at Athens, Antipater and Alexander appeared as ambassadors,[7] and Philip, who had always shown the greatest bitterness and malice against Athens, as we see from his letters, especially from the one preserved by Demosthenes,[8] now all at once assumed the appearance as if he had been most deeply grieved at being obliged to fight against Athens, and as if his heart was bent upon nothing so much as upon conciliating the Athenians; but this was only a cunning political trick, and certainly not generosity; it is inconceivable how the ancients can have been deceived on this point, for even very intelligent men interpret his conduct as generosity. His motives are perfectly obvious.

Every one saw clearly, that Philip would not rest satisfied with Europe. The conquest of Greece was completed, except that Athens was not occupied by a Macedonian garrison; he could not stand still, but was obliged to go on conquering; just as, in 1811, every one knew that Napoleon would be obliged to wage war against Russia, so then every one saw, that Philip must go to Asia. He could not be inactive, and in Europe he had nothing to do; for it could not be his wish to try his strength against the poor Illyrians, and the still poorer Triballians, Dacians, etc. He was an extraordinary man, but his objects were those of a common conqueror—money and plunder—which Asia offered to him in abundance. Even the attacks upon Byzantium and Perinthus had been preparatory to the war against Persia; and his attempts to establish himself in the Hellespont were intended more to lead to a war with Persia than to injure Athens. The commanders in western Asia were already expecting him, and making preparations, each in his own way. Two of them, both Rhodians, were particularly active; they were both distinguished men, and Memnon, especially, was great as a man and as a general. The Persians then had Phoenician and Cyprian ships, and Egypt had been re-conquered. As, therefore, Persia had a

[7] *Or. de Lit. Philip.*

[8] " Justin states, that Alexander accompanied Antipater; but Polybius (v. 10) and Plutarch do not mention Alexander on that occasion, and neither of them would have omitted the fact if he had known it. Justin often relates falsehoods, whence we cannot trust him in regard to the names of this embassy."—1825.

large fleet, its natural policy was, to prevent the war by supporting Athens, and sending its fleet to Piraeeus. Athens herself also still had large fleets. If, therefore, the Athenians had only withstood the first attack—and Philip could hardly have taken it quickly, as the city was strongly fortified, and better prepared than towards the end of the Peloponnesian war—Persia would have sent as many millions as were required. As the sea was open, Athens might have received her supplies from thence, and the siege might have been endlessly protracted.

I cannot comprehend how it is, that no one has yet understood this simple relation between Persia and Athens. Philip, as a great man, clearly saw through it; he perceived that not a moment was to be lost, and that he must avail himself of the very first moment to exercise his influence upon Athens. For Demosthenes, not caring what people said, was already urging the necessity of forming an alliance with Persia. Chios, Rhodes (which was then dependent on Persia), Byzantium, and Lesbos, would have supported Athens with all their might, and Memnon would have sent over his mercenaries. After a few years of increasing oppression and Macedonian insolence, ten or twenty other Greek cities, instead of five, would have declared for Athens, and Philip in the end would probably have been obliged to withdraw. But even if he had destroyed Athens, such a revenge would have been of no use to him, and he would have been prevented from waging war against Persia, to which all his desires had long been directed. Philip, accordingly, was obliged to endeavour to finish the war in Greece, and his best policy manifestly was to play the part of a generous man and a friend.

In the meantime, before the embassy of Philip arrived, the Athenians had made every possible effort to enable themselves to stand out against a besieging army. "On that occasion they again showed their greatness: they did not reproach Demosthenes, but gave themselves entirely up to his guidance. How different was this conduct from that of the English during the American war! for among a hundred Englishmen there was not one who gave up the idea of the war; and after its unfortunate issue, there was not one in a hundred who did not curse the author of the war, which they themselves had wished for." Demosthenes had made proposals for the most determined defence, and they had been unanimously adopted by the citizens.   They looked upon the approaching events as decisive of life and death; the walls were immediately put in a state of defence, and the country people were placed in the frontier fortresses for protection.   Demosthenes was appointed one of the commissioners to superintend the repairs of the walls, and not only carried out this business in the most excellent manner, but contributed from his own property three talents towards defraying the expenses of the defence.   He was also commissioned by the people to purchase grain, and sailed out with a ship of war.   Aeschines calumniously makes this the subject of a charge of cowardice, as if Demosthenes had only wished to escape in safety.   It was a time of great tumults; one of those remarkable periods in which the Areopagus acted with dictatorial power.   That council appointed Phocion strategus, while the restless party which had voted for the war against Philip in a different spirit from that of Demosthenes, demanded Charidemus as commander.

Antipater now appeared as ambassador at Athens.   Philip accepted all the terms which were agreeable to the Athenians; no investigations were to be instituted against his enemies, and none of them was to be sent into exile.   Athens was not only to remain a perfectly sovereign city, but retain Lemnos, Imbros, and Scyros, nay even Samos and Chersonnesus, though he might have taken the latter without any difficulty, and though the Athenians had most cleruchiae in Samos.   Thus he bought over the Athenians through this peace, against which Demosthenes and others who saw farther, could not venture to protest, because Philip offered more than they could give him in return.   This was the greatest mistake on the part of the Athenians, but great as it was, it was still pardonable.   " No popular assembly could comprehend the advice of Demosthenes to hold out, until Philip should be worn out: a monarchical state might have followed it."

The only thing which the Athenians conceded to Philip, was, that they concluded a symmachia with him, and conferred upon him the supreme command in the Persian war.

For with great cunning Philip summoned an assembly of the Greeks whom he called his allies, to Corinth, to deliberate upon the war against Persia.   The war of revenge against the Persians had already become a popular idea in Greece, that is one of those ideas of which every one expected that it would sooner or later be realised. All the rhetoricians now raised their voices, they called all Greece to arms, following the example which had been set them by the foolish old Isocrates. All reiterated the standing phrase, that the crimes of Xerxes must be avenged. Isocrates himself had died after the battle of Chaeronea; he had come to see that that which had been the end and aim of all his wishes, was the ruin of Greece and the abyss in which everything must perish, and was ashamed of the folly of his attachment to Philip. But his successors preached revenge, called on all the Greeks to take up arms, to take vengeance for the temples and towns burnt by Xerxes. One hundred and forty years had elapsed from that time, circumstances had become altered, and Philip had razed to the ground thirty-two Greek towns on the coasts of Thrace and Macedonia alone. And it was he that was called upon by the rhetoricians to avenge the destruction of those towns which had long since risen again from their ashes! There cannot be a greater contrast than that between the sublime eloquence of Demosthenes and those wretched rhetoricians.

" The states of Greece, with the exception of Sparta, Chios, Lesbos, and Rhodes, now recognised Philip as generalissimo for the war against Persia;" and owing to the mediation of Demades, who, even before the peace of Antipater, and probably without the sanction of the people, had exerted himself with Philip to bring about a peace,[9] the Athenian people now

---

[9] " In the fragment of Demades, which is printed even in the 'Aldine edition of the orators, there is nothing about his having been taken prisoner; but his influence with Philip is mentioned, and it is moreover stated, that he effected the liberation of 2,000 prisoners and the burial of the dead, and that he procured for the Athenians the possession of the town of Oropus. This was a small place in Boeotia, which after the Peloponnesian war had probably placed itself under the protection of Athens. It was formerly of great importance to Athens, because it had a great harbour, and seems to have been a particularly busy commercial place. After the battle of Leuctra, the Thebans had taken it from the Athenians; on which occasion Callistratus delivered a speech. After this, it remained in the hands of the Boeotians, until the tyrant of Eretria took possession of it. The Athenians endeavoured to recover Oropus, but in vain; afterwards, however, they were again in possession of it, and they must have recovered it at some time; but whether this happened during the embassy of Antipater or afterwards, is uncertain. This fragment of Demades has been declared spurious at an early time, especially on the ground of a passage in Cicero, *Brutus* (9, 11), where it is stated that Demades left no writing behind him: *Demadis nulla extant scripta.* Cicero, however, is not a very great authority

likewise recognised Philip as commander in chief of the Greeks, and became a party to the general peace of Greece: μετέχειν τοὺς Ἀθηναίους τῆς κοινῆς εἰρήνης, says Plutarch in in the life of Phocion. This κοινὴ εἰρήνη is the real expression to designate Philip's hegemonia and protectorate (see Demosth. *De Coron*. p. 212)[10]. It was a regular federative constitution for Greece as a confederation of states, in which at the same time the contributions of every particular state were fixed, and what amount Philip might demand of each for the war against Persia. The contents of that federal constitution may be pretty accurately seen from the speech of Demosthenes περὶ τῶν πρὸς Ἀλέξανδρον συνθηκῶν. But as it was afterwards modified, I shall speak of it more fully, when I come to the conclusion of the treaty with Alexander. The number of the troops mentioned by Justin is evidently exaggerated.

For this treaty Demades has been censured; but it must not be understood as if he had been bribed by Philip to draw up the resolution, that the Athenians should serve (δουλεῦσαι) Philip. It is, however, true, that Philip afterwards made him a present of estates in Boeotia, and the property which Demades possessed in that country originated, probably, in the confiscations which Philip made at Thebes. When the decree was put to the vote, Demosthenes, probably, retired. Phocion then opposed it, saying, that it went too far, and that they ought not to go so far out of their way to meet Philip with their eyes shut; Phocion here appears labouring under a good-natured delusion. But the Athenian people, although an intense national hatred still prevailed, saw no way of

---

on this point. Suidas, who invents nothing, but only gives in a mutilated form what he took from ancient and good authors, speaks in an obscure passage of writings of Demades. The fragment, moreover, is of a kind, that it cannot be the production of an imitator or a literary impostor. Internal evidence shows that it cannot be a modern forgery: its whole form and the historical facts contained in it, show that it is ancient and genuine. It is true, that as early as the time of Dionysius of Halicarnassus, several orations were forged under the names of great orators; but if this fragment had been fabricated in the spirit of Demades, we should not find in it so many extremely important and genuine historical statements. The speech, moreover, has something so fresh and novel, so natural and genuine, that it is impossible to suppose it to be the work of a rhetorician, for that class of men neither possessed so much knowledge, nor could they write in so simple and beautiful a style."—1825.

[10] Comp. *Klein. Schrift.*, vol. ii. p. 166.

escaping, for there were no heroes, and the people were unwilling to run into evident destruction. Hence Phocion's advice was rejected, and the proposal of Demades was accepted. Afterwards, when Philip came forward with his demands, they felt vexed at having done so.

Philip now entered Peloponnesus with his whole army, and went to the diet at Corinth, where the Greek deputies received his orders. In Peloponnesus he acted as mediator, for he was invited as such by the Arcadians, Messenians, and Argives, to decide their disputes with Lacedaemon, and they demanded that he should restore to them their ancient territories. The Arcadians had formerly possessed many places on the Eurotas, and the Messenians were still very far from having recovered all their ancient territories. He accordingly fixed the boundaries, and greatly diminished the extent of Laconia. It is quite undeniable, and perfectly evident from Polybius and others, that he restored to those nations the places they claimed.[11] He advanced as far as the frontiers of Laconia, and sat in judgment in a place which had long belonged to the Spartans. As to how far the Lacedaemonians recognised the validity of his decisions, is another question; certain it is, that their neighbours recovered possession of those places which Philip adjudged to them, without the Spartans being able to oppose it.[12] The Spartans, on that occasion, behaved in a dignified manner; they were the only ones who refused to acknowledge Philip as generalissimo against Persia, " and to accede to the κοινὴ εἰρήνη." Philip was indifferent to this, not caring for the shadow of ancient Sparta, and allowed them to say and protest as much as they pleased. Such a protestation very rarely deserves to be taken notice of, and is often disregarded. Their refusal to submit to Philip is noble, but if the protest was to be anything more than the expression of their sentiments, it was childish.

Diodorus, passing over the Spartans, mentions the Arcadians as the only people that refused to recognise Philip as commander-in-chief; but the other statement is, probably, more authentic, and although the account of Philip's

[11] Paus. *Achaic.* p. 216, D. ed. Sylburg; Strab. viii. p. 361, B.; Polyb. ii. 48, 2, xvii, 14, 6.—1825.

[12] In 1825, Niebuhr said, that Philip distinctly appeared as arbitrator chosen by the Spartans of their own accord.—ED.

correspondence with the Spartans is found only in the Apophthegmata, yet it is of more weight.[13]

The battle of Chaeronea was fought in the same year in which Rome, by the conquest of the Volscians and Latins, laid the foundation of her sovereignty over all Italy. This is a remarkable coincidence; the old state of things perished, and a new order of things arose. Even the ancients regarded the day of Chaeronea as the death-day of Greece; every principle of life was cut off; the Greeks, indeed, continued to exist, but in spirit, and politically, they were dead. We can hardly conceive how Demosthenes and Aristotle could so long survive that day.

Philip was now at the height of his power. Byzantium, and the other allied cities, had submitted to the conqueror, when he sent his army against them,[14] and he was already trying to establish himself in Asia. " A detachment of troops, under Attalus, had been sent across, to keep open the road for the great expedition, and had encamped on mount Ida." Philip was thus enabled to commence his passage across the Hellespont whenever he pleased.

But the close of his career was already at hand. His family had latterly been in a very distracted state. His wife, Olympias, to whose brother he had given the kingdom of the Molottians, and who was the mother of Alexander, was a real fury in the form of a woman; she was hated by the Macedonians as a foreigner, and all who knew her could not help hating her. But Alexander and his mother were greatly attached to each other; he seems to have felt more affection for her than for his father; Alexander was looked upon as an Epirot, and the Macedonians hated the Epirots. In addition to this, the sons by a foreign woman, according to the notions of the ancients, were considered as νόθοι, or bastards; this was the case even among those barbarous tribes, and the Macedonians, no doubt, did not regard Alexander as

[13] It said that the Spartans having declined the first command of Philip, answered to his threat: " Measure thy shadow, and see whether after the battle of Chaeronea it has become greater." When he replied, " If I come to Sparta, not one stone shall remain upon another:" they answered, " Yes, if."—1825.

[14] " It must have been about this time that he subdued Acarnania, which from early times had been allied with Athens, because the towns by which it was surrounded were of Corinthian origin, and belonged to the opponents of Athens."—1825.

a γνήσιος. There accordingly arose among them a desire to have an heir of genuine Macedonian origin, whose mother also should be a Macedonian. The Macedonians, possessed the right of connubium with their kings; for though they were governed by kings, they belonged to the system of free nations, just as Neufchatel has its princes, though it belongs to Switzerland. " We may form a clear notion of such a state of things, by comparing it with the relation subsisting between the princes and the people during the middle ages. The kings, during these latter periods, also sometimes exercised absolute power, but it was not legitimate; when they were conquerors they, indeed, had absolute power over the nations which they had subdued, but not over that to which they belonged. Thus the Frankish kings were princes over a free nation, but they were absolute lords over the provincials. They had a retinue assisting them in the exercise of their power; and this retinue they constantly increased, especially from the provincials; and by this means they were enabled, at times, to satisfy their love of power, and their lusts, in a bloody and criminal manner. The Macedonian kings also were not absolute. We have traces of a βουλή; and when a free Macedonian was charged with a crime, he was tried by the community. Philip, it is true, acted as an absolute ruler, but he was, at the same time, the man of the people which he had, as it were, called into existence. The Macedonians might have said of him, what the Romans said of Romulus, *Tu produxisti nos extra liminum fores.*

A serious enmity also had arisen between Philip and Olympias in the course of their union; he had good reasons for hating and mistrusting her. Between him and Alexander there had likewise been a bad feeling for some time. In such states, there are always treacherous interlopers between father and son; and, in a truly oriental manner, they had roused in Philip suspicions of his son. Philip seems to have long suspected Alexander of plotting against him; and he had, therefore, the more reason to marry Cleopatra, a Macedonian lady of noble family: she was the niece of Attalus, one of his generals. It seems to have been an ancient custom among the Macedonians, to have several concubines, besides the legitimate wife.

The nation hailed this step with enthusiasm; but the bitterness in the royal family rose to the highest pitch, and this marriage gave rise to an open rupture, the consequences of which led to the murder of Philip. During a banquet, Attalus, the uncle of Cleopatra, forgetting the presence of Alexander, said, in a fit of drunkenness, to the Macedonians who were present, that they might now rejoice at the prospect of having a successor to the throne of genuine Macedonian origin. Alexander was beside himself, and began to rave at Attalus. This, again, provoked Philip, and the exasperation rose so high, that Philip drew his sword, and was on the point of stabbing Alexander. The latter, however, escaped, and Philip fell down. Alexander ridiculed his father for this; and matters came to such a point, that Olympias and her son, Alexander, fled to her brother in Epirus, prince of the Molottians, to whom Philip had assigned precisely the same position as Napoleon did to his brothers, and who was, no doubt, as dissatisfied with it as the brothers of Napoleon were, when they were treated by him as his subjects. Though he had the title of king, yet he was altogether powerless. Philip was in possession of the fortress of Ambracia, in Epirus, and the prince of the Molottians was, in reality, nothing but a wealthy landed proprietor. Such a position assuredly did not satisfy him. Alexander was altogether in disgrace, and would have remained in it, had not a Greek brought about a reconciliation between father and son. Philip accordingly recalled his son, and Alexander returned, but without having forgiven his father.

Meantime, Cleopatra had given birth to a son, to whom Philip appears to have been particularly partial. The name Caranus, which was given to the boy, was very significant, being, according to one of their genealogies, that of the mythical ancestor of the Macedonian kings. If Philip had lived longer, he would, probably, have chosen him for his successor; and, in that case, Macedonia might easily have been torn to pieces by civil war, and Greece might have been saved.

But Philip seems to have been somewhat good-natured, for he could not live long at enmity with his family. He showed his desire to become reconciled to Olympias by giving his eldest daughter Cleopatra in marriage to Alexander of Epirus, the brother of Olympias. This marriage was celebrated in the ancient town of Aegeae, and not in the capital of Pella, with such great pomp and splendour as Greece had never witnessed.

During these solemnities, Philip was at the height of his glory. He was proud of being able now to enter upon his long-contemplated Asiatic campaign; all nations seemed to be reconciled to him, and all the Greek states sent ambassadors and presents to him. Demades brought from Athens a psephisma, in which the people congratulated him, and promised not to afford an asylum at Athens to those who conspired against him. But in the midst of these festivities he was murdered by Pausanias, one of his own guards (Olymp. 111, 1).

It is well known, that the pretext for this deed was, that Pausanias had been mortally offended by Attalus, and that Philip had shewn great partiality towards Attalus as the uncle of his wife, etc. But there can be no question, that the general opinion of antiquity is well founded, that Olympias, at the head of a court faction, was the real instigator of the murder. It is a well-attested fact, that, according to an oriental fashion, the murderer was killed by the instigators, because he could not escape; and because it was feared lest he should betray the secret. Olympias, however, had appointed relays for him, that he might get away; and had he been able to reach the horses, he would have escaped; but as he fell, the instigators themselves stabbed him. Olympias was almost frantic with joy, and she so little concealed her delight, that she hung up the dagger with which Philip had been murdered, in a temple, and dedicated it to the God under the name of Myrtale, which she had borne herself when a child. The body of Pausanias was nailed on a cross; and soon after a golden crown was found upon his head. The unhappy Cleopatra was tortured to death with red-hot irons; her infant was murdered in her arms, and Attalus and his whole family experienced the same fate.

Alexander was no doubt deeply implicated in this murder: A jury would have condemned him as an accomplice. But he was prudent enough to make away with the participators in the conspiracy, who might have betrayed him, just as Charles XIII. of Sudermannland, who also knew of the conspiracy against his brother Gustavus III., severely punished all those that might have borne witness against himself. Thus Alexander sat in judgment upon the conspirators, and their blood was shed, that he might not become known as a parricide.

He consented to Olympias taking vengeance on her rival and her infant, " and he was no less cruel himself against others whom he dreaded as probable avengers of the murder of Philip, and against all the true Macedonian party. Nearly the whole of the royal family was at that time extirpated."[15]

LECTURE LXX.

In accordance with my plan, I have deferred relating the history of Persia until the time when Philip's long-contemplated expedition directs our attention to Asia. We shall accordingly take up Persian history at the point where we left it, after the battle of Cunaxa[1] (Olymp. 94, 4).

I cannot relate to you the history of Persia as minutely as Plutarch, in his life of Artaxerxes, has done; for it is the moral and intellectual importance that determines our treatment of history ; and this importance is very small with those nations, and incomparably smaller than the period of time over which the history extends.

The manner in which Plutarch relates the history of Artaxerxes after Ctesias and Dinon, has no personal interest at all; and I do not understand what induced Plutarch to write that biography. " If it was not written altogether without any plan, we may conceive that he wrote it only with the intention of contrasting Artaxerxes with the great men of the West: he appears to us only as a great king of an immense empire, but otherwise altogether weak and little enterprising. The biography, however, should not be classed among the βίοι

[15] This is the last Lecture delivered by Niebuhr during the winter of 1829 and 1830. In the night following (between the 5th and 6th of February, 1830), his house was burnt down; and this calamity, which laid the first foundation of his fatal illness, made it impossible for him to continue his lectures during that winter. The following Lectures, therefore, were delivered during the summer of 1830.—ED.

[1] The history of the relations between Persia and Greece, from the battle of Cunaxa to that of Leuctra, was given very completely in this place in 1826, less completely in the history of Greece. In 1830, it was only related once in connection with the history of Greece.—ED.

παράλληλοι, for Artaxerxes has not the least resemblance to Aratus, nor is he intended to be compared with him; some of Plutarch's biographies stand quite isolated, and should not be confounded with the parallel ones.

That of Artaxerxes is remarkable on account of the description of the customs, manners, and mode of acting in the East, and we see from it, that it does not require any deep insight into Eastern affairs in order to comprehend them. Those who have read the history of the Sofis and the Mongole kings, must own that they find exactly the same things in Plutarch, with only a few exceptions arising from the Mahommedan religion; and if you read the history of the Hindoo and Mahratta reigns, you will find in it a complete picture of the Persian court. The despotism of a sultan is altogether opposed to the European type, such as it was established by the Greeks. Slight exceptions occurred as long as the enthusiasm about Islam lasted, that is, during the first period of the Khalifs; but as early as the time of the Ommaiads, that Eastern character shows itself, and under the Abassids, who commenced well, it displayed itself at last in its full extent. We cannot deny that it also crept into the history of Constantinople, and the western dynasties of the Morabeths, Edrisids, etc., present the same spectacle."

Artaxerxes was, properly speaking, not a tyrant; but as he was merely an Eastern despot, his history is full of the greatest cruelties, which were committed as things that must happen in the natural course of events. Severe sentences are in Persia only the expressions of arbitrary despotism; thus a person is fastened between two boats with his head free, but smeared over with honey, etc., as a punishment for high treason. Similar things are done by pashas otherwise humane; and lovers of the middle ages would rather see a leg or an arm cut off than go through the process of a long lawsuit. " Little as we can desire to become acquainted with such horrors, we must mention some in order to characterise the time.

The battle of Cunaxa is related by Plutarch in a very characteristic manner. When Cyrus was slain, and the bloody tiara was brought to his brother, Artaxerxes, beside himself with joy, immediately hastened to the corpse, ordered in his presence the head and right hand to be cut off, and displayed them as trophies. Those who had slain him were richly rewarded, but were desired not to mention that they had killed him, and Artaxerxes caused himself to be proclaimed and complimented as the chastiser and murderer of his brother. Such is Persia, and in all the histories of the East we find fratricide regarded not only as something pardonable, but even as something glorious. I might mention plenty of examples from the history of the Edrisids, Morabeths, etc., in which one brother murders another; it seems that in the East two brothers were deemed to be equal, but that the one who overcame his equal by fraud or violence was thought superior.

But Parysatis took fearful vengeance on the murderers of Cyrus. It first fell upon him who, by the king's command, had severed the head and arm from the body. She first demanded of the king to deliver up the man to her; and as the king refused, she allowed years to pass without showing any signs of mortification. At last she played a game of dice with the king; and playing, no doubt, with false dice, she allowed the king at first to win a thousand darics; she then stipulated that each party should select three court slaves, and that the winning party should be allowed to select one from the remainder, that should be entirely at the discretion of the winner. It unfortunately happened that the slave who had cut off the head of Cyrus was not one of the three chosen by king: the game continued, Parysatis won, and demanded the wretched man on whom she meant to wreak all her vengeance. The king, terrified, endeavoured to evade, but she reminded him of his royal word, and ordered the slave to be publicly tortured to death in the most fearful manner. In like manner she brought destruction upon all who had participated in the deed, and in the end, even Statira, the king's wife, experienced her revenge. She had long endeavoured to get rid of her; but Statira had been on her guard, neither taking her meals with her, nor accepting anything from her, lest it should be poisoned. At length, Parysatis invited her to eat with her from the same dish: she then used a knife poisoned on one side, and gave to Statira the part of the meat which had been cut with it on the poisoned side. The queen died in consequence, and Parysatis was banished from the court; but Artaxerxes was so weak that after a short time he recalled her."

But the life of Artaxerxes is particularly important, because it reveals to us the state of dissolution of the Persian empire, which greatly resembles the condition of Turkey at the end of the eighteenth century.

In the very centre of the empire we find nations which do not obey the king. " Even under Darius the organisation of the empire had not been quite complete, inasmuch as many parts entirely governed themselves, and had only to pay tribute; as Cilicia, which was perhaps still governed by the same dynasty which had been found there by Cyrus; for in the time of Alyattes it was governed by a king Syennesis, and Cyrus the younger also met a Syennesis there; the same was the case with the Phoenician cities, and the Graeco-Phoenician cities in Cyprus. Yet until the time of Xerxes, the authority of the great king was equally acknowledged in all parts of the country by direct intimidation, and the most inaccessible districts at least paid tribute. But when the government became feeble, when there occurred not only national insurrections, like those of the Medes, Babylonians, and Egyptians, but also of satraps, many small tribes in countries difficult of access made themselves independent, and were never subdued again till the time of Alexander. In like manner, while the Roman empire was sinking, the Isaurians in Asia became perfectly independent even before the time of Theodosius, '' and maintained their independence for two centuries and a half." In later times, also, many parallels occur, as in the empire of the Moguls, and in that of the Turks. Under the first Moguls all the native Rajahs were subdued and paid tribute, but this changed even in the reign of Aurengzeb, under whom the Mahrattas and other bold tribes revolted, and there were large districts of his own empire in which the great Mogul had no authority. Such also is the case in Turkey, where the supremacy of the Sultan is not recognised, not only by the nomadic nations, such as the Kurds, but also Egypt, and foreign tribes settled in his dominions, both Christian and Mohammedan, such as the Druses, maintain their independence.

Such also was the state of the Persian empire. " Several nations are known to have been independent, and in the case of others it is very probable. The Pisidians, in the mountains between the coast of Pamphylia and Phrygia (afterwards the country of the Isaurians), whence in the Macedonian period vast numbers of mercenaries proceeded, were always at war with the Persians. The Carduchi, or Kurds, likewise were hostile against Persia: that race maintained its liberty also against the Chaldaeans, the Persian Sofis, and the Turks, and the Kurds have submitted only for the sake of appearances, to take their country from the Turks as a fief with the horse's tail. The Cadusii, a people not belonging to the Persian race," who dwelt in the frontier hills of Media, towards the Caspian, were perfectly unsubdued; they were the ancestors of the bold Delemites (in the heroic epic of the Persians, the Cadusii are called Delemites), who were independent even under the later Khalifs, and first appeared as a barbarous people, while afterwards they formed an independent state. They were extremely powerful. Artaxerxes set out against them with a very large army, and would certainly have perished in the mountains with it, had not the princes apparently submitted, in order to get rid of the invaders; but no sooner had Artaxerxes left their country than they were again independent. That bold nation certainly occupied the most impassable districts of mount Taurus, behind the *pylae Caspiae.* Another people, the Uxii, was unconquerable in the passes between Ecbatana and Susa, and thus entirely obstructed " the straight road between the two cities; the king of Persia was even obliged to pay tribute to them, in order to keep open the communication: the most evident symptom of an empire in a state of dissolution."

Egypt, which had risen against Persia, and had been reconquered, had become permanently independent as early as the reign of Darius, and under Artaxerxes only a feeble attempt was made to subdue it again. For this reason the Egyptian kings of that period appear in Manetho as a distinct dynasty: Psammetichus II., to whom the inscription of Ipsambul refers, belongs to that dynasty. The residence of those kings was at Memphis(?).

The Egyptian state of that time may be fitly compared with that of Constantinople, after it had been recovered from the Franks by Michael Palaeologus, which was equally powerless and equally poor in comparison with what it had been before. Such was then the condition of the Persian empire, which may be further compared with the Roman empire under Augustus and Trajan, and with the lower empire under Michael and Andronicus Palaeologus. The weakness and poverty of the Egyptian empire is evident from the monuments of that period: scarcely any inscriptions are extant, and all the buildings

belonging to it are mean and poor.   The warlike spirit of the
Egyptians had disappeared long before, and the whole strength
of the kingdom consisted in mercenaries.   As the Byzantines
after the recovery of Constantinople from the Franks, employed
Catalanians and Franks, so the Egyptians kept Greek mercenaries, who were quite demoralised and untrustworthy like those
of the Byzantines, and whom they were obliged to attach to
themselves by constantly increasing their pay: the safety of
the kingdom depended upon those troops.

" Artaxerxes also undertook the subjugation of Egypt with
Greek mercenaries (Olymp. 102).   The most celebrated Greek
generals were not ashamed, for the sake of the pay, to engage
in the service of barbarians, and to submit to the yoke of a
Persian satrap; they had no scruples in enriching themselves
by any means: to such a degree had the sense of honour
become extinct in the Greeks.   Iphicrates was a real military
genius, but he was a robber like the rest, a man without
principle, and his accusation at Athens was by no means
unjust.   He did not scruple to train an army of mercenaries
for the Persians according to his own system, nor to conquer
Egypt for a tyrant, and to expose the unhappy country to all
the horrors of a hostile invasion.   The undertaking was conducted by Iphicrates and Pharnabazus.   The Egyptians had
no fleet, and the Persians none of any consequence; but they
still had ships, as the Phoenicians who in the reign of Evagoras
of Cyprus had for a time been in a state of insurrection, had
been subdued again.   The Egyptians, therefore, were exposed
to a landing of the enemy at all the seven mouths of the Nile,
and the Persians might sail up the Nile as far as Memphis; a
thing which was then still easy, but now the mouths of the
river are obstructed by sand-banks. The Egyptians had indeed
fortified the entrances to the river with forts, block-houses,
chains, and armed river-boats, but their forces were by this
means too much divided, and their main army was not of much
importance.   The latter was stationed near Pelusium, because
there the approach of the Persians was expected.   But the
main army of the Persians had embarked, and, on the advice
of Iphicrates sailed past Pelusium, landed at one of the mouths
of the Nile, marched against the fortifications, and took them
by storm: the Egyptians were thus outflanked.   Iphicrates
then advised the Persians to proceed straightway to Memphis,

and in the confusion of the moment to terminate the war with one blow; but Pharnabazus opposed him, we do no know for what reason. The Egyptians thus obtained time to rally, to fortify Memphis, and build new forts along the river. And in this manner they were saved by the same mistake which Louis the Saint made, and the great expedition was obliged to return without having effected anything."

It was, however, not Egypt alone that had separated itself as an independent kingdom, but throughout the reign of Artaxerxes, the consequences of the revolt of Cyrus continued in Asia Minor: the authority of the king of Susa was not restored there, and insurrections of satraps were of frequent occurrence. The king's rule was continued only by his being satisfied with receiving the tributes, by allowing the satraps to act as they pleased, and even to wage war against one another, as the Turkish pashas did at the end of the eighteenth century. " And according to a principle universal in the East, care was taken that the governors of neighbouring provinces should be enemies, that they might watch one another and keep one another in check, as in the case of Pharnabazus and Tissaphernes." Nothing was more common than an insurrection; " every commander who apprehended any danger from the faithless court, seeking safety in insurrection. But the satraps did not revolt with a view to mount the throne; they had no other object but to secure their existence by making themselves independent." Mehemed Ali cannot conceive the idea of making himself independent; so long as he pays tribute, he has authority over the troops, and if he ceased to pay it, he would perhaps lose that authority. This circumstance makes the Sultan formidable, and his authority is still very great.

The great insurrection of Evagoras in Cyprus (Olymp. 98, foll.), which is highly characteristic, gave rise to one of the wars originating in the defection of dependencies. Evagoras was a Greek king of Salamis; he had been educated in the Greek fashion, and was respected in Greece; with the sophists in particular he is uncommonly celebrated; he was liberal towards all men of letters in Greece, whence he is praised by Isocrates, for instance, with all his might. We find in him a man of enterprise and decision of character, but of a degraded and thoroughly barbarised mind. Such a Greek had other notions than a Persian, and his thoughts reached farther than

those of the satraps.   He entertained the idea of making
himself the ruler of all Cyprus; " and by various means he
had already taken possession of several Phoenician towns in
the island."   But his undertaking failed; for a large Persian
armament was sent out against him, and he was obliged to
capitulate.   According to general Oriental principles, he
obtained a tolerably favourable capitulation, being only confined to his original possessions, and recognised in them as a
tributary prince, " on condition that he should call himself the
servant of the great king; this, however, was not a disgrace, for
the Orientals are proud of being slaves."   But this treaty was
also kept in the Oriental fashion; for not long after the Persians
expelled him, and subsequently he again won the favour of
the Persian king, who employed him in quelling another
insurrection in Cyprus;[2] just as, seven years ago, the grandson
of Ali Pasha was sent from his prison to Epirus to crush
another rebellious party.   This is the misery of Eastern
despotism.

This war in Cyprus was not the only one of the kind.   A
number of insurrections, headed by Persians, broke out in
Asia Minor; but more especially after the campaign against
Egypt, when Ariobarzanes in Phrygia and Datames rose.
The latter was a remarkable man, and different from the
majority of Orientals; his life in Cornelius Nepos is very
instructive.   He was driven into an open and implacable
rebellion by a succession of circumstances, and took the matter
more seriously than others.   His example, however, was
followed by many, and for a time the satraps of Lydia and
Mysia also were in a state of insurrection.

" In some satrapies the hereditary succession was beginning
to be established; in this manner there arose in Pontus the
principality of the Achaemenidae, who availed themselves of
the unconquerable situation of that country; and there Ariobarzanes was the first who left his satrapy as an hereditary
principality to his son Mithridates, the ancestor of the kings
of Pontus."   In Caria, the princely dynasty of Mausolus had
established a regular kingdom, which, owing to the fertility of
that country, though it was of small extent, became extremely
wealthy and prosperous; the great king was quite unconcerned

---

[2] Niebuhr here appears to confound the younger Evagoras, who went with
Phocion against Cyprus, with the elder one.—Ed.

about it; and it sometimes recognised his supremacy and sometimes not.

These insurrections are characteristic, in as much as they reveal the most fearful depravity, and acts of treachery at which we shudder, but there was no faith and no honour. Datames, who was a man of honour, forms an exception; but it would scarcely be possible to find other exceptions, and we may safely assert, that otherwise fidelity and good faith had ceased to exist. Everything was venal, and when an insurrection did not succeed, none of the rebels hesitated to send the head of his rival as an atonement for his own offence, if he could hope thereby to become reconciled to the court. Under the successor of Artaxerxes, however, these insurrections were suppressed.

" But during the long reign of Artaxerxes, the state of dissolution was ever increasing, so that at the end of his life the empire was weaker than it had ever been before. He had many sons, and wished to prevent a war about the succession breaking out after his death. Hence he appointed Darius, the eldest, his successor, and crowned him. But Darius thinking that Artaxerxes was living too long, entered into a conspiracy with his brothers and other noble Persians against the life of his father, who, however, discovered the plot, and cautiously thwarted it. The prince and his accomplices were put to death. Artaxerxes now selected Ochus, a younger son, as his successor; but he, too, was dissatisfied with his father's long life, and it is probable that Artaxerxes was poisoned after a reign of forty-five years (Olymp. 105, 2)."

Under Ochus, we see the regular development of Asiatic states : when a dynasty has been for some time in possession of a throne, the princes sink into voluptuousness, which they regard as the highest privilege of their sovereignty, and abandon themselves to the most perfect indolence. The military commanders then taking the reins of government into their hands, exercise the functions of the government, so that the prince becomes a complete nullity; they leave his title, but govern at their own discretion, like the major-domos under the Merovingians, and the emirs-al-omra under the Khalifs. In India, matters went so far, that, at first, the Maharadsha of the family of Sewadshi was sent by the minister into an honourable prison, like the Merovingians, and next, the Peishwas, who were as contemptible as the Maharadshas, and were likewise locked up by their ministers.   Ochus appears in history as an active enterprising prince, and in his fate somewhat resembles the present sultan, Mahmud, who has reduced the rebels; but there is this difference, that Mahmud is himself the personal ruler, whereas the energy of Ochus proceeded entirely from his vizier, an officer like the major-domo and the emir-al-omra.   We do not know how the dignity was styled in Persia; the Greeks call the officer chiliarch.   When the Macedonian dynasty adopted the Persian ceremonial, as was done even by Alexander, a chiliarch also was the next to the king, and thus Perdiccas succeeded Alexander, because he was the chiliarch, and therefore the person highest in rank next to the king.

Bagoas, the chiliarch of Ochus, was a eunuch, a cruel and inhuman monster, " like the eunuch Achmed Mehemed Chan (the uncle of Feth-Ali-Shah, the present king of Persia), who restored the Persian empire at the end of the eighteenth century.   Achmed Mehemed Chan, during a time of confusion, after a long period of dissolution, again united most parts of the Persian kingdom; but he was a most cold-blooded tiger, to whom cruelty was a delight."   Bagoas completely ruled in the name of the king.   The wars of Ochus appear as his personal undertakings; but Bagoas carried Ochus with him, to prevent his rebelling against him at Susa, and appointing another chiliarch.   In cruelty, Ochus was not inferior to his major-domo, and it seems that he was ambitious to show his power as king, in giving himself the command for the commission of any atrocity.

" When Ochus ascended the throne, nearly all parts of the empire were in a state of insurrection, and the rebellions were extending further and further.   All Asia Minor had then revolted; but, under him, the monarchy, outwardly, and for a time, was restored by means of money and Greek mercenaries."

During the first period of his reign, the revolts in Asia Minor were crushed by the king's generals by means of gold, one rebel being bought over to assist against another.   Among these rebels there was one Artabazus, who had been the most powerful man in western Asia, and is particularly remarkable on account of his connexion with the two Rhodian brothers,

Mentor and Memnon, whose sister was married to him. " Rhodes had then thrown itself into the arms of the Carian queen, Artemisia, the oligarchical party preferring submission to liberty ; and thus it was closely connected with the Asiatic satraps. These two brothers found in this relation the means of satisfying their base and brutal tastes, which they could not have indulged in under Greek laws." In regard to their ability and moral worthlessness, they perfectly resembled the leaders of the League, in the thirty years' war ; they were Greeks by birth, but in no way better than the barbarians.

During that unhappy period, the satanic element in man had gained the most perfect ascendancy : all that is pure and noble, the power of conscience, and an abhorrence of what is bad and base, from which even the wicked cannot always escape, had entirely disappeared ; just as was the case with the commanders of the League, the generals of Wallenstein's army, and all the Spanish commanders of that period. Whatever people may say of Castilian honour, there is nothing more base than those commanders, ever since the time of Ferdinand, and that not only in America : Spinola, indeed, forms an honourable exception, but one swallow does not make a summer. The enterprising and able men of that period, Greeks as well as barbarians, entertained such views as we find in Machiavelli's Prince, that men are a rabble, and that it is not true, that we ought to regard men as our brothers, and beings made after the image of God : that love, self-sacrifice, and devotion, are follies and lies, and that the whole aim and end should be dominion and the gratification of lust. Machiavelli himself did not follow these principles, but they were those of his age ; and he saw no other motives of human actions, and regarded these as the most practical. To keep one's word was looked upon as folly, and an oath was nothing more than a strong assurance, to make deception the more easy. This fearful demoralisation was quite general. Philip also was under its influence, and often acted according to such principles, although at bottom he was of a nobler nature, and often displayed a genuine humanity, of which most men knew nothing. Memnon afterwards acts a conspicuous part in history ; and it is the curse of such times, that men of his class become such powerful agents in history, that the noblest must form connexions wish them, in order to attain that

.which is attainable, Thus even Demosthenes and the patriots
were obliged to enter into negociations with Memnon, and
expected support and safety at his hands, although they
knew him quite well. This is the most dreadful fate that
a nation can experience; and one must know and be able to
estimate it, in order to form a conception of the misfortunes
of such a period.

After the failure of the revolt, those brothers had fled from
Asia with Artabazus; all eyes were directed towards them,
because they were the greatest military geniuses of the age.
They were now drawn into the current of events by the insurrection of the Phoenicians.

These wars, while reducing the extent of the empire, at the
same time increased the wants of the great king. We hear, it
is true, nothing about the eastern provinces, but we see, from
the conquests of Alexander, that there too the empire was
reduced to narrower limits, and we no longer find the state of
things described by Herodotus. In his time, India, on the
Indus, belonged to Persia, and Bactria was one of the principal provinces; but, in the time of Alexander, Bactria was
so loosely connected with the empire, that its satraps could
easily make themselves independent, and India was altogether lost. Egypt also was independent. In this manner
some of the richest provinces were gone, while, owing to
the wars, the need of money was not less than before; and
the yoke, therefore, pressed all the more heavily on the yet
remaining provinces. Tyrannical measures were particularly
common in the Phoenician cities.

The form of the Phoenician state had remained unchanged
under the Persians, but there were Persian governors, as
everywhere else where organised cities existed. Cyrus seems
to have granted to the Phoenicians favorable terms, which,
however, were not kept. Sidon, Tyre, and Aradus, were
then the three chief cities of Phoenicia, and they had a
common colony, Tripolis, which belonged to the three cities
together, just as e. g., the Romans, Latins, and Hernicans,
possessed the colony of Antium as a federative town, which is
much more reasonable than the colony of Washington, intended
to stand by itself.[3] " At Tripolis the three cities had their

_____

[3] " This may teach us how foolish it is to draw inferences from a resemblance
of circumstances. The town of Acca in the middle ages consisted of four parts,

centre, and held their diets.   Each separate city, however, had its own government;" their constitution was republican, but with kings, generally hereditary; but sometimes, as we learn from Menander of Tyre, Tyre had elective kings, although there existed a royal dynasty.   So the king of Babylon, at different times when there was no son to succeed him elected some person from the royal family to undertake the government, so that Babylon, under such circumstances, was an elective monarchy; but under the Persians the kingdom again became hereditary.   The Persian governors had their residence, and exercised their power at Sidon.

Some of these Persian satraps may have been unusually cruel, and have provoked the Phoenicians by acts of oppression; and, driven to madness by inhuman barbarities, the Phoenicians revolted, and treated the Persians in so horrible a manner that reconciliation was impossible.

LECTURE LXXI.

IT is generally supposed that the rule of barbarians is less galling, when they do not interfere in the internal administration of the civilised people that are subject to them, but are satisfied with exercising the supremacy. This certainly contributes to the preservation of the originality of such nations, as well as of their customs and laws; but if we inquire without any bias, it appears very questionable as to whether this advantage is not outweighed by greater disadvantages. Barbarism, with a sudden, overpowering, and violent interference, both despotic and personal, leaves in the end nothing but anarchy, and under the government of barbarians this disadvantage outweighs everything, for it draws the governed people away from their own civilisation.   The direct despotic

---

one belonging to Pisa, the second to the knights of St. John, the third to the patriarch of Jerusalem, etc.; and this gave rise to the belief, that this arrangement was of Phoenician origin.   Such inferences are correct in some cases; but we must not immediately draw such inferences wherever we meet with such resemblances."—1826.

interference of such nations leads to acts of violence without end; and if, in addition to this, the tribute is exorbitant, the yoke becomes insufferable.   In the distant mountains, conquered nations cannot be so easily reached, but near the seat of power the oppression is quite unbearable. Hence insurrections against such a government are accompanied by numberless acts of inhuman cruelty: such was the insurrection of the Greeks against the Turks, such that of the Phoenicians against the Persians; and these acts of cruelty are returned by the conquerors, and in each successive rebellion in the East, cruelties, atrocities, and reaction, continue to increase. Thus the personal tyranny of the Persian governors was most insufferable at Sidon, the residence of the satraps, and the Phoenicians during their insurrection took inhuman vengeance on those Persians whom they could lay hold of; they scorned and insulted the king wherever they could, and destroyed the palace of the satrap and all the king's property.

Under the circumstances of the times the insurrection was by no means hopeless. The Phoenicians allied themselves with Nectanebos, king of Egypt, "who had recently gained honour for his country by the expulsion of Iphicrates and Pharnabazus. Cyprus too was in a state of insurrection against Persia." The condition of Egypt, however, was no less deplorable than that of the Persian empire, and patriotism was altogether out of the question. The Egyptian king had his worst enemies among his own subjects, and among those who stood nearest his own person. Thus it happened that the predecessor of Nectanebos, who lost his throne during a rebellion, so far forgot his sense of honour, that in order to take vengeance on his own kingdom, he applied to the court of Susa, endeavouring again to reduce Egypt under the dominion of the great king. The position of Phoenicia was indeed very unfavourable for defensive operations, as in most parts the country did not extend farther than four or five miles from the sea to the interior, and by its navy alone it could not defend itself; but if the insurrection had been managed only with moderate prudence, the Phoenicians, might have maintained themselves. But they, like the Egyptians, at that time were only a great name; what remained to them was nothing but the tradition of their ancient splendour, and the recollection of great inventions in arts and sciences; they had outlived themselves and had become effete: their fate itself shows to what extent this was the case. They too knew of no other means of defending themselves than that of employing mercenaries, and Mentor was their commander.

"Ochus made preparations (Olymp. 107 and 108) to reconquer Phoenicia, Egypt, and Cyprus, and accordingly sent for Greek troops and Greek commanders. At this time Phocion entered the service of Persia; his exemplary virtue did not scruple to fight against a brave people defending its liberty, and the Thebans were base enough to sell to the king of Persia a body of troops against Phoenicia and Egypt. The infamy of the Greeks thus restored the Persian monarchy. Bagoas now induced the king to place himself at the head of his troops against Phoenicia and Egypt. The best part of his army consisted of 10,000 Greeks; the rest only swelled the numbers, and were good for nothing but to fill up ditches with them." The fearful demoralisation of the time shows itself most awfully during the Phoenician insurrection, in the fate of Sidon—a demoralisation which makes us feel deeply, how unhappy the great men of that period, especially a Demosthenes, must have been.

Tyre and Aradus are not mentioned by Diodorus in his account of the catastrophe,[1] and his narrative is our only authority on these events. Accordingly we do not know whether they submitted to the Persians immediately on their arrival, or whether they held out till after the destruction of Sidon, which fell by double treachery; not only was it betrayed by the mercenaries and Mentor, who sacrificed the Phoenicians in order to regain for himself, his brother, and Artabazus, the favour of the Persians, and thus recovered their possessions in western Asia; it was betrayed also by Tennes, the king of Sidon, himself, who was base enough to sell his own country for advantages which the Persian king willingly secured to him. As an earnest of his treachery, he first delivered up to the Persians one hundred of the noblest Sidonians, whom, under the pretext of an embassy, he led to Tripolis, to deliberate there what was to be done. "The Persians were evidently not encamped before Sidon, but in some other part of Phoenicia, so that the citizens could freely go in and out. The one hundred Sidonians were murdered,

---

[1] Compare, however, Diodorus, xvi. 45, in fin.—ED.

Tennes was protected," and, as this treachery did not yet bring about the surrender of the city, he continued his treason step by step. " The Persians now advanced before the panic-stricken city; five hundred of the noblest were sent out to implore mercy and a capitulation. But Ochus asked the traitor, if he could answer for the city being taken by treachery, adding, that if it could, he would at once make an example. Tennes answered, that its surrender was quite certain; whereupon all the five hundred were killed with arrows." With the assistance of Mentor, Tennes now opened a gate to the king. The fate of Sidon is one of the most fearful catastrophes recorded in history, for it was treated as a city taken by storm; the inhabitants, in despair, set fire to the city, and most of them made away with themselves, in order to save themselves and their friends from the cruelties of the enemy. " All parts of the city were in flames, and the whole was soon one heap of ashes; more than forty thousand human beings perished. The king then sold the heap of ruins, that the melted gold and silver might be recovered." Tennes himself, when the great king could no longer make any use of him, received the well-merited reward for his treachery: he was put to death, and Mentor entered the service of Persia.

After this the campaign against Egypt was continued. There, too, Nectanēbos (for thus it is to be pronounced, and not Nectanebos, which false pronunciation has been the effect of the Latinised form, *Nectanebus*) defended himself, for the most part, like Psammenitus, with mercenary troops; he had also an Egyptian army, but that was of no use. At first his troops were faithful to him, but he himself showed a great want of courage and skill. " He was stationed with the main army near Pelusium, in a fortified camp, when Ochus arrived there. The situation of Egypt was now more favorable than during the preceding campaign, when the Persians sailed past Pelusium; for, owing to the fate of Phoenicia, the Persians had no fleet, and, as they had not sufficient courage to march across the desert, they were obliged to pass by Pelusium in order to enter Egypt. The whole Pelusian arm of the Nile, however, was strongly fortified and well garrisoned, and at Pelusium itself a Greek corps was stationed." But the position of Pelusium was evaded, " a Greek general in the

Persian army succeeded in carrying a column across the Bubastian arm, and the Egyptians were defeated in a battle," whereupon Nectanebos fled to Memphis. The corps at Pelusium being forsaken, surrendered; and the Persian army, spreading over Egypt, took one town after another. The Egyptian king neglected the formation of a new army, and all resistance in the field was given up.

Nectanebos, despairing of everything, fled into Ethiopia. Egypt was frightfully plundered; the temples were broken open, and the sacred books were carried off by Bagoas, in order to compel the priests to ransom them with immense sums; just as the Mongoles in India carried away the idols from the pagodas, and afterwards sold them again to the Brahmins for large sums of money. " In what manner Egypt was treated, may be easily inferred from the fact, that Alexander was received as its deliverer."

It is most remarkable on that occasion, to see how Mentor and Bagoas intrigued against each other, in order to deprive one another of the advantages of the conquest. Similar things also occurred during the seventeenth century, and the same baseness shows itself during the latter period of the thirty years' war, when cowardice and treachery were so common, that no one was ashamed of them; Odowalski even wrote a justification of his not paying just claims that were made on him, saying, that as he himself had not been paid, he had availed himself of the opportunity for not paying others. After this, when Mentor and Bagoas became convinced that both might maintain their posts, they made an arrangement, by which they were to govern the empire in common. " Ochus was completely in their hands." He now proceeded to Asia Minor, the whole of which he contrived to reduce to submission; even Cilicia no longer appears under its own kings. Pisidia alone remained free.

The presence of Bagoas, at this time, at Jerusalem is mentioned by Josephus: it is the only occurrence which he introduces into his history of the Jews; he might have given more if he had searched more carefully.

When Ochus had returned to Persia, he fell out with Bagoas for some unknown reason, and after a reign of twenty-one years, he was murdered, together with his sons, except one

Arses (Olymp. 110, 3), whom Bagoas raised to the throne. But Arses was only a nominal king, like the Roman emperors under Ricimer. Bagoas, however, having soon become tired of him, murdered him also, and then, for a time, endeavoured to govern the empire himself. But this was too precarious; and, as he dreaded to be overthrown, he raised the unfortunate Darius Codomannus to the throne.

"With Arses, the direct male line of Darius appears to have become extinct; Darius Codomannus was, only on the mother's side, a grandson of a brother of the second Artaxerxes and Cyrus, the sons of Darius Nothus. Bagoas probably placed him on the throne only to render the Persians familiar to the idea, that a person might wear the diadem without belonging to the race of Darius. He contemplated murdering him also; but Darius was prepared, and compelled him to drink the poison prepared for the king."

In his private station, Darius had acquired great reputation in the Persian army, which has been transferred to him in his position as king, and the general opinion in history is favourable to him. But I cannot see that he did anything to justify that reputation: he did not know how to use the resources of his immense empire against Alexander. In the battle of Arbela, he is said to have been brave; but this is a very insignificant quality, which he shared with thousands of others, and the absence of which is only a disgrace. A fallen prince always leaves behind him a feeling of sympathy, and this is increased in the present case by the fact that Darius was a man of a humane disposition. Not a single act of cruelty is recorded of him, though cruelty is generally found even in the best Oriental rulers, who rarely regard men as anything more than mere insects. He must have been a man of a gentle, mild, and humane disposition.

The Persian empire, until the war with Alexander broke out, was apparently in the enjoyment of perfect tranquillity from the Hellespont to the Nile; but from the events which afterwards took place, and from the condition in which Alexander found the empire, it is manifest that this was only the stillness of death, that the empire was an old, decrepit, and decayed body, with absolutely no strength. "For a time it might yet have continued in that state, had not Alexander undertaken his expedition; one satrap would then probably have revolted after another, and the empire would have fallen to pieces."

The conquest of the Persian empire had long been a favorite topic with the Greek rhetoricians, especially with Isocrates in his speech to Philip. I believe that Isocrates looked upon Persia as a really great power, and imagined that he would be doing the Greek people a great service, if he could persuade Philip to direct his arms against Persia. It cannot be denied, that Ochus spoke to the Greeks, and even to the Athenians, in an insolent manner, and the satraps were threatening the islands. Rhodes was Persian, and Chios and Lesbos were under the influence of Persian gold. It was, moreover, a very general notion among the Greeks, that it would be a glorious thing for Europe to throw itself into Asia, and to avenge the invasion of Xerxes. Ever since the expedition of the 10,000, it was generally known that such an undertaking would not be difficult, " and it had now become evident, that Persia was kept together only by Greek mercenaries."

But the wise men at Athens regarded the Persian empire, compared with Macedonia, as the lesser evil, and as the only means by which Athens and Greece might possibly be enabled to maintain their liberty against Macedonia. Hence we cannot wonder, nor ought it to be censured, that Demosthenes had for a long time past been in communication with Persia against Macedonia, in order to protect the interests of his own country: there has been much declamation about this point, but it is the simplest matter in the world. The mere negative existence of Persia saved Athens after the battle of Chaeronea; the fear lest the Persian and Athenian fleets should attack Macedonia, induced Philip to grant to the Athenians such favourable terms. Hence the favour and generosity of Philip! So long as the Persian empire existed, the servitude of Greece was anything but irretrievable; it was only necessary for the Peloponnesians to be informed about their true position, and to have their eyes opened to the tyranny of Macedonia to put an end to its power. When, therefore, we read in the ordinary histories, that Demosthenes received money from Persia, in order that he might bring about an alliance with the great king, we must regard such things as calumnies no less vulgar, than the French bulletins in the time of the war with

Napoleon, which spoke of the Tyrolese, as if they had been stirred up by English money.

Peace was concluded between Athens and Philip, and at the time nothing better could be done;[2] it was the period of the usurpation of Bagoas. Darius was indolent, though he may have been ever so good a man. The circumstance that the two Rhodians and Artabazus had come down to Asia Minor, opened a favourable prospect to the Greeks; but Artabazus died soon after. Mentor was an atrocious man; Memnon does not appear to have been such a monster, but I am very far from considering him as an honourable man: he was assuredly no better than others of the same time. He was a man of great parts, and of decided talent as a military commander. Nothing could be done but to form connections with him. The Athenian patriots, accordingly, entered into direct relations with Mentor; among them I will mention Ephialtes, an excellent man, "altogether a great military genius, extremely bold, and without either fear or reproach; Dinarchus, his enemy, mentions him in a manner (κ. Δημοσθ. § 33), which clearly shows that his personal character was highly esteemed;" he was perhaps a descendant of the Ephialtes who distinguished himself as a friend of the people during the early career of Pericles, and who is known to us only from those passages in which he is spoken of along with his friend Pericles. This Ephialtes left Greece, just as the best of the German officers, during the wars of 1805 and 1806, went wherever a state was in arms against Napoleon, to fight against him, without scrupulously inquiring whether in other respects those states were deserving of blame or praise. With such feelings, Ephialtes, a certain Miltiades (probably a descendant of the great Miltiades), and Critias, the son of Iphicrates, and great-grandson of the Critias who had been a nephew of Solon, —all men of the most illustrious families of Athens,—went to Memnon and the Persians. Ephialtes was the soul of the defence of Halicarnassus. Many volunteers from Athens fought against Alexander in the battle of the Granicus; in that near Paropamisus, many Greeks were engaged; and Greeks were repeatedly taken prisoners.

For these reasons, we must regard the war of Alexander from its beginning in a very different light from that in which

[2] Compare the opposite opinion in p. 301, foll.

it is usually described. At the beginning we cannot side with him; afterwards, when all is decided, it is no longer possible to sympathise with either party; we can only look on, and do as the grand vizir did in the time of Louis XIV., who was quite indifferent when pigs and dogs were fighting with one another. In like manner, we feel indifferent as to how the rest fare, seeing that there is no longer any help for Athens: the Persians and Macedonians were equally good and equally bad. Asia, however, was effete; ancient Asia had disappeared long before, and intelligence and vigorous mental activity were benefited by its subjugation.

It is singular that the first acts of hostility are not mentioned in Arrian. He confines himself to Alexander, and according to him, it would seem as if Alexander was the first to cross over into Asia. But a statement in Diodorus shows, that three years before the passage of Alexander, Philip had sent an army under Attalus and Parmenio across the Hellespont — this happened in the reign of Arses. That army spread over Mysia and Troas without meeting with any resistance, took possession of the Lesbian towns and of Tenedos, and occupied a large extent of country. Cyzicus had already joined them, and it was only by a bold march in the hot season of the year, that Mentor recovered the place from them. That army, however, did not remain in Asia until the arrival of Alexander. Attalus was put to death by Alexander, on the ground that he had been implicated in the conspiracy against Philip; but there is a strong suspicion that the real motive with Alexander for this execution, was the circumstance that Attalus was the uncle of Cleopatra, the youngest wife of Philip. The Macedonian army had either been recalled from Asia, or had been forced by Mentor to retreat across the Hellespont. This is a remarkable instance of the manner in which history is put to rights: otherwise the circumstance is not of much importance.

Let us now turn our attention to the intellectual life of the Greeks during this and the preceding periods. In a literary point of view this period bears a very different character, not only from the time about the close of the Peloponnesian war, but from the age of Pericles, about ninety years before the time we have now reached.

Poetry had assumed a different form even as early as the age of Pericles: the objective or epic had already become

united with the lyric. The peculiarity of lyric poetry consists
in the poet breathing out his own feelings in song, or in describing the impressions which events make upon him. A lyric
poet is like a bird in the air, his life melts into song; and such
were the poets of the true lyric period. The last of them,
though he forms already the transition to another period, and
applies the highest of the divine gifts to other persons, not
confining himself to his own feelings, was Simonides, and still
more Pindar. Both transfer themselves from their own positions
into those of others; and Pindar did so even where he was
strictly in his own domain. This poetry then combined with
the epic or dramatic; " and the poet, by transferring himself
into the position and persons of other men, sometimes singing
like the bold Titan Prometheus, and sometimes like the
unhappy and oppressed, the dialogue of tragedy arose, the
development of which is most perfect in Sophocles."

Epic poetry was produced even immediately before the outbreak of the Peloponnesian war, by Rhianus,[3] who in his way
was a very important poet; and afterwards by Panyasis, a poet
whom we are not able so well to judge of. At a later time,
epic poetry was altogether extinct, which was quite natural,
tradition and its thriving productiveness being lost; tradition
had lost its plasticity—it was completed and dead.

LECTURE LXXII.

THE extinction of what was really poetical distinguishes this
period from that of Pericles, as well as from the one preceding
the age of Pericles. Modern times furnish a parallel to this.
If we compare the Greeks under Philip and Alexander, with
those before the Peloponnesian war, we shall find that among
the former, culture and skill are far more widely spread than
among those of the earlier and more unpolished period. But
in the later times poetical geniuses are altogether less frequent;
and wherever one does appear, he moves in quite a different
sphere, dealing with the external world, and with reality,
whereas the earlier poets moved in an ideal world. We find a

---

[3] The name Rhianus here seems to be a *lapsus linguae* for Chœrilus, as in
vol. i. p. 263, Rhianus is said to have lived about Olymp. 100.—ED.

similar difference in English literature, if we compare the age of Shakespere and Milton with the present; and in our own country the same difference exists between the period of Goethe's youth and the present time, and will be still more marked in the period which is coming.

It is true that in Greece, considering the richness and variety of its intellectual activity, the poetical vein continued for a very long time, but the extinction of lyric poetry shows itself not only in the fact, that after Sophocles we find no great poetical genius, but also in the disappearance of the ancient lyric element in tragedy, which even Euripides did not exactly know how to make use of. Freshness and boldness had perished in the Peloponnesian war; that long and melancholy struggle had extinguished all poetical visions and enthusiasm. Men had made too bitter experiments to allow themselves to be deceived about the actual state of things; and no one could conceal from himself what that state really was. At Athens, as well as in all other parts of Greece, there had arisen very great poverty in comparison with former times. Proofs of this are found in Xenophon's History, and especially in his work περὶ πόρων, where he states that Athens contained numerous unoccupied places for buildings.

Lyrics, as an independent species of poetry, was at this time cultivated only in Sicily by Philoxenus and Telestes; but it was already degenerate; from the drama lyric poetry vanishes, and in comedy it disappears altogether soon after the Peloponnesian war; one of the reasons perhaps also being the general poverty which rendered it impossible or difficult to meet the expenses of the chorus. We have no specimens of tragedy belonging to that time, but there can be no doubt that it was very inferior. Of the middle comedy we can form a definite idea; it stands in the middle between the ancient and new comedy, in the same manner as a building of the sixteenth century stands between the Gothic and modern architecture; in secondary points and in little details, it reminds us of the ancient form, but in its leading features there is a vagueness which forms the transition to the new comedy; it is altogether something very insignificant, and confined to trifling and every-day occurrences.

If we except philosophy, the whole period was only one of transition. The true tendency of the age was towards prose,

and towards the realities of life, which were treated of in the
forms which had been developed during the ideal and creative
period. But the substance was the ordinary and real life with
its common incidents.

In the earliest times there existed no art of oratory. Thucydides indeed had the models of his master Antiphon, but no
one ever thought of instruction in the art. Whoever had
oratorical talent created his own form for himself, in which
he clothed the deep thoughts of his mind, just as they arose
and developed themselves in him. With the exception of
the ancient gnomes, there was no commonplace of oratory.
Hence the gulf between the powerful and eloquent, and those
who only expressed their sentiments plainly and simply, as in
ordinary life, and in the same manner in which we may conceive the early Roman orators to have spoken. These are the
ἐνθυμήματα, an ancient rhetorical term, which it is difficult to
explain, and for which I do not know a modern equivalent.
These ἐνθυμήματα constitute the greatness of Thucydides, and
on them his art rests. The subject controls the orator, and
his oratory spontaneously develops itself in him, just as the
Pythia gives forth her oracles without adding anything of her
own; there was no reflection. But after the Peloponnesian
war, things became altered: men began to reflect upon the
art of speaking, and this reflection gave rise to the rhetorical
schools of Isaeus and especially of Isocrates.

We are enabled to form some notion of the great master
Antiphon, although only two λόγοι ἰδιωτικοὶ of his have
come down to us; but even these enable us to recognise the
analogy between him and Thucydides. The speech which he
delivered when he was accused, must have been thoroughly
Thucydidean. One of his contemporaries was a man who has
nothing of the art or of really deep eloquence; nothing
poetical, and not a mind that can be compared with Thucydides and Antiphon, but an animated, bold, warm, and
instructive orator. I mean Lysias, who is eloquent from deep
political emotion, patriotism, and love of liberty; he is distinguished by uncommon clearness and vigour, propriety and
animation; but the rhetoricians previous to the age of Cicero,
are not agreed in their opinions about him. He was a puzzle
to them: they venerated the ancient Attic orators, but in
reality they did not feel at ease with them, though they were

unwilling to own it; they were not sincere, for they revered the ancient Athenians, although there were others whom they much preferred; but with Cicero the case was different.

Isaeus is generally admired by the ancients; but he is only an ordinary man, and greatly inferior to those I have mentioned before. He and Andocides are proofs that, among those whom we call classical authors, there are some inferior to many of our own contemporaries. Andocides is an adroit speaker in the way of Lysias, but scarcely anything beyond it; the muse of Lysias is patriotism and love of liberty, but Andocides has nothing of this. Even among the present French orators, there is more than one whose speeches I like better than those of Andocides, not to mention the great orators of the revolution, as Mirabeau, and at a later time, De Serre, an orator as great as Mirabeau, though in a different way, and not so passionate. In like manner, many of our contemporaries in England and France far surpass Isaeus. Every exaggerated admiration destroys itself: it is either not honest, or it becomes stupid. The general question, Who were greater, the ancients or moderns? which was asked by men like Perrault and Chapelain, belongs to the infancy of these discussions, and is extremely absurd. Among what are called the classical writers, there are many who are greatly inferior to modern authors; but there are others who have never been equalled and never will be equalled. No modern has ever come up to Thucydides and Demosthenes, and no one ever will come up to them; Shakespere, on the other hand, is in his way quite as great as Sophocles, although he has not his beauty: he stands on a different line.

Isocrates also is a thoroughly worthless and miserable author, and one of the most thoughtless and poorest minds. He made an art for himself, but it is an art of appearances, of words, and of a manner of speaking, or rather an art of phrases, not an art of thought. It is inconceivable to me how the ancients could so much esteem and admire him. When men applied this art of externals to rich thought, deep feeling, wit, and genius, such forms served as pleasing modes of expression, and became very useful; but if the art had not been fructified by better men, it would have remained the most wretched of all arts.

Demosthenes was not a disciple of Isocrates; he entirely educated himself, except that he passed through the school of

Isaeus in order to make himself acquainted with the civil law and the mode of procedure. The λόγοι δικανικοί afforded a person a sufficient income. The study of the civil law at Athens was very peculiar: there was no public school of law, and when a man wished to become acquainted with it, he visited, as at Rome, the places where legal business was carried on. Isaeus was a barrister, and he was particularly occupied with civil cases; Demosthenes learned of him; but this was all, and Isaeus had nothing else to communicate to him.

Athens was in a state of indolence and weariness until Demosthenes appeared. He did not look back to a by-gone time, nor did he lament that the good old times were past, but he set to work with warm love and faithfulness towards his countrymen such as they actually were. He did not idly walk up and down, declaiming about the good old time of Pericles, Sophocles, Solon, and even Theseus; he did not recite charms to call them back, but with spirit and boldness he seized the present, and did not despair, under the most trying circumstances, of effecting the most arduous things; he was supported by the strongest mind, which he infused, in the noblest form, into his treatment of actual circumstances. Most of his contemporaries resigned themselves to the oppression of the time; but he rose against it, trying to raise his people above the present, and to bring them to a level with himself. "The noblest spectacle," says an ancient Stoic, "is to see a great man struggling against fate;" and never has any one done this more than Demosthenes. After a period of great poverty, there arose at Athens an extraordinary degree of intelligence, and quite a new spirit, which were called forth partly by the urgency of circumstances, and partly by the impulse given by the one great man. The condition of Athens had been in a manner jejune, though with much more elegance than that of Germany, during the period from the thirty years' war until the middle of the eighteenth century.   .

Demosthenes had many talented contemporaries, but all were far below him; and there were among them many who by their moral obliquity were directly opposed and hostile to him. One of these was Demades, the rude and vulgar sailor, though he was then, next to Demosthenes, the first man in point of talent. He was the son of a common boatman, and had himself, in his early youth, been engaged in the same trade, when all at once his genius impelled him to come forward as an orator in the popular assembly, where, without any previous study, by his wit and talent, and more especially by his gift as an improvisatore, he rose so high, that he exercised great influence upon the people, and sometimes was more popular even than Demosthenes. With a shamelessness amounting to honesty, he bluntly told the people everything which he felt, and what all the populace felt with him. When hearing such a man, the populace felt at their ease; he roused in them the feeling that they might be wicked without being disgraced; and this excites with such people a feeling of gratitude. There is a remarkable passage in Plato, where he shows, that those who deliver hollow speeches without being in earnest, have no power nor influence; whereas others, who are devoid of mental culture, but say in a straightforward manner what they think and feel, exercise great power. It was this circumstance, which, during the eighteenth century, gave the materialistic philosophy in France such enormous influence with the higher classes; for they were told that there was no need for being ashamed of the vulgarest sensuality; formerly people had been ashamed, but now a man learned that he might be a beastly sensualist, provided he did not offend against elegance. People rejoiced at hearing a man openly and honestly say what they themselves felt. Demades is a remarkable character; he was not a bad man, and I like him much better than Aeschines. The latter made all the pretensions of a good citizen, and even had the audacity to vilify those who really were good citizens: but all in him is untrue and false. His hatred of Demosthenes is as much the hatred of mediocrity against genius, as that of political aversion: it is the hatred of antipathy and envy, of mental and moral depravity against that which is excellent. Demades, on the other hand, took matters in an extremely naïve manner, and said, in plain words, that there had indeed been different times, when this or that would not have done, but that now everything was lost, and that it was every man's business to feather his own nest; that they must undertake public duties in order to obtain from the state as much money as possible, so as to be able to lead a merry life. Such things he said without any misgivings; but he hated no man. This accounts for his conduct towards Demosthenes, whom he did not hate, but whom he thought exceedingly stupid. Sometimes he actually did

essential service to the republic; as in evil times the best man
often does harm, while the worst is useful.   In the whole of
modern history there never was a purer or more unblemished
statesman than Pitt, and yet at times a bad one was more useful,
nay more necessary than he.   In like manner, there have often
been bad patriots who, nevertheless, did good service to their
country.

The other contemporaries of Demosthenes were much more
insignificant.   Of Aeschines I have already spoken.   The next
after Demosthenes, *sed magno intervallo proximus*, as Cicero says,
seems to have been Hyperïdes or Hyperīdes (for the ending is
both εἴδης and ἴδης). He is probably the author of the speech
on the treaty with Alexander, which is printed among the
orations of Demosthenes, but cannot belong to him, as was
seen· and proved even by the ancient critics.[1]   It is a much
better speech than those of the other contemporaries; and if
it is actually his, we may unhesitatingly agree with Cicero's
judgment of him.

Prose literature thus prevailed, and of poetry nothing
remained except the worst,—the middle comedy.   When
oratory, which had acquired a substance by being inspired by
politics, was afterwards paralysed, men of talent turned their
minds to science in the proper sense of the term, and to the
new comedy, in which there was more scope for the display of
intellect than in the middle.

This is also the great period in which the Platonic philosophy appeared, into which the ancient and higher poetry
was merged, for Plato himself was a thoroughly poetical mind.
It is remarkable, that the Greek philosophers of that period
changed the substance and the objects of their speculations.
With the earlier philosophers, we find a philosophy of nature,
with concrete views of nature, in which a great deal of natural
philosophy and mathematics was embodied.   That philosophy
of nature then breaks up, and out of it are developed mathematics, and, perhaps, also natural history and mathematical

---

[1] " As Libanius had read Hyperides, his remark that he considered this
speech to be a work of Hyperides, ought certainly not to be rejected.   The
orations of Hyperides existed in the library of Matthias Corvinus: they remained at Ofen until the Turks destroyed the greater part of that library, and
during that conflagration the MS. disappeared.   But we hope to recover a fragment in the Eclogae of Constantine Porphyrogenitus from a codex in the
Vatican library."—1825.

geography. It is scarcely possible to believe, that the natural history in Aristotle should have become at once so perfect, if there had been no predecessors. The earlier philosophers had certain formulae for mathematics and mathematical geography, which they had received from foreigners : Thales, *e.g.*, calculated the eclipse of the sun — if he actually did calculate it— not by means of his own mathematical knowledge, but by means of certain formulae obtained from the East, as is still done by the Chinese. Mathematics did not yet exist at all ; it was then only developing itself, and was taken up with great interest. As a proof of this, I may mention the extraordinary development of mechanics, which, ever since the Peloponnesian war, was cultivated for definite purposes, in different places, with the greatest zeal and success. Philosophy is no longer a philosophy of nature, but becomes altogether transcendental, theological, and dialectical.

The totally different character of its tendency is perfectly accounted for by the circumstances of the time. All the theology and national faith which had existed before was now extinct; they survived only in mere forms, and the worship of nature had become changed into contemptible idolatry. Hence the want of a theology and a new faith was felt by every mind.

Aristotle appeared at the same time with Demosthenes, and as the latter directed all his energies to the actual present, so the former also applied his gigantic mental powers to the realities in the state and in nature. Everything that existed was of interest to him, and because it existed, it had a right to be investigated by him.

—◆—

LECTURE LXXIII.

HISTORICAL literature and its different epochs have already been considered on a former occasion. At first, history consisted in annalistic records of ancient, especially mythical, traditions ; next came the combination of the accounts of countries and nations with ancient traditions, and the first beginnings of records of contemporary events, as in the narratives of Hecataeus and Herodotus. In regard to the

z 2

description of nations (ethnology) Hecataeus gave the impulse; we do not sufficiently value him, and Herodotus is unjust towards him. After this, there came the history of the time through which the historian himself had passed, which kind of history was first attempted by Hellanicus, who, however, seems to have been an author of very indifferent merit. But history then appears all at once in its highest perfection in Thucydides. After him, the art of writing history became dormant; and, for a period of upwards of thirty years, no history was composed. It was not till after the battle of Mantinea that it was taken up again by Anaximenes and Xenophon, who had commenced a supplement of Thucydides even at an earlier date; its miserable character has been already pointed out.

As soon as the Greeks believed that they possessed the art by which oratory might be produced, that art also became the basis of prose in general, and of history, and upon this foundation it was continued. Thus two celebrated historians, Ephorus and Theopompus, proceeded from the school of Isocrates. Ephorus was an author of uncommon merit and value. Next to the loss of the lyric poets, whose excellence surpassed everything, there is no loss that we feel more painfully, than that of the history of Ephorus. He was a most truthful man, possessed of historical talent for criticism and investigation; he is the first who applied truly historical criticism on a large scale, " and with whom history appeared as a distinct branch of systematic knowledge." He wrote without any affectation, and it is for this reason, that, at the time when the rhetoricians were supreme judges in matters of taste, Ephorus, as an author, was very much less valued than he would be valued by us. Our judgment of Theopompus, who was somewhat younger than Demosthenes, would be the very opposite. His eloquence is praised, but he was a rhetorician of the bad and spurious kind: he combined a faulty mannerism, an inflated style, and diffuseness, with highly-objectionable sentiments, falsehood, and a malicious character. The main requisite of a man who is to treat history in the right way, is, to have sound and correct feelings. Why should we be concerned in the history of by-gone ages, unless we take a delight in noble acts and undertakings, and unless our hearts beat for the great things done in past ages ? Nothing is more detestable than to see the history of a great period written by men who take a pleasure in always setting forth its weaknesses and defects, in order to arrive, as Pope says, at the conclusion, "that Cato was as great a knave as they themselves." I will mention only one man of this class, Menzel of Breslau, who tries to drag down everything for which our hearts beat. This tendency is a disease under which many labour. Theopompus also was a man of this kind: he vilified everything that was great and noble in the history of Greece; he lived at Athens, but he nevertheless endeavoured, in every possible way, to represent that city in the most unfavourable light. "This animosity was, indeed, inherited, for Athens had formerly been guilty of many acts of injustice against his country; but Chios ad been the cause of the deplorable social war which overthrew Greece, and it had subsequently altogether renounced the cause of Greece, and thrown itself into the arms of Persia." The work of Theopompus is no longer extant. He had taken Herodotus for his model, and interspersed his history with episodes like Herodotus; but his style of writing was something studied and artificial. In addition to this, he was very credulous, and introduced into history and ethnology a great number of exaggerations and absurdities, as well as many calumnies of excellent men. But, along with these absurdities and false-hoods, his work contained many historical facts; and it is on account of these that we could wish to have it. " Through him we should be enabled to arrive at a thorough understanding of Demosthenes. He also embraced the history of the non-Hellenic nations which came in contact with the Greeks." His character was that of a man of the opposition, and he could not help attacking. He was angry with the Athenians, but could not make up his mind to side with the Macedonians, and thus he was at war with all the world. This makes him appear, morally, in a better light than if he had been servile to the Macedonians.

" About the same time, Callisthenes wrote the history from the peace of Antalcidas down to the end of the Phocian war. His work enjoyed great reputation on account of his talent, but his personal character was evidently by no means blameless. He was a sophist, though he was a relation of Aristotle."

These are the principal authors; my object is only to give

you a general outline of intellectual culture among the Greeks, and not a history of Greek literature, which would here be out of place.

The arts underwent exactly the same change as literature. With the earlier Greeks, art was ideal; but its ideal character with them widely differed from that which we find in the school of the Caracci, and in the later period of decay during the seventeenth and eighteenth centuries, when a great number of beauties were gleaned and collected, so that beautiful pictures were produced by copying the beautiful points of several others, the nose being taken from one, a beautiful hand from another, etc. The ancients took a very different course in the creation of their ideal works. They accurately seized the outlines, the scaffolding of life, and in their minds formed a careful image of what was produced by the creative powers of nature; that is, they conceived the idea which she endeavoured to develop in refractory matter. Thus they themselves created the image in their minds, and represented in a tractable material the object which in a defective material had always remained defective. Hence portrait-statues and paintings appeared to the earlier Greeks as something unworthy of art. They did indeed exist, but only as masks in wax; it was certainly not the Romans alone that had such masks. The Greeks reasoned thus: if I form, e. g., an image of Sopocles, I do not make him as he looked at the time when I saw him, when he was perhaps unwell or recovering from an illness; but I try to seize the man's countenance, and put to myself the question, how would this man look in his highest perfection, if this life were not subject to so many misfortunes, if the defects and ravages of circumstances had not distorted his features? It was in this spirit that they made their portrait-statues, as, for example, those of the victors in the great games. This is expressly attested. Our method of making portraits in paintings and statues first commenced in the time of Alexander.

The ancient, severe, and Dante-like manner in painting and sculpture, as well as in architecture, disappeared as early as the Peloponnesian war. Corinthian architecture begins under Alexander, the Ionic order having sprung up before, and having gradually supplanted the Doric order. The last-mentioned now altogether ceased to be applied. There had now arisen a style of great elegance and greater finish in forms, a greater variety of colours and a better mixture were introduced, and in the drawings everything sharp and unpleasing was avoided. The objects aimed at were gracefulness and loveliness. Ancient art had in some points been intentionally stationary, which was not right, for progress is necessary. Now, however, it had arrived at the dangerous point, from which no advance was possible, but only decay. Along with this development of the beautiful in art, there now also appeared the desire to be historically true. Even Lysippus made portraits, and an elder brother of his was the first who made his statues perfect portraits.

Even before the Peloponnesian war the Greek constitutions had ceased to be developments of the ancient institutions: the ancient basis had consumed itself. Whatever constitutions there were, they were only conventional forms of the period. In ancient times people had lived in their early traditions, regarding them as that which was really glorious; on them their minds feasted with delight; every-day life was too ordinary, and it seemed hardly worth while to speak of it. Men lived on in joy, but all the years were alike, and when the new year came, the old one was forgotten; as we forget the flowers and trees of last year while we are enjoying those of the present. They lived only in the enjoyment of the actual present, and the ancient legends engaged their minds. Hence men were at that time so thoroughly poetical: in every mouth those legends underwent a thousand changes. That beautiful life in the traditions of the past received a decisive shock at the time when the present became great and more glorious than the past; when men began at first to look to the times of their ancestors with less interest, and soon even with complete disregard. When I passed from the age of boyhood into that of youth, and even after having passed through a few years of youth, I used to blush at the thought of the foolish things I had said and done; but when I grew older, the recollection of my childhood again became dear to me, and in my maturer years I understood the beauty of my boyish dreams. I believe most of you will experience the same thing. Such also is the case with nations: there is a time when they are ashamed of that which has been handed down. The same thing happened to the Romans and to the Germans after the thirty years' war, when they began to abandon themselves to a foreign literature. During the Persian war, the Greeks had already forgotten much of their past history, although Herodotus was still able to collect λόγοι. Then came the Peloponnessian war of twenty-eight years' duration, with all its misery, with all its devastations and demoralisation, during which people merely to maintain their present existence, had to make the greatest exertions: such things could not but make them forget the past. And thus the period subsequent to the Peloponnesian war was separated from the earlier ones by a deep chasm. This was one of the chief causes of the decay of ancient poetry, for tradition had ceased to live among the people. Aeschylus and Sophocles had learned the ancient legends from their nurses and from the people, for every one knew some stories of the olden times. But the subsequent generations had nothing but what they found already treated of in the earlier poets. Hence the creative, poetical power disappeared.

The question as to what subjects are fit for epic poetry has often been discussed; and many strange things have been said on this point by our neighbours and by the Germans themselves. It has often been seriously asserted, that every epic subject must have a certain age, and that then only it becomes ripe and available. The crusades, it is said, were just ripe for Tasso, and at present there is no subject thoroughly fit for epic poetry. But the truth is, it is not age that renders an event epic, and no subject can properly be epic, unless it has, as it were, become national property, unless it has become a universally known popular tradition; forming and enriching itself in the mouth of the people, until in the hands of a poet it receives a permanent epic form. Tasso's subject was so little ripe, that the honest Italians even now confess that his " Jerusalem Delivered" is a failure. Whoever still praises it, shows that he has no judgment, and only repeats what others have said before him. Painful as it is, it must be confessed, that it makes a sad impression to find that a really great genius undertook such a work.

This change in the mode of thinking among the Greeks exercised a very extensive influence, and hence also the hereditary national laws lost their meaning and their power: they were no longer the peculiar expression of the Ionic or Doric constitution, or the hereditary substance of their nationality.

The Greek states of that time were in the same condition, in which we at present find all the nations of Europe, where new social institutions are to be formed, and must be formed solely according to the conventional circumstances of the present, because the past has lost its vitality. When the past has become effete, it is a carcase, and it is a folly productive of absurdities, if we cling to it, and insist upon appealing to it. We must, as far as possible, endeavour to comprehend present circumstances, and to give to the best the greatest stability: this alone can create healthy and manly characters. It must, however, be owned, that in this respect our present circumstances are less favourable than those of the times that are gone by. The connection between the past and the present, was at that time in Greece completely torn asunder.

Manners and customs had been changed, and the fearful demoralisation, combined with extreme misery, had commenced during the Peloponnesian war. Not only were all the tribes and towns exasperated against one another; but in all the towns themselves the most violent divisions had arisen, which were incomparably worse than the ancient parties, because they were factious and altogether personal. A faction is a party consisting of men who unite for their own interest and their own individuality; but there may also be factions for good. Parties, on the other hand, exist where the divisions which neither can nor ought to be wanting in a state for the preservation of its vitality, exist for the purpose of supporting certain opinions and hereditary institutions. Parties can very well exist without the bitterness peculiar to factions. What ought to be a party, becomes but too often a faction. The party of Demosthenes was indeed a *factio bonorum*, but it cannot be denied after all, that the divisions of that time were factions. It is true, that divisions had existed at Athens even at earlier times; but when, for example, under Pericles, the questions as to the power of the Areopagus and democracy were opposed to each other, they were parties, at least up to a certain point. Now, however, these divisions had become personal. No one wished to introduce any change of form, but the question was, who was to rule in the existing forms. Wherever, in our days, there is what is called a free political life, the divisions become factions: whigs and tories once were parties, but have now become factions.

At the time of his father's death, Alexander was twenty years old.   He is the first instance of a prince, to whose education all the advantages of regal resources were applied. Philip's judgment and intelligence, even if we had no other proof, is evident from what he did for the education of his son, from the trouble he took to induce Aristotle, the greatest among his contemporaries, to leave Athens and undertake the training of Alexander's mind.   But Philip does not seem to have formed a very accurate idea of what Aristotle was going to teach his pupil, nor of the fact that the philosopher would regard the moral training and the cultivation of the heart as a matter of greater importance than the cultivation of the intellect; it cannot be supposed that this was Philip's intention, for he was a barbarian, though a barbarian of a most powerful intellect and judgment, and a man who, no doubt, spoke Greek as well as the Greeks themselves, just as noble barbarians in modern times speak French as perfectly as it is spoken at Paris.   Aristotle, therefore, cannot be made responsible for Alexander's moral character.   But it does, notwithstanding, great credit to Philip to have valued Aristotle so much as to do all he could for the purpose of winning him, and he even restored the native place of the philosopher, which had been destroyed, at his special request; a great concession !

In his early youth, Alexander had been on very good terms with his father ; but, some years before Philip's death, a vehement aversion arose between them,[1] and there can be no doubt that Alexander knew about the murder of his father.

LECTURE LXXIV.

VERY few men have acquired such an immense celebrity, both in Asia and Europe, as Alexander; and among all the great men of history, if we except Charlemagne, and, in a less degree, Constantine, he is the only one that has become a

[1] The MSS. notes here contain a minute account of the disputes in Philip's family, and the murder of the king; the greater part has been incorporated in the 69th Lecture, and needs not to be repeated here. —ED.

poetical being.   Alexander is, for the East, what Charlemagne is for the West; and, next to Rustam, he is the chief hero of the Persian fairy tales and romances.   To us also he is a man of extraordinary importance, inasmuch as he gave a new appearance to the whole world.   He began what will now be completed, in spite of all obstacles—the dominion of Europe over Asia; he was the first that led the victorious Europeans to the East.   Asia had played its part in history, and was destined to become the slave of Europe.   He has also become the national hero of the Greeks, although he was as foreign to them as Napoleon was to the French, notwithstanding that he traced his family to the mythical heroes of Greece.   From certain statements referring to his earlier career, we must infer, that, even during his life-time, and immediately after his death, his name enjoyed that popularity among the Greeks.   In the beginning of his reign, he inflicted fearful sufferings upon them, but he left Greece so soon after, and the Greeks were so quickly ready to ascribe to themselves the laurels which he won for Macedonia, and which he complaisantly shared with them, that he soon became popular among them.   And when he wrote, " Alexander, king of the Macedonians and Greeks," they were rather pleased with it.

But his personal character will appear to us in a different light.   Many a rhetorician, even in antiquity, formed a correct judgment of him.   Who does not know the story of the pirate, who was condemned to death by Alexander, and, on being brought before him, said, that there was no difference between them !   The orientals still call him, " Alexander the robber."   I will not judge of him from this point of view, for the whole history of the world turns upon war and conquest; I speak only of his personal character.   But, without agreeing with the declamations which have so often been made about him, I unhesitatingly declare, that I have formed a very unfavorable opinion of him.   When I behold a young man, who, in his twentieth year, ascends the throne, after having conspired against his father—who then displays in his policy a cruelty like that of the house of the Medici in the sixteenth century, like Cosmo de Medici and his two sons —who not only sacrifices his step-mother to Olympias, but causes the innocent infant of the unhappy Cleopatra, as well as several other near relatives, to be murdered (we do not know their names, as Arrian skilfully evades mentioning them)—who despatched all that knew anything of his complicity, as well as those who had previously offended him—such a young man is condemned for all time to come.

Plutarch shows a foolish and unfounded partiality towards him, and such was universally the case among the Greeks. His drunkenness cannot be denied, and with it they excuse his murders, as, for example, that of Clitus; and, in order poetically to complete the indescribable folly committed by later Greeks, they compare him with Dionysus. Bacchus, it is said, at all times allows a Macedonian, in his intoxication, to commit more serious offences than others; the Clodones and Mimallones are talked of, and the Thracian women who tear Orpheus to pieces, and other similar trivialities of the Greek sophists, are brought forward as analogies. But his drunkenness does not account for all he did. He caused the most innocent and most faithful servant, the best general of his father, to be maliciously assassinated in a truly oriental manner; the man had been frank and open, and knew that Alexander was what he was through him. Things like these are passed over in silence. The murder of his friend Clitus, who told him the truth, was a fearful act. " I do not comprehend how persons can excuse Alexander by saying, that he was an unusually great man; if he was so, was he not then responsible for his unusually great powers?" All his actions, which are praised as generous, are of a theatrical nature and mere ostentation. He was indeed attached to Aristotle; but even lions and tigers show a certain kindness to those who have fed and nursed them in their youth, until the beast of prey awakens in them in all its ferocity. His friendship for Aristotle did not save Callisthenes, and when this man had been sacrificed, Aristotle too thought it advisable to return to Athens. His attachment to Hephaestion was not friendship, but a disgrace. His generosity towards the captive Persian princesses is nothing extraordinary; if it be not ostentation, it is something quite natural, and of every-day occurrence; but it is mere ostentation.

It must, indeed, be acknowledged, that Alexander is a most remarkable phenomenon; but the praise bestowed on him can apply only to his great intelligence and his talents. He was altogether an extraordinary man, with the vision of a prophet, a power for which Napoleon also was greatly distinguished; when he came to a place, he immediately perceived its capability and its destination; he had the eye which makes the practical man. If we had no other example of the keenness of his judgment, the fact that he built Alexandria would alone furnish sufficient evidence; he discovered the point which was destined, for fifteen hundred years, to form the link between Egypt, Europe, and Asia. Although at the time, when the course of the Nile was not obstructed by deposits of mud, that point did not yet possess its importance, still Alexander, at any rate, saw at a glance what nature had destined that place to be. " It was only required to build a city there, to make it the great emporium of the world." That city was to be the corner-stone of his empire, and, as such, he probably intended it to be his capital. It would be the height of injustice not to ascribe the skilful management of the war to him, but to the generals of Philip. The Persians, it is true, were incredibly wretched, and the senseless manner in which they opposed him rendered it easy for him to subdue them; but, at the same time, Alexander's arrangement was so sure and so correct, even under the most difficult circum-stances, and his expedition to the Indus was so skilful, so well planned and chosen, that it is impossible not to concede to him the praise of a great general. Nay, a most competent judge, Hannibal, declared him to be the greatest general. It must not, however, be forgotten, that he had most excellent instruments — distinguished generals, and a splendid army. If he had had to create his army, his undertaking would not have succeeded so well. Parmenio, Philotas, Ptolemaeus, Seleucus, and Antigonus, were all distinguished captains, all proceeded from the school of his father, and had acquired great reputation even under him; and, if we except the single Eumenes, we may assert, that no great commander was trained under Alexander. In like manner, King Frederick II. inherited an army already trained by his father; and most of his generals had served in the army before his time.

Alexander was a man of cultivated intellect, and he could not have been otherwise, having received the careful instruction of Aristotle; he was, moreover, as intimately acquainted with Greek literature as the best educated Greeks of his age.

The authorities for the history of Alexander which we

possess, are no longer the original ones, for all of them have perished. The current histories of Alexander are altogether fabulous. The historians of Alexander may be divided into two classes; the first comprising his contemporaries and companions, and the second the later authors, who wrote his history generally as rhetoricians.

Two among his contemporaries and companions, Aristobulus and Ptolemaeus Lagi, the first king of Egypt, deserve to be distinguished from the rest; they certainly did not confine themselves to the absolute truth, but were very well able to report the truth, and may on the whole be relied upon. The works of both are lost, but we know Alexander as well, as if we possessed them, and it is only in the detail that we miss them. Their substance is preserved in the excellent history of Arrian, who took them as his basis. Arrian was a Bithynian of Nicomedia in the time of Trajan, and one of the first provincials who obtained the highest dignities at Rome. He is at once a Greek and a Roman, and not only a rhetorician, but a practical military man. It is quite evident from his history, that he understands what he is writing about: it is the work of a man who made everything perfectly clear to himself. " It is, moreover, written with critical skill, although as far as its sentiments are concerned, it is a panegyric on Alexander; its style is very beautiful, and in the manner of Xenophon. It stands indeed to ancient history in the same relation in which the new comedy stands to the ancient one, but it is at all events a happy imitation. The remarks on Oriental affairs render the book extremely interesting." This history is truly invaluable.

The most popular among the many lost works on Alexander was that of Clitarchus, one of the elegant Greek writers of later times, that crept in among the classical authors, and were read as much as Thucydides. Clitarchus lived somewhat later than Alexander, and did not accompany him on his expedition; he wrote uncritically, and many fabulous stories originated with him. But Onesicritus was altogether fabulous, for he wrote without any regard for truth. Curtius is for the most part based upon him and Clitarchus. " Curtius imitated Livy at a time when classical Latinity had disappeared, under Septimius Severus,[1] as Arrian imitated Xenophon." The history of

---

[1] Comp. *Klein. Schrift.*, vol. i. p. 305.

Alexander in Diodorus is made up of several others, and probably shows how the continuations of Ephorus, especially that of Duris, related it; " but it is important for chronology." St. Croix has written a criticism on the historians of Alexander ; but his work is very unsatisfactory to a German scholar, and must be treated by us as if it did not exist. The whole work must be done over again. As regards the facts in the life of Alexander, we need not hesitate to follow Arrian.

While the history of Charlemagne is faithfully and truly related by Eginhard and a few contemporary chronicles, avowedly fabulous stories about him occur at a very early time : an expedition to Palestine is mentioned very early; this tradition was afterwards further developed; the expedition to Spain also assumes a fabulous form; the first traces of romantic histories of Charlemagne occur as early as 150 years after his time; and they were generally believed as early as the tenth century. In like manner, a fabulous history of Alexander existed in Egypt at an early period, under the name of Aesopus; it was not a purely Graeco-Alexandrian story, but rather a combination of Egyptian and Eastern traditions. In it Alexander was connected with Nectanebos and the East: it is full of sorcery, miracles, and most extravagant fables. A. Mai has discovered an ancient Latin translation of it, of which the beginning unfortunately is wanting. Peyron of Turin discovered the beginning, but destroyed it, in order to be able to read what was written underneath, and did not think it worth while to publish it. The Greek original was rewritten several times, like our popular stories of Siegfried, Genoveva, and the like; and under the name of Callisthenes, it was read in the Byzantine empire as a popular book down to the year 1453. This Pseudo-Callisthenes, in bad ancient and modern Greek, still exists in several libraries. The same has been the fate of the fables of Aesop. The Latin popular version made by Julius Valerius from Aesopus, continued to be read in the West as Callisthenes was in the East. The Spanish poem on Alexander, by Garselo, of the thirteenth century, is based on the Pseudo-Callisthenes, and in like manner Aesopus was translated into Eastern languages. There can be no doubt that the Eastern Aesopus forms the basis of the Persian poems of Nisami. It is an interesting subject, which I should like to see one day given out as a prize essay, to show in what manner the history of Alexander was spread in the East. There is even a Hebrew version of the romance of Alexander, and also an Arabic one in the ancient dialect. All these stories depart more and more from the truth. Afterwards Alexander disappears from the romances, and their substance is transferred to other romances; thus in the ancient German romance about Duke Ernest of Suabia, this hero is simply substituted for Alexander. To trace such poetical compositions is difficult, indeed; but the labour is well rewarded.

The death of Philip (Olymp. 111, 2) created an immense sensation throughout his empire; for it was as yet by no means firmly established. Philip had accelerated his contemplated expedition against the East, and had certainly hoped to live to see its successful issue; as at his death he was only forty-eight years old, such a hope was not unreasonable. However, his conquests would have been of a different kind from those of Alexander; he would certainly not have carried them so far as in the end to involve the dissolution of his own empire; he would perhaps have been satisfied with Western Asia, Syria, and Egypt. His character at least justifies such a conjecture, for it was his maxim to do one thing thoroughly rather than to attempt many things which he could not compass. He had not yet been able to consolidate his own empire, for his Macedonians had every year been led to fresh campaigns, and had been weakened; and most of his veterans had, through their wounds, become disabled.

"All the tribes round Macedonia believed, that the empire had been kept together only by Philip's personal character; the Macedonian supremacy was connected only with his name, and it was believed that the kingdom was now reduced to the limited power, which it had possessed in the times of Amyntas, and no one imagined that Alexander would be able to maintain himself. His faults were better known than his brilliant qualities, and in Macedonia itself, the national party was opposed to him."

Commotions thus arose in several places, but at first they were nowhere of a decisive character. The most determined was that in Ambracia, where the inhabitants expelled the Macedonian garrison. But all Greece was in a state of ferment, and threatened to revolt, and nowhere was this the case more than at Athens, which was guided by Demosthenes. When the news of Philip's death reached Athens—Olympias seems to have formed connections even there to spread the news, and, in case matters should not turn out well through a victory of the party of Attalus, to place herself under the protection of the Greeks—the people were completely intoxicated with joy. Demosthenes, adorned with flowers and in festal attire, appeared before them to announce the tidings of Philip's death, although he was suffering from a domestic affliction, his daughter having died only a few days before. This is stupidly brought forward by Aeschines as an offence against nature: the Romans, too, put off their mourning, when the republic met with some great success. The Athenians allowed themselves to be carried away by their joy, and although shortly before they had sent to Philip a servile psephisma to congratulate him on his marriage, they now resolved to afford protection to Pausanias, and to confer distinctions upon him, for they believed that he had escaped. The Illyrians and Thracians also, and, in fact, all other hostile tribes were in commotion.

It was just now, at the beginning of his reign, if ever, that Alexander showed his ability and greatness by a prompt and judicious mode of action. He assembled an army in a very short time: in Macedonia he crushed every movement by terror, and hastily set out against Thessaly, which refused to recognise him as king. As Philip had divided that country into four cantons, which had produced jealousy and disunion among them, it was not very difficult to maintain his authority there. The Thessalians accordingly submitted as soon as he approached, and at once recognised him as their protector, transferring to him their revenues and the tributes from their subject tribes, which were applied εἰς κοινόν. In the same manner, the first excitement throughout Greece gave way to a feeling of the necessity of submission. After having pacified Thessaly, he quickly marched with his army to Corinth, whither he summoned a general congress of all the Greek allies. The Spartans alone did not appear at this congress: according to Arrian, it was attended by all the nations ἐντὸς Πελοποννήσου; but this is an error in the text, which is on the whole very faulty, the true reading being ἐντὸς Πυλῶν, as opposed to the Thessalians. Young Alexander was recognised by all, and they renewed with him the treaty which had been concluded with Philip; that is, they conceded to him the same kind of supremacy which had formerly belonged to Sparta and Athens, and he obtained the supreme command in the contemplated war against Persia. The κοινὴ εἰρήνη was renewed.

The Athenians were then in a difficult position: Demades was again sent as ambassador to sue for pardon, and strange to say, the Athenians obtained a peace. But it was necessary for Alexander to win them over, because he wanted their fleet. On that occasion Demosthenes refused to go as ambassador to Alexander, and his enemies do not blush to blame him for it. He mistrusted Alexander, and he had not concealed either his joy at Philip's death or his contempt for Alexander. Wherever he could gain allies for his country, he was not behind hand; but why should he have gone there? Under other circumstances, he would have done it, even if he had had to pass an army of demons; but to demand of him to compliment a hated enemy, is more than disgraceful. Alexander, moreover, would not have been very scrupulous about the laws of nations, for he was even then threatening, and spoke of the surrender of disturbers of the peace.

The Athenians made even larger concessions to Alexander than they had done to Philip. The substance of the κοινὴ εἰρήνη, and the concessions made by the Athenians, are known from the speech περὶ τῶν πρὸς Ἀλέξανδρον συνθηκῶν. The principal articles of the peace were:—

1. All the Greeks shall be free and independent. By this clause all the towns which had hitherto been under the supremacy of another, became emancipated; Thebes, e. g., lost all its power over the Boeotian towns.

2. Whoever changes the constitution of the states existing at the time when an enemy joins the confederacy, shall be a public enemy.

3. Whoever recalls an exiled enemy or tyrant, shall be a public enemy, and all shall take up arms against him and his country.

4. Exiles and other armed persons shall not be permitted to proceed from an allied town to their native place. Any town permitting this, or neglecting to prevent it, shall be outlawed.

5. The allies and guardians of the peace shall watch, that in the allied states no one be put to death or sent into exile contrary to the existing laws, that no confiscations, no

cancelling of debts, no distribution of lands, and no revolutionary manumissions take place.

6. Every one shall be free to sail at sea without molestation, and no ships of any nation shall be captured; whoever acts contrary to this shall be treated as a public enemy.

7. Another stipulation of this treaty, which, however, can be stated only vaguely, seems to have been, that armed ships should not be allowed to enter the harbours of the allies, if they should object to it.

It requires no proof to show that such a treaty on the part of the protector was a mere farce. Hyperides mentions these points only for the purpose of showing how they were violated by Alexander. The second and sixth were openly disregarded. At Pellene, *e. g.*, the very ancient democratic constitution was abolished in a revolution, supported by Macedonia, during which the rich were murdered, their property confiscated, slaves set free, and exiles recalled. Alexander's ships, moreover, took away whole fleets of the Athenians laden with corn, and stationed near Tenedos.

Greece thus groaned under the yoke of Macedonia: Macedonians were in Peloponnesus, and the Cadmea was in the hands of a Macedonian garrison. There remained nothing but a successful attack of the Persians, which might have broken the Macedonian empire, and burst the chains.

Alexander now returned to Macedonia (Olymp. 111, 2), and continued his preparations. It may have been during this interval, that the troops standing in Asia were expelled or withdrawn. A rebellion in the north of Thrace called him thither, for he felt the necessity of setting a terrifying example. In order to chastise those tribes, he undertook an expedition across mount Haemus against the Triballians. They had driven the Getae across the Danube, "and now dwelt in Bulgaria, which in the time of Herodotus had been occupied by the Getae. The Getae in their turn had pushed the Scythians eastward.[2] There Alexander showed himself for the first time as a great general." He forced the passes of mount Haemus with great difficulty and loss; but he succeeded. He then quickly, and with great energy, quelled the insurrection and crossed the Danube. " This last undertaking, however, was not a campaign, but only a reconnoitring expedition to

[2] Comp. *Klein. Schrift.*, vol. i. p. 374, foll.

A A 2

show that he did not dread such distances." The question here presents itself whether the island of Peuce, means the islands at the present mouths of the Danube, or whether it is one island at the ancient mouth of the river, behind which stands the ancient *vallum Trajanum* towards Silistria, north of Varna, where even now there is an ancient but insignificant arm of the Danube, which in ancient times must have been much deeper. This question cannot be determined, though I think the latter supposition highly probable; for those Danubian islands are in reality scarcely inhabitable, whereas the island of Peuce is spoken of as a very populous country. Alexander crossed the Danube at its mouth, near the Euxine; his galleys sailed into the river and came up to him. Having there received the homage of the Getae, and concluded peace, he returned across the river. Thence he proceeded to Illyricum, which was likewise in a state of insurrection. He there had to wage war against Glaucias, king of the Taulantians, by whom he had at one time been protected for several years,—when suddenly he was informed of the revolt of Thebes.

His absence in a remote country had produced a singular state of feeling in Greece. Those northern nations were regarded as very dangerous, it was hoped that they would overcome Alexander, and as Memnon seemed to command the Persian army, it was thought, that fortune might be favorable to the Greeks. In short, the insurrection broke out in several places.

The Thebans, in particular, revolted because a report reached them, that Alexander had been slain. The communication with his army had been interrupted for a time, and for this reason the credulous Greeks believed, that he had been destroyed with all his forces. This unfortunate report induced the Thebans to revolt; they were exasperated in the highest degree at the treacherous conduct of Philip, and it was the general opinion in Greece, that everything would be easily accomplished, if they could but destroy the Macedonian garrisons.

The garrison in the Cadmea indulged in the most revolting cruelties against ἐλεύθερα σώματα, and, under the protection of the soldiers, the returned exiles, to whom Philip had entrusted the government, took the most fearful vengeance for private wrongs, and did everything that could be suggested by Boeotian brutality, and by the general unscrupulousness of the time. When, therefore, the report of Alexander's death became general, some exiles returning to Thebes stirred up their fellow-citizens. Demosthenes, no doubt, knew of this undertaking, and it is probably not a false report, that he provided the returning exiles with the means of carrying out their plan; for in everything that concerned the liberty of Greece, there was no one else to whom to apply. Nor does there seem to be any good reason for doubting the statement, that Demosthenes, at his own expense, furnished the Thebans, and those who joined them, with arms. The conspiracy at Thebes soon ripened into insurrection,[3] which was not confined to the city, but spread over the country around. It was easy to overpower the Macedonian party, as the garrison of the Cadmea was not numerous; the Thebans, however, seem to have considered it impossible to take the Cadmea; hence they surrounded it with double palisades, that no reinforcements might be introduced, and the garrison might be compelled to surrender by famine.

At Athens also violent speeches were made, and violent resolutions passed. " We may well imagine that Demosthenes did not allow such an opportunity to pass, or remained

[3] " Arrian relates, that the insurrection commenced with the people seizing and murdering Amyntas and Timolaus, who had come down into the lower city. Wesseling, on Diodorus Siculus, considers these two men to have been commanders of the Macedonian garrison; but I believe that the name Amyntas is a mistake, and that we ought to read Anemoetas, whom Demosthenes, pro. Coron., mentions among the Theban traitors. From Aeschines' speech against Ctesiphon, and from Dinarchus, it is clear, that the garrison of the Cadmea was then inclined to accept a bribe on condition of its evacuating the citadel. This is probable enough, and quite intelligible, the garrison consisting of mercenaries. But the statement of Aeschines, that it was quite impossible to obtain the five talents for the purchase of the surrender, is inconceivable; it is assuredly not probable that the mercenaries would have surrendered the Cadmea for so small a sum. The same Aeschines and Dinarchus blame Demosthenes for having refused to advance those five talents when they were asked of him, although he had received and appropriated to himself 300 talents from the Persian king. But this must be regarded as a base falsehood, for it is morally impossible. Considering the general depravity of all the men who then took part in public affairs, we cannot wonder any more than in the case of the Italians at the end of the fifteenth and the beginning of the sixteenth century, if they utter the most fearful falsehoods against one another with the most reckless impudence. If we can draw an inference from this accusation, it is just possible, that, before the rebellion broke out, very suspicious and unauthorised persons may have applied to Demosthenes to ensnare him, intending, if the undertaking should fail, to denounce him as the man who had attempted to excite a rebellion."—1825.

inactive : but, from the very fact, that we have no speeches
of that time, we may infer, that he was not very pressing in
urging his countrymen on to war. But Ephialtes did call
upon them to take up arms."

But all was in vain ; Alexander was on his return, and
already approaching.   As soon as he heard of the insurrection
of the Thebans, he forthwith set out to take vengeance upon
them, " and, with indescribable rapidity, he accomplished
his celebrated march through Upper Macedonia, across the
highest frontier mountains and mount Pindus, * instead
of taking the ordinary road through the valley of the Peneus ;
and thus he all at once appeared at Pellina, in Thessaly,
while in Greece they were still imagining that he had perished
among the Triballians."   The Greeks, therefore, learned at
once that he was on his return, and that he was rapidly
advancing against Greece.

Meantime the garrison of the Cadmea, under the command
of Philotas, had been reduced to great distress by the Thebans.
The ruins of Thebes are less fitted than those of any other
city to give us an idea of its topography. In the time of
Pausanias the Cadmea alone was inhabited. The work of St.
Croix on the historians of Alexander contains a plan of Thebes
by the otherwise very able Barbier du Bocage, which, like
all his maps of Greece, is apt to mislead by the appearance of
accuracy and careful study of the authorities, but it is quite
arbitrary and erroneous.   He imagines that the Cadmea was
situated in the centre of the city, and had a great circumference, and that the city was built concentrically round the
Cadmea. But this is impossible. The Cadmea, like almost all
Greek acropoleis, was indeed surrounded by the city, and was
situated within the walls; but from our historians, it is quite
evident, that one side of the Cadmea touched upon the wall of
the city, and upon this supposition alone the siege can be
understood.

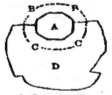

A. The Cadmea.

B B, C C. Fortifications of the Thebans
       against the Cadmea.

D. The city of Thebes.

* Comp. *Hist. of Rome*, vol. iii., note 811.—ED.

Thebes, compared with its small population, had a very large extent; but the citizens might still have been able to defend their city, had not the acropolis been in the hands of the garrison, so that the city had to be defended against two enemies at once. They had built fortifications round the Cadmea, and barricaded the streets (near C), while on the outside (at B) the garrison had been surrounded with a wall.

Alexander appeared south of Thermopylae before the pass could be closed against him, as no one yet expected him there. He had reached the banks of the lake of Onchestus before the Thebans had heard of his arrival, and the fact that the Thebans were panic-struck by the mere thought of seeing the enemy at their gates, was equal to half the victory of Alexander. He now appeared, and after some severe skirmishing with the Thebans, marched round the walls, to occupy the road leading to Attica, and to cut off any support that might come from that quarter. There he encamped and blockaded the city.

The Athenians were likewise surprised and affrighted in the highest degree, when they were informed of his approach. They were not yet prepared; they had indeed determined upon a general levy in arms, and had commenced operations, but they had made no great progress, and no troops were yet sent out.

All the other Greeks had kept aloof. It is true I assign to this time the general commotion in Peloponnesus, where the ancient partizans of Philip, the Arcadians, Eleans, and Argives, as well as the Lacedaemonians, declared against Macedonia— a commotion which Diodorus places immediately after the death of Philip—and the Aetolians also expelled at the same time the governments instituted in Acarnania by the Macedonians,[5] but the greater part of Peloponnesus was in the hands of rulers appointed by the Macedonians, who with the aid of mercenaries kept the citizens down.

The Lacedaemonians, who, in the battle of Chaeronea, might have turned the balance in favour of Greece, now declared themselves against Macedonia, but did nothing. Antipater sent an embassy into Peloponnesus, calling upon the people to march against the Thebans and subdue them; but the Athenians

---

[5] In 1825, Niebuhr assigned the insurrection of Ambracia to this time, while in 1830 he placed it immediately after Philip's death. Compare above, p. 352. —ED.

by another embassy persuaded the Lacedaemonians not to send any support to the Macedonians. Things, however, might have gone farther. In Arcadia, the Greek party had become more powerful than the Macedonian, and had gone so far as to call the militia to arms. But it was impossible to come to the determination to support the Thebans otherwise than by bribing the strategi. Calumny said of Demosthenes, that he had indeed money from Persia in his possession, but that he refused to give it up, when he was requested by the Thebans to bribe the Arcadians. But this is incredible. The Arcadians were indeed ready to assist the Thebans, but were at the same time opposed to the Macedonians being altogether excluded from the affairs of Greece, because they dreaded the reviving power of Lacedaemon. This very circumstance, that the Greeks were jealous of one another, drew foreign nations into their affairs, and was the cause of the ruin of the Greek states. If Cleomenes, who was not born till 100 years later, had then been king, Greece would have been saved. The policy which he adopted, could no longer produce any good results in his day, but in the time of Alexander it might have done so. As he then offered to the Achaeans a share in the supremacy, he certainly would now have been prudent enough to make the same concession to the Athenians, who had far greater claims to it.

The Thebans thus received no assistance from Peloponnesus, and when Alexander appeared before their city, they were helpless, and knew not what to do. " Their conduct towards the unfortunate Phocians was now avenged upon them: the Phocian towns had been destroyed, and the Phocians had been cruelly treated; but they were still living, and now availed themselves of the opportunity of taking revenge upon the Thebans. It was indeed Philip that had ruined them, but Thebes had been the cause of their misfortune." Alexander now showed himself kind to them, and promised to restore their state. The other Boeotians, offended by Thebes, joined the Phocians with double alacrity. Alexander's army is said to have consisted of 30,000 men, Macedonians, Thessalians, and Phocians; but this number seems to be somewhat exaggerated.

Thebes could do nothing but capitulate on as favorable terms as circumstances permitted: to think of anything else, or to imagine that the city could maintain itself, was absurd.

Alexander offered tolerable terms; and it is probable that they would actually have obtained them, as Alexander did not wish to be detained, for every day that he was kept from his Asiatic expedition, was unbearable to him. But the Thebans were infatuated, and would listen to no proposal of reconciliation, although they were in want of arms, provisions, men, and commanders. Alexander caused peace and pardon to be announced to them by a herald, demanding of them only to surrender Phoenix and Proetidas, two of the most conspicuous leaders of the insurrection. But the men who had returned from exile stirred up the people, and haughtily answered that if there was to be peace, Antipater and Philotas ought to be given up to them; and when Alexander offered safety and protection to those who would come to the Macedonian camp, they proclaimed that every Greek who would come to them, should enjoy the same honour as those who for the independence of Greece allied themselves with Persia.

After a few days (Alexander is said to have been encamped three days before the walls of Thebes) he made an assault upon the city, the Thebans having made an unsuccessful sally and having been driven back into the city. Perdiccas made an attack upon the fortifications nearest to the Cadmea[6]; he was very successful, and without difficulty broke through the fortications and the first lines; the garrison gave way, and he now tried to force the second line also. Amyntas immediately followed him with his 3,000 men (a τάξις), and as the contest became hot, Alexander sent his light-armed troops, the Boeotian archers, to support them. The Thebans now offered a powerful resistance, and fought bravely; Perdiccas was wounded, and the Macedonians were nearly repelled by the Thebans, when Alexander came up with his picked troops and body guards. The Thebans were now repulsed, and thrown into such confusion that they fled into the city in complete disorder. Their cavalry too fled, trampling down the infantry, and in the general consternation the gates were left feebly guarded. The Macedonians

---

[6] " His object evidently was to put himself in connection with the Cadmea, and thence to effect his entrance into the city. This was also the object of the attack upon the Theban fortifications. As he was supported by the other corps, his operations were probably not unauthorised, as would appear from Arrian, who, on the authority of Ptolemaeus, says, that it was not Alexander's plan to attack the city, but to penetrate into it from the Cadmea. Arrian seems to have misunderstood Ptolemaeus."—1825.

scaled the ill-protected walls and the towers near the gates, in which the Thebans were nearly crushed. The garrison of the Cadmea now likewise broke through, and forcing the barricades which had been thrown up (at C) against the citadel, penetrated to the agora. The Thebans were thus attacked both in their front and in their rear: the Macedonians were already fighting in the city, while the storm against the walls was still continued. A gate was now broken open, the city was taken by storm, and destroyed with the same fury as Magdeburg. The massacre was going on everywhere. Alexander had in his army many Thracians who were rude barbarians, and the Thespians, Plataeans, Phocians, and Orchomenians, were the most exasperated enemies of the Thebans. The murder and bloodshed was continued the whole day till late at night. It is childish to attach any importance to the fact, that Alexander ordered to spare the house and family of Pindar, while all the rest was destroyed. Such an act deserves no praise, when a whole city and people are annihilated.[7]

That he might have the appearance of justice on his side, Alexander summoned a congress of the Greek allies, Phocians, Thespians, Orchomenians, and the other Boeotian towns, to sit in judgment on the Thebans. This was on the day after the storming of Thebes: the city contained nothing but corpses and slaves, and in the midst of these horrors, the hypocritical tyrant called upon the Greeks to pass judgment. The Phocians and Boeotians pictured in glaring colours the cruelties of which the Thebans had been guilty for years. The ancient sins during the Persian war, since which time 150 years had elapsed, nay, the crimes of the house of Oedipus were laid to their charge, and adduced as cogent reasons for destroying the city. Such things are quite in accordance with the character of the time. The Thebans were allowed to defend themselves, and Cleadas, one of their prisoners, rose to plead for the devoted city, imploring the conquerors not to

[7] " The books of anecdotes relate, that the descendants of Pindar, foreseeing that the city would be taken, caused an inscription to be made upon their house. This is not quite true; but it was probably done after the destruction of the city had already been decreed, and freedom and safety had been promised to the Pindarids. Then, and not until then, the verse was inscribed upon the house to commemorate the event. The sum of money realised by the sale of the booty amounted to 440 talents, which shows that Thebes must have been very poor. Diodorus, however, regards this as the price of 30,000 Thebans who were sold."—1825.

destroy it, and to set the prisoners free.   But it was, notwithstanding, decreed to raze it to the ground, and to sell all the prisoners as slaves: every fugitive was declared an outlaw, and the whole territory, with the exception of what belonged to the temples, was distributed among the allies.   The priests, the friends of Philip and Alexander, the proxeni of the Macedonians,[a] and the descendants of Pindar, alone retained their liberty, and probably also their property.   " The Thebans had indeed greatly sinned against Greece, but still the destruction of a city which was perhaps the most ancient in Greece, and the distribution of its territory among its neighbours, was a terrible visitation."

----◆----

LECTURE LXXV.

THE destruction of Thebes produced great consternation throughout Greece, similar to that which followed a decidedly lost battle against the French in our own days.   Before this catastrophe some had entertained sanguine hopes, the more intelligent had looked with heavy hearts towards the future, and others had indulged at least a feeble hope, that after all, things might improve a little; but now, all at once, the most fearful reality had destroyed every prospect, and complete dependence on Macedonia was the result.

When the Athenians received the tidings, they were just celebrating the mysteries: it was the twentieth of Boedromion (in September).   All ceremonies were immediately suspended, the gates were closed, and preparations were made for a siege. The Athenians were seriously compromised, by the measures they had adopted immediately after the death of Philip, when they declared themselves independent, and still more at the time when Alexander was north of mount Haemus.   Their leaders in particular had to dread the king's vengeance. Among the orators, Demosthenes and Hyperides, and among

[a] " These proxeni (προξενοι) had the same obligations towards a country which a ξένος had towards an individual and his family.   They enjoyed in the city greater privileges than the μέτοικοι, for they were allowed to marry a citizen, and to inherit property."—1825.

the generals, Ephialtes and Leosthenes, had unreservedly expressed their sentiments. Alexander was now with his army on mount Cithaeron, and his watch-fires must have been visible at Athens. The people assembled and deliberated what was to be done. Taken by surprise as they were, it was impossible to think of defending themselves. We need not suppose that they came to a decision at once; weeks may have passed away, for Alexander, like Philip before him, was afraid lest Piraeeus, should be opened to the Persians. In the midst of these difficulties, the Athenians displayed a nobleness of character which was quite peculiar to the republic. The outlawry pronounced by the allies against the Thebans was the same as that proclaimed by the Spartans at the end of the Peloponnesian war, when every fugitive Athenian was declared an outlaw; and the princes of the confederacy of the Rhine would not have been slow to decree the same against Prussia, if it had been the pleasure of Napoleon. But in the midst of this distress, the Athenians resolved that the Thebans who had taken refuge among them should be protected, and that none should be delivered up. This was done to shew their gratitude; for the ancestors of the Thebans, after the Peloponnesian war, had offered an asylum to the fugitive Athenians, though, as we have seen, they had not done so from generous motives, but because their eyes were opened to the arrogance of the Spartans. But the Athenians overlooked their motives; since that time seventeen Olympiads (sixty-eight years) had passed away, and only the oldest people recollected those days.

But what was to be done against Alexander? A reconciliation with him was now thought of. If there had been a sufficiently prepared fleet, they might have opened the communication with Persia, and the city might have been supplied with provisions; the country people might then have been drawn into the city, and they might have ventured upon war. But as the Athenian fleet had not yet been got ready, and the 170 ships of the Macedonians and their allies had the control at sea, such a determination would have been highly dangerous. But they were, after all, not so far reduced as to be obliged to surrender to Alexander at discretion: matters were in that state, that they could enter into negotiations.

It was therefore resolved at Athens to send an embassy to Alexander to congratulate him upon his victory over the

Illyrians and Triballians, as if they did not yet know anything about the destruction of Thebes. But Alexander treated the ambassadors very haughtily, and throwing the psephisma on the ground, turned his back upon them. He then wrote a very angry letter to the Athenians, in which he recounted all their offences, and, in the end, demanded the surrender of Demosthenes and of the most eminent and distinguished men, who were to be tried by the highest court in Greece.

It is commonly said, that Alexander demanded the surrender of the ten orators. This is a strange point. In consequence of certain changes, about which history furnishes no information, there must have existed at Athens at that time something like the tribunes of the people at Rome. Demosthenes himself says: formerly you marched into the field according to phylae, νῦν δὲ πολιτεύεσθε κατὰ φυλάς; and from several passages, it seems to be quite evident, that an arrangement had been made by which each phyle appointed a spokesman,[1] who was chosen from among those who were most distinguished for their eloquence. We should be utterly ignorant of the Athenian constitution, were it not for the fragments from Aristotle's Politics, preserved by Harpocration and Pollux. We must, therefore, suppose that during the anarchy the want of some fixed government gave rise to a constitution different from that which we commonly imagine to have existed at Athens. Although the power of the assembly had become greater than was compatible with the good of the state, and although it interfered in everything, and confined the influence of the βουλή, yet during the period after the Peloponnesian war, a form was developed in which measures were brought before the people. This is, indeed, a very obscure point, but there can be no question that, probably after Olymp. 100, a reform was brought about by which each phyle chose a spokesman, " who, though every Athenian was at liberty to speak, yet came forward with great weight as the representative of a phyle, and as *the* man whose particular duty it was to speak and discuss measures; but he had not the same power as a Roman tribune." Their functions, rights, and qualifications, were fixed by special laws; a man, *e. g.*, to become a spokesman, was obliged to be father of a family, and to be possessed of landed property. It was this peculiar form that made the

---

[1] " The Swiss call such a man *Fürsprecher*."

power of the speaker so great. Such a representative of a
phyle bore the title of rhetor, and there being ten phylae, and
each being represented by one, the number of rhetors was ten.
This is the sense in which we must understand the ten orators
in the time of Demosthenes, who himself, as well as Aeschines,
belonged to the number.

The ten orators mentioned in later times, belong to the
history of literature alone, and consist of a series of orators
belonging to different periods, beginning with Antiphon and
ending with Dinarchus, who lived 100 years later. These latter
ten orators are found in all the works on Greek literature. Plutarch and Dionysius saw in them only an accidental enumeration of ten classical orators. But if the classical character
alone is taken into consideration, it may be asked, why is not
Demetrius Phalereus included among them?   The fact is this:
that the designation of " the ten orators," which often occurs in
the time of Demosthenes, was afterwards, in a playful allusion,
transferred by the Alexandrian grammarians, who knew the
Athenian institutions from Aristotle's Politics, to those whose
orations they admitted into the canon as classical.   In the
time of Philip and Alexander, moreover, the expression, "the
ten orators," is used, without real orators being meant; and
the ten whose surrender Alexander demanded, were not all
orators, for, to mention one instance, there is no trace of
Ephialtes having been an orator. Alexander demanded ten
men, and Plutarch and others hastily assumed that they were
ten orators; especially as Plutarch imagines that the Athenians had no other arms than those of oratory, just as if at
present we were to estimate the strength of a country by its
journalists.[2]

[2] " What men Alexander demanded is not quite certain.   Arrian names
Demosthenes, Lycurgus, Hyperides, Chares, Ephialtes, Polyeuctus, Moerocles,
Diotimus, and Charidemus.   Plutarch, in his life of Demosthenes, does not
notice Hyperides, Diotimus, and Chares, and mentions in their stead Damon
and Callisthenes.   Arrian is a high authority and must be followed, whereas
Plutarch is highly uncritical.   The fact that the surrender of Hyperides was
demanded is mentioned by several authors, so that his name may possibly have
dropped out of Plutarch's account by the mistake of a copyist. As regards
Damon and Callisthenes, the former is entirely unknown, and there is no
doubt a mistake in the name, which occurs only among Doric tribes; I know
of no Athenian of the name of Damon.   Callisthenes was a friend of Demosthenes; his name was, perhaps, the tenth in Arrian, and may easily have
dropped out.   It is true, that it does not occur in any of the MSS. of Arrian,

Alexander had demanded the surrender of the very flower of the Athenian people, in order to deprive it of all its strength; but his demand called forth the highest exasperation. Phocion then came forward in the assembly, scornfully calling upon the Ten to comply with the demand, and saying, that as they were such noble and good men, they ought to prove their patriotism by imitating the example of the daughters of Leos and of Erechtheus, and willingly sacrifice themselves for their country which they had so seriously compromised.

Phocion was a hero, not among his contemporaries, but in the schools of the rhetoricians; hence he is also a hero with Plutarch, who undertook the biographies with the opinions which had already become current.[3] A wise posterity saw that Demosthenes and the patriots of Athens had much damaged the prosperity of their country, that it would have been infinitely better, if their ancestors had in good time submitted to Macedonia, that Philip must be admired, and Alexander

---

but all of them can be traced to one codex, which has not yet been discovered; those which are known, are of little value. Besides Demosthenes, Hyperides— a patriotic soul, though he afterwards wavered—Lycurgus, and Ephialtes, who are all well known, we have mention of Polyeuctus, an intimate friend of Demosthenes, and a man who, in conjunction with him and Lycurgus, travelled about in Greece to stir up his countrymen, took part in the most important affairs, and became a martyr to his love of liberty. Moerocles always appears as one of the good and honourable citizens; but there was one point which brought him into bad repute. In the third of the apocryphal letters of Demosthenes, he is mentioned as the person who persecuted the children of Lycurgus. But this report is not mentioned anywhere else. He is said to have been thrown into prison for debt, and afterwards his surrender was demanded by Antipater because he had been a partisan of Demosthenes, and he is said to have been murdered for the good cause. Diotimus was one of those who had come forward against Philip; he fought in the battle of Chaeronea as hipparchus, having armed some Athenian horsemen at his own expense. He was older than Demosthenes; and it is doubtful whether he belonged to the ten orators. Chares must then have been very old, having been a commander even in the Social war. Charidemus was that wretched commander of mercenaries, and had obtained the Athenian franchise. Dinarchus speaks of him as one of the first men of the nation. He now went to the court of Darius, where he was very favourably received, and drawn into the king's council. But having, just before the battle of Issus, given some arrogant advice—he claimed the command in chief for himself—he fell into disgrace with the king, and was put to death, because the satraps were hurt by his conduct. Callisthenes, an able statesman and friend of Demosthenes, is otherwise scarcely known."—1825.

[3] An opinion on Plutarch, which here occurs in the notes, has been omitted, because it is nearly the same as the one occurring in Lecture LXIX., with which it has been incorporated.—ED.

deified.   From such sentiments they started, and thus the
opinion naturally became established, that Phocion, who had
accidentally foretold the misfortune, had hit upon the right
mode of acting.

Phocion was called by his contemporaries " the Honest"
(ὁ χρηστός), and this title he deserved in a certain sense; but
to call him a hero of virtue, to regard him as the only noble-
minded man at Athens, so as to detract from the merit of
Demosthenes and other illustrious men, is intolerable, and I
cannot concede it.   While, in general, men with but few
exceptions strive after wealth and outward comfort, people are
in the habit of indulging in a kind of idolatry of poverty, as
if thereby they could make amends for their own love of
wealth.   Aristotle and every practical and honest man would
say, that a man ought not to allow himself to be drawn away
from the path of virtue by any treasures that the world contains; but that wealth is a great power, that it affords us the
means of accomplishing much and of embellishing life.   A
cynic speaks contemptuously of wealth, but to an intelligent
man it is an *adiaphoron*.   People who are given to sensual
lusts imagine that they are doing a pious act by a temporary
and irrational mortification of the flesh: the Indian penitent,
the Mahommedan fakir, and the cynic, are degenerate men,
and their actions are blasphemies.   Whence arises this declaiming against riches, but from the fact that the declaimers
themselves regard wealth as affording a very strong temptation,
and possessing irresistible charms?   All the treasures of the
world could not have induced Demosthenes to betray his
country; and we cannot claim any praise for not being cannibals.
There is no merit in this any more than in the fact of our not
committing any horrors which are repulsive to nature.   When
people make so much ado about Phocion's poverty, they only
confess, that, if they had been in his situation, they would have
accepted the hundred talents from Antipater.   The contemporaries of Phocion called him " the Honest," not as contrasted
with Demosthenes, Leosthenes, and Ephialtes — I mention
Leosthenes and Ephialtes along with Demosthenes as honourable names of the time for which I entertain profound respect
—but because they compared him with Chares and Charidemus, and to them Phocion could not but stand in a
favourable contrast.   It was indeed a disgrace for Athens to

compare him with such men, for both were dissolute and venal creatures; Charidemus was the most faithless man, for being engaged in the service of Athens, he sold himself to those who offered him higher pay; and when, *e. g.*, he was sent out by the Athenians on an expedition, he did not scruple to carry on war for king Cotys of Thrace, leaving the Athenian expedition to take care of itself. It was the greatest misfortune for the Athenians to appoint him and Chares as generals. And yet, as if bound by a spell, Athens could not get rid of those thoroughly bad men. There ought to have been a central board for the election of generals at Athens; a single man like Demosthenes could not exercise sufficient influence in such matters. " But what are we to say to the fact that Phocion entered the service of Persia? Was it perhaps to show his dilettantism, that he marched against a people which defended its liberty? If so, it is so much the worse. Or was it a desire to plunder and enrich himself, that drove him to it? If so, how can he be praised for having despised money? The exemplary and virtuous character of his life turns in reality upon this fact alone, that he was inaccessible to bribes."

But the one fact of his calling upon Demosthenes to go into death, is enough to characterise the man; this alone must deprive him of the nimbus of virtue. He was personally hostile to Demosthenes: an aversion which is intelligible to those who have observed the conduct of men at the time of the confederacy of the Rhine. I have known people, whom I am very far from believing to have been dishonest, but who were incapable of any enthusiasm, sacrifice, and confidence, and who imagined, that misery did not really consist in being enslaved by a foreign ruler, but in the evils which follow in the train of war, and in personal sufferings; and that nothing was more foolish than sacrifices .of any kind, for that there was extremely little prospect of success, and that many thousands were indifferent as to who ruled over them. When they were told, that with such principles all nationality was sacrificed, as well as that existence by which human life is raised above the mere animal comfort; or when they were asked, what great misfortune it could be, under such circumstances, to die? or what is death, what is any misfortune, compared with servitude?—How often have I wished to die together with all those that were dear to me! and I would have thanked God for it, and for the fact that I had as yet no children;—they would answer, " You are an enthusiast," adding, with indignation, " You are answerable for all our misfortunes." Those who dissented from them were even in danger of being denounced by them as fanatics, and as the authors of all mischief. Phocion belongs to that class of people, to whom in modern times no honest man will erect a monument; he will pardon them, for they are not indeed wicked, but stand extremely low in a moral point of view, and are quite indifferent and utterly incapable of any enthusiasm. Such men are full of hate and venom : I have seen them triumph over things, which, in calmer moods, they would have deplored, but their wisdom had foreseen them, and they insultingly wounded their opponents. Traitors they were not. In this manner, Phocion was as bad a citizen as Demosthenes was an excellent one. I may yet have the honour of being decried as a calumniator for these sentiments. From my early youth I have felt a healthy aversion to Phocion; and this aversion in the course of years has only increased. I have been in circumstances, where I could gain experience in such things, and a man can speak of history when he feels it as completely as if he had been living at the time. I should have joined Demosthenes unconditionally; he was not an enthusiast, but a man free from all folly. What was he to do? Was he to try to form an alliance with Philip for the purpose of promoting the good of Athens, or was he quietly to look on? This question he himself puts in his speech on the crown.

Phocion, then, as I have said, scornfully demanded, that the man who was then, beyond all comparison, the first at Athens, should be surrendered to the Macedonian tyrant, in order that the city might be restored to favour with him. But the people of Athens showed themselves in their true character; they rejected the disgraceful proposal, and resolved not only not to sacrifice any citizen, but not to conclude peace even if the surrender of the Theban exiles should be demanded; they were determined rather to endure any calamity. It was the πολιτεία of Demosthenes that strengthened the Athenians in their noble resolution to protect the Thebans. After such a resolution, we surely should speak of Athens with respect, and acknowledge the influence which a great man could exercise upon the people. The difficulty, however, now was to find some one to go to the tiger's den to negotiate; and I see no reason for doubting the statement, that Demosthenes offered to Demades 4000 crowns (four talents) to induce him to go to Alexander and to negotiate with him. Demades accepted the offer, and he could venture to go without fear; for neither Alexander nor any one else believed him to be an enthusiast. He was in reality a good fellow, without malice, and he made no one unhappy; if he could but get money, he was ready to do the best. There are cases in which a man of honour is not fit to enter into negotiations, and when no one can ask him to do it; and in such cases a man like Demades is the very person that is needed. He did his business well, and settled the whole affair in an admirable manner; Alexander was actually induced to give up his demand. " The firmness of the Athenians compelled him to yield, for he had no choice but either to conclude peace now, or to besiege Athens; and and if he had done the latter, the Persians might have endangered his position by transferring the war to Greece. But panegyrists have not been slow in praising his giving way, as an act of generosity proceeding from his great regard for Athens."

He only stipulated that some of the Athenian generals should be exiled, namely, those who had already gone away for the purpose of fighting against him: a decree of exile was sent after them with the good intention of recalling it, as soon as circumstances should permit it. " The little importance of this sentence of exile is evident, from the fact that Demosthenes and his friends remained at Athens." The exiled generals, like our officers in the wars of independence, went wherever opposition was offered to the tyrant. In like manner, our excellent general, Grolmann, in 1809, when we were unfortunate, first went to the Austrians, and then to the Spaniards, among whom he wanted to serve even as a common soldier, if he could not be employed otherwise: he felt the irresistible necessity of fighting and struggling against the common enemy. Thus Ephialtes went to the Persians, and was afterwards slain at Halicarnassus, and several other men acted under the influence of the same feeling. Dinarchus was at first one of them, but afterwards changing his politics, he became an apostate. It is asked, why Demosthenes, if he was such a patriot, did not likewise go to

Persia? The answer is simply this, because Demosthenes, at his advanced age, could not have done much; and who informs us that he had any ability as a military officer? If he had had such abilities, he would no doubt have been appointed strategus; and he with justice did not feel called upon, at his advanced age, to engage as a common soldier. Accordingly, he remained in Attica, guiding the Athenians in the city in the right way, and boldly counselling them to do, as far as was possible, nothing that was unworthy of them. As long as he was there, he was a silent protest against anything that might injure the honour of Athens, and a promoter of her independence and dignity.

The Athenians were obliged to send cavalry and twenty galleys as a contingent, and at the same time as security, to Alexander. He shewed himself on that occasion really gracious, for he reconciled himself with the Athenians, and told them that they must undertake the supremacy in Greece, if he should be unsuccessful in Asia.

Thus Athens, though no longer able to act a brilliant part, yet preserved her dignity. "And above all things, the Athenians maintained their character; for, in bestowing honours upon Alexander, they only followed an ancient custom. But it is a proof of their moral greatness, that at this time, and under the terrors of the Macedonian power, they reinforced the ancient law, that whoever possessed a free-born Greek as a slave should be put to death, and that they actually did put some persons to death for purchasing Greeks who had been made slaves by the Macedonians; that while Alexander had reached the highest point of his greatness, they awarded the golden crown to Demosthenes on the proposal of Ctesiphon, and acquitted him of all the accusations of the sycophants; and lastly, that they never accused him for having disappointed them in their expectations, and the relatives of those who had fallen in the battle of Chaeronea assured him, that even after the death of their friends they did not repent of having followed his advice."

Meanwhile every effort was made to prepare themselves. The Athenian navy was increased to an extent far exceeding that which it had ever attained since the Peloponnesian war. Lycurgus greatly distinguished himself in the administration of the finances: he is the only man in antiquity that has gained a reputation as a financier. He cannot otherwise be compared with Demosthenes, but it is almost incredible to what amount he increased the revenues, embellished Athens, and augmented the fleet. He was intrusted for three successive *pentaëterides* with the administration of the finances; and several departments of the government acquired, under him, a more consolidated constitution than even at Rome. Lycurgus himself had proposed and carried a law, that no one should be invested with that office for a longer period than five years; but the people, one time after another, conferred it upon him in such a manner, that one of his friends was nominally intrusted with the office, while he himself performed all the duties of it. He really did wonders in his administration, for he built 400 galleys, erected arsenals in Piraeeus, and stocked them with arms. He also did everything in his power to maintain a taste and respect for poetry, which had already sunk : he appointed choruses and new theatrical contests, and a fund from which the victors received their rewards; he caused authentic copies to made of the tragedies of Aeschylus, Sophocles, and Euripides, to be deposited in the archives, and to be recited in public; for none but new pieces could be performed on the stage. Fourteen thousand talents passed through his hands, and he rendered a faithful account of them. Although proud of his ancestors—he belonged to the ancient and noble family of the Butadae[4]—he was greatly attached to the people, and their ancient institutions and laws. When he was already near his death, he caused himself to be carried to the popular assembly, and in a dying state he rendered his accounts to the people, calling upon any one to come forward who had a charge to prefer against him : a wretch who had sold himself to the Macedonians, actually did come forward to calumniate him in his hour of death. But, notwithstanding all this, he was widely different from Demosthenes.

[4] In the notes, Niebuhr here, in opposition to his earlier as well as later views, remarks, that the ancient Athenian nobility, the εὐγένεια, was not enrolled in the demi, but consisted in separate bodies, the γένη, by themselves. We might understand this to mean, that they were not enrolled in the *local demi*, and that remaining in their γένη they formed separate demi, which would agree with Niebuhr's general opinion. But he further observes, that Lycurgus, as a noble was excluded from all privileges, which renders the above interpretation impossible.—ED.

When Alexander had thus settled his affairs with Athens, all the other Greek states which had risen against him, came to him as penitents, and prostrated themselves before his throne. The Arcadians, who had advanced as far as the Isthmus, condemned those who had urged them on to the expedition, to death; the Eleans recalled their exiles, and the Aetolians implored his pardon. The last-mentioned sent ambassadors κατὰ ἔθνη, a proof that they did not yet form one state, but that the separate tribes there co-operated together like those of Arcadia. It was probably at this time that the revolution in Pellene broke out, which clearly shows the fate of the Greeks under the dominion of Macedonia.

Hereupon Alexander, in the spring, about the close of the second year of Olymp. 111, crossed the Hellespont, and began the Persian war, which I will not treat minutely, as I can refer you at once to the account in Arrian.

LECTURE LXXVI.

ALEXANDER undertook the Asiatic expedition as a true adventurer. I never desire to be paradoxical, which, on the contrary, I avoid and detest. I regard the κοιναὶ δόξαι as something very respectable. When, therefore, I speak thus of Alexander, I have no wish whatever of uttering a paradox. To be an adventurer, is in my mind, to undertake a thing in such a way that all depends upon its success. Circumstances may be such that a man *must* commence war and stake everything, there being no choice between victory or destruction. This was Hannibal's situation when he undertook his expedition into Italy; he could do nothing else, for Carthage could not restore her fleet, and war was unavoidable. But such was not the case with Alexander, who commenced the war only because the dominion over wealthy Asia had an irresistible charm for him. He, moreover, undertook the war without a reserve; for the troops which under the command of Antipater remained in Macedonia and Greece, were necessary to maintain his dominion there. The population of Macedonia cannot have

been large, and had already been much affected by the wars of
Philip.   He commenced the war with a fleet of one hundred
and seventy ships, which was altogether insufficient for a naval
engagement with the fleet from Phoenicia and Cyprus. He also
had no money; it is not improbable, as is said, that when he
set out, he had not more with him than seventy talents, so that
in case of a protracted war he could not have existed more
than six months.   But notwithstanding all this, Alexander, in
the spirit of a gambler, sacrificed everything in Macedonia,
exempting the Macedonians from taxes, and giving away his
domains.   When told by thinking friends that nothing remained for himself, he replied, " but hope."   This shews the
adventurer.   If Memnon had had the command against him,
Alexander's plan would of necessity have failed, and he would
have returned to Macedonia disgraced and weakened; he
would then have been obliged to take back his presents.

Had Darius come to the throne in consequence of great
personal qualities, had he descended from his palace to the
provinces to see the state of things with his own eyes, had he
entrusted to Memnon, in whom he had confidence, the unlimited
command, and had Memnon been able to maintain himself
against the personal jealousies of the satraps, Alexander would
have been lost to a certainty.   Memnon's plan was that which
in modern times has been tried very successfully even under
more unfavourable circumstances; it was, not to engage in any
open battle, but to protract the war; to apply all his energy
to the fleet, and to make the greatest exertions for it; to take
the islands from Alexander and to bring about a general
insurrection in Greece; to employ all the treasures of Susa and
Ecbatana for the purpose of enlisting thousands in Greece and
forming an army there to attack Macedonia, but to act merely
on the defensive against Alexander; strongly to garrison all
fortified places, to obstruct his progress in every possible way, to
cut off his reinforcements, and to lay waste all the country before
him.   Memnon's plan was to hold out only a few months
in this manner, to lay waste the coast districts, to withdraw himself into impassable countries, and thus to entice
Alexander into the interior of the country, to oblige him to
consume his stores, and thus to allow his army to wear itself
out.   This wise and excellent plan—by which the Duke of
Wellington, in the Peninsular war, saved Portugal — was

opposed by the mean jealousy of the Persian satraps, and in part also by their own interest, as they probably had rich possessions on the coast. Memnon without any definite orders was in the most painful situation. He solely depended on the personal confidence of the king, who, however, thought it too dangerous a proceeding to put him, as a foreigner, in a position where he could command. Memnon had only one vote, which was overruled by the ignorant and miserable satraps. They trusted in the superiority of their cavalry, which, especially in regard to the horses, far excelled that of the Macedonians.

The army which Alexander led into Asia consisted of 30,000 foot, and 4,500 horse; this account is authentic with the exception of a few points of detail. In proportion to his infantry, his cavalry was much more numerous than it had ever been in any Greek army. The phalanx or militia, formed about one half of these forces. The real military resources of Macedonia were so small, that Alexander had 5,000 mercenaries in his employ. The Macedonian phalanx was calculated to employ the untrained militia in masses, and thus, through masses, to make use of them; in later times the phalanx was generally disbanded during the winter, and met again in spring; but the mercenaries were in arms throughout the year; they were constantly drilled, and formed the real core of the army.

Alexander crossed the Hellespont (Olymp. 111, 2) and advanced as far as the Granicus without meeting with any resistance. The Persian army, no doubt, was not very superior to his even in numbers; the statements mentioning enormous numbers are apocryphal, and the genuine account in Arrian does not mention any such large numbers. It was only in their cavalry that the Persians were greatly superior. They met the Macedonians on the little river Granicus (Olymp. 111, 3). Even the very excellent Arrian often mentions only the movements, leaving us to guess their objects. It seems that the Persians were assembled in the plain of Dascyleum, the seat of the governor of Lower Phrygia, where they had their head quarters; thence they proceeded to meet Alexander, believing that he would march along the coast towards Cyzicus. The Persian cavalry, on account of its excellence and numerical superiority, ought to have gained the victory in that battle, but it was defeated by the superiority of Europeans over

Asiatics; as has always been the case, except at the time of the Khalifs and the Turkish conquest, when the Europeans had become half Asiatics. Alexander, in that battle, as everywhere else, deserves the praise of great youthful valour, of a great and talented commander, and of the quick and correct judgment which is altogether peculiar to him in all material arrangements he had to make. For moral or intellectual arrangements he had no skill, nay, he had not the least idea of their necessity; but in all material affairs his perception was as quick as that of Napoleon. These circumstances, and the desperate situation of the Macedonian army, which was compelled either to conquer or to retreat—and in the latter case would have ended as disgracefully as Mack did near Ulm,—rendered the victory possible. The Macedonians thus gained the day, and the Persian army was so completely dispersed, that until the battle of Issus we do not hear of any assembled forces. Nor was it even attempted to form a new army.

It is inconceivable how Darius could remain so quietly in his golden palace, without trying to raise an army. Greek mercenaries were indeed enlisted; but three months before this time all the passages from Asia Minor to the interior ought to have been occupied by innumerable forces. Instead of this, the army was gradually assembled in the neighbourhood of Damascus, and did not meet Alexander till he reached Issus. The battle near that place might still have saved Persia, and if fortune had been favourable, Memnon might have carried out his plans in another quarter; for his counsels were now appreciated, and the king, who had made up his mind to give him the command of an army where he should not have to contend against jealousy, appointed him commander-in-chief of the fleet, and provided him with money to enlist an army of Greeks. He first went to Halicarnassus, and there collected Greek mercenaries and a fleet. This fleet became so powerful, that Alexander broke up his own fleet in order not to expose his men to certain defeat.

Meantime he advanced along the coast with the same determination as the French commanders did in Spain. He everywhere found the symptoms of an effete and decayed empire. The Persian commanders in their fortresses did not think of defending themselves, and the invincible acropolis of Sardes, with all its treasures, was surrendered to him at once and without any resistance.   In the Greek cities on the coast, Alexander appeared as a deliverer, and he everywhere proclaimed the democratic form of government.   There were only a few places, as Miletus and Halicarnassus, which being in the hands of strong Persian garrisons of Greek mercenaries, offered a determined resistance.   Miletus was soon taken, but Halicarnassus defended itself for a long time.   That city was no longer entirely Greek; it had for a considerable time been the seat of the Carian dynasty, which was less barbarous than that of Macedonia.   Those princes did very much for the embellishment of the city; and Halicarnassus was then one of the most splendid towns.   Ever since the time of the Persian wars, the peculiar and inexplicable power of the Greek language and of Greek manners had exercised, even under the dominion of the Persians, such an influence, that those districts became hellenised without there being any Greek immigration or any political ascendancy of Greeks.   The Carians had at first been βαρβαρόφωνοι, and now the Carian princes were the patrons of Greek art and literature.   Everything was Greek; the Carians did not consider their own language worth writing, any more than the Macedonians or the Goths under Theodoric in Italy wrote theirs; the Goths wrote their own language only in cases of extreme necessity.   The siege of Halicarnassus is one of the most remarkable in history.   The merit of its defence belongs to Ephialtes, the Athenian exile: the barbarians had very little share in it; but Ephialtes, with his Greeks and Carians, defended the city against Alexander with real enthusiasm, and was supported by Memnon, who had his head quarters at Cos, from the sea.   But Alexander's situation was now greatly improved: he was in possession of Mysia, Lydia, and Ionia, the rich coast districts, in which he levied large contributions.   He was thus enabled to furnish his army with ample supplies, and had the means of ever increasing it with fresh mercenaries.   He no doubt also obtained reinforcements of Carians and other warlike people.   His victories are like those of Frederick II. during the latter period of the seven years' war: the mercenaries became more and more numerous in proportion to his Macedonians.   The possession of Halicarnassus was a point of decisive moment; if the siege had not succeeded, the whole expedition would have been a failure; public opinion would have turned against him, and an army of

Persian cavalry might have come from Phrygia in his rear, ravaged Lydia, and ruined him. He was, therefore, obliged to take Halicarnassus at any cost, and Providence gave him the victory. Ephialtes fell in a sally, in which he had destroyed the besieging engines of the Macedonians; and with him the soul of the defence was gone. The city was taken first, and the acropolis then capitulated. It was only through the death of Ephialtes, that Halicarnassus fell into the hands of Alexander.

Memnon had not been able to prevent Alexander's success; but he was undaunted, and now formed a grand plan: he allowed Alexander to proceed, trying in the mean time to deprive him of his possessions in the Aegean, and to transfer the war into Greece. Chios received him as its deliverer, and he then went to Lesbos, which had recognised the supremacy of Alexander even before his passage into Asia; and that island, with the exception of Mitylene, likewise joined Memnon. Mitylene was in league with Alexander,[1] and had to be conquered; Memnon took it after an obstinate siege. King Agis of Sparta, who had likewise been gained over, had already assembled an army for him; Persian troops had already landed in Euboea, and Memnon himself intended to follow them, wishing, no doubt, to draw Antipater from one place to another. There can be no doubt that he would have roused the Athenians also, and he would then have obliged the Macedonians to recall Alexander, who would have been unable to reach his own country. But all at once Memnon was taken ill and died. There was so little of a guiding spirit, and everything was in such a state of dissolution, that there was no one to take the command in his place. Pharnabazus indeed obtained the command of the fleet, and took Tenedos, but after this he cruised inactively among the islands off the coast of Asia Minor. He also continued the negotiations with king Agis, and had a meeting with him in the island of Siphnos, and gave him money and ten galleys, but he himself then returned to Asia and did nothing with his large fleet.

[1] " To this league I refer an inscription in Dodwell's work (Boeckh, *Corp. Inscript.* 2166) which is of palaeographical interest, and is written in the pure Aeolic dialect. The stone, however, has been intentionally broken. The treaty refers to the return of the Macedonians sent home from Persia, for whom special authorities are appointed to prevent their estates being confiscated."— 1825.

In addition to this, when, after the battle of Issus (Olymp. 111, 4), the Phoenician towns and Cyprus surrendered, the Phoenician fleet refused to serve any longer and returned. The whole army, with all its treasures, and the fleet then dispersed. Lesbos, Chios, and in short all the islands off Asia Minor, surrendered to Alexander. Thus ended this undertaking. King Agis, however, had been stirred up, and I shall afterwards have occasion to speak of his undertakings.

During these commotions, which must have caused him great uneasiness, Alexander continued to advance (Olymp. 111. 3), and energetically pursued the only path which lay open to him, that is, he marched forwards. He could do nothing but advance into the interior, meet the Persian army, defeat it, and destroy the Persian fleet by taking the towns and districts of the coast which furnished it. He accordingly penetrated into Lycia. Lycia and Pamphylia were highly civilised countries, as we see even from the coins with inscriptions in an unknown language, which display the highest perfection of art. Their civilisation was perfectly Greek, and although they were not Greeks, they were in possession of the arts of Greece, as is evident also from other monuments. Their architecture was of the most perfect style of Greek art. It is unfortunately difficult for travellers to visit those countries. Their inhabitants had republican constitutions, and were treated by the Persians like the Greek cities in Ionia; they had the same feeling of hatred and contempt of despotism as the Greeks; for in an intellectual point of view they were akin to the Greeks and foreign to the Asiatics. In addition to this, there was a collision of a different kind, which I have not found mentioned anywhere, namely, the opposite character of their religions. For the idolatry of the Greeks and kindred nations was a horror to the Persians, and their sacrifices, by which, in the opinion of the Persians, the fire was polluted, were unbearable to them; their whole mythology was despised, because the Persians had a much purer theology; and these circumstances were an everlasting source of conflicts. This alone accounts for the fact that the Persians were hated by the Lycians and Pamphylians, while the Greeks were liked and fraternally regarded by them. It cannot, moreover be doubted that among those nations, as among the Italians, the influence of Greek literature was very great, and that they were inti-

mately acquainted with Greek mythology, language and literature, and the Macedonians were regarded as Greeks; whence
we cannot wonder, that Alexander was everywhere received
with joy. It was only in a very few places that he met with
a most determined resistance ; this was the case especially
where the intelligent conviction, that they would get a strong
and powerful ruler, who was more formidable than the powerless and distant king of Susa, stirred the people up to defend
themselves, as at Termessus. But Alexander was victorious
everywhere. He overawed and dazzled his opponents by
undertakings and dangers, which perhaps were altogether
unnecessary; as for example by that celebrated march, when
instead of conquering a mountain pass, he went around it, and
made a regular march over a beach which was covered by the
sea, leading his men as it were through the sea. Such exploits
dazzled his enemies far and wide, and he speedily inspired
them with enthusiasm for himself, so that there sprang up a
feeling of ambition to acknowledge the young hero in his
glory. By this means they excused themselves in their own
eyes for their servility, and appropriated to themselves a portion
of his honour. This feeling also prevailed at Athens. The
fact that the poet Menander mentions Alexander's march
through the sea,[2] is in my opinion not a *captatio benevolentiae*,
to receive a handful of gold, for Menander was an honest man,
but he was really an enthusiastic admirer of the young hero.
Alexander also flattered the Greeks, and after every victory he
sent reports and trophies to Athens; for it was by the Athenians that he wanted to be praised. At a somewhat later
time a person said, " The Athenians alone have the privilege
of raising a man to heaven." A decree of praise passed by the
Athenians at that time was the highest honour to which an
ambitious prince could aspire; it was the same as at present a
title or an order of knighthood is to a vain private person.
Such was the intellectual height on which the Athenians then
stood. " The conquest of the west of Asia Minor, as far as the
river Halys, was the result of one summer's campaign; and
Alexander sent his army into winter quarters at an early
season of the year."

He then advanced towards Cilicia, where mount Taurus
forms the natural boundary between Asia and Europe. The

[2] Plut. *Alex.* 17.

Hellespont is not the natural boundary, any more than a river can separate two nations. Mount Taurus is the natural boundary, so that the coasts of Cilicia, properly speaking, belong to Asia. The nations in the west of Asia Minor were either themselves of European origin, or were akin to them; nearly all those nations had, like the Greeks, thoroughly republican institutions. The Phrygians on the heights formed an exception, for they had no free cities, and their character was altogether Asiatic, but the same was the case with some nations belonging to Europe proper; and yet the Phrygians were nearly akin to the great European race of the Thracians. But it is nature that forms the boundary, for if a defence is possible anywhere, it is on the frontier of Asia, which is doubly closed, first by the Cilician passes which lead down to Tarsus, and secondly by the Syrian passes situated between mount Amanus and the sea. Mountains everywhere form the natural boundaries, and such is the case with mount Taurus, for on the further side of it the Semitic tribes begin. Eastern despotism was then quite familiar to all those nations except the Phoenician towns, which were analogous to those of Europe; they had quite a different religion, founded upon a basis altogether different, and not in the least akin to that of the Greeks. Their art also was of quite a different style: it never rose to the ideal, and was at the utmost skilful in combination, but was always deficient in a general idea from which further development might have proceeded. They also spoke a language which had no connection with those of Europe. The Persian language in its origin is perhaps akin to those spoken in Europe, but those other languages are radically different from them: they are not only wholly distinct, but are altogether opposed to them, and proceed from quite different foundations. " The Cilicians were indeed attached to the Persians, but did not defend their country."

There Alexander might have been stopped, and ought to have been stopped, if the Persian commanders had done their duty. Darius himself had by this time taken the field, and there now ensued the battle of Issus.

LECTURE LXXVII.

BATTLES against barbarians are very different from those against civilised nations, such, for example, as the battles of Hannibal, which are interesting in themselves, even without regard to their results. The battles against the Persians and other eastern nations have all the same character, and are in a measure contemptible. I do not mean to say that those who gained them are to be undervalued; but the confusion and the absence of plan and energy on the part of the conquered, deprive those battles of their charms. The battle of Issus was lost, because it could not but be lost; everything that ought to have been done, having been left undone, and all preparations and precautions having been neglected.

The passes leading from Cappadocia and Phrygia down to Cilicia are among the strongest in the world. In modern times armies usually endeavour to evade such passes and not to storm them; but the general custom in the wars of the ancients was to take the bull by the horns, and to storm the passes. Hence they might have been admirably defended. I know from travellers that those passes are among the most difficult that separate one country from another. But they were altogether unguarded, so that Alexander crossed mount Taurus without any difficulty. In like manner Tarsus, where the passage of the broad and rapid river Cydnus might have been defended, was neither garrisoned nor fortified. " The Persians now ought at least to have kept possession of the Syrian passes; to accept a battle was quite irrational;" but the whole Persian army, consisting, it is said, of 300,000 men, did nothing, and had not even formed a fortified encampment.

" On this occasion (Olymp. 111, 4) again, Alexander showed himself as a great general, by forcing the Persians to accept a battle in a position in which they had to contend with the greatest difficulties." Not one of the things that might have been expected of the Persians, was done in the battle; nowhere did their cavalry do its duty, although their horses were the best in the world, and although the whole education of the Persian nobles consisted in their being trained in horsemanship.

The only soldiers that did their duty, were the Greek mercenaries, most of whom were commanded by the excellent Athenian, Leosthenes(?). Those brave men, abandoned by the Persians, did their utmost: I call them brave in reference to the battle, for otherwise they were a rabble like the mercenaries during the seventeenth century. Many were slain in the battle; the others having received an honorable capitulation, returned to Phoenicia. Some forced their way to Syria. In their rear, the Persians had the narrow Syrian passes, and in their front a defile which they had not guarded, and a broad rapid river; quite close behind them was another defile, in which during their flight their baggage was so crammed together that neither vehicles nor men could get through: their measures were of the most senseless kind. No wonder, therefore, that the whole Persian army were dispersed like chaff, as soon as the Greek mercenaries were lost; and when the army was thus routed, the whole Persian camp, full of immense treasures, fell into the hands of the conqueror. "This rich booty of the war caused the Macedonians greater joy than anything else."

The manner in which Alexander made use of this victory, does great honor to his judgment, his strategics, and his keen perception. He is one of those that are born generals, and understood how to make use of a victory in its whole extent. Some can only gain battles with great skill and often with small means, but are blind as to the object of the victory, regarding it only as a game of chess, and are thus in the end necessarily worsted, if they are opposed by able generals. Others look upon a victory only as a means, and it was with this view that Alexander advanced, and did what may easily be recognised as the only right thing, but which yet is done only by a general of great talent. Alexander proceeded along the Phoenician coast. Cyrus, the younger, also would have acted more wisely, if he had marched along the Syrian coast instead of penetrating into the interior. The Phoenician towns threw off the Persian dominion, and opened their gates to Alexander, for they remembered the fearful fate, especially that of Sidon, which fourteen years before this time they had experienced at the hands of Ochus. Tyre alone kept its gates closed against Alexander, and wanted to remain neutral. What can have been the cause of this? "It was certainly not blind passion." I can mention it only as a conjecture that Tyre, perhaps, enjoyed the privilege of not having a Persian garrison within its walls. It is possible also that it may have arisen from jealousy of Sidon: these two cities had long been jealous of each other, and even in the last war Tyre had been gently dealt with by the Persians, especially as compared with Sidon, and it had separated itself from Phoenicia. "Tyre, after the destruction of Sidon, had perhaps been raised to the rank of metropolis among the other Phoenician towns." But it seems probable that it enjoyed that great privilege of being exempted from the necessity of keeping a Persian garrison; and what this privilege means, is evident from the example of Hamburgh, and afterwards Frankfort on the Main, in the thirty years' war: it is the greatest favor that can be conferred on a city in such circumstances. I believe that the Tyrians were ready to submit to Alexander, to recognise and support him in his war, if he would promise not to enter their city; but this provoked his anger. His conduct may be called senseless, for being determined to force the city, he spent seven long months in besieging it. "Tyre was situated in an island, and was strongly fortified; it was four stadia from the main land, and had been built by the inhabitants of ancient Tyre, in the time of Nebucadnezar. The latter place was not entirely abandoned, but had become an insignificant place, and New Tyre was probably the seat of the government." This siege is highly interesting, but my time does not allow me to give you a minute account of it. You must read it in Arrian, who gives an excellent description of it; he is a very pleasant writer, and is uncommonly easy to read. He is an intelligent and thinking author, who speaks of all military matters as a man well acquainted with them, whence his accounts are very clear and of great value. Alexander's efforts were immense, until at length he succeeded in making a quay through the sea to the island, "notwithstanding the strong current of the water, whereupon he set his besieging engines to play against the walls of the city. The Tyrians defended themselves with the courage of despair: the besieged and the besiegers fought with equal bravery, until at length the city was taken by storm" (Olymp. 112, 1). A siege which, after a long defence, is in the end successful, is always very painful to contemplate; it is very melancholy to see a small heroic band overpowered

VOL. II.   C C

and destroyed by overwhelming numbers: and such was the case at Tyre.   The city experienced the most fearful fate, and the population would have been extirpated, if the Tyrians had not previously sent their wives and children to Carthage, " so that afterwards Tyre could again be peopled with Tyrians."

Alexander now proceeded to Egypt.   There, too, he met with a determined resistance at Gaza on the frontier, where the brave governor defended himself with two thousand men for the space of two months: he was the only Persian that made a gallant defence.   Otherwise the resistance in Egypt itself (Olymp. 112, 2) was quite insignificant; most of the Persian troops had been drawn to Issus, and the forces in Egypt were powerless, while the Egyptians, having experienced under Ochus all the horrors of Asiatic cruelty and avarice, regarded the Macedonians as their deliverers.   " The Egyptians, moreover, had of old been allied with the Greeks against the Persians as their common enemies."   The religious antipathy between the Egyptians, as idolaters, and the Persians had reached the highest pitch: it had become a true religious hatred.   The Persians justly despised the Egyptians, on account of their worship of animals; and the Egyptians, in their turn, detested the Persians for despising the objects of their veneration: a Persian did not scruple, for example, to strike a cat or an ox, although in the eyes of the Egyptians such an act was most atrocious.   The Macedonians, in this respect, were not more delicate than the Persians, but Alexander behaved with great prudence; he had, no doubt, given strict orders not to offend the Egyptians, and he himself affected to entertain great veneration for Anubis.   His celebrated expedition to the oracle of Jupiter Ammon also seems to have been undertaken for the purpose of showing to the Egyptians how much he honoured their chief divinity.   Escorted by a select retinue, he proceeded to Siwah—an undertaking for which he might easily have had to pay dearly.   Independently of political motives, however, he was probably drawn to that place by curiosity; it was an object of interest to him, for there was the famous spring of Siwah and the oracle of Ammon, the only barbarian oracle that was consulted by Greeks, and many other things which possessed attractions for him. He attained his object perfectly, for the Egyptians regarded him as the friend of their nation.   " Nor did Alexander impose

any heavy burdens upon them, for he demanded neither troops
nor anything else beyond tribute, so that all Egypt as far as
Nubia was quite devoted to him."

There he founded Alexandria, the greatest of his creations,
on a site the immense advantages of which had hitherto not
been perceived by any one.   When the oracle told those who
went to Byzantium to settle opposite the blind, the term *blind*
was meant to describe the Egyptians.   He at once destined
Alexandria to become the greatest city; and its rapidly increasing prosperity, so that it actually did become the greatest
city, is truly oriental.   In the East, every new dynasty either
founds a new capital, or raises some existing town to that rank,
by making it the seat of the government.   This new capital
being the centre of a new power, must throw the old capital
into the shade.   Such has been the case, for example, in
Bengal, where the capital was shifted several times, until at
last Calcutta was raised to that rank: the same occurred in
the empire of the Great Mogul.   Such, also, is now the case
in Persia, of which the successive capitals have been Kasbin,
Ispahan, Shiraz, and Teheran; and in Egypt itself, Thebes,
Memphis, Sais, Bubastis and Heliopolis had been capitals at
different times, and now Alexandria succeeded.   There can
be no question that Alexander then entertained the idea of
making Alexandria the seat of his empire, and that he wished
to unite all the countries round the Mediterranean into one
vast kingdom.

" Alexander then returned to Syria, and thence proceeded
to the Euphrates." He was now in possession of immense
treasures: Parmenio had traced the Persian treasures to Damascus and there taken them, so that Alexander had become
enormously rich.

In the meantime, Darius had assembled an immense army
from the provinces to the east of the Tigris, on the river Zab,
on the frontiers of Kurdistan.   But his confidence was shaken,
and his hopes were greatly diminished; he endeavoured to
make peace with Alexander, offering him one half of his
empire, as far as the Euphrates, and to give him his daughter,
who was a prisoner in the hands of Alexander, in marriage,
" as a security that the Persians would not claim back the
empire ceded to him."   Parmenio was wise and intelligent,
and advised Alexander to accept the offer.   A later and

degenerate age admired Alexander for his answer, " If I were Parmenio, I would do so;" but his real greatness would have consisted in accepting it, for the greatest of all things is moderation: " whatever is to be lasting must not be immoderate. Such an empire as that offered to Alexander would have had a form, and might have been governed; and although it consisted of heterogeneous elements, it would afterwards have become hellenised." But Alexander, who did not see why he should stand still and not take all the king's treasures—why he should not advance eastward as far as possible towards the gold regions, the accounts of which were even exaggerated— Alexander, for whom something unlimited possessed the greatest charms, and who would not have known what to do with himself without a war, rejected everything, advanced through Mesopotamia, crossed both rivers (Olymp. 112, 2), and met Darius at Arbela, in the fourth year of the expedition. There the battle was fought which decided the fate of Asia, but concerning which I will not enter into detail any more than I have done in the case of that of Issus, for it does not deserve it. Darius is said to have fought bravely, and he may have done so; but his bravery was no more than that of a man who when all else was lost, endeavoured to save his honour. The victory was easy; it was a victory over Asiatic cowardice and barbarian disorder, like that of Lord Clive at Plassey, who with a few thousand men defeated an army of a hundred thousand Indians. So also Alexander conquered a very numerous army, said to have consisted of three hundred thousand, five hundred thousand, or even one million of men, with a comparatively small force, " although the plain in which the battle was fought was favourable to the Persians." He defeated them so completely, that afterwards we do not find a trace of the immense army. No portion of it rallied anywhere: even when the Romans were completely beaten at Cannae, Varro, whom I do not regard as an eminent man, was enabled after some days to assemble a few thousand men, so that Hannibal thought it advisable to leave him behind the walls of Canusium. But such was never the case with the Persians.

Alexander now could direct his arms wherever he pleased. His road led him first to the mighty Babylon, the walls of which must have been demolished before that time, but which, even after the Persians had plundered it, still contained sufficient treasures to excite great astonishment among the Macedonians. There, too, Alexander was highly welcome. The fertile country of Babylonia seems to have been drained by the Persians with particular avarice. But notwithstanding all this, it was, even under their tyranny, cultivated like a garden, or like the Netherlands ; at present it is a wilderness. Thence Alexander directed his march to Susa in Chusistan, a half-Persian country : I consider it to have originally been Semitic, but it was taken by the Persians, very many of whom settled in it, so that there existed a strong mixture of Elamites (Persians in the Old Testament) and Semites. Susa contained the very strong citadel of the Persian empire, which was surrendered to him with all its treasures and without any resistance. All the Persians already regarded themselves so much as his servants, that they surrendered to him everything as his property, "and the treasurer handed over to him his treasury as if he had been his lawful master, although Darius was still alive; whereas in other countries at such times every one takes what he can save." From Susa he marched to Persepolis, the real capital of the Persians in the strict sense of the term. The Persian nation, the Iranians, also comprises the inhabitants of Sistan, Chorassan, Balkh, and the tribes all around as far as Mawaralnahar, Bokhara, and the country of the Afghans, where a Persian tribe, under the name of Tadjik, living in towns, are engaged as artizans, and some also as agriculturists. Thus far extended the ancient Persian race. The Medes were akin to them without being the same nation; but the real Persian nation, in its narrower sense, consisted of the tribes of Fars and Kerman: the Arians and Drangianians in Sistan and Chorassan, although kindred nations, were yet treated by them as subjects. The magnificent remains of Persepolis are no doubt monuments of the ancient national capital, built in the time of the greatest splendour of the Persian nation, by the kings, as ornaments of their real national seat; though they visited it only from time to time. Susa was their residence in winter, and Ecbatana in summer. " But Persepolis was the centre of the ancient Persian nobility, and filled with immense treasures." There Alexander at first assumed the appearance of a generous conqueror, anxious to spare the vanquished; but in direct contradiction to this he caused the city to be reduced to ashes. This shows that he was only a barbarian in disguise: whatever motive he may have had, it was a most unworthy action, and it is evident that he sought only an excuse, when he asserted, that he meant to retaliate upon the Persians for having burnt the temples in Greece. The buildings of Persepolis, with all their elaborateness and richly-ornamented pillars, yet have something tasteless, and are deficient in ideas; even their rich bas-reliefs are remarkable for their total want of beauty and creative ideas. It is singular that they show no traces of fire, for they are of marble, which is very easily injured by fire. Even if only the beams were of wood, I do not understand how they can have been burnt, without injury being done to the columns. The ground-floor also is not injured, and we must, therefore, conclude that the fire did not rage there. Hence it is very possible that the buildings which were then reduced to ashes, were different ones; that the city of the Persians itself which was situated close by, did suffer, but not the palaces or temples; and that the buildings which were burnt, have disappeared altogether, whereas the still existing ruins did not belong to those buildings. The ruins themselves are the most magnificent in all Asia.

Alexander had now no difficulty except that of deciding whither he should proceed; but nature guided him. Just before him in the East there was the immense desert, which, commencing in India between the Ganges and Indus, is traversed by the valley of the Indus; and on the west of the Indus extends through Mekran and Kerman as far as the heights of Media and Masanderan. There was now no occasion to march through this desert, as he afterwards did. He was tempted to proceed to Ecbatana (Olymp. 112, 3). During this expedition we catch a glimpse at the condition of the Persian empire: Alexander was obliged to force his way through the mountains, inhabited by savage nations, who in the midst of the Persian empire had not recognised the supremacy of the Persian kings, and to whom the great king, whenever he wanted to go from Ecbatana to Susa, was obliged, for the)ake of peace, to pay tribute under the name of a present. From Ecbatana Alexander turned eastward, and then descended through the pass of the Elbur down to Masanderan.

Darius fled before him as Jezdegerd did before the Arab

conquerors. Bessus, a monster of baseness of every kind, who in the midst of the ruin of his country formed the disgraceful plan of usurping the throne, now revolted against his master, made him his prisoner, and dragged him away with him. Alexander pursued him for the very good reason of preventing his gaining ground, for Bessus was perhaps an able man. It is quite foolish to believe that Alexander followed him for the purpose of saving Darius. Bessus, or one of his accomplices, then caused Darius to be murdered : this is the common though not undisputed account. Alexander now very prudently assumed the air as if he wanted to avenge the legitimate and unfortunate monarch; he received a brother of Darius with great kindness, and having given him a satrapy pursued Bessus (Olymp. 112, 4 foll). He thus traversed eastern Persia, penetrating through Parthia and across the Oxus into Sogdiana. It is difficult for geographers to identify the marches he made, and it would be inconsistent with our brief survey to examine how he proceeded until he reached the eastern bank of the Jaxartes. "But there, in Jagatai, he was obliged to return, for he could not penetrate into the Scythian steppes, and he also felt that he had already arrived in a very cold country. We wonder when we are told by the ancients, that Alexander advanced as far as the arctic circle; but we must remember that in those high steppes the cold is extremely severe and truly Siberian, and we cannot be surprised at the soldiers, who made no geographical measurements, believing that they had reached the 60th degree, from which they were yet far distant." The difficulties which he overcame on those expeditions, both by his skill and good fortune, are brilliant exploits: he succeeded in every enterprise. With what prudence he conducted the war, I leave you to read in Arrian.

LECTURE LXXVIII.

THE order of Justin's narrative leads us to two digressions in the history of Alexander, the wars of king Agis in Greece and of Alexander of Epirus in Italy, and the unfortunate expedition of Zopyrion in Pontus against the Scythians. After Alexander had overthrown the Persian empire, he received from Antipater the threefold news of the death of Agis, of Alexander of Epirus, and of his general Zopyrion in Scythia. Of the expedition of Zopyrion little is known. If he was really commander in Pontus, it is evident that it is erroneous to say, that Pontus was not touched upon by Alexander's expedition; and moreover, the Scythians attacked by Zopyrion, are, in this case, not the wandering Scythians of the Ister, but those about mount Caucasus. But how is it, that these reports were sent to Alexander by Antipater, and not by Parmenio, the governor of Media, from whom the news would most naturally have come?

I have already briefly noticed, that king Agis, son of Archidamus and grandson of Agesilaus, received Persian subsidies from Memnon, with which he raised an army. The great recruiting place for all mercenaries was at that time in the territory of Sparta, near mount Taenarus; a recruiting establishment had existed there for the last thirty years, and continued to exist for a long time afterwards, and mercenaries from all parts of Greece repaired thither and found quarters. A remarkable phenomenon! There was a temple of Poseidon with an asylum, and from this circumstance that district had in the course of time become neutral ground. During the general distress in Greece at that time, every one sought to gain his bread by engaging as a mercenary; every strong fellow enlisted himself, took the pike instead of struggling with difficulties at home—just as in the thirty years' war—and plundered the property of his equals in all countries; an evil of which nations sometimes never recover. The more places were laid waste, the greater became the number of those ready to serve as mercenaries, and war fed war.

Agis, therefore, collected troops at Taenarus; he had received large sums from Memnon, and was already on the point of striking a blow, when the death of Memnon changed everything.

About, or after Memnon's death, Agis went to Crete to find occupation for his troops. This undertaking is involved in very great obscurity. The Cretans had long been quiet but for some time they had been in a state of decay, Cnossus and Lyctus being at war with each other, and distressed

Cretans seeking the protection of the Persians and of king Agis, who sent to them his brother Agesilaus. The details are unknown, except that Agis established himself in Crete. When Alexander had conquered Phoenicia, he sent an expedition to Crete to drive the Spartans from the island. He appears to have been successful; and this is perhaps the war alluded to by Aristotle in the second book of his Politics; for the affair of Phalaecus was too short and too insignificant.

Meantime, however, Alexander gained the battle of Issus, and owing to this event, together with the death of Memnon and the conquest of Phoenicia, the condition of Greece had become such, that thinking and intelligent men could place no hopes on any undertaking; " so long as Persia was in a condition to help, men could indulge hopes, but it was now too late." It is a proof of Demosthenes' deep insight and freedom from blind passion, that he did not allow himself to be drawn into a commotion at the time when Agis was endeavouring to rouse all Greece; Demosthenes kept the Athenians back, and for this he was blamed by his detractors at the time. These accusations brought forward by Aeschines and Dinarchus have been taken up by simpletons in modern times, who have unblushingly asserted that Demosthenes was not in earnest about the liberty of Greece. The venal Aeschines and the unprincipled Dinarchus reproached him for not having followed the example of Ephialtes, for not having taken up arms when Agis was ready to act, and for not having come forward at the time when a Macedonian corps under Corrhagus was cut to pieces; nay, it is even insinuated that he might possibly have been bribed with Macedonian gold. We cannot wonder that the party-men of the time spoke thus; for they did their business, and told falsehoods fully conscious of what they were doing; but posterity ought to know the truth. The eastern proverb says, " to speak is silver, and to be silent is gold, each in its time," and Demosthenes knew this well; he possessed the heroism of patience. He saw that with Memnon's death all was lost, and that it was necessary to wait for new and more favorable circumstances. Agis, it is true, was a bold heroic adventurer, who died as a hero, but he was not the man from whom a Demosthenes could hope much. He, who saw things when they were yet far distant, and, no doubt, was in possession of intelligence of which others knew nothing, assuredly discovered in the circumstances of Macedonia and in the heart of the Macedonian government and power, the germ of division and dissolution; and upon this alone he based his hope, though it was a sad one. As Agis fought so bravely, " and as Alexander had so much exhausted Macedonia by his levies, Antipater might certainly have been reduced to great straits, if the Athenians had joined Agis; this is true, but if Alexander had sent home a portion of his army, all would nevertheless have been in vain. If the insurrection had broken out at a later time, when Alexander was beyond the Oxus and Indus, and when the disaffection in his army had already become more general, some hopes might have been entertained, and Demosthenes would perhaps have ventured more; but now, when Alexander was in Media, and could send back a portion of his army whenever he pleased, it would have been folly to rise. The circumstances of the time were very like those of Prussia in 1811, when Napoleon had gone to Russia, when good men were hopeful, and thought that some desperate undertaking must be ventured upon, and that the people of Germany must rise; the more thoughtful were of a different opinion, and thanked God that nothing of the kind was done. I myself fell out with friends on this point at the time, but I rejoiced to be one of those who hoped with impatience. Demosthenes was perhaps too cautious, but he could not possibly calculate the consequences of the commotion. That he was not kept back by mean jealousy of Sparta, was evident from his conduct when peace and alliances were concluded, for he always yielded, and from the relation in which he placed Thebes to Athens: he expected that the spirit which reigned at Athens, would of itself gain the ascendancy.[1]

Meantime Agis actually continued to enlist mercenaries (Olymp. 112, 3). After the battle of Issus, the Greek troops for the most part quitted the Persian service. Some of them went to Phoenicia, under Amyntas, and thence sailed to Cyprus and Egypt, where they are said to have been cut to

---

[1] In 1825, Niebuhr judged differently; he then said, " The fault was probably equal on the side of the Spartans and Athenians, neither of whom were willing to waive any of their pretensions. It is possible that Agis thought he might carry his point without the aid of the Athenians, and he had probably formed the idea of restoring and governing Greece from Peloponnesus."

pieces. This account, however, must be taken with great limitation, for most of them must have escaped to Taenarus. Before the battle of Arbela nothing of importance was done.

During this period one Memnon, the governor of Thrace, had revolted, and a prince of the Perrhaebians in Thessaly had likewise risen in arms (Aesch. *c. Ctesiph.*). Under these circumstances Agis began the war against the Macedonians. The Lacedaemonians marched out accompanied by the Eleans, Achaeans, and a part of the Arcadians. Agis had 10,000 mercenaries, mostly Greeks who had escaped from the battle of Issus. Diodorus states that, besides the Peloponnesians, some Greeks from the countries beyond the Isthmus served under Agis; but these cannot have been any others but Aetolians.

It is evident that this war threw Antipater into great difficulties, especially as he had at the same time to combat the insurgents in Thrace. An army of Macedonians, under Corrhagus, which had invaded Peloponnesus, was destroyed. Corrhagus is misunderstood as the name of a place; but it is a Macedonian name, which is mentioned also in an anecdote in the history of Alexander.[2]

Meantime Agis met with difficulties in Peloponnesus, which arose in consequence of the cruelty of the Spartans in former times, and of their unfortunate efforts against the Athenians. The Argives were hostile to Lacedaemon, and he found the Arcadians full of jealousy of Sparta; they were inclined to submit to Macedonian rule, for they thoroughly detested the dependence upon Sparta, especially on account of the enmity existing between the Spartans and Megalopolis. Had the Spartans, after the battle of Mantinea, been in any way accessible to reason, had they offered to the Arcadians the hand of reconciliation, and made up their minds to leave Megalopolis in the possession of the lands assigned to it by Epaminondas, this state of feeling would not have arisen, and things would have gone on well ; but now Philip had fixed for Megalopolis the disputed boundaries between it and Sparta, and the former could maintain itself only by the protection of Macedonia. Megalopolis is one of those places which greatly increased the misfortunes of Greece.

The first thing which Agis in his undertaking had to do,

[2] Diod. xvii. 100.

was to lay siege to Megalopolis, "in order to be safe in his rear," and this detained him so long, that old Antipater, who was still a fresh and vigorous warrior, was enabled to approach with a Macedonian army consisting of the Macedonian militia and mercenaries. He seems to have had no difficulty in subduing the Thracians and Perrhaebians, and all their princes now joined him and accompanied him into Peloponnesus, anxious to show their devotion to him. He appeared before Megalopolis and forced Agis to accept a battle:[3] the Macedonians were far superior to him in numbers, and he was utterly defeated; but he ended his hasty undertaking in a glorious manner. The Peloponnesian allies had 20,000 foot and 2,000 horse; but Antipater, according to Diodorus, had an army of double that number. Curtius states, that the contest was very severe, and the ancient Spartan bravery once more displayed itself, though it must be observed, that only few Spartans and Lacedaemonians were in the army of Agis, which consisted for the most part of mercenaries. The Spartans had at first been victorious; but Antipater then threw himself into the battle, and continued pushing the Spartans backwards, until they found a favorable position. There they resisted until Agis was so severely wounded that he had to be carried away; and as the overwhelming power of the Macedonians continued to press onward, the allies retreated, leaving

---

[3] " The place of the battle is not quite certain; it is commonly called the battle of Mantinea, but I know of no authority for it. Megalopolis was in reality the scene of the action, and the battle itself was an attempt of Antipater to relieve that city. The common name may be a mistake, this battle being confounded with one fought near Mantinea by a later Agis, son of Eudamidas. In Plutarch's *Apophthegm. Lacon.* p. 216, a battle of Mantinea is mentioned, and it is related that some one advised Agis not to fight at Mantinea, because his enemies surpassed him in numbers, and that Agis answered, " Whoever wishes to rule over many, must fight against many." But this statement does not refer to our battle, but to another, probably the victory over Corrhagus. This passage may have contributed to establish the error more firmly. In the same work, p. 219, there occurs a passage, from which it is evident that the battle was fought at Megalopolis, but we must read there 'Αντίπατρον instead of 'Αντίγονον. There are several other isolated allusions in Plutarch to the war of Agis. It would seem, that in this war the Argives acted decidedly against the Spartans. Agis fought a battle against them, and defeated them, but afterwards they again advanced against him. A fact which is more certain is, that Agis advanced as far as Corinth, but again retreated as far as Megalopolis, when Antipater was approaching with all his forces from Macedonia. On the day of the battle, Agis wanted to send back to Sparta an officer who was eighty years old, but the soldier answered, " It is fairer to die here than at Sparta."—1825.

the flanks unprotected. The Spartans then likewise gave way, though they did not flee; and at first, at least according to Diodorus, they retreated in good order: such a retreat, however, cannot remain orderly for any length of time. It was one of the most bloody battles that had ever been fought within the bounds of ancient Hellas: 5000 men fell on each side.[4] Agis did not survive the defeat, for being wounded in one foot, and being carried away by his men on his shield, he was overtaken. He then ordered the men to stop, demanded his armour, and chose the spot where he wanted to die. On being put down there he fought on his knees against the pursuing Macedonians, until a spear entered his heart and put an end to his life.

The Spartans sent ambassadors to Antipater and obtained peace. He did not advance against Sparta, but referred them to the diet of the Greeks, and there they were referred to Alexander; but in the meantime they gave to Antipater fifty hostages belonging to the most illustrious families.[5] All further details are unknown. Whether they were then obliged to cede to the Argives the places that had been promised to them, is uncertain; but there can be no doubt that the leaders were sent into exile. The other peoples of Peloponnesus, the Arcadians, Eleans, etc., were, no doubt, dealt with far more severely than the Spartans. Antipater at this time levied a considerable number of troops, and sent them to Alexander. This was a political artifice, for the strength of Greece was thereby sufficiently weakened. But Antipater saved them from a worse fate.

The relation subsisting between Antipater and Alexander was unquestionably one of the circumstances on which the farseeing Demosthenes based his hopes: Antipater feared the

---

[4] " The Peloponnesians had 5300 dead, and the Macedonians upwards of 3,000. Curtius mentions 5,360 on the part of the Spartans, but this number is corrupt, the latter part of the number (60) containing something else, as is evident from the writing in the MSS."—1825.

[5] " The Spartans are reported to have said, ' Impose sacrifices upon us, but no disgrace,' and represented to Antipater that they could not give him young men, because they would become estranged from the Spartan manners, but that they would give him double the number of old men. The diet of the Greeks was held at Corinth. The Isthmian and Pythian games probably did not commence till the time when the meetings took place (Aeschin. c. Ctesiph. p. 89, ed. Steph.), and its seems. therefore, probable, that the σύνεδροι were present at all the four games."—1825.

king and negotiated with the Greeks for the sake of his own
safety, and of having something to fall back upon. When
Alexander received intelligence of the battle, which was far
more important than all the battles in which he gained victories over the Persians; he said, with haughty contempt, that
he had received news of a quarrel among mice in Arcadia.
Such expressions were not calculated to conciliate Antipater,
and we cannot wonder that he became an exasperated enemy
of Alexander.

"The condition of Greece henceforth remained unchanged,
until Alexander and his army had reached India." For Athens,
this was a period of great prosperity. Lycurgus was as skilful
an administrator as he was a bad orator; if his orations were
not well-known to be genuine, we might believe them to be
the work of a declaimer; in the earlier literature of Greece,
there are few which are equally bad. Athens abounded in
good-natured admirers of Alexander, and one of them, the
poet Menander, like many other honest men, was really enthusiastic for him; just as we have seen many admirers of
Napoleon in Germany and even in England. Menander was
a very amiable person, but totally devoid of judgment; I
believe that Demosthenes, being an active, great, and powerful
man, entertained an indescribable contempt for him, and considered him useful only in his peculiar sphere. "Alexander's
victories were dazzling, and his expedition was regarded as a
national undertaking. This feeling afterwards changed, but
at the time when Agis entered upon his enterprise, the general
voice had not yet risen against Alexander."

We now come to the undertaking of Alexander of Epirus.[6]
He was a brother of Alexander's mother, and Philip had
established for him a small principality in Epirus, though he
himself retained possession of the fortresses in the midst of the
principality, "such as Ambracia, which might crush all Epirus
at once. Alexander, therefore, derived indeed revenues from his
dominion but as far as his condition as a prince is concerned, he
was like the Indian prince whose capital is situated a few miles
from Seringapatam, which is garrisoned by the English, and
who is controlled in his own capital by an English commissioner,
carefully watching the administration of the prince. Alex-

* Comp. *Hist. of Rome*, iii. p. 159, foll.; *Lectures on Roman History*, i. p. 426.
The early history of Epirus is given in the account of Pyrrhus.—ED.

ander may have felt his dependence; and he, like Agìs, shared the despondency and the adventurous spirit of the age. It was insupportable to him to think, that his nephew should subdue Asia, and conquer for himself a world-wide empire, while he was to remain inactive and dependent in those countries. Hence he joyfully complied with the request of the Tarentines to bring an army over to them (Olymp. 112, 1). It is one of the absurdities of later Greek writers to blame the Tarentines as cowards, because they carried on war by means of mercenaries, for Sparta herself did the same, and Alexander and every one else made use of mercenaries; and how could that city of seamen have carried on wars with its own militia against shepherds and peasants? They are called cowards for it, while others escape uncensured. They are also blamed for having engaged the service of a foreign prince with an army; but this censure too is unjust. Such an army kept much better together, and was much more trustworthy than 10,000 Greeks composed of twelve or twenty different tribes, and the prince was engaged as the cementing element of the army. The same faithlessness which they had to fear from such a prince, would also have threatened from an army of mercenaries gathered from all parts; while they had much more security in the honour of such a prince. On a former occasion they had engaged the services of king Archidamus, the father of Agis, against the Lucanians and Sallentines. Archidamus fell, and his army was dispersed; but it seems that they nevertheless made great progress, and that the Sallentines were compelled to recognise their supremacy, and remain in this condition. The Tarentines were now involved in a war against the Lucanians, and were more particularly concerned about the protection of Heraclea on the Siris. Nearly all the Greek colonies on the coast of Lucania had been destroyed or ruined by the Lucanians, while Tarentum continued to rise in prosperity. About fifty years after this time, when the war with Rome commenced, it was at its height, but it was a great and important city even as early as the time of Alexander.

It is much to be lamented, that we know absolutely nothing of this war. The seventeenth and eighteenth books of Diodorus, consisted each of two halves, and were, in fact, double books. Of the latter, we have only the first half, and that too not without great gaps, which are often concealed, the parts which might show the gap being cut off in the MS. to deceive the purchaser. In the first half, Diodorus related the history of the successors of Alexander; and in the second, the history of the other nations of Greece, Sicily, Italy, Africa, etc., during the same period and in the age of Alexander, that is, a period of about nineteen or twenty years. This defect is not mentioned anywhere; neither in Fabricius' *Bibliotheca Graeca*, nor in any other work on Diodorus. But the fact is nevertheless true, and hence we are deprived of the history of Alexander of Epirus, which is particularly painful in regard to the history of Italy.[7] I have collected the fragments relating to this war. In the *Mémoires de l'Académie des Inscriptions et des Belles Lettres*, there is a collection of the passages and fragments referring to it, but I have collected far more than is there printed, though that collection is called complete. The chronological confusion is very great, for by a false application of Roman chronology, some events are assigned to too early, and others to too late a date. The war itself, it may be observed, did not last long.

Alexander assisted the Tarentines at first with great success, and defeated the Lucanians and Apulians; but afterwards he quarrelled with the Tarentines. The latter are charged with ingratitude, but I believe that they are much wronged. Alexander reversed his relation to Tarentum, wishing to be in the West what his nephew was in the East, and first of all to be king of Italy and Sicily. This excited distrust and aversion among the Tarentines, and these feelings ended in complete hostility, so that Tarentum broke off the connection with him, and concluded, it would seem, peace with the Lucanians. Alexander then continued the war against the latter on his own responsibility, and with his own means. The smaller Greek towns on the coast of Lucania and Bruttium were protected by him, and many of them naturally supported him, especially those governed by Thurii, and apparently those also which were dependent on Croton. With the Romans he concluded a treaty of friendship, which does them no honour; but they did it because the Samnites had joined the Lucanians, and with the Samnites they were then, publicly, in relations of friendship. This friendship, however, was the second of three kinds, described by Chamford, as occurring in private affairs,

[7] Comp. *Hist. of Rome*, iii. p. 166, note 297.

when he says: " *il y ʿa trois sortes d'amis, des amis qui nous aiment, qui nous détestent, et qui nous sont indifférens.*"

The Lucanians were always disunited among themselves. A Sabellian colony ruled among them, though it was not very numerous. In the census of the Cisalpine war, the number of the citizens in the extensive country of Lucania is extremely small, being stated to have amounted only to 34,000 citizens, while the total number of the inhabitants must have been half a million. This shows that the ancient Oenotrian population were *penestae*, or subjects. People are generally much surprised at finding, that in the Samnite war the Oenotrians were so powerless, while in our maps their country appears so extensive; but the cause of this lies in the unfortunate circumstance of a ruling and a subject people, notwithstanding a free constitution. A prince can amalgamate such nations, but in a republic this is impossible.

Alexander of Epirus, as I said before, continued the war; for he saw no other way of acting, even after his hopes had vanished. He lost his life in a battle through the treachery of Lucanian emigrants, who wanted thereby to make peace with their countrymen (Olymp, 112, 4 and 113, 1). I have published in the *Rheinisches Museum*[a] an interesting passage from Lycophron and Tzetzes on these matters; it is one of the most remarkable complications which has arisen from a confusion, and from which we may derive some valuable historical results. I shall hereafter have occasion to return to the affairs of Magna Graecia.

Alexander of Macedonia had now annihilated the Persian empire, and was constantly advancing farther eastward. He found everything in a state of dissolution, and met with as little resistance as Nadir Shah in India, after the capture of Delhi, when he was opposed only by a few Subadars.

Alexander was already developing his plans. His task was extremely difficult, like that of every conqueror. Fortune sometimes carried him onward with full sails, but the question now was, What should be done? Institutions had to be founded, and a government to be established; but the constitution and government of conquered countries was a task beyond the powers of the ancients in general, and this is a point in which they are surpassed by the moderns.

[a] *Klein. Schrift.*, vol. i. p. 438, especially p. 446.

However, we generally imagine the ancients vastly more childish than they really were. We fancy, *e. g.*, that in their administration, they had an αὐτοσχεδιασμὸς of quite a peculiar kind; it is not believed that there was much writing, and the governments of antiquity are commonly imagined to have been like the rudest governments of the East; it is supposed that all important business was settled by word of mouth. This false notion, like all others, has some foundation of truth. The relation subsisting between the highest authority and those entrusted with the administration, was extremely simple, and the former interfered but rarely, as was the case also in the middle ages. But in reference to the civil law and the finances, there was an immense deal of writing in antiquity, as is still the case in India. I have seen specimens of Indian writing relating to taxation, which prove that matters are controlled there with immense care. A friend of mine has brought from Bengal an excellent collection of such documents in the Persian language, where the accuracy in the description of portions of land, is as great as in any good administration among ourselves. The Romans wrote immense quantities, even in the time of the republic. There can be no doubt that they had already certain formulae for notaries, like those of which we have specimens belonging to the period of the empire. The law-suits also were conducted according to certain forms, as we can clearly see from the law proceedings against St. Cyprian the martyr. The ancients, then, were not so rude as is commonly imagined; but a conquered country was generally left in the condition in which it was found, and the only care was to secure from it the same advantages which the preceding ruler had derived from it. These institutions, however, did not engage Alexander's attention, who was absorbed by the idea of uniting the nations of Europe and Asia. This idea has something captivating, and Alexander is praised for it. But his indulging it was in every respect unwise and hasty, not to mention how ungrateful he thereby became towards his own nation, and his companions in arms.

LECTURE LXXIX.

ALEXANDER ought to have attached to himself not only the Greeks, but those nations which resembled them; he ought to have hellenised the Pamphylians, Lycians, and Carians, and drawn them towards himself; he ought to have made them, together with the Macedonians, the ruling nation, and to have formed his armies of them, so that the Orientals were constantly kept distinct from them, and subordinate to the Hellenic races. It would have been quite natural to do this. The fact that he established a number of colonies all over the empire for the purpose of keeping the nations in submission, was indeed a very wise undertaking; but everything else he did was most perverse, and does not allow us to regard him as a great man. He wanted to amalgamate all his nations, and to assimilate them to one another, by means of his adopting, together with his Macedonians, the customs of the Orientals. The Macedonians, in comparison with the nations of Upper Asia, were as a handful compared with millions, and by assimilating themselves to the Persians, they were obliged to adopt every bad custom of the Orientals, and soon had to learn the most contemptible part of Eastern luxury. He had conceived the senseless project of forming an army of Persians with Macedonian discipline; and the Macedonian and Greek soldiers were to adopt the Persian dress and manners alternately with their own: they were not to cease to be Macedonians and to wear Macedonian armour, but sometimes they were to wear the Persian dress and sometimes again the Macedonian. He caused able-bodied Persians to be enlisted, and this exasperated his veterans. They said to themselves: " If this plan succeeds, those nations will swallow us up; and if it does not succeed, our children will degenerate and become Orientals." This was the case with the second generation of the crusaders, the Pullahs, who were the most wretched of all Orientals. In this feeling the old veterans were quite correct.

He himself adopted the most contemptible pomp of Eastern despotism, " and took pleasure in the vanities and follies of the Persians; the Orientals, who were accustomed to prostrate themselves before him, were his darlings. He forgot the respect due to his old soldiers, and demanded of them, who were free men, the prostration of the Persians. All this called forth a general feeling of indignation in his army.

Alexander was a young man surrounded by a generation much older than himself; all his generals were older, and some of them were at a very advanced age, older even than Philip; and the reproaches of these men were disagreeable to him. Among the men of his own age there were very few of any note. This is a very remarkable phenomenon: it is a startling fact, that genius is often limited to a certain period. Among all those of his age there was none that could be compared with the veterans of Philip. Craterus was the only eminent man among the younger officers. Eumenes of Cardia was indeed brought forward by Alexander, but was much older than himself, and had belonged to the army of Philip. The older the generals were, the bitterer they were against Alexander's innovations; they felt that they had established his dominion, and there arose a decided aversion between him and them, which they did not indeed express, but sometimes they put themselves to him in the same relation as some of the older generals of the revolution did to Napoleon; as, for example, Massena, who made a show of his opposition before everybody. Parmenio, who had probably been the most important among Philip's generals, was a man of this kind. Alexander had appointed him governor of Media, and entrusted to him the treasures of Ecbatana, for the purpose of removing him from the army.

Alexander had spent a long time in the East, and that period does all honour to his military talent; but in it also occurred the execution of Philotas and the beginning of the estrangement from his nation and army. Philotas, a son of Parmenio, was a man of the same age as Philip; he held a high office at the court of Alexander, which was regulated according to the Persian fashion, although as yet Alexander conferred most of the offices upon Macedonians.

The Asiatic army which Alexander formed, and which was to be independent, created the greatest exasperation. It would have been better if he had formed a phalanx of Asiatics with Macedonians as its lochagi; but as it was, there was great discontent among the Macedonians; outbreaks of indignation were not uncommon among them, and the desire to get rid of Alexander was expressed no less frequently. Such expressions are rarely the sign of a conspiracy, but rather thoughtless gossip, such as, in the time of Napoleon, was often heard in Germany and France, and was frequently followed by the most unhappy consequences for individuals. Dimnus, a Macedonian, made himself particularly conspicuous (Olymp. 112, 3), by his saying that Alexander ought to be got rid of, and the like. This talk was reported to Philotas, and as the office he held may be regarded as that of a chamberlain to Alexander, we might expect him to have given information to the prince; but his silence was, nevertheless, quite natural, supposing that many of the old officers, friends of his father, who may have expressed themselves in the same way, would have been endangered, for Alexander had already shown symptoms of cruelty. There cannot, however, be any doubt but that the whole was mere talk, and would not have been followed by any consequences. But as those who had communicated the matter to Philotas, began to suspect that he had kept it secret, and as they feared lest it should reach the ears of Alexander through others, they, anxious to be beforehand, gave information to the king himself, declaring that Philotas had known of it long before. Alexander, imagining that a conspiracy was discovered, ordered Philotas to be tried for high treason by the army, as the representative of the Macedonian nation. The guards condemned him to death, and he was executed without delay. Meantime, Alexander quickly sent an officer to Ecbatana to despatch Parmenio, like a Capiji Bashi; the officer arrived at Ecbatana quite unexpectedly, and while Parmenio was reading the letter brought to him, the assassin murdered him. And in order that there might be no survivor that could avenge these deeds, the last of Parmenio's sons (?), and many other persons were put to death. Parmenio had had three sons, one of whom had already fallen in the service of Alexander. These murders are of the most detestable kind, and not a shadow of an excuse can be found for them.

" The aversion of his old soldiers against him was thus constantly increasing, and the feeling that he owed his victories to them was oppressive to him." Among the young men, there were two whom Alexander treated as friends: the first Hephaestion, for whom he entertained an unnatural affection;

he was a flatterer, and a complete servant of his master in everything, even in the basest. Craterus, the second, was a very different man; he was an unlucky personage in the world's history, for his arrival decided the unfortunate issue of the Lamian war against the Greeks. But he was by far the best among the Macedonians, and there is none among them in whom we can feel a deeper interest. He and his wife Phila, the daughter of Antipater, are a noble couple, such as is not otherwise known in the history of Macedonia. They stand alone among the Macedonians, who were removed as far as they could be from everything that is noble. Phila, like the whole family of Antipater, was indescribably unhappy, but in her misfortunes she displayed her noble mind. The blessing of both parents descended upon their son, who was a man of great talent and extensive knowledge, and of quite a different character from the other Macedonians: he wrote a diplomatic history of Athens, for which he derived his materials from original documents. All three are far above their nation, and are quite isolated phenomena. Craterus, in his close connection with Alexander, was never guilty of flattery towards him, and he used to say, that he was serving only the king and not Alexander. Alexander respected and feared him until the end of his life, even during its worst period. Devils themselves believe and tremble, and the same is the case also with vicious men: they recognise goodness, and find it honorable and useful, though in reality they think it ridiculous; but they must acknowledge that it too is a power.

Under these circumstances, there arose in Alexander a peculiar bitterness of feeling, which occasioned the murder of Clitus (Olymp. 113, 1). Clitus was his faithful friend, and was nearly related to him through his sister, who had been Alexander's nurse or *bonne* in his infancy. Nurses are very highly esteemed in the East, and enter into as close a relation with the families in which they are engaged, as if they were relatives. This murder ought not to be ascribed to his drunkenness alone; it is characteristic on account of the circumstances which occasioned it. Alexander, in the midst of his victories, was jealous of his generals. I have already mentioned the defeat of Zopyrion; at this he was rather pleased, for he thought: " the Macedonians may now see what they can do without me." He treated the whole affair very lightly, and at a banquet, the defeated army was even ridiculed in burlesque songs. This exasperated the old soldiers, and Clitus rising, requested the king to put a stop to those songs which ridiculed the misfortunes of their own countrymen. But Alexander, who was already drunk, answered with an unseemly shout of laughter, and commanded the songs to be continued. This occasioned a dispute: Clitus was altogether beside himself, and became infuriated, as was quite natural. Imagine to yourselves the situation of Clitus, who stands face to face with a prince laughing at his own defeat, and rejoicing at the misfortune of his own soldiers: in such a situation, no man can be sure of keeping his temper. I therefore excuse Clitus becoming enraged and provoking Alexander, who would not listen to him, to such a degree that he murdered him. Alexander's lamentation and whining about his death, and the affected imitation of Achilles bewailing the death of Patroclus, are to my mind, on the whole, a mere farce and a piece of acting. If he was in earnest, he certainly made no reparation.

After this occurrence, he did not by any means alter his conduct, but showed more and more defiance; he demanded of the Greeks and Macedonians to prostrate themselves before him according to the Persian fashion. On the whole, he was obeyed with inconceivable readiness, for the terror of Parmenio's fate had intimidated the men in the highest degree, and when, under the influence of terror, cowardly actions have once been submitted to, people know of no bounds. This accounts for the slavish servility of Callisthenes (Olymp. 113, 2). This man, a near relation of Aristotle, who had sent him with Alexander, was then in the king's retinue. His real office may have been to accompany Alexander as a sort of courtly scholar and historiographer, for which, however, he was absolutely unfit. Polybius quotes him in his account of the battle of Issus. Of military matters he understood about as much as Voltaire in his Life of Charles XII.; and Polybius, an able officer, is particularly annoyed at him. The loss of his history, therefore, is no loss at all; he is celebrated, however, as the source from which Plutarch derived his information. His personal character too is despised, but he appears in a much more favourable light than is commonly believed. He is treated as a bad man, whereas in reality he was only weak.

He was celebrated for being able to speak *in utramque partem*, and the manner in which he did this, gives me a deep insight into his character. At a princely banquet he was called upon to make a eulogy on the Macedonian nation. He made a most brilliant one. Alexander then ordered him to make also a speech against the Macedonians. He now completely unburdened his mind, breaking out into a most fearful invective, and spoke of the misery which they had brought upon Greece —the object of his accompanying Alexander was to effect the restoration of his native town which had been destroyed by Philip;—as he had before praised the Macedonians, so he now painted them in the darkest colours, and described the misery and destruction which they had inflicted upon Greece in a manner which startled all who were present. This reveals to me the man completely; it clearly shows his mind and his real feelings. There are men who, when in a state of dependence, can control their tongues, but still cannot conceal their inward feelings, and although they may be in servitude, yet never allow a word to cross their lips that would dishonour a free man. I think I am a man of this character myself: I have often been employed in negotiations, where I had to face the most powerful; but I never was able to conceal my sentiments, though I always honoured every kind of merit, esteeming a good statesman and a good military man each by himself. Other minds are of a more pliable nature: they have a desire not to stand aloof from their age, but to fit themselves into it, although it may be quite opposed to their own nature. They assume an outward appearance by means of which they please those with whom they come in contact, outwardly joining the powerful, and doing homage to the *causa victrix*, *quae Diis placuit*, but in reality they are filled with a feeling of pain and indignation because things are as they are, and because they cannot alter them. Callisthenes was a man of this latter kind. Sometimes, however, their feelings burst through all restraints, and such was then his case. The words he then uttered were not punished at the time, but were not forgotten, for the cruel treatment which he afterwards experienced, was no doubt the result of that day. When the words had once crossed his lips, he may have thought that all was lost, that it would be of no use disguising his feelings any longer, and that henceforth he ought, without fear, to act as an honest man. The noble

Macedonians who slavishly bowed before Alexander, were yet always enraged at being obliged to do it; they acted just as the old generals of the revolution did towards Napoleon; these latter were men without any moral firmness, for whenever Napoleon appeared, they could not bow low enough, but when he had turned his back, they spoke unreservedly against him, never calling him emperor, but speaking of him only as *cet homme ;* yet they received from him every fresh decoration with the greatest gratitude and delight. Such also were the Macedonian generals; and it is possible that Callisthenes who knew their low state of mind, often conversed with them. When Alexander demanded the humiliating salutations—for it is not always meant that they had to prostrate themselves on the ground—Callisthenes who avoided the low obeisances, was denounced by them. Alexander treated him for this as a man guilty of high treason, and ordered him to be locked up in a cage, in which he was carried about with the army for seven months, until in the end he died in filth and wretchedness.

Alexander's exasperation against the old Macedonians was so great, that Antipater no longer thought his life safe; and fearing some secret dagger he entered into negotiations with the Aetolians to prepare himself for a revolt in case Alexander should attack him as he had attacked Parmenio. This situation was the more dangerous, as he was living in the proximity of Olympias, who entertained a bitter hatred against him. He had always been at enmity with her, for Olympias wanted to exercise an influence upon the government, and Antipater ruled with despotic power.

" Meantime Alexander advanced farther and farther, but without any definite object, and merely because he felt that he must go on. Such a conqueror always gets into the fearful condition of a gambler, being unable to stop, and obliged to carry on war and to stake his own existence upon it. This was the position of Alexander, and he advanced on and on; but this feeling of his could not be communicated to the army; and the commander in such circumstances is unconcerned about the army. The troops of Alexander were obliged to march onward, although the men greatly longed for rest, to recover from their hardships, and enjoy the fruits of their labours; and as they deserved rest, they claimed it, and with justice. The admirers of Alexander act foolishly in decrying his men for not having entered into his grand ideas, for he was only dragged onwards like a gambler who cannot retrace his steps, and were his Macedonians to sacrifice their lives for *this* idea?"

After these occurrences, Alexander undertook his expedition to India (Olymp. 113, 2). As soon as he enters upon military undertakings, he is admirable. But the manner in which he, before this, deceived his soldiers by the promises that he would send a part of them home, is disgraceful; for he intercepted the letters which they had sent home, opened them, and having picked out the suspected individuals he sent them to distant places, or employed them in desperate undertakings. But great is his march over the mountains, the Indian Caucasus, the lofty range of Paropamisus, and a portion of the Himalayah, in order to penetrate into India; great also are his contests there, where he met with a desperate resistance from warlike nations—for to their utter astonishment, the Macedonians did not find the Indians effeminate, but warlike. The frontiers of the country were inhabited by warlike tribes, whose manners were those of Ravistan and the modern Rajpoots about Ajmir, and not those of the Bengalese—but he nevertheless advanced and overcame all difficulties: these are brilliant exploits, and the Indian campaign is as truly glorious for Alexander, as it is honorable to the Indians who opposed him.

From Paropamisus, the army descended into the paradise-like country of India. Cashmir was not reached by Alexander; but he entered the splendid country of Moultan and Lahore. There he was opposed by the Indians in the most resolute manner; but he defeated two of their princes, and forced his way across all the mountains and rivers. He continued to advance, and crossed five rivers: from the Indus across the Acesines, as far as the last river of the Pentapotamia, where the valley of the Indus is separated by the desert from the India of the Ganges." He penetrated as far as the neighbourhood of Delhi, evidently with the view of reaching the Ganges. Although his generals had no knowledge of the Ganges,—Herodotus knew nothing of it, nor, perhaps, Ctesias —yet Alexander no doubt possessed accurate information about those countries. His object was to subdue all India, and he would perhaps have succeeded. Between the Jumna and Hyphasis, there is indeed a barren desert, but not so barren as

on the south in Rajpootana, and Alexander might have led
his troops through it without any difficulty. On the Jumna
he might have built a fleet; and by means of it he might
have sailed down that river and the Ganges into Bengal. But
his Macedonians now refused to go farther, because they had
heard that they would come to a river, the course of which
would lead them into quite different regions, and into quite a
different hemisphere. They accordingly rebelled, because they
knew well enough that such an adventure would be tempting
to Alexander. He therefore returned (Olymp. 113, 3); and
advancing to the Indus, he followed the course of that river,
with a large part of his army, as far as its mouth. Another
part was sent through Candahar and the beautiful country of
Sistan, the most splendid parts of the Persian empire.

On the Indus he caused a fleet to be built, which, under the
command of Nearchus, sailed down the river, as he would
have sailed down the Ganges, and was commissioned to examine the coasts of the Erythraean sea as far as Gedrosia.
This voyage was undertaken for the benefit of the Greeks, for
the Persians had already made it under Darius, sailing in
Carian ships from Cashmir as far as the Euphrates or Egypt.
This undertaking of Alexander was noble and praiseworthy,
and did great service to geography.

LECTURE LXXX.

THE appointment of Nearchus to this undertaking, was a very
happy choice. The description of his voyage has been preserved by Arrian. But he was sent out at an unfavourable
season, as the monsoons were against him; in consequence of
which he spent six times more time upon the undertaking,
than would otherwise have been required.

Alexander might have returned by going up the Indus
some way, and then taking the road by Gasna and Candahar;
and he did send a part of his army that way, but he himself
with the greater part went by another road, the difficulties of
which were enormous, and cannot have been unknown to him.

But he chose it either recklessly from a desire to accomplish something extraordinary, and to overcome enormous difficulties, in which princes always suffer least, or else from hatred of his army, and a wish to punish them for their resistance: this latter supposition is very probable.   He had wished to advance as far as the Ganges, to sail down that river, circumnavigate India, and perhaps to penetrate even farther; and he actually hated the Macedonians for having thwarted this plan. For this reason, he led them through the terrible country of Beloochistan, which is much worse even than the desert of Arabia or the Sahara; for days no human habitations are met with, and they are situated like islands far separated from one another.   The desert is altogether of a very peculiar kind. In the Sahara and the Arabian desert, there are some districts formed of quicksands, but they are only an exception, and on the whole the ground is firm, and consists of small pebbles. But the countries from the frontiers of Kerman as far as the Indus, Mekoan, and Beloochistan itself, are infinitely more dangerous.   Lieutenant Pottinger, an Englishman, about twelve or thirteen years ago, travelled through that country in disguise —for its inhabitants are in the lowest stage of civilisation, they are fanatical Mahommedans, and form the dregs of mankind—and his description has given me a clear idea of the march of Alexander.   That immense district does not seem to consist of real sand; Pottinger compares it with volcanic ashes of extreme fineness; he probably did not examine whether it resembles ashes in its chemical properties also.   We may form a faint idea of the difficulties of the country, by comparing it with the sandy districts in the north of Germany, where the foot sinks deep into the ground, and the traveller becomes extremely tired.   The dust, for so we may call it, of the country through which Alexander marched, is so extremely fine, that it not only rises during the slightest breath of air, but is made to rise even by the rays of the sun, when they fall upon it perpendicularly.   When the sun is high in the heavens, Pottinger says, the atmosphere, as it were, consists of dust, and by means of the slightest wind, it becomes so mixed with the air, as to penetrate into both mouth and nose.   The human habitations are not so far removed from one another as in Arabia, and in the Sahara; and wherever there are such settlements of a few wretched families, there is water;

but while in Arabia and in the Sahara those inhabited spots are marked by green vegetation, the whole fearful extent of that Indian desert does not show anything of the kind; and real grass does not exist anywhere. " The miserable population on the coast are ichthyophagi living upon whales and seals, and their habitations are made of the ribs of whales."

Through that fearful country Alexander led his army; the march lasted for a whole month, and the hardships and sufferings of the soldiers, though they were of an opposite kind, were like those of the French army on its retreat from Russia. But the long duration made the distress much greater. " The fleet which, under Nearchus, sailed from the Indus along the coast, might have alleviated, at least to some extent, the difficulties of the march, if it had established magazines with stores at certain intervals; but no precautions had been taken, and the army took with it only such an amount of provisions and water as everyone could carry. A frightful thirst, bordering upon madness, seized upon the army, and the greatest torture was, that every now and then they imagined they saw water and were disappointed." Many thousands perished. Alexander did not bring back the fourth part of the troops which he had led across the range of Paropamisus into India, although the corps which he had sent back by Candahar, returned in safety, so that certainly one third of his troops must have perished in the desert. In theatrical historians, we read the moving tale of the water which a soldier brought to Alexander, and how he poured it out in order to show them that he would share all their sufferings with them. I suspect it was with Alexander as it was with another great general, who ate a piece of coarse bread, but is said to have had a delicate morsel concealed in it.

After this march, when he arrived in Kerman (Olymp. 113, 4), he is reported to have imitated the triumphal progress of Bacchus on his passage through that country; after having sufficiently tortured his soldiers, he allowed them to refresh themselves in that beautiful wine-growing country, which is the easternmost of the country of Asia that produces wine. This march was one of his deplorable farces. It is a very true remark of Goethe's, that the later Romans, even during the latter period of the republic,[1] and afterwards under the

---

[1] Comp. *Lectures on Rom. Hist.*, vol. iii. p. 215.

emperors, fell into the extravagant and the monstrous, whenever they wanted to do anything grand. Such also is the character of the great festivities and games of Alexander. An architect proposed to change mount Athos into a reclining statue of him, and Alexander declined it only because it was impossible. How the gigantic and not the beautiful was his element, may be seen from the regulations contained in his will, from the works he intended to execute, "such as, a pyramid in honor of Philip, then seven temples, for the construction of each of which he set apart 1,500,000 crowns," plans requiring immense efforts, but which were, after all, no better than the magic palaces in eastern tales. All the immense resources of Asia were at his disposal, but the beautiful which had flourished at Athens in the time of Pericles was not his element.

He now returned to Persia, and from this time he conducted himself completely as a Persian, aping the manners of the Persian kings, in consequence of which the discontent among the Macedonians increased from day to day. It had been the custom of the ancient Persian kings, when entering the real country of their race, to give a certain *congiarium* consisting of a piece of gold for every woman in the mother country; and Alexander now did the same. With the Persian kings this act had an appropriate meaning, but in the case of Alexander it was an obvious renunciation of his nation. He had selected 30,000 young Persians, he had conferred upon them military honours and a military education, and caused them to learn Greek; and they were to be his phalanx. But he would have been greatly disappointed if he had employed them as a phalanx without Macedonian lochagi; they would have been as useless as sepoys are without European officers. The Asiatics are deficient in what Aristotle calls the architectonic, *i. e.*, the directing and constructive power: the Asiatics are mere masses. Men like Sewaji, Mahommed, and the first Khalifs, are exceptions, and it is only isolated individuals among the Asiatics that have this gift; a single mind can indeed by enthusiasm carry his nation onward, but can never be its soul. The degree of ability and power of a nation consists in the possibility of individuals being the soul of many; whenever this is not the case, much remains to be done. We Germans also are unfortunately deficient in this; we should be much stronger, if we possessed this requisite along with our many good qualities.   A machine is often nothing else but a lifeless organism.   Aristotle would have told Alexander this, for he well knew the difference between Europeans and Asiatics, and even went so far as to say, that the Asiatics were incapable of being free, that is, incapable of guiding both themselves and others.   An Asiatic officer can never be the soul of Asiatics.   The Macedonian system of military training is quite simple, and we may form as clear a notion of it, as if we had seen it ourselves.   I know it quite accurately; I have often drawn it on paper with all its evolutions; and we may well imagine that the Persians when passing in review before the king, completely satisfied him.   But anything beyond this they could not learn.

But Alexander thinking that he could now do without the old Macedonians, wanted to get rid of them.   This design became manifest in the first instance by his proclamation, that the veterans who had served their time should be dismissed. He had even before this left a great many, even against their will, in the most distant countries on the Jaxartes and Oxus, some as settlers, and others as garrisons.   The others were now to be dismissed from their service.   These Macedonians however were demoralised warriors, whose prospects at home were not attractive; they knew not what to do at home; they had fearfully plundered in Asia, but had squandered everything, and in Macedonia they could be nothing else but either beggars or robbers.   Hence they wished to remain; they had their Asiatic women with then, who formed an immense host, as they generally do in the armies of Asiatics.   The national feeling however was aroused in them, and a general insurrection broke out; they demanded that, if he dismissed one, he should dismiss all.   He accordingly formed the right resolution, and dismissed them all; but this had not been their object.   They were overawed by it; some of them had, by his command, already laid down their arms, and were entirely in his power.   Hence they soon sued for his pardon.   This pardon too has been praised by sophists as something noble; but all I can say, is, that he acted on that occasion with firmness and skill.   " All his efforts were now evidently directed towards emancipating himself from the Macedonians, a desire which also shows itself in his plan of despotically transplanting the nations of Asia into Europe, and those of Europe into Asia.

He wanted to unite them into one mass, which would have been without any nationality. If twenty different tribes had constituted the population of a country, if among 10,000 inhabitants there had been 500 Greeks, 500 Persians, 500 Egyptians, etc., a nation would have arisen without any peculiarity, without any bond of language or any other connection—the most detestable and injurious arrangement that can be conceived — and by this Babylonian confusion of languages, he would have jumbled the nations together in such a manner, that none would have been gainers but all losers, and Alexander himself would have been obliged to abandon his plan.

He had by this time become quite hardened against all feelings of humanity, and abandoned himself more and more to his fierce passions. His worthless friend Hephaestion died; and Alexander celebrated his burial in a manner which showed utter senselessness and absurdity, in his prodigality and in his perpetration of oriental horrors. In order to offer to the deceased a worthy sacrifice, he undertook an expedition against a free people of mountaineers, and extirpated the whole nation; and according to a truly Eastern fashion, he slaughtered all the prisoners in honour of his deceased friend. All that is related of this period is disgraceful; insensible to all that is good, and dissatisfied with himself, he abandoned himself more and more to frightful drunkenness. He offered prizes for the best drinkers, and an $\dot{\alpha}\gamma\grave{\omega}\nu$ $\pi o\lambda\upsilon\pi o\sigma\acute{\iota}\alpha\varsigma$ ended with some thirty persons drinking themselves to death: a proceeding which we can contemplate only with the most complete disgust.

But at the same time he made great preparations; for he was obliged to undertake something to amuse himself. In the East he had no more to do; he could not lead his soldiers a second time to India, without again causing an insurrection among them. He accordingly turned his attention to the west; and the western nations were actually looking towards him with great apprehension. He ordered ships to be built in Phoenicia, and at Thapsacus on the Euphrates, which were then to be transported by land to the Mediterranean. The pieces were probably made ready to be transported, and to be put together on their arrival on the coast of the Mediterranean. His plan was to equip a fleet of 1,000 galleys, quadriremes and quinqueremes, everything was intended to be of a colossal nature. He probably intended to circumnavigate Africa and to conquer Carthage. His generals were to subdue Arabia, while he himself was to proceed westward and take Carthage, in which undertaking the Phoenicians, in spite of their reluctance, would have been obliged to fight against their own country- men and colonists. Carthage would not have detained him long: he would have easily taken it, as we may infer from the subsequent landings of Agathocles and Regulus; for when an enemy approached it, it was only a colossus on a rotten foun- dation; Carthage had no perseverance. He would then have continued his expedition " in order to conquer all the countries as far as the pillars of Hercules. For the purpose of connecting the provinces he then intended to make a road along the coast of the Mediterranean from Cyrene to Carthage."

Embassies from all the western countries were already ap- pearing before him, from the Celts, Iberians, and the Italian nations. The Greeks in Italy and Sicily hailed his expected approach. Freedom they no longer concerned themselves about; and to be governed by a mighty king had nothing derogatory in their eyes; they were willing to sacrifice their independence as small states for the splendour of such an empire. Clitarchus relates, that Roman ambassadors also came to him, and we cannot well say that this statement is false.[2] We cannot, it is true, say that Clitarchus had no inducement to mention the Romans; " it is true also, that the Romans, at the time he wrote were, not yet so celebrated as to induce a Greek to name them from mere vanity, but" they were already known, and might easily be mentioned in an enumeration of the other Italian nations. The modern Italians likewise often introduce well-known things where they are out of place, and on all occasions they mention together things they are in the habit of naming together. The Italian always goes on enu- merating the acting nations together with those well-known in the vicinity; thus when he is to relate an undertaking of Milan, Genoa, or Florence, he not only enumerates these cities, but also those situated between them, and if you tell him, that they are out of place, he will say that this makes no difference. This accordingly may have been the origin of Clitarchus' statement; but if we consider, on the other hand,

[2] Comp. *Hist. of Rome*, vol. iii. p. 169; *Lectures on Rom. Hist.*, vol. i. p. 434.

that the Romans had just concluded a treaty with Alexander of Epirus, I see no reason why they should not also have carried on negotiations with Alexander the Great, for the purpose of providing for the threatening tempest. Livy's belief that the Romans were unacquainted with the name of Alexander, is extremely thoughtless; the Romans knew very well that the Persian empire was overthrown, and that Alexander had made immense conquests. Maritime communications in antiquity were very active and extensive, and the notions commonly entertained on this subject are quite erroneous: after the expulsion of the kings, Roman ships sailed as far as Spain, as we see from the treaty with Carthage. The Romans therefore might very well know about Alexander. At the present time reports of European occurrences reach the interior of Africa, Persia, and China, with inconceivable rapidity. Thus the French revolution was known in the distant east at an early period, but in a peculiar manner; the people in Persia and on the coast of Arabia could not understand it. I have heard strange things from those who had travelled in those countries; even in China it was very soon known. The present insurrection of the Greeks was known in the interior of Africa; in the year 1823, the attention of everybody in Sacatoo and Borneo was occupied with it; it was imagined to be a general war between Christians and Mahommedans. As nations little more than half savages knew of these things, why should not the highly civilised nations of ancient Italy have heard of Alexander's progress and conquests? Whoever could tell of these things, was no doubt listened to by thousands. During the seven years' war, my father met in Yemen the minister Fati Achmed, who knew about the war, and by the many questions he asked about the relations between England and France, he showed that he took great interest in them. He had maps of countries, of which he could not read the names, but he nevertheless formed some notions from them. In Japan, there exists a complete European atlas in Japanese characters; and from it the geography of Europe has been learned for the last forty years, although the Japanese exclude Europeans. "It is asked, how did the Romans find their way to Babylon"? If Etruscan and even Spanish ambassadors found their way, why should not the Romans have found it? Our notions of the real condition of the ancient world are so deplorably perverse, because the study of antiquity withdraws us from the contemplation of actual life. As our own life becomes necessarily more and more prosaic, we should endeavour to rescue that of the ancients from its shadowy obscurity, and conceive it as a living reality.

Crowds of foreign ambassadors appeared at Babylon, which was to Alexander what Dresden was to Napoleon before he went to Russia: the scene of the most brilliant period of his life, on account of the homage which he there received. But his soothsayers cautioned him not to enter Babylon; whether this was a deception, or whether God's inscrutable providence actually allowed them for once to catch a glimpse of the future, are questions of which it would be folly to believe either the one or the other, and I merely mention them. The first cannot be unconditionally maintained, nor can it be said that the latter actually happened in any given case; but it would be a gross mistake to assume, that all the oracles and prophecies of antiquity were based upon nothing but imposition. The soothsayers of Alexander may have been perfect fools, for we have no traces to shew what reason they had for cautioning him. But Alexander did not resist the temptation, and went to Babylon as if it had been his capital (Olymp. 114, 1). He knew that that city was the cradle of all Asiatic empires—as such it is also described in the Bible—and this circumstance drew him to it, although its walls were demolished and the city laid waste: Babylon was like the present Delhi, compared with what it once was according to the description of Bernier. Fate attracted him towards Babylon, as often man is drawn by an irresistible power towards the place where he is destined to die. Whether Alexander there died of poison or of a fever, which he had brought upon himself by his brutal intemperance, cannot be decided. Those who state that he was poisoned, relate that the drug was administered to him by Cassander, the son of Antipater, against whom he was highly exasperated, through the instrumentality of his cup-bearer, Iollas, another son of Antipater. " If we consider the course of events, and the fact that poisoning was so common a thing in the Macedonian empire, together with the inveterate hatred of Antipater's family against Alexander, we might be inclined with most of his contemporaries to believe that he was poisoned; and Plutarch's arguments against it are not convincing." But all the bulletins which Arrian gives of the illness of Alexander rather indicate that he was suffering from a fever in consequence of his beastly manner of living, and render this supposition very probable. His illness, moreover, lasted too long to allow us to suppose that he died of poison. All poison in antiquity produces its fatal effects within twenty-four hours, or it acts very slowly; but Alexander's illness lasted from ten to twelve days.

Perhaps no man has personally exercised a greater historical influence than Alexander; this cannot be questioned. But what influence he exercised, and whether it was beneficial, is a question on which opinions are divided. Owing to Plutarch and other late writers, public opinion is generally in his favour; this cannot be wholly denied, though I must protest against its correctness.

In regard to Greece, his conquests were altogether injurious. Through him the Greek nation was, as it were, seized with consumption, for he reduced its numbers immensely. A vast number of recruits must have gone from Greece and Macedonia to India and upper Asia, whom he for ever withdrew from their country by assigning to them settlements in those countries. It lay in the nature of things, that Greece should be lost, and should fall into a state of complete weakness, when a new wealthy and military state arose by the side of it. Even the good which arose from the establishment of this Macedonico-Asiatic empire, was injurious to Greece. Commerce was tranferred to Alexandria; and Athens ceased to be spoken of as a commercial city.

Alexander's influence upon the nearer and remoter parts of conquered Asia was different in different countries. Upon Egypt it was beneficial, for that country was evidently better off under the Ptolemies than it had been under the Persians. The first three Macedonian kings of Egypt were excellent princes, and raised the country to a degree of prosperity, which it never enjoyed either before or after: and that period was sufficient for such a country to heal its ancient wounds.

The nations of Asia Minor endeavoured to hellenise themselves under the Macedonian dominion, and this was effected in a wonderfully short time: the ancient languages disappeared within the first century after Alexander, and Greek was so generally diffused in Lycia and Caria, that the popular orators spoke Greek. This might be regarded as a compensation for Greece, which became itself more and more desolate; but the Greek which they spoke was poor and artificial, and the literary men of those countries were the wretched Asiatic rhetoricians, a few fragments of whose productions furnish us with sufficient evidence to show how miserable their literature was, when compared with that of ancient Greece. Those nations did not, in fact, gain many real advantages, though it cannot be denied that many buildings were erected in their towns, and that some of them acquired a certain celebrity and importance.

Syria obtained some advantages, but Phoenicia was a loser: Alexandria and Rhodes became the great seats of commerce. It is scarcely conceivable how the Phoenician cities could become so insignificant. That Tyre became a deserted place, is quite natural; and the fact that Sidon, Aradus, and others, experienced the same fate, is clear from the circumstances of the time. Subsequently, Antioch arose in those parts—a splendid city, and full of talent, which spread life around it, but it was a strangely mixed life.

The upper satrapies of Mesopotamia, Babylonia, and Persia, were only injured by Alexander's conquests; they were indeed hellenised, but their ancient arts and sciences were lost, and nothing new took root in them. His colonies were in most cases unsuccessful; it was only the efforts of a few among his successors, that produced somewhat more favourable results. Seleucia was an island in the midst of a barbarous country.

Alexander's contemporaries among the Greeks were not mistaken as to the influence which he exercised. He died detested and cursed by Greece and Macedonia. If he had lived longer, he would perhaps himself have seen the downfall of the structure he had reared. He could not be otherwise than active and stirring, and he could not have gone on without bringing ruin upon himself. His intention was not to hellenise Asia, but to make Greece Persian; hence if he had longer remained in Asia, we should have seen the formation of a Graeco-Persico-Macedonian empire. As he wanted to arm the Greeks and Macedonians in the Persian fashion, those nations would afterwards probably have revolted and put him to death. The only means by which Greece might have been saved, and have recovered its liberty, would have been, if Alexander had passed through the natural course of his life, and had fallen with the glory of his exploits.

END OF VOLUME II.

1 *vol. 8vo., with a Map, price 12s. 6d. cloth.*

THE

GERMANIA OF TACITUS,

WITH

ETHNOLOGICAL DISSERTATIONS
AND NOTES.

By R. G. LATHAM, M.D., F.R.S.,

LATE FELLOW OF KING'S COLLEGE, CAMBRIDGE, MEMBER OF THE ETHNOLOGICAL
SOCIETY, NEW YORK.

LONDON:

TAYLOR, WALTON, AND MABERLY,

UPPER GOWER STREET; AND IVY LANE, PATERNOSTER ROW.

Post 8vo., price 5s. 6d., cloth,

REGAL ROME:

AN INTRODUCTION TO ROMAN HISTORY.

BY

FRANCIS W. NEWMAN,

PROFESSOR OF LATIN IN UNIVERSITY COLLEGE, LONDON.

Contents.

LONDON:
TAYLOR, WALTON, AND MABERLY,
UPPER GOWER STREET; AND IVY LANE, PATERNOSTER ROW.

CPSIA information can be obtained
at www.ICGtesting.com
Printed in the USA
BVHW081614220819
556561BV00018B/3994/P